Easy
Knitting

kp books

Iola, Wisconsin

TABLE OF
contents

Design & Knit the
Sweater of Your Dreams

Vintage
to Vogue

INTRODUCTION

Whether you're a new or experienced knitter, this book offers you more than 80 projects to gratify your creative talents. You'll get tips, tricks, and techniques, along with detailed instructions and diagrams for handy reference. This book is easy-to-follow, with step-by-step instructions. In fact you can even learn how to tailor to your own size and figure, or that of a family member.

Easy Knitting also includes styles from the world's hottest yarn companies, including Lion Brand, Berroco, Tahki Stacy Charles, Coats & Clark, Cascade and Handy Hands. A wide variety of projects for all skill levels means you will be able to use this book for years to come!

Knitting
in the
Fast Lane

Christina L. Holmes
and Mary Colucci

Creative Director: Christina L. Holmes
Technical Editor: Evie Rosen
Illustrations: Jan Wojtech

Acknowledgments

We would like to thank the knitting yarn companies who generously provided designs for this book, and the creative staff who worked with us on these projects: Sara Arblaster of Bernat Yarns; Margery Winter of Berroco, Inc.; Kathleen Sams of Coats & Clark; and Adina Klein of Lion Brand Yarns.

Special thanks also go to Anne Chua Greenwald for knitting the Weekend Chic Rollneck Pullover in a week; and to Arlene Levine for knitting the base scarf for our Loop Trim Scarf.

We'd also like to thank long-suffering husbands Irving Greenwald and Philip Weinstein, and our patient, supportive animal friends: Mary's Moustan and Christina's Shy, Mao-Me, Sir Beasley and Tony the Tiger.

A big thank-you to our wonderful models: Felicia Allen, Brett Bivona, Carole Grajek, Irving Greenwald, Michael Greenwald, Rachel Greenwald, Barry Holmes, Caitlin Holmes, "Daisy" Holmes, Lauren Holmes, Jake Levine, Shari Levine, Zachary Levine, Lisa McLaughlin, Lauren Rudman, Jeremy Weinstein, and Dolores Zipfel. Thanks too, to Colin Campbell-Harris for his lighting expertise.

Last but not least, special thanks to Evie Rosen, who has always been our favorite teacher and problem-solver, and with whose help *Knitting in the Fast Lane* stayed on track.

More about Evie...

Evie Rosen is the creator of Warm Up America!, and owned the Knitting Nook, a retail specialty store in Wausau, WI, for over 30 years. Evie is a noted knitting authority who teaches extensively for associations and professional guilds and has authored more than 25 books and leaflets, including the best-selling book, *The All New Teach Yourself to Knit*. Rosen divides her time between teaching and traveling on behalf of Warm Up America!

Evie Rosen, technical editor on this project.

Table Of Contents

Introduction

Who has time to knit?

You do!

You don't have to be living in a big city to be living "in the fast lane" these days. Whether you're caught up in the electronic and digital wonders that have sped up our lives so much, or running non-stop juggling kids, work, and home, it's easy to run out of time for the things that make you feel good. Working with the wonderful texture of yarn, being creative, and making gifts that warm the heart are important things to make time for.

We feel the same way. That's why we wanted to write a book that makes knitting a bit more manageable for the fast pace of today's lifestyle. It combines fun, wearable, fashion-right designs with bulky yarns, or multi-stranding, and most are worked on larger needles. Or sometimes it's just a small-size project. Whatever it is, we want you to be able to finish it and enjoy it within a reasonable amount of time.

We don't consider ourselves "expert" knitters (we don't knit away while looking out the window and carrying on a conversation and think intricate intarsia designs are a snap). Basically, we're "average." But we really do enjoy the creativity of knitting and working with wonderful yarns. You'll find some helpful tips we've picked up along the way on working with the yarns used here, and with the help of technical editor Evie Rosen, the answers to some Frequently Asked Questions that come up when you're on a roll at 11 p.m. and have no one to call.

We've used traffic signs to draw your attention to items you might not notice if you're reading too fast, such as needle or stitch changes, or special pattern notes.

You'll find stitch instructions in the back of this book that should cover just about every stitch used in the patterns contained here, so you can have a reference guide handy instead of taking the time to look up stitches or techniques for correcting mistakes elsewhere.

We hope you'll find these designs fun to work and great to wear. So, put it in gear and start knitting!

Christina & Mary

Chapter 1

Starting Out

Welcome to *Knitting in the Fast Lane*. This book is about projects you can realistically complete without making them your life's work, depending on your skill level and the time you have available for knitting. We've tried to give you an idea of the complexity of the project in our introduction to each design, but it's all subjective, based on your skill level and what you like to do. Some designs are worked in one piece so they'll require fewer steps in assembling; others are worked in separate pieces because having it all on one needle would be much too heavy and bulky to work comfortably. In fact, most are worked on the larger-size needles.

This book is also about having some (though not all) of the answers you need in one convenient place. We have some obvious advice for getting organized (which few of us heed until we get stuck on the roadside); answers to frequently asked questions that come up from knitters of all skill levels; and stitch instructions so you don't have to search for your basic instruction book when you want to keep going on a project.

What this book is most about, however, is having fun and being creative—at your own speed.

Getting Organized

Knitting is like any other journey: You'll save a lot of time by being prepared in advance for your trip. For today's fast-lane knitters this means:

Choosing a do-able project (destination). If you're only comfortable travelling quickly on smooth roads, then stick to projects you feel you can finish realistically. This means choosing:

❖ Small projects with no fitting necessary and a minimum of finishing required;

❖ Bulky yarns or multi-stranding (two or more strands held together, which give you the option of combining different colors for tweedy or graduated color effects);

❖ Projects worked on larger needles.

For beginners, the general recommendation is to use smooth, non-textured yarns versus more highly-textured ones (although many of the new textured yarns can also be wonderfully easy to work with).

"I don't like the yarn used…" If you don't like the yarn shown in the pattern, or feel it's too expensive, buy a skein of a yarn you like and work up a gauge swatch to see if it matches and how the yarn you prefer drapes compared to that shown in the project. (Sorry, we still have to make gauge swatches in the fast lane to avoid going off the road!) *IT ALL COMES DOWN TO GAUGE AND HOW THE YARN DRAPES.* If you substitute a yarn in a different fiber, it should have the same elasticity as the original fiber used. For example, a cotton yarn will not have the elasticity of wool. Check the

yardage on your substitute yarn as well, to be sure you have enough to finish the project. While we can't guarantee the same results as shown in our photos when you change yarns (and for that matter, results are subject to individual knitting quirks such as tension), you will get a good idea from a 6" x 6" gauge swatch how your new yarn works up.

*Speaking of gauge, that swatch need not be wasted. You may choose to put your gauge swatches in a notebook with notes about the pattern or use it to test-clean for washing methods. If you make a 7" X 9" swatch, you may donate it to Warm Up America!, c/o Craft Yarn Council of America, P.O. Box 9, Gastonia, NC 28053. Warm Up America! is the brainchild of Evie Rosen, our technical editor on this book. Your donated swatches are joined with others to make wonderful warm blankets that are distributed throughout the U.S. to everyone from homeless children to victims of hurricanes and fires. We work with CYCA to promote that program, and can tell you first-hand how heartwarming it is to see and hear how grateful recipients are for these warm, handmade blankets. **NOTE:** For obvious reasons, the yarn used should be washable and durable.*

Experiment with different yarns. You might want to mix a smooth yarn with a highly-textured one for an interesting effect that's still easy to handle and because it's multi-stranded, it works up quickly. Remember, you can also achieve great effects from textured or variegated-color yarns using the simplest of stitches.

"Packing" For Your Trip

Pack tools and supplies in advance. If you can't find the needles or stitch marker or crochet hook or yarn needle you need, when you need it, time will be lost, and frustration will be high. Read the list of needed materials and be sure you have the right size of everything you'll need before you want to sit down and begin the project.

When choosing your yarn, buy all the yarn you need at once. Even though there are many "no dye lot" yarns these days, it's best to have all of each color you need and from the same lot number if possible; no sense being frustrated by running out of yarn.

Planning Your Route (reading instructions)

You'd never set out on a trip without looking at the map first to review your route, would you? The same principle applies to knitting. Review the whole pattern, from start to finish. You should know where you'll be every step of the way. Trust us, it will prevent you from getting confused and angry. When you read the pattern through (and it doesn't hurt to do it more than once), you'll know what to expect. The diagrams will give you the measurements of the pieces *before* they're assembled, while the measurements shown with the sizes will show the *finished* measurements.

About Sizing...

The patterns in this book represent the talents of many different designers, so sizing will vary. To decide which size is right for you, refer to the pattern diagram, measure your own body, and even measure a sweater that has a similar silhouette and fits you well.

If you want to make the body or sleeve longer or shorter, look for the place in the pattern where the instructions say, "continue knitting in the pattern established for X number of rows or inches." That's generally a good place to increase or decrease the number of rows to adjust the fit. Check your gauge information in each pattern to determine how many rows equal an inch. For example, if you want to lengthen a sleeve from 19" to 20" and the gauge is 12 rows = 2", then add six rows to add that inch. If that's too complicated, lay your knitting on a flat, smooth surface and measure it against another sweater. Just remember to make a note of any change on the pattern and make the same change on the corresponding sleeve or sweater body. Always maintain the established stitch pattern.

Traffic Signs

Throughout the patterns in this book, you'll see traffic signs that alert you to changes or draw your attention to a special stitch or technique, or an area that needs a bit more attention. Generally, we've gone by the following guidelines:

 Read through and understand before going further.

 Special tips on working this section.

 Change here (yarns or needle sizes).

The intent is to save you time by helping prevent "wrong turns," i.e., changes you might miss if you're reading too fast.

About Gauge

Think of your gauge swatch as "stitches and rows per inch." You will have more patience for gauge than you will if you have to rip out half a sweater because the gauge is way off. Gauge is probably the single most important thing you can do to ensure the correct size of your knitted project. (And by the time you've finished complaining about it, you could have finished it!)

Using the yarn, needles and pattern stitch called for at the pattern's beginning, cast on four times the speci-fied number of stitches per inch. For example, if 5 sts = 1", cast on 20 stitches and work in the pattern stitch for 4 inches. Your swatch *should* be 4" square.

To check your gauge, slip the work off your needle, lay it right side up on a smooth, hard surface and measure across the center. If your swatch doesn't measure exactly 4" square (or whatever size was specified for the gauge), you will have to make adjustments. If the swatch came out too small, knit another one with the next size larger needles. If it was too large, try it with the next size smaller needles. Work it out until you come as close as possible to the gauge required. While you're working on your project, measure across the width of the whole piece every 3" to be sure that your gauge hasn't changed.

Working With Specialty Yarns

Several projects in this book use very large needles and/or multi-strands of yarn, incorporate faux fur yarns, highly-textured fibers or hand-dyed yarns, any of which you may not have worked with before. Here are some tips we've picked up working on this book.

On Big Needles...

Sizes 17 and above generally come in different materials—metal alloys and plastics. Many knitters prefer the plastic needles to help control the more slippery yarns.

If you're into row counters, they won't fit on the really big needles. At one of Christina's favorite local shops, The Stitchery in Pearl River, NY, owners Judi and Adam Leber recommend using a safety pin to affix the row counter right to the garment.

Markers don't come big enough for sizes 17 and above either; the Lebers use bone rings or pieces of yarn as markers.

On Multi-Stranding...

Make believe you're working with one big strand, and hold the strands together in your hands as you would a single strand.

It's important that the different skeins you're pulling from remain untangled. This can be managed from two ends: First, keep the skeins in separate bags or baskets or whatever storage units you're using. Then, use a favorite trick from the Lebers: Depending on the thickness of your yarn, take a thread spool or a spool from an empty adding machine tape and thread the multi-strands of yarn through the spool before you cast on. The weight of the spool on the yarn will help keep the yarn manageable as you knit.

As with the faux fur yarns, this is one place where you have to keep your eyes on the road. It's easy to put your needle through the middle of a multi-strand stitch and wind up with extra stitches, so don't go into cruise control and look away too much.

On Fur & Other Novelties...

A few hints for getting the smoothest ride from some of these luxury or sporty vehicles:

❖ With any fur, hairy or highly textured yarn, watch what you are doing. Otherwise, you can easily add extra stitches or drop stitches, and take it from us, you don't want to have to rip out rows in a fur yarn. It's very difficult to pick up dropped stitches, and the long fibers in these yarns make it just about impossible to unravel.

❖ Count stitches and count rows. A good gauge swatch will be helpful here, since fur yarns tend to be stretchy. (You can use that gauge swatch to test-clean later.)

❖ Join your new ball of yarn at the beginning of a row, for ease of weaving in (and hiding) ends. (This is a good rule to follow in general.)

❖ Cast on loosely with fur yarns because there will be very little give in the cast-on row.

❖ When finishing, use a smooth yarn in a matching color for the seaming; brushing the fur gently and lightly with a hairbrush will conceal the seam if it happens to show.

❖ Don't block or steam fur yarns; it will flatten the fibers.

❖ Another general rule that applies here is to be sure to make your stitches over the full circumference (thickness) of the needle (the shaft rather than the point), for uniformity and to meet the gauge (and so you don't have to fight to get your needle in the stitch in the next row!).

❖ Don't worry about ribbon yarns twisting as you knit: *it doesn't matter.*

If you work with hand-dyed or "hand-painted" yarns, you may see a lot of variance in color between individual hanks or skeins. The designers behind the Colinette Yarns used in our Fur-Trimmed Tabard and Weekend Chic Rollneck Pullover recommend that knitters alternate two skeins throughout the knitting, alternating the skeins every other row and carrying the yarns. We have to confess, we didn't. Instead, we tried to pick colors and skeins that seemed to be even and similar in color, and we were happy with the results.

Facts About Finishing

You're almost done! When it comes to finishing, Evie Rosen, knitting teacher and knitting maven, offers some helpful hints…

Finishing Seams

Back Stitch: This is a strong, not bulky stitch that is very acceptable for shoulders and armholes. (See Stitch Instructions for the technique in Diagram 53.)

Mattress Stitch: This is a perfect stitch for side seams and sleeve seams, and is also called Vertical Weaving or Invisible Stitch. You work under a bar between the first and second stitches on each side, alternating sides. (See Stitch Instructions for the technique.)

Three Needle Bind-Off: This is used as a shoulder bind off and shoulder seam. Hold the right sides together with knitting needles pointing in the same direction. With a third knitting needle, knit one stitch from the front needle and one from the back needle together and move the new stitch to the third needle. Knit the next two stitches together and move to the third needle. Lift the first stitch on the third needle over the second stitch to bind it off. Continue in this manner and binding off across the row. Fasten off.

Blocking

Blocking will even out your stitches, flatten your seams and give your garment a more finished, professional appearance.

Wet Blocking: If the garment is machine washable, wash it in the machine and machine dry according to manufacturer's directions on the yarn label. Otherwise, hand wash it carefully, pressing as much moisture out of it as you can. Then put it in the last four minutes of the spin cycle in your washer to remove the rest of the water. Spread on bath towels to desired size, shaping with your hands, and let it dry, checking it often for size. You may pin it to size if desired, using rust-free pins.

Steam: This will be easier with a wool yarn. Keeping the iron (or steamer) at least a half inch above the garment, steam the entire garment on the wrong side. Acrylics should only be steamed (or wet-blocked), not pressed. You can change a garment's size slightly when it is damp from the steam. Let it dry before moving it.

Pattern Coding

The introduction to each project provides an overview of the pattern instructions. In addition, we have added a coding system more detailed than the usual Easy/Intermediate/Advanced ratings, which defines the quickest and easiest patterns as Beginner1, 2 and 3, followed by Intermediate and finally, Experienced.

Beginner1, for instance, is a good first-time project with no shaping and garter and stockinette stitches.

Beginner2 projects also have simple shapes and stitches, but involve changing yarn colors and working with very textured or multiple strands of yarn, simple increases and decreases and stitch holders.

Beginner3 projects still feature simple shapes, and may use textured yarn or multiple strands, and can introduce different stitch combinations, circular needles, decreasing, increasing, and picking up stitches.

Chapter 2

Quick Trips

Speedy Girl's Poncho

Designed by Lion Brand Yarn Co.

It's fun, fashion and easy to wear. And you'll be cruising in the fast lane with this design: one rectangle, one seam and steam—you're done!

Sizes:

Girl's sizes 4/6 (6/8, 10/12)
Block to 11 x 30" (13 x 32", 15 x 34") or as desired

Gauge:

In pattern on size 13 needles, 3 sts = 1"
To ensure proper fit, take time to check gauge.

Instructions:

Row 1: Slip 1, *k2, p2; repeat from *, end k3.
Row 2: Slip 1, *p2, k2; rep from *, end p2, k1.
Repeat rows 1 and 2 for pattern.

Cast on 32 (40, 44) sts. Work in pattern, beginning with Row 1 for 30 (32, 34)". Bind off.

Finishing:

Block. Sew bound off edge to the first 11 (13, 15)" of side edge as pictured.

MATERIALS:

❖ Lion Brand *Woolspun*
    (wool/acrylic/polyester,100 yd) skein
    Raspberry (#112)—2 (2, 3) skeins

❖ Size 13 knitting needles or size
    needed to obtain gauge

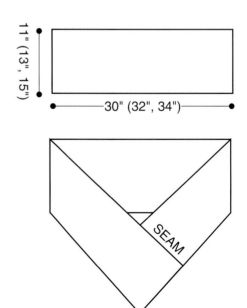

Photo: Christina L. Holmes

Sleeveless High Neck

Designed by Lion Brand Yarn Co.

This easy-to-wear design is fashion-right and fast—a straight road to style! Worked on size 13 needles, the thick-and-thin yarn makes this a quick but interesting trip.

Sizes:

Directions are for women's sizes Small
   (Medium, Large, X-Large)
Finished garment at chest measures 36 (38, 40, 42)"

Gauge:

In Stockinette stitch on size 13 needles,
   5 sts and 7 rows = 2"
To ensure the proper size, be sure to check your gauge.

Instructions:

Back

With size 13 straight needles cast on 48 (50, 52, 54) sts. Work in k1, p1 rib for 6 rows. Continue in St st until piece measures 14" from beginning, end by doing WS row.

Armhole Shaping

Bind off 3 sts at beginning of next 2 rows. Decrease row (RS): Slip 1 st, p1, k1, p1, k2tog, knit to last 6 sts, ssk, p1, k1, p1, k1. In all WS rows slip 1st st, k1, p1, k1, purl to last 4 sts, k1, p1, k1, p1. Repeat decreases one more time, 38 (40, 42, 44) sts. Work as following: (RS) slip first st, p1, k1, p1 to last 4 sts, p1, k1, p1, k1; (WS) slip first st, k1, p1, k1, purl to last 4 sts, k1, p1, k1, p1. Repeat these 2 rows until armhole measures 7 (8, 8, 9)". Bind off 10 (11, 12, 12) sts at beginning of next 2 rows. Place remaining 18 (18, 18, 20) sts onto stitch holder for back neck.

MATERIALS:

❖ Lion Brand *Woolspun*
   (wool/acrylic/polyester, 100 yd skein)
   Sky Blue (#106)—4, (4, 5, 5) skeins

❖ Size 13 (9 mm) straight knitting needles

❖ Size 13 (9 mm) 16" (40 cm) circular needles,
   or size needed to obtain the correct
   gauge

❖ 2 Stitch holders

❖ Yarn or tapestry needle for weaving in ends

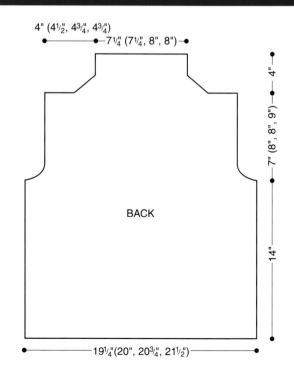

4" (4½", 4¾", 4¾")

7¼" (7¼", 8", 8")

4"

7" (8", 8", 9")

BACK

14"

19¼" (20", 20¾", 21½")

Front

Work as for back until armhole measures 5 (6, 6, 7)".

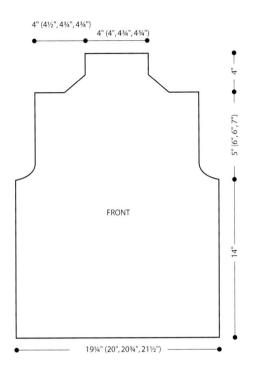

4" (4½", 4¾", 4¾")

4" (4", 4¾", 4¾")

4"

5" (6", 6", 7")

FRONT

14"

19¼" (20", 20¾", 21½")

Front Neckline Shaping

Slip 1, p1, k1, p1, k7 (8, 8, 9), ssk, k1, place next 10 (10, 12, 12) sts onto stitch holder. Attach a separate strand of yarn to other side and work remaining sts as following: k1, k2tog, k7 (8, 8, 9), p1, k1, p1, k1. Working both shoulders at the same time, repeat decreases every other row 3 more times. When front measures same as back, bind off 10 (11, 12, 12) sts from each shoulder edge.

Neck

Sew shoulders together. With RS facing and circular needle, work across 18 (18, 18, 20) sts from Back holder, pick up 5 sts on left side of neck, work across 10 (10, 12, 12) sts from front holder, pick up 5 sts on the right side of the neck—38 (38, 42, 42) sts. Next round: Work in k1, p1. Work around until neckband measures 4". Bind off loosely.

Finishing:

Sew side seams. Weave ends. Block.

Photo: Christina L. Holmes

Quick Cropped Top

Designed by Elena Malo

Simply stylish, this flattering, capped-sleeve top is made in one piece on size 11 needles. Be sure to use a soft yarn as shown, so the top drapes properly.

Sizes:

Directions are for women's sizes Small (Medium, Large, X-Large)
Finished garment at chest measures 36 (38, 40, 42)"

Gauge:

In Stockinette stitch on size 11 needles, 3 sts and 4 rows = 1"
To ensure proper fit, take time to check the gauge.

Instructions:

Top is made in one piece, beginning at lower back edge.

With size 11 straight needles, cast on 48 (51, 54, 57) sts. Work in St st for 10 rows. Increase 1 st each side, repeat increase every 10 rows, 2 more times. Repeat increase every other row 3 times, 60 (63, 66, 69) sts. Work until piece measures 18 (19, 19½, 20)".

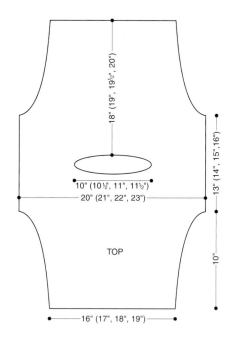

18" (19", 19½", 20")

10" (10½", 11", 11½")
20" (21", 22", 23")

13" (14", 15", 16")

TOP

10"

16" (17", 18", 19")

Neckline

Work over first 15 (16, 18, 19) sts. Bind off next 30 (31, 30, 31) sts, work to end of row. Next row work first 15 (16, 18, 19) sts, cast on 30 (31, 30, 31) sts, work to end of row. Continue even on 60 (63, 66, 69) sts until piece measures 6 (6½, 7, 7½)" from neckline cast on. Decrease 1 st each side every other row 3 times. Work 10 rows. Repeat decrease. Repeat decrease every 10 rows, 2 more times. Work 10 rows, bind off with a knit row on WS.

Finishing:

Holding work RS up, with circular needle pick up 60 (63, 60, 62) sts around neckline. Bind off with a knit row from WS.
Sew side seams. With circular needle repeat this same finishing around each armhole picking up 30 (42, 45, 48) sts and around lower edge, picking up 96 (102, 108, 114). Finish off all ends.

Materials:

❖ Berroco, *Pronto*
(cotton/acrylic, 55 yds/50 gm ball)
So Blue #4450—7 balls

❖ Size 11 straight needles, or needle size to obtain gauge

❖ Size 11 circular needle—16" (for finishing)

❖ Yarn or tapestry needle for finishing

Photo: Christina L. Holmes

Plushest Pullover

Designed by Elena Malo

Picture a luxurious limo—this is the softest ride imaginable, and lightweight too! Knit mostly on size 15 needles using two strands, with the body made in one piece, this is a loose-fitting design everyone can wear.

Sizes:

Directions are for women's sizes Small
(Medium, Large, X-Large)
Finished garment at chest measures 36 (40, 44, 48)"

Gauge:

In Stockinette stitch, using 2 strands of Plush and
size 15 needles, 8 sts and 12 rows = 4".
To ensure proper fit, take time to check the gauge.

Instructions:

▽ Sweater is knit in the round, using circular needles. See page 126 for information on working with circular needles.

Body

With longer circular needles size 13 and A, cast on 72 (80, 88, 96) sts. Work in rounds in k1, p1 ribbing for 3 rows.
▽ (Place a marker at the end of first row, to help you determine when you are about to begin a new row.)
◇ Change to circular needles size 15 and 2 strands of MC. Knit all rows until piece measures 14" from start.

⬟ Divide work in half for back and front.

Back

Work over 36 (40, 44, 48) sts, place remaining sts on holder. Work in St st until piece measures 7½ (8, 8½, 9)".

Place first 12 (14, 15, 17) sts on a holder for left shoulder, center 12 (12, 14, 14) sts on a separate holder for back neckline, last 12 (14, 15, 17) sts for right shoulder.

MATERIALS:

❖ Berroco *Plush* (acrylic, 90 yds/50 gm ball) Java Purple (#1916)—10 (10, 12, 12) balls—Main Color (MC)

❖ Berroco *X-Press* (wool/acrylic, 42 yds/ 50 gm balls) Java Plum—2 balls—Color A

❖ Size 13 circular needle—16"

❖ Size 13 circular needles—24"

❖ Size 15 circular needle—24" or size to obtain gauge

❖ 6 stitch holders

❖ Yarn or tapestry needle for finishing

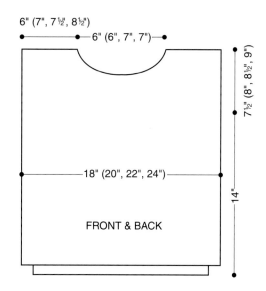

6" (7", 7½", 8½")

6" (6", 7", 7")

7½" (8", 8½", 9")

18" (20", 22", 24")

14"

FRONT & BACK

Front

Pick up remaining sts. Join 2 new strands of MC, work in St st until piece measures 6 (6, 6½, 6½)".

Neckline Shaping

Work over first 15 (17, 18, 20) sts, leave next 6 (6, 8, 8) sts on holder. Join 2 new strands of MC, work each shoulder separately. Bind off 2 sts at neck edge once, decrease 1 st once. Work even until front corresponds to back. Place remaining 12 (14, 15, 17) sts of each shoulder on holders.

Sleeves

Make 2. With size 13 needles (short circulars) and A, cast on 23 (23, 25, 27) sts. Work in rounds in k1 p1 ribbing for 3 rows.

Change to size 15 needles and 2 strands of MC, work in St st for 8 rows. Increase 1 st each end. Repeat increase every 8th row 4 (5, 5, 5) times; 33 (35, 37, 39) sts. Work even until piece measures 19" from the beginning. Bind off.

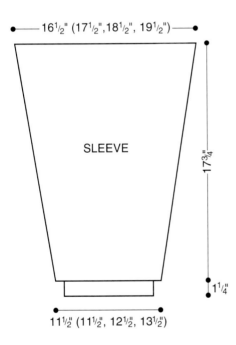

16½" (17½", 18½", 19½")

SLEEVE

17¾"

1¼"

11½" (11½", 12½", 13½")

Photo: Christina L. Holmes

Finishing:

STOP Three-needle finishing: Place front and back shoulder sts on 2 separate needles (13 and 15 circulars). Holding work with WS together, with a third size 13 needle, *knit 1 st from front and 1 from back together.* Repeat from * 1 more time and bind off first st. Repeat across. Repeat for other shoulder.

With the RS of the sweater facing you, using size 13 needles (short circular) and color A, pick up 34 (36, 36, 38) sts around neckline. Work 5 rows in k1, p1 ribbing. Bind off in ribbing loosely. Pin sleeves to armholes and sew together using backstitch. Sew sleeve seams.

Fringed Necklace & Beaded Necklace

Designed by Arnetta Kenney

Depending on the yarn and beads you choose, these little necklaces can have the fashionable look of the 1970s or be elegantly Victorian. Beads are added to the fringe or threaded onto the yarn in advance and later knitted into the stitches.

Gauge:

In garter stitch and size 6 needles, 23 sts = 4"
To ensure proper fit, take time to check gauge.

Instructions:

Using 1 strand cast on 3 sts.
Row 1: K1, yo, k1, yo, end k1.
Row 2: K1, yo, k to end of row—6 sts.
Row 3: K1, yo, k to last st, yo, k1—8 sts.
Row 4: K.
Repeat rows 3 & 4 until there are a total of 22 sts, end with Row 4.

🛑 To create the straps for the necklace, you will cast on stitches at end of Row 4, which is one of the top corners of the necklace triangle. Then you will knit across these new stitches, continuing knitting across the necklace and then at the other top corner, cast on stitches for the second strap.

Necklace Strap

Row 1: At the end of Row 4, cast on 32 sts, by knitting into the end stitch, and placing the newly formed st onto the left needle 🛑 Do not remove old st from left

FRINGED NECKLACE MATERIALS:

- ❖ J & P Coats *Speed–Cro–Sheen*
  (cotton, 100 yd ball)
  Size 3 Vanilla (#007)—1 ball

- ❖ 1 large center bead

- ❖ 12 medium-to-large beads for fringe

- ❖ 1 small-to-medium button for necklace closure

- ❖ Size 6 needle (or size needed to obtain gauge)

- ❖ Needle for threading beads

needle.) Continue adding new sts, until you have cast on 32 new sts.

▽ Strap length is approximately 6½". Adjust length as desired by increasing or decreasing the number of stitches you cast on.

Row 2: K into the back loop of the new 32 sts. Work the 22 necklace sts in pattern established: K1, yo, knit to last st, yo, k1. Following instructions as in row 1, cast on 32 sts creating the second strap.

Row 3: K into the back loop of the new 32 sts. K the 22 necklace sts in pattern established and k the sts of the first strap.

Row 4-6: K every st, yo above previous yarn overs every other row.

Row 7: Bind off across row.

Finishing:

To make the necklace fringe, cut 18, 12 " lengths of yarn. (Two lengths per fringe.)

Loop one set of fringe through the eyelet hole at the center bottom. Loop the remaining fringe through the eyelet holes along side edges of necklace. There should be 4 strands in each fringe.

(STOP) To make twisted fringe: Separate each fringe into 2 groups (2 strands per group), twist each group to the right tightly, while twisted place both groups together then twist in the opposite direction (to the left). While maintaining twist, thread a bead(s) onto twisted fringe, then knot the twisted fringe closely to bead. Repeat with other fringe. For a graduated look, cut each fringe shorter than the bottom one.

▽ Making twisted cord can be tricky, especially when you are twisting two threads. It's helpful to place the necklace on a hard, flat surface, twist one set of threads tightly, tape the ends to the surface with regular adhesive tape so they can't unravel, and then twist the second set of threads. To twist the two sides of fringe together, it's helpful to hold the two sides together with one hand and twist with the other. Experiment with bead placement and the number of beads.

Sew a loop to the back of one strap and add a button to the other.

Gauge:

In garter stitch, 23 sts = 4"
To ensure proper fit, take time to check gauge.

Instructions:

STOP Thread 10 beads onto the yarn before you begin. Beads will be held behind your knitting and when you are ready to position them on the necklace, you simply pull the bead up to your needles.

Using 1 strand, cast on 3 sts. Follow Fringed Necklace pattern, positioning the beads where desired on the necklace triangle. **STOP** To position the bead, bring the bead forward, close to work, slip the next st (bead sits in front of this stitch), knit next stitch. Knit the slipped stitch on the next row. Continue following the Fringed Necklace pattern until there are a total of 22 sts, ending with Row 4.

Necklace Strap

Continue to follow pattern for Fringed Necklace, binding off on Row 6.

Finishing:

Sew beads onto necklace edge, just below eyelet holes. Sew a loop at end of one strap and button at the end of the other.

BEADED NECKLACE MATERIALS:

❖ J & P Coats® *"Speed–Cro–Sheen"* (cotton, 100 yd ball) Size 3 Navy (#486)—1 ball

❖ 10 medium-to-large beads

❖ 1 small-to-medium button for necklace closure

❖ Size 6 needle, or size needed to obtain gauge

❖ Needle for threading beads

Country Weekend

Fur-Trimmed Tabard & Cowl

Designed by Elena Malo

From Aspen to Zermatt, this chic tabard in hand-dyed yarn with faux fur trim would look great wherever you are! Worked on size 15 needles for speed, and secured with twisted ties on each side for adjustable fit. With the option of a separate "fur" cowl and ski band, you'll be fashionably warm.

Sizes:

Womens sizes Small (Medium, Large, X-Large)
Finished chest size, 40 (44, 48, 52)"

Gauge:

In Stockinette stitch, using *Point Five* yarn and size 15 needles,
 11 sts and 15 rows = 5"
To ensure the proper size, take time to check your gauge.

Tabard Instructions:

Back

With straight needles and A, cast on 42 (46, 51, 55) sts. Knit for 3 rows, ending with WS row. Work in St st; for selvedge slip first st of every row. Work until piece measures 24". Work first 13 (15, 17, 19) sts and place on holder, bind off next 16 (16, 17, 17) sts for the back of the neck, place remaining 13 (15, 17, 19) sts on a stitch holder for left shoulder.

MATERIALS:

❖ Colinette Hand-Dyed *Point Five*
 (wool, 54 yds/100 gm hank)
 Summer Berries (#109)
 Color A—6 (6, 7, 7) hanks

❖ Mondial *Fur* (wool/acrylic/polyester, 50 gm hank/49 yds) (color #85)
 Color B—4 hanks
NOTE: This is sufficient yarn to trim tabard and complete cowl and ski band.

❖ Size 15 straight needles, or size to obtain gauge

❖ Size 15 circular needles, 24" long (for finishing)

❖ 4 stitch holders

Photo: Christina L. Holmes

Front

Work the same as for back until 21½" from beginning, end with WS row.

Neckline Shape and Shoulders

K first 17 (19, 21, 23) sts. Place remaining sts on holder. Row 1: Bind off first 2 sts, p to end. Row 2-4: K to last 3 sts, slip 1, k1, psso (pass slip stitch over knit stitch), k1. Work on remaining 13 (15, 17, 19) sts until front measures the same as back. Place stitches on holder. Pick up sts on holder. Join A, bind off next 8 (8, 9, 9) sts and k to end of row. Work on remaining 17 (19, 21, 23) sts. Shape right shoulder as for left but reverse shaping. Place stitches on holder.

Finishing:

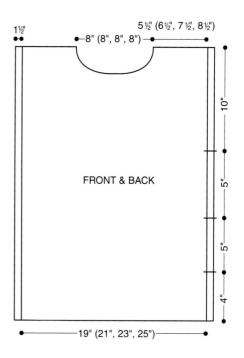

▽ Following is an alternate method of joining seams which is called three-needle bind off. It is the neatest finish for shoulder seams. As its name suggests, you use three needles. Try this or you can bind off the shoulder stitches and join the shoulder seams using backstitch. Place front and back shoulder sts on separate needles. Holding work with RS facing, with another size 15 needle, knit 1 st from front and 1 st from back together and at the same time, bind off. Repeat on other shoulder.

Finish Side Edge: With RS facing, size 15 circular needles and 2 strands of B, pick up the first st (selvedge stitch) every 2nd row, from beginning of back to beginning of front. Work in St st for 3 rows, bind off on 4th row loosely.

Side Ties

There are six, 12" long twisted-cord ties on each side of the tabard, approximately 5" apart. (See illustration for exact placement.) Each tie is made by twisting four strands of yarn.

Cut 24, 36" long strands of color A. For each tie, hold together two strands, fold them in half and draw the loop end through the side edge of the tabard, at the designated point. Using your fingers or a crochet hook, draw the ends through the loop to secure the tie just as you would if you were making a fringe. Take two of the four strands and twist them to the right. Secure them so they do not unravel and take the second two strands and twist them to the right. Then hold the two twisted cords together and twist them tightly to the left. Make a knot at the end and trim close to the knot. Finished cord will measure approximately 12" long.

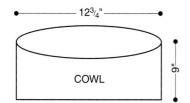

Detachable Cowl

With circular needles and 2 strands of B, cast on 36 sts. Work in rounds, knit each round, until piece measures 9". Bind off very loosely. Fasten off and weave in all ends.

Fur Ski Band

Designed by Christina L. Holmes

This is a real downhill racer! Worked in two strands of *Fur*, knit stitch all the way, it's fast and easy. (You can also use this basic pattern to make a man's ski band in another, more masculine yarn. Guys whose occupation demands they work outside in the cold weather especially appreciate these in bright, neon colors that motorists can see.)

Size:

Measure the head you want to fit. Keep in mind that this is worked in knit stitches in a "stretchy" direction, so you'll want to make it a little snug to allow for stretch (about an inch smaller than the head size). Ours measures 3" x 22½".

Instructions:

Working with two strands of *Fur* yarn on size 15 needles, cast on 7 stitches. Knit until piece measures 22½" long (or size desired). Bind off, leaving a 12" tail of yarn for seaming. Try on the band for fit, and seam as desired, using overcast stitch.

3" | SKIBAND | —22½"—

Silvery "Shearling" Vest & Hat

Designed by Lion Brand Yarn Co.

We love the look of shearling—why not knit it? The vest is made in one piece, with a single strand of this bulky chenille on size 10½ needles. The "fur" yarn is worked with two strands held together on size 7 needles. Be sure to measure for the head size on the hat, which is sized for a generous fit; some may prefer a more snug fit.

Sizes:

Women's sizing Small (Medium, Large, Extra Large)
Finished chest measurement: 36 (39, 42, 46)"

Gauge:

With *Chenille* yarn on size 10½ needles in Stockinette stitch,
    2½ sts and 3 rows = 1"
With *daVinci* yarn on size 7 needles in Stockinette stitch with two
    strands of yarn held together, 4½ sts and 6 rows = 1"
To ensure proper fit, take time to check your gauge.

Instructions:

Vest Back & Front (knit in one continuous piece)

With single strand of *Chenille* and size 10½ needles, cast on 45 (49, 53, 58) sts. Work in St st for 18 (18½, 18½, 19)".
  ▽ Make length adjustments at this point. ◇CAUTION◇ Work one row of Reverse St st, then continue working in St st until piece measures 24½ (25, 25½, 26)" from start.

Neck Shaping

Work 13 (14, 16, 18) sts, bind off center 19 (21, 21, 22) sts. Join a second ball of yarn and work remaining 13 (14, 16, 18) sts.

MATERIALS:

❖ Lion Brand *Chenille "Thick & Quick®"* (acrylic/rayon, 100yd skein) grey (#149)
  Vest (all sizes)—4 skeins
  Hat (all sizes)—1 skein

❖ Lion Brand *daVinci* (nylon, 1¾ oz/50 gm/121 yd ball)
  Marble (#152) for faux fur trim
  Vest (all sizes)—2 skeins
  Hat (all sizes)—1 skein

❖ Worsted-weight yarn—a small quantity of grey (approximately 6 yards) for finishing seams (See finishing notes in the pattern.)

❖ Size 10½/6.5mm circular needles, or size to obtain gauge

❖ Size 7/4.5mm circular needles

❖ Size 9/5.5mm circular needles

❖ Size H/8 crochet hook

❖ 7 fur hook closures

❖ Yarn or tapestry needle for finishing

❖ Yarn markers

Photo: Christina L. Holmes

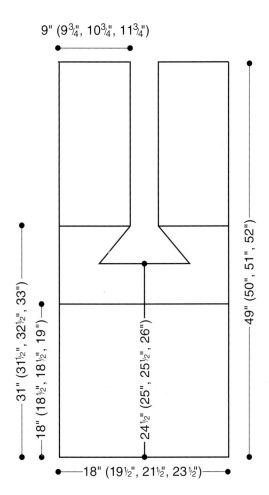

9" (9¾", 10¾", 11¾")

49" (50", 51", 52")

31" (31½", 32½", 33")

18" (18½", 18½", 19")

24½" (25", 25½", 26")

18" (19½", 21½", 23½")

Working both sides at once, work even for 2 rows. Increase 1 st at neck edge every other row 9 (10, 10, 11) times, 22 (24, 26, 29) sts, and at same time when piece measures 31 (31½, 32½, 33)" from start work, 1 row of Reverse St st. Continue working in St st until piece measures 49 (50, 51, 52)" from start. Bind off all sts.

Finishing:

Sew side seams. ▽ Chenille is difficult to sew with. We recommend weaving together the side seams using a similar color of a worsted-weight yarn.

Front Faux Fur Edging

With size 7 needles and two strands of *daVinci* faux fur yarn, pick up 70 (70, 72, 72) sts along one of the front edges from bottom of piece to start of neck shaping. Work in Reverse St st (so that the fur rolls inward toward the WS of the sweater) for 6 rows. ◇ Bind off all sts with size 10½ needles. Repeat pattern on the other front edge.

Neck Edging

With a size 7 needle and a double strand of *daVinci* faux fur yarn, pick up 72 (74, 81, 83) sts around neck edge starting at neck shaping. Work in garter stitch for 9 rows.
◇ Bind off all sts with size 10½ needles.

Bottom Edging

With RS facing, size 7 needles and two strands of *daVinci* "fur" yarn, pick up 153 (171, 189, 207) sts along bottom edge. Work in St st (so that the fur rolls outward toward the right side of the sweater) for 6 rows. ◇ Bind off all sts with size 10½ needles.

Armhole Edging

With RS facing, size 7 needles and a double strand of daVinci "fur" yarn, pick up 90 (100, 102, 104) sts around armhole edge. Work in St st (so that the fur rolls outward toward the right side of the sweater) for 6 rows. ◇ Bind off all sts with size 10½ needles.

Yoke "Seams"

With size 7 needles and two strands of *daVinci* "fur" yarn, pick up 38 (43, 47, 51) sts along Reverse St st yoke ridge along each front. Work in garter st for 2 rows.
◇ Bind off all sts with size 10½ needles. Again, using size 7 needles, pick up 77 (85, 95, 103) sts along Reverse St st ridge at back yoke, and work in garter st for 2 rows. ◇ Bind off all sts with size 10½ needles.
Sew 7 fur hooks and loops along the front opening, spaced evenly from bottom of vest to start of neck opening.

Hat (generous sizing):

With size 10½ needles and one strand of *Chenille Thick & Quick*, cast on 4 sts. Working in St st, increase 1 st into each stitch (8 sts). Next row: Purl. Next row: Knit all! sts, increase 1 st into every other stitch (12 sts). Continue working in St st, placing a marker every 3 sts (4 markers total). Increase 1 st before each marker every other round until there are 13 sts between each marker, 52 sts total. Work even until piece measures 7". Switch to size 9 circular needles and continue working in St st until piece measures 9½". With two strands of *daVinci* "fur" yarn and size 7 circular needles, k1, increase 1 st into each stitch across the row, k1 (102 sts). Work in St st for 2½". Bind off all sts with size 10½ needles.

Finishing:

▽ **NOTE:** Sizing adjustments can be made when you are finishing the hat. For instance, before sewing the hat seam, pin it and try it on to make sure you like the fit. Do the same thing before you fold and stitch the fur trim cuff.

Sew hat seam. Turn up bottom 5". At the point where the fur trim starts, tack cuff to the hat all the way around. Turn down fur so that it completely covers cuff. With a double strand of fur and a yarn or tapestry needle whipstitch the bottom of the fur trim to the bottom of the cuff, securing it all the way around the hat.

Lay hat flat. Make a faux fur "seam" with a double strand of *daVinci* yarn and a size H crochet hook. Work one row of single crochet beginning from the fur cuff, along the diameter of the hat dome to the opposite side of the cuff. Lay hat flat so that fur seam is in the direct center of the hat and make a second faux seam perpendicular to the first so that both seams intersect at the hat's tip.

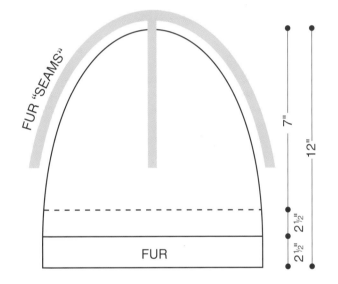

Sporty Slip-Stitch Turtleneck

Designed by Brenda A. Lewis for Coats & Clark

Three strands held together make a cozy, oversized turtleneck that's easy to wear. The pattern stitch creates a woven look, but you won't have to do any weaving on this one. Try out the pattern stitch first, by making a swatch, and it will be a much easier project.

Sizes:

Directions are for women's sizes Small (Medium, Large)
Finished chest size: 40 (44, 48)"
Sleeve length: 19 (20, 21)"

Gauge:

In pattern stitch with size 17 needles, 12 sts
   and 18 rows = 4".
To ensure the proper fit, take time to check your gauge.
NOTE: Hold 3 strands together throughout.

Pattern Stitch:

Row 1: Using 17 needles and MC knit.
Row 2: MC purl.
Row 3: CC k1, *slip 1 purlwise, k1, repeat from *.
Row 4: CC k1, *(yarn forward, slip 1 purlwise, yarn back), k1 repeat from *.
Rows 5 & 6: As rows 1 & 2.
Rows 7 & 8: As rows 3 & 4.
Rows 9 & 10: As rows 1 & 2.
Rows 11 & 12: ◇CAUTION Using **MC** as rows 3 & 4.
Rows 13 & 14: As rows 1 & 2.
Rows 15 & 16: As rows 3 & 4.
Rows 17 & 18: As rows 1 & 2.
Rows 19 & 20: As rows 11 & 12.

MATERIALS:

❖ Red Heart® *Soft* (Bounce-Back® acrylic, 5 oz/328 yd skein)
   Light Yellow Green (#7672), Main Color (MC)—7 (7, 9) skeins
   Dark Yellow Green (#7675), Contrasting Color (CC)—2 skeins

❖ Size 11/8mm knitting needles

❖ Size 17/12.75mm knitting needles, or size needed to obtain gauge

❖ Size 10 circular knitting needles, 16"

❖ Yarn or tapestry needle for finishing

❖ 3 stitch holders

Photo: Mary Colucci

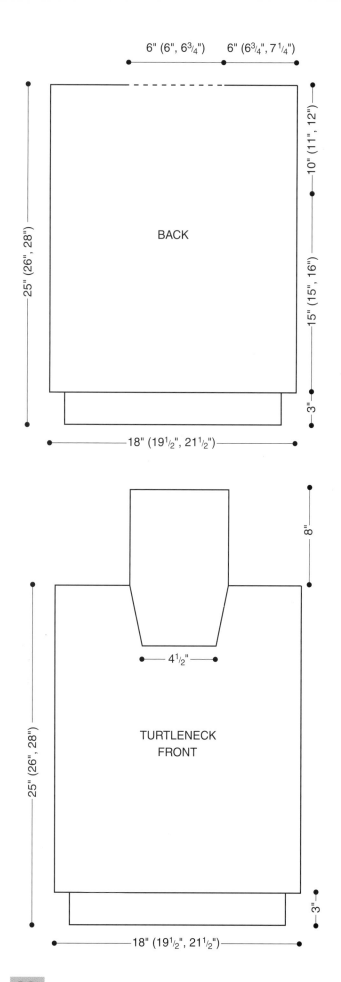

Instructions:

Back

Using size 11 needles and MC cast on 45 (49, 53) sts. Work k1, p1 ribbing for 3" ending with WS row. Repeat rows 1–20 for pattern and work in established pattern until back measures 25 (26, 28)" ending with a WS row. Bind off 15 (17, 18) sts at the beginning of each of the next 2 rows. Slip remaining 15 (15, 17) sts onto holder for neck back.

Front

Work the same as back until front measures 22 (23, 25)", ending with a WS row.

Neck Shaping

Next row work 17 (19, 21) sts in established pattern for left shoulder, slip next 11 (11, 11) sts onto holder for front neck, slip next 17 (19, 21) sts onto holder for the right shoulder. Work shoulder in established pattern and decrease 1 st at the neck edge every RS row 2 (2, 3) times. Work even until front measures 25 (26, 28)", ending with WS row. Bind off. With RS facing, leave center 11 sts on a holder, join yarn to remaining sts. Complete to correspond to first side, reversing shaping.

Sleeves

With size 10 circular needle and MC cast on 25 (25, 29) sts. Work k1, p1 ribbing for 3" ending with a WS row. 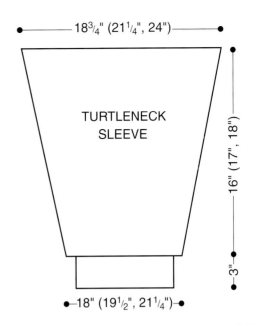 Change to size 17 needle, knit next row, increasing 6 sts evenly spaced across row. (Counts as row 1 of pattern.) Continue to work in pattern and increase 1 st each end of needle every 6th row until there are 45 (47, 53) sts. Work even in established pattern until sleeve measures 19 (20, 21)", ending with WS row. Bind off.

Finishing:

Sew shoulder seams.

Turtleneck

With size 10 circular needles, RS facing and MC, knit the 15 (15, 17) sts from holder for back neck. Pick up and knit 10 sts along side edge of neck, knit the 11 sts from holder for front neck, pick up and knit 10 sts along side edge. Place marker on needle. Work k1, p1 ribbing in rounds until neck measures 8".

▽ Bind off **loosely** in ribbing.

Measure down 10 (11, 12)" from each side of the shoulder seam and place a marker. Mark the center of the sleeve's top. Matching center of the sleeve top to shoulder seam, sew sleeve between markers.

Sew sleeve and side seam. Weave in yarn ends.

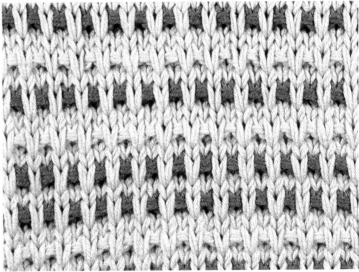

18³/₄" (21¹/₄", 24")

TURTLENECK SLEEVE

16" (17", 18")

3"

18" (19¹/₂", 21¹/₄")

Closeup of pattern stitch, right side.

Tunic With Optional Cowl

Designed by Elena Malo

We like the look of tunics as an elongated alternative to vests, and a separate cowl neck lets you add warmth and a fashion touch. Those who don't like something around their neck can go with this easy-to-wear tunic on its own. The yarn is bulky enough to use single stranded on size 13 needles and still move quickly.

Sizes:

Women's Small (Medium, Large, Extra Large)
Finished garment at chest measures 36 (40, 44, 48)"

Gauge:

On size 13 needles in Stockinette stitch, 13 sts and 7 rows = 5"
To ensure the proper size, take time to check your gauge.

Instructions:

Back

With straight needles, cast on 52 (56, 62, 66) sts. Work even in St st until piece measures 16" from start.

Armholes

Bind off 2 sts at the beginning of next 2 rows. Decrease 1 st each side as follows: K1, k2tog, work to last 3 sts, ssk (slip, slip, knit), k1. Purl one row repeat decrease row one more time. Work even until 8 (8½, 9, 9½)" from start of armhole. Place first 11 (13, 15, 17) sts on holder for left shoulder, bind off next 22 (22, 24, 24) sts for back neckline, place remaining 11 (13, 15, 17) sts on holder for right shoulder.

MATERIALS:

❖ Reynolds *Bulky Lopi* (wool, 100gms/ 66 yd ball)—7 skeins

❖ Size 13/9mm straight needles, or size to obtain gauge

❖ Size 13/9mm circular needles, 16"

❖ 4 stitch holders

❖ Yarn or tapestry needle for finishing

Front

Work same as for back to 6 (6, 6½, 6½)" from beginning of armholes.

Neck Shaping

Work over first 17 (19, 21, 23) sts, place center 10 (10, 12, 12) sts on holder. Join a second ball and knit over last 17 (19, 21, 23) sts. Work each shoulder separately. Bind off at each neck edge 3 sts once, 2 sts once, decrease 1 st each side of neckline once. Work until front length corresponds to back.

Finishing:

▽ Following is an alternate method of joining seams which is called three-needle bind off. It is the neatest finish for shoulder seams. As its name suggests, you use three needles. Try it or you can use the more common weaving (invisible) method.

Place front and back shoulder sts each on separate needles. Holding work with RS together, with another size 13 needle, knit 1 st from front needle and 1 from back needle together and at the same time, bind off. Repeat for other shoulder. Sew side seams.

Cowl Neck Piece

Photo: Christina L. Holmes

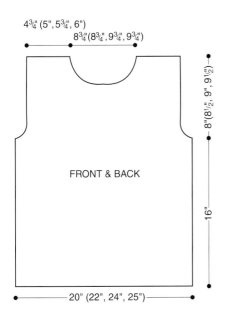

4¾" (5", 5¾", 6")
8¾" (8¾", 9¾", 9¾")
8" (8½", 9", 9½")
FRONT & BACK
16"
20" (22", 24", 25")

With circular needles, cast on 66 sts. Work in the round in St st (knit all rows) for 9". Bind off loosely on a purl row. This can be done on straight needles and seamed (short edges) on wrong sides.

▽

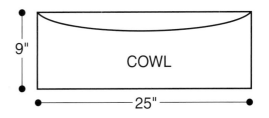

9"
COWL
25"

Weekend Chic Pullover

Designed by Evie Rosen

For those who like a little closer silhouette, this simple roll-neck pullover is a great option for day or relaxed evening, and the hand-dyed yarn revs up the style. Worked on size 17 needles, with some shaping and set-in sleeves, you also can choose to finish this with a jewel-neck collar if you prefer.

Sizes:

Women's sizes Small (Medium, Large, Extra Large)
Finished chest size 36 (40, 44, 48)"

Gauge:

On #17 needles in Stockinette stitch, 2 sts = 1"
To ensure the proper fit, take time to check gauge.

Instructions:

Back

Cast on 40 (44, 48, 52) stitches. Working in St st, decrease 1 st each end, every 1", 3 times. Continue in St st to 3½" from beginning. Next row, increase 1 st each end every 1", 3 times, then work even until piece measures 17" from the beginning. ▽ (Because of the slightly fitted style of this pattern, you might wish to adjust the length of the sweater body. Just remember, if you make an adjustment to the length in the back, to make the corresponding change for the front.)

Armhole Shaping

On the next row, continuing in pattern established, bind off 2 sts at the beginning of the next 2 rows, then decrease 1 st at each end every other row 3 times. Work even until armhole measures 9 (9½, 10, 10½)".
   Bind off 4 (5, 5, 6) sts at beginning of next 4 rows. Place 14 (14, 18, 18) sts on holder for neck.

Front

Work as for back until armhole measures 6 (6½, 7, 7½)". Work across 11 (13, 13, 15) sts, slip next 8 (8, 12, 12) sts on holder.
Joining a second ball of yarn, work the remaining 11 (13, 13, 15) sts. Continue working both sides of the front, decreasing 1 st at each neck

MATERIALS:

- ❖ Colinette Hand-Dyed *Point Five* (wool, 55 yds/100 gm hanks)— 8 (10, 12, 13) hanks

- ❖ Small amount of smooth-textured sport weight yarn for sewing seams

- ❖ Size 17 straight needles, or size to obtain gauge

- ❖ 2 stitch holders

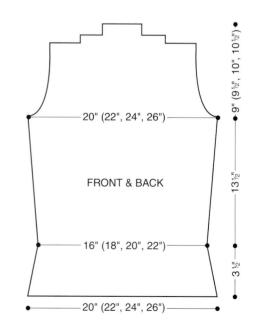

9" (9½", 10", 10½")

20" (22", 24", 26")

FRONT & BACK

13½"

16" (18", 20", 22")

3½"

20" (22", 24", 26")

edge every row 2 times, then every other row once. Work even until front is the same length as for back. Bind off as for shoulders on back.

Sleeves

Cast on 16 (16, 18, 20) sts. Increase 1 st at each end every 1½", 9 times, then work even until piece measures 17". Bind off 2 sts at beginning of next 2 rows. Decrease 1 st at each end every other row until sleeve cap measures 6 (6½, 7, 7½)". Decrease 2 sts at beginning of next 2 rows, then bind off remaining stitches.

🛑 In the finishing steps that follow, we repeatedly say, "bind off loosely," and there's a good reason for that. If you bind off tightly, the sweater will be difficult to get over your head and feel uncomfortable when you wear it. And when we say "loose," we mean real loose, so your stitches look oversized. (You will not even notice these loose stitches once you start wearing or block your sweater.) If you knit tightly, try binding off using a larger size needle.

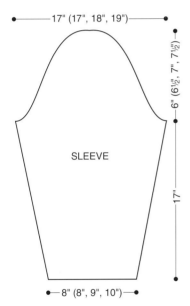

17" (17", 18", 19")

6" (6½", 7", 7½")

17"

SLEEVE

8" (8", 9", 10")

Photo: Christina L. Holmes

Finishing:

▽ Because of the texture of this yarn, we recommend sewing the seams with a smooth textured sport or worsted weight yarn, in a color that will blend in with the sweater yarn. Sew the left shoulder seam.

Collar

With RS facing, pick up neck sts on the holder, pick up sts along left neckline, sts from front neck holder and sts along front right neckline, approximately 44 (46, 52, 60) sts.

For those who prefer the jewel-neck collar, bind off the sts that you have picked up along the neck loosely and work one row of reverse single crochet (crab stitch) around it.

For the roll collar as pictured, work 6 rows of St st knit side out so it will roll and the purl side will show. Bind off loosely.

Sew right shoulder seam and collar. Sew side seams and sleeve seams, then set in sleeves. Work 1 row of reverse single crochet around the bottom of the bodice and sleeves.

Steam lightly if desired.

Chenille Scarf & Hat

Designed by Mary Colucci

Solid and printed yarns in coordinating colors give this scarf and hat set its subtle tweed look. Narrow shaping makes this scarf especially comfortable for wrapping, and it's light.

Scarf Size:

Scarf is approximately 6" wide and 54" long

Gauge:

With size 11 needle in Stockinette stitch, 5 sts = 3"
To ensure the proper size, take time to check your gauge.

Instructions:

The scarf is worked in Stockinette stitch, alternating colors every two rows. You do not have to cut the yarn when you change to the other color; simply drop one color yarn and pick up the second color. As you switch back and forth between colors, remember not to pull the yarn at the edges or the edges will pucker.
With color A cast on 10 sts.
Row 1: Knit
Row 2: Purl
Row 3: Pick up Color B, knit.
Row 4: Purl.
Repeat Rows 1 through 4 until the scarf measures 54" or the scarf length you desire, ending with two rows of Color A. Bind off and work in the yarn ends.

Hat Size:

This snug-fitting hat will fit head sizes 19-21". To increase the size, add two stitches per inch.

Instructions:

With size 15 needles and working with one strand of Color A and one strand Color B held together, cast on 25 stitches.
Rows 1-10: Working with Color A and Color B held together, k every stitch. Piece should measure approximately 3" from beginning.

SCARF MATERIALS:

❖ Lion Brand's Chenille *"Thick & Quick®"* (acrylic/rayon, 100 yd skein)
Wine (#189), Color A—1 skein
Ruby Print (#213), Color B—1 skein

❖ Size 11 needles, or size to obtain gauge

❖ Yarn needle to work in ends

HAT MATERIALS:

❖ Lion Brand's Chenille *"Thick & Quick®"* (acrylic/rayon, 100 yd skein)
Wine (#189), Color A—1 skein
Ruby Print (#213), Color B—1 skein

❖ Size 11 needles

❖ Size 15 needles

❖ Yarn needle to work in ends

*NOTE: One skein of each color will be sufficient to complete a hat and scarf of the approximate size noted in the scarf and hat pattern. Purchase additional yarn to ensure that you have enough yarn in the same dye lot if you plan to make significantly larger sizes.

⬦ CAUTION Beginning with Row 11, switch to size 11 needles and begin St st pattern. (To switch needle size, simply hold one of the size 11 needles in your right hand and work the stitches off of the size 15 needle, following the pattern and continue knitting with the size 11 needles. Beginning with Row 11, you also will work with a single strand of yarn, rather than holding two strands together.

Row 11: With one strand of Color A, knit.

Row 12: Purl. (See note under Chenille Scarf pattern about alternating colors.)

Row 13: Pick up Color B, knit.

Row 14: Purl.

Repeat Rows 11 through 14 until the Stockinette piece measures approximately 6". Bind off leaving a long end of yarn to use for finishing.

Finishing:

You have knitted a rectangle. To finish the hat, sew the side seam with

Photo: Christina L. Holmes

the right side of the fabric facing the inside. The garter stitch panel frames your face. To complete the hat you have to join the stockinette end at the top. Thread a yarn needle with an 18" length of yarn (or the yarn end from the bind-off row) and carefully pick up the edges of stitches around the top of the hat. Gently gather the edges together, closing the top. To cover any open spaces, simply criss-cross the yarn several times, and secure by weaving in the ends. Cut the thread.

NOTE: Because *Thick & Quick* is a very furry yarn, using a non-textured sport or worsted weight yarn in a matching color might be easier for finishing. If you use *Thick & Quick* for finishing, remember to pull the yarn gently.

Loop-Trim Scarf

Designed by Christina L. Holmes

Tired of tassels? Frustrated with fringe? Here's a fast and easy—but different look, knitted with two strands and using a backstitch for the loop embellishment. An easy jaunt in cruise control at the speed limit!

Size:

Scarf measures 9½" x 48"

Gauge:

2 stitches = 1"
To ensure proper size, take time to check your gauge.

Instructions:

Holding two strands of MC, cast on 19 stitches. Work in St st, ▽ To form a selvedge to prevent rolling, knit the first 2 sts of each purl row. Work until scarf measures 48", then bind off and weave in any loose ends.

Finishing:

Loop Trim

Cut eight, 24' lengths of B; four, 24' lengths of A; and four, 24' lengths of C.

NOTE: Yes, we threaded our needles with all 24' of yarn. When we say *Knitting in the Fast Lane*, we mean it! We didn't want to weave in lots of ends. However, working with such a long "strand" can be challenging and unless you pull carefully, very wearing on the yarn, so it's best to cut it into more manageable lengths.

Thread four strands of A into yarn needle. Working in the last row lengthwise, secure yarn in first stitch, then work in backstitch the length of the scarf. Work each stitch over one stitch on the right side, leaving two stitches space between each loop. 🛑 To form loops, loop all four strands of yarn over forefinger when you bring the needle up on the right side of the scarf. Secure with knot at end of the scarf.

Follow this same pattern to make three more rows of loop trim, in B, C, then B again, leaving one stitch between rows.

MATERIALS:

❖ Lion Brand *Jiffy®*, (acrylic, 3 oz/ 115 yd ball)

  Denver (#307) Main Color (MC)— 3 balls
  Violet (#191), Color A—1 ball
  Teal (#178), Color B—1 ball
  Navy (#110), Color C—1 ball

❖ Size 15 straight needles, or size to obtain gauge

❖ Yarn or tapestry needle with eye large enough to hold 4 strands of yarn

Photo: Christina L. Holmes

The Warmest Scarf Ever!

Designed by Christina L. Holmes

Sometimes you prefer a scarf, sometimes a shawl; why not both? This hybrid measures 12" wide (not including the 5" fringe along the length) and 6' long, so it can double as a scarf or a shawl, depending on your mood, and it's warm as toast. You'll be breaking the speed limit on those size 35 needles with this lofty, lush yarn!

Size:

12" x 72" (not including fringe)

Gauge:

In Stockinette stitch with size 35 needle, 2½ stitches and 4 rows = 2"
To ensure the proper size, take time to check your gauge.

Instructions:

△CAUTION You will knit the first two stitches of every purl row to form a selvedge edge to prevent rolling.
Cast on 16 stitches in A. K 8 rows (garter stitch) for border. Join MC and work in St st until piece measures approximately 68½". STOP Be sure to knit the first two stitches of every purl row for a selvedge edge to prevent rolling. Remember to move the yarn to the front of your knitting for your purl stitches, then to the back of the knitting for the last two knit stitches in the row.
Join A and work for 8 rows in garter stitch for border. Bind off. Weave in yarn ends throughout.

MATERIALS:

❖ Horstia's *Marokko* from Muench Yarns (wool, 200 gm/80 meter hank)
Off White (#117) Main Color (MC)—3 hanks
Charcoal (#103), Color A—1 hank

❖ Size 35/19mm needles, or size to obtain gauge

❖ Large crochet hook for fringe (size J, for example, optional)

Fringe:

Hold one strand of MC and one strand of A together. Cut 53, 12" lengths. Fold each set in half, pull folded end through the last knit stitch, pull the end through that loop, and tighten. Attach at every other stitch along the length. (You can use a large crochet hook or even your fingers to pull the doubled yarn through each stitch, since the yarn is so thick.)

Photo: Christina L. Holmes

Cabled & Cozy Afghan

Designed by Lion Brand Yarn Co.

Love those cables! Three plump cable panels knitted with three strands held together on size 19 needles will give you the warmest blanket ever—and a decorating showpiece as well.

Size:

Approximately 41" by 56" without border
NOTE: Entire afghan is worked holding three strands of yarn held together.

Because of the thickness of the yarns, the afghan is constructed in panels of 40 stitches. Make three. Each panel measures approximately 14" wide.

Gauge:

Holding 3 strands of yarn on size 19 needles in Stockinette stitch, 3 sts = 2"
To ensure proper size, take time to check your gauge.

Pattern Stitch:

Rows 1, 3, 5, 7, 9 & 11: P2, k2, p32, k2, p2.
Rows 2, 4, 8, 10, & 12: K2, p2, k32, p2, k2.
Row 6 (cable row): K2, p2, sl 8 sts to cable needle and hold in back, k 8 sts; k the 8 from cable needle; slip next 8 sts and hold in front; k 8; k 8 from cable needle, p2, k2.

Afghan Panel (make three):

With size 19 needles and holding 3 strands of yarn together, cast on 40 sts. Work in pattern for 11 repeats, ending with Row 12. Panel measures approximately 56". Bind off.

Finishing:

Using 2 strands of yarn held together, sew the panels together, taking 1 stitch from each side. Tack the edges of each cable on the cast on and bind off rows so that they do not fan out and are in proportion to the rest of the cables.

MATERIALS:

❖ Lion Brand's *Jiffy*™ (acrylic, 3 oz/ 115 yd ball)

  Fisherman (#099)—33 balls

❖ Size 17 knitting needles

❖ Size 19 knitting needles, or size to obtain gauge

❖ Cable needle ▽ (Because you will be working with three strands of yarn, you may not be able to find a large enough cable needle to hold 8 stitches. Substitute a double pointed needle.)

❖ Yarn or tapestry needle for finishing

Borders:

Top and Bottom

Using size 17 needles and 3 strands of yarn, cast on 7 sts. Work in Seed St as follows:
Row 1: K1, *p1, k1; rep from *. Repeat this row for 42".

Using 2 strands of yarn held together, sew the borders to the top and bottom edges, taking a full st from each piece.

Side Borders

Cast on and work as for top and bottom borders for 63". Position side borders along afghan and top and bottom borders and sew as above.

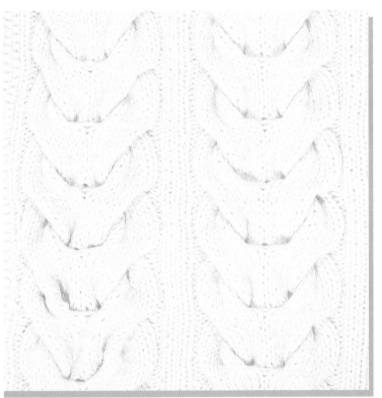

Photo: Christina L. Holmes

Button-Down Bag

Designed by Arnetta Kenney

This shoulder bag has no gussets, just two sides in an interesting stitch, worked with three strands held together on size 13 needles. Throw it over your shoulder for a sporty, fashion look with the luxury feel of alpaca.

Size:

Approximately 12" by 15" flat (when flap is folded over approximate size 12" by 9")

Gauge:

With size 13 needle in garter stitch and 3 strands of yarn, 11 sts = 4".
To ensure proper sizing, take time to check gauge.

MATERIALS:

❖ Lion Brand's AL*PA*KA (alpaca/wool/acrylic, 50 gm/107 yd ball)
  Camel (#124)—9 skeins

❖ Size 13 straight knitting needles, or needle size to obtain gauge

❖ 1 Large button for closure

❖ Yarn or tapestry needle for finishing

Loop Pattern:

🛑 Slip all sts purlwise.
Row 1: (right side): Knit.
Row 2: * K1, slip 1; repeat from * to last 2 sts, k2.
Row 3: Knit.
Row 4: K2, * slip 1, k1; repeat from * to end.
Repeat these 4 rows.

Instructions:

NOTE: Bag is knitted with three strands of yarn together.

Side 1

Using 3 strands of yarn held together, cast on 34 sts.

Rows 1–6: Work 6 rows in Garter St.

Rows 7–13: Beginning with Row 1 of loop pattern (WS), work from row 1 to row 4 of loop pattern once. Then work from row 1 to row 3 of pattern once. (WS should be facing). Repeat rows 1-13 until piece measures 14", ending with all or part of Rows 1-6 in garter st.

Flap

Row 1: Purl.
Row 2: Knit.
Row 3: Purl.
Row 4: Purl.
Rows 5–7: K 1 row, p1 row, ending with WS facing.
Rows 8–11: Work from row 1 to row 4 of loop pattern once.
Rows 12–13: Work garter st pattern for two rows. Bind off.

Side 2

Work the same as Side 1, until piece measures 14", ending with right side facing, before beginning the flap.

Strap

Using size 13 needles and three strands held together, cast on 6 sts. Work in garter stitch until strap measures 25" (or desired length). ▽ Avoid making the strap too long as it will stretch with use.

Finishing:

Using a large tapestry needle, with two strands of yarn and right sides facing, sew the bag together at bottom and side edges using an overcast stitch.

To attach the strap, fold down the top edge of the bag approximately 5½". Fasten strap ends along the fold edge on both sides with an overcast stitch.

For the loop closure, cut two lengths of yarn approximately 4" long, twist loosely and attach to the top piece of the back flap just above the garter stitch border. Sew a large button onto front side of the bag, below the button loop.

Doggie Bed Pillow

Designed by Kathleen Sams for Coats & Clark

Woof, woof. Sweaters aren't the only things to knit for your dog. Here's another idea, a bed pillow shaped like a bone. Your dog will love the cushy thickness of the yarn and you'll love the fact that it's fast to knit and easy care.

Size:
21" x 27"

Gauge:
In Stockinette stitch and size 17 needles, 2 sts = 1".
To ensure proper sizing, take time to check your gauge.

Instructions:

Back & Front
With 3 strands of yarn held together as one, cast on 48 sts.
Row 1 (RS): Knit.
Row 2: Purl.
*Row 3: K 11; TURN. To shape the dog bed pillow, you will work what are called "short rows," which like its name suggests you knit only part of a row, in this case 11 stitches. With 11 stitches on your right needle, simply turn your work so the 11 stitches are now in your left hand and the other stitches in your right. Now you are ready to purl the 11 stitches. In subsequent rows when it says to knit 12, 13 and 14 stitches, simply pick up an additional stitch and continue working. At Row 20 you will work the 14 stitches of the short row and continue knitting the remaining 34 stitches.

MATERIALS:

- Red Heart® *Super Saver*® (acrylic, 6 oz/348 yd skein) Shaded Browns (#992)—3 skeins

- Size 17/12.75mm, or size to obtain gauge

- Filling (See note below.)

▽ Some dogs will love this bed pillow without any stuffing. If you want a really soft bed, consider using 2, 14" pillow forms for the center of the bone and 4, 8" round pillows for the ends. Another option is creating a casing from an old towel or pillowcase, filling it with a large bag of polyester fiberfill and stuffing the bed.

Row 4: P 11.	**Row 16:** P 13; turn.	**Row 28:** K 12.	**Row 40:** K 48 sts.
Row 5: K 12; turn.	**Row 17:** K 13.	**Row 29:** P 11; turn.	**Row 41:** P 14; turn.
Row 6: P 12.	**Row 18:** P 14; turn.	**Row 30:** K 11.	**Row 42:** K 14.
Row 7: K 13; turn.	**Row 19:** K 14.	**Row 31:** P 48 sts.	**Row 43:** P 13; turn.
Row 8: P 13.	**Row 20:** P 48 sts.	**Row 32:** K 14; turn.	**Row 44:** K 13.
Row 9: K 14; turn.	**Row 21:** K 48 sts.	**Row 33:** P 14.	**Row 45:** P 12; turn.
Row 10: P 14.	**Row 22:** P 48 sts.	**Row 34:** K 13; turn.	**Row 46:** K 12.
Row 11: K across 48 sts.	**Row 23:** P 14; turn.	**Row 35:** P 13.	**Row 47:** P 11; turn.
Row 12: P 11; turn.	**Row 24:** K 14.	**Row 36:** K 12; turn.	**Row 48**: K 11.
Row 13: K 11.	**Row 25:** P 13; turn.	**Row 37:** P 12.	**Row 49:** P 48 sts. **
Row 14: P 12; turn.	**Row 26:** K 13.	**Row 38:** K 11; turn.	
Row 15: K 12.	**Row 27:** P 12; turn.	**Row 39:** P 11.	

Photo: Christina L. Holmes

Bind off 14 sts, k across. Next Row: Bind off 14 sts, p across. Beginning with k row, work in St st to 14", end p row.

Cast on 14 sts. K across—34 sts. Cast on 14 sts. P across—48 sts. Repeat from * to **. Bind off.

Finishing:

With right sides together, sew seams. Leave opening if you plan to stuff.

Chapter 4

Around Town

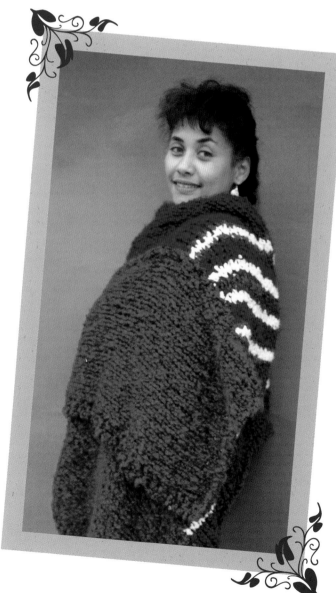

Hooded Seed-Stitch Jacket

Designed by Ann E. Smith for Coats & Clark

Casual and comfy, this hooded jacket is worked in seed stitch using three strands of yarn on size 15 needles for speed. The simple stitch creates a pattern of texture, and contrast edging is worked in crochet.

Sizes:

Directions are for women's sizes Small (Medium, Large, X-Large)
Finished bust size (buttoned), 40 (42, 44, 46)"
Finished Length: 19½ (20½, 21½, 22½)"

Gauge:

With size 15 needles in seed stitch and 3 strands of yarn held
together, 5 sts and 7 rows = 2"
To ensure the proper fit, take time to check your gauge.

Pattern Stitch:

NOTE: Use 3 strands of yarn held together throughout this project.
Seed Stitch (also known as Moss Stitch)
Row 1: * K1, p1 repeat from * across row
Row 2: * P1, k1 repeat from * across row
Repeat these two rows for pattern.

Instructions:

Back

With MC and three strands of yarn, cast on 50 (52, 55, 57) sts.
Work seed st to 17½ (18½, 19½, 20½)" from beginning.
Bind off in seed st.

MATERIALS:

* Red Heart® *Soft* (Bounce-Back® acrylic, 5 oz/328 yd skein) New Aran (#7313), Main Color (MC)—7 (9, 9, 10) skeins Dk. Yellow Green (#7675) Contrasting Color (CC)—3 skeins

* Size 15/10mm knitting needles, or size to obtain gauge

* Size K/10½ aluminum crochet hook

* Yarn or tapestry needle for finishing

* 5, 1⅛" buttons

* 2 stitch markers

Front

(Make two): With MC and three strands of yarn cast on 22 (24, 25, 26) sts. Work seed st for 1".
For Pocket Opening: At the beginning of the next row, bind off 3 sts in seed st. Work even for 5". Cast on 3 sts above pocket opening. Continue as established to 15½ (16½, 17½, 18½)" from beginning.

Photo: Christina L. Holmes

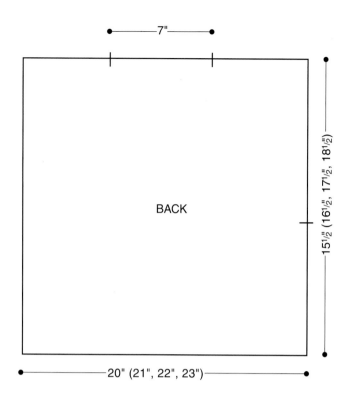

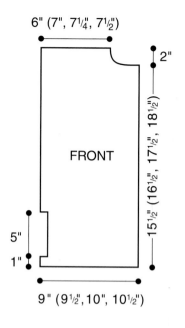

Neck Shaping

At the beginning of the next row (on opposite edge from pocket opening), bind off 5 sts in seed st. Decrease 1 st at neck every other row twice. Work even on remaining 15 (17, 18, 19) sts to same length as back. Bind off in seed st.

Sleeve (Make two)

With MC and three strands of yarn, cast on 25 (26, 27, 29) sts. Work in seed st, increase 1 st each edge every 4th row 10 (11, 12, 12) times; include these new sts into pattern 45 (48, 51, 53) sts. When piece measures 14 (14½, 14¾, 15)" from beginning, bind off in seed st.

Pocket (Make two)

With MC, cast on 12 sts. Work seed st for 5". Bind off in seed st.

Hood

With MC, cast on 54 sts. Work seed st for 9". At the beginning of the next 2 rows, bind off 18 sts in seed st.

For Back

Work even on center 18 sts until piece measures 16" from beginning. Bind off in seed st. Using one strand of yarn, sew bound-off sts of each side to sides of hood back.

Finishing:

Join shoulder seams. From each side of the shoulder seams, measure down 9½ (10, 10½, 11)" and place markers. Set in sleeves between markers.

With WS facing, place pocket onto front so that it covers the indention at side opening. Leaving an opening at seam, sew pockets to inside of fronts. With the RS facing, using crochet hook, join MC with a slip st to edge of pocket opening on front only.

Row 1: Ch 1, sc evenly across; DO NOT TURN.
Row 2: Ch 1, working from left to right, sc in each sc across for reverse sc. Fasten off. Join sides of pocket edging to sides of pocket opening. Join sleeve and side seams, sewing pockets (not the crochet border) into seam.

Body Edging

With the RS facing using 3 strands of CC and crochet hook, join with a slip st in corner of left front neck edge. Ch 1, work 28 (30, 32, 34) sc evenly spaced to corner, 3 sc in corner, sc evenly along lower edge. ▽ (For an attractive edge, do not sc crochet into every stitch across the bottom. Skip approximately every 6th st) 78 (84, 90, 96) sts, 3 sc in corner, 28 (30, 32, 34) sc along right front; turn.

Row 2: Ch 3, dc in each sc around working 3 dc in each corner; turn.
Row 3: Ch 1, sc in each dc around; DO NOT TURN.
Row 4: Ch 1, working from left to right, sc in each sc around for reverse sc; fasten off.

Cuff

With the WS facing and crochet hook, join CC with slip st in lower sleeve seam. Ch 1, work 25 (26, 27, 29) dc around; join with slip st in 3rd ch of beginning ch 3.
Round 2: Ch 3, dc in each st around; join with slip st in 3rd ch of beginning ch 3. Repeat Round 2 for 4 times more. Ch 1, work reverse sc around and fasten off.

Hood

RSs together, pin hood onto MC neck edge at each side of Body Edging and ease to fit. With crochet hook and MC, slip st in place. With RS of hood facing, join CC with slip st in edge.

Row 1: Ch 1, work about 55 sc evenly spaced across; DO NOT TURN.
Row 2: Ch 1, working from left to right, sc in each sc for reverse sc; fasten off.

Buttons

Sew buttons 1" from neck and lower edges then space remaining 3 buttons at even intervals between the first 2. Push buttons through the dc row. Turn back cuffs.

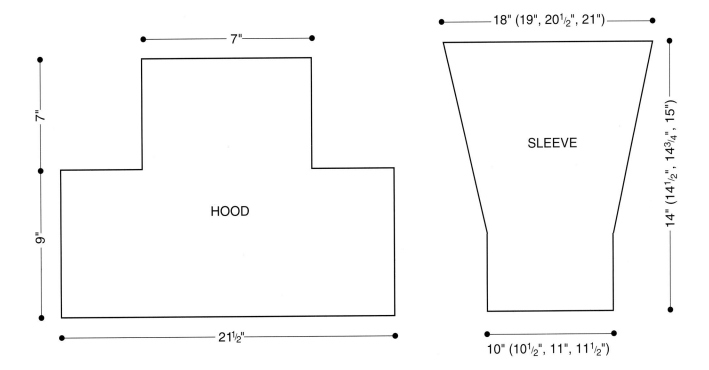

Basketweave Jacket

Designed by Ann E. Smith for Coats & Clark

Toss on this raglan-sleeved cardigan for running errands and you'll always feel "dressed." The textured yarn and stitch jazz up this practical look, rounded out by handy pockets. Test drive the Body Pattern before you begin. Once you master the combination of knit and purl stitches, you'll understand why basketweave is a favorite knitters' route.

Sizes:

Instructions are for women's sizes Small (Medium, Large, and X-large)

Finished Bust (Buttoned): 41½ (45½, 49, 52½)"

Finished Length: 26 (26½, 27, 28)"

Gauge:

In Body Pattern with size 11 needles, 11 sts and 15 rows = 5"

MATERIALS:

❖ Red Heart® *Light & Lofty*™ (acrylic, 6 oz/148 yd skein)
   Cafe Au Lait (# 9334)—5(6, 6, 7) skeins

❖ Size 10 knitting needles

❖ Size 11 knitting needles, or size needed to obtain gauge

❖ Yarn needle

❖ 3 stitch holders

❖ Five, 1⅛ inch diameter buttons

The following Body Pattern creates a basketweave pattern (alternating blocks of knit and purl stitches). The designer added rows of rib stitch to separate and define the basketweave pattern. Please note that throughout the instructions, the phrase: "keep continuity of pattern, adjusting stitches accordingly" is mentioned. This means that in certain sizing changes and when increasing or decreasing stitches be careful to maintain the established pattern (Body Pattern) on the main part of the sweater and adjust the pattern along the side edges.

Photo: Christina L. Holmes

Basketweave Jacket 63

Body Pattern (multiple of 10 + 5):

Row 1 (RS): *(K1, p1) 2 times, k1, p5; repeat from * across to last 5 sts (k1, p1) 2 times, k1.

Row 2: *(P1, k1) 2 times, p6; repeat from * across to last 5, (p1, k1) 2 times, p1.

Row 3: *(K1, p1) 2 times, k6; repeat from * across to last 5, (k1, p1) 2 times, k1.

Row 4: *(P1, k1) 2 times, p1, k5; repeat from * across to last 5 sts, (p1, k1) 2 times, p1.

Row 5: Repeat Row 3.

Row 6: Repeat Row 2.

Row 7: Repeat Row 1.

Row 8: Repeat Row 2.

Row 9: Repeat Row 3.

Row 10: Repeat Row 4.

Row 11: Repeat Row 3.

Row 12: *K5, (p1, k1) 2 times, p1; repeat from * across.

Row 13: *K6, (p1, k1) 2 times; repeat from * across to last 5 sts, k5.

Row 14: *P6, *(k1, p1) 2 times; repeat from * across to last 5 sts, p5.

Row 15: *P5, (k1, p1) 2 times, k1; repeat from * across.

Row 16: Repeat Row 14.

Row 17: Repeat Row 13.

Row 18: Repeat Row 12.

Row 19: Repeat Row 13.

Row 20: Repeat Row 14.

Row 21: Repeat Row 15.

Row 22: Repeat Row 14.

Repeat Rows 1-22 for Body Pattern.

Instructions:

Jacket Back

With size 10 needles cast on 41 (45, 49, 53) sts. Work in ribbing as follows:

Row 1 (RS): K1, * p1, k1; repeat from * across.

Row 2: P1, *k1, p1; repeat from * across. Repeat Rows 1 and 2 for 3", increase 4 (5, 6, 7) sts evenly on last row, end Row 2 – 45 (50, 55, 60) sts. Change to size 11 needles and work in Body Pattern, adjusting stitches accordingly.

Keeping continuity of pattern, adjusting stitches accordingly, work until 16¼ (16¼, 16½, 17)" from beginning, end WS row.

Shape Raglans

Bind off 3 (3, 4, 4) sts at beginning of next 2 rows. K1, slip 1, k1, psso, work in pattern to last 3 sts, k2tog, k1. Work 1 row even. Decrease 1 st each edge as before every other row until there are 11 (14, 15, 18) sts. Work even to 26 (26½, 27, 28)" from beginning, end WS row. Place sts on a holder.

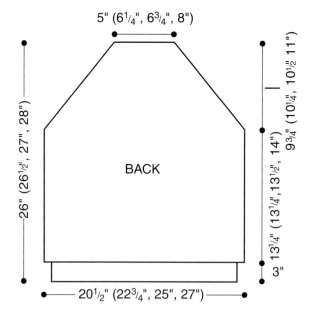

5" (6¼", 6¾", 8")

BACK

26" (26½", 27", 28")

9¾" (10¼", 10½", 11")

13¼" (13¼", 13½", 14")

3"

20½" (22¾", 25", 27")

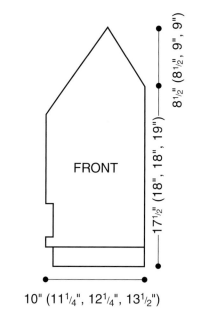

8½" (8½", 9", 9")

FRONT

17½" (18", 18", 19")

10" (11¼", 12¼", 13½")

Left Front

With size 10 needles, cast on 19 (21, 23, 25) sts. Work in ribbing same as for Back for 3", increase 3 (4, 4, 5) sts evenly spaced on last row, end Row 2—22 (25, 27, 30) sts. Change to size 11 needles and work in Body Pattern, adjusting stitches accordingly. AT THE SAME TIME when piece measures 6" from beginning, bind off 3 sts at beginning of next row for Pocket Opening. Work even on remaining 19 (22, 24, 27) sts for 15 rows. Keeping continuity of pattern, cast on 3 sts at end of next row – 22 (25, 27, 30) sts. Continue in pattern to 16¼ (16¼, 16½, 17)", end WS row.

Shape Raglan as for back. AT THE SAME TIME when 17½ (18, 18, 19)" from beginning, begin V-neck shaping.

V-Neck Shaping

Decrease 1 st at neck edge on next row, then every right side row 1 (1, 1, 2) times, then every 6th row 2 (3, 3, 3) times. Work same as for back. Place sts on a holder.

Right Front

Work same as left front, reversing shaping.

Sleeves

With size 10 needles, cast on 21 (21, 23, 23) sts. Work in ribbing same as for back for 3" increase 4 (4, 7, 7) sts evenly spaced on last row, end Row 2—25 (25, 30, 30) sts. 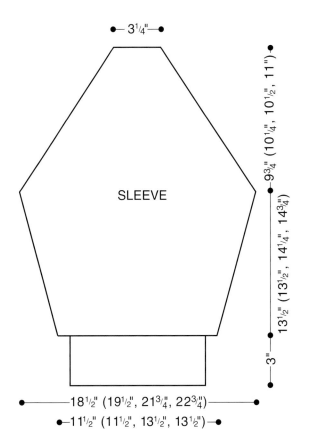 Change to size 11 needles and work in pattern as for back, shaping sides by increasing 1 st each end of next row, then every 6th row until there are 41 (43, 48, 50) sts. Work even in established pattern until 16½ (16½, 17¼, 18)" from beginning, end WS row.

Shape Raglans

Work same as for back until there are 7 sts. Continue in pattern until 26¼ (27, 28, 29)" from beginning, end WS row. Place sts on a holder.

Pocket Linings (Make 2)

With size 10 needles, cast on 11 sts. Beginning with Purl row, work 17 rows in St st. Bind off loosely.

Finishing:

Pocket Trim

With RS facing and size 10 needles, pick up and k 11 sts evenly spaced along opening. Work 3 rows ribbing as for back. Bind off loosely in ribbing. Join sides of pocket to top and bottom of opening. Join pocket lining to back opening so RS is next to WS of front. Sew pocket in place.

Sew raglan seams. Join side and arm seams, leaving pocket open.

Right Front Band and Buttonholes

With right side facing and size 10 needles, pick up and k 43 (45, 45, 47) sts evenly spaced up edge to V-neck. Work 2 rows ribbing same as for Back.

Row 3: Rib 2 (2, 2, 4) sts, yo, k2tog; *(p1, k1) 3 times, p1, yo, p2tog, (k1, p1) 3 times, k1, yo, k2tog; repeat from * again, rib to end. Work 3 more rows in ribbing. Bind off loosely in ribbing.

Left Front Band

With RS facing and size 10 needles, begin at V-neck, pick up and k 43 (45, 45, 47) sts evenly spaced down edge. Work in ribbing as for back for 6 rows. Bind off loosely in ribbing. Sew buttons opposite buttonholes.

Collar

With RS facing and size 10 needles, pick up and k 6 sts evenly along top of right front band, stitches from the holders and 6 sts along top of left band. Work 7 rows in ribbing as for back. At beginning of next 8 rows, bind off 7 sts loosely in ribbing. Bind off remaining sts.

SLEEVE

3¼"

9¾" (10¼", 10½", 11")

13½" (13½", 14¼", 14¾")

3"

18½" (19½", 21¾", 22¾")

11½" (11½", 13½", 13½")

Weekend Wrap-Up

Designed by Kathleen Sams for Coats & Clark

Wrap up for any trip around town with this sporty ruana. There are "no detours" with this pattern, just a "fork" in the road where you work two sides of the center panel (there are three panels), creating the front opening. This lightweight yarn is comfortable to wear in addition to being fast to knit, especially on size 17s.

Size:

Measures 43" across back, 24" at center and 32" at inner front edge

Gauge:

In Stockinette stitch and size 17 needles, 12 rows and 8 sts = 4". To ensure proper fit, take time to check your gauge.

Instructions:

Back

With A, cast on 46 sts. Work in St st (k1 row, p1 row) for 10 rows. Continuing in St st, work in stripe pattern as follows:

1 Row B	1 Row A	4 Rows A
2 Rows C	2 Rows B	1 Row B
1 Row B	1 Row A	2 Rows C
4 Rows A	2 Rows C	1 Row B
2 Rows C		

Change to A and continue in St st for 25". Next Row: K across 23 sts. Put remaining 23 sts on a holder. Continue in St st working stripe pattern in reverse, then change to A and work an additional 11 rows, end purl row. Bind off. With RS facing, join yarn to remaining 23 sts, k to end. Complete to correspond to first side. Bind off.

Side Panels (Make 2)

With B cast on 23 sts. **Row 1 (RS):** Knit. **Row 2:** P to last 3 sts, k3. Repeat Rows 1 and 2 to 48". Bind off.

Finishing:

Keeping garter stitch of side panels on outer edge, sew side panels to the sides of the back panel.

MATERIALS:

❖ Red Heart® *Light & Lofty*™ (acrylic, 6 oz/148 yd skein)
   Navy Grape (#9387), Color A—2 skeins
   Wine (#9376), Color B—2 skeins
   Creamsicle (#9322), Color C—1 skein

❖ Size 17/12.75mm circular knitting needles, or size to obtain gauge

❖ Stitch holder

❖ Yarn or tapestry needle for finishing

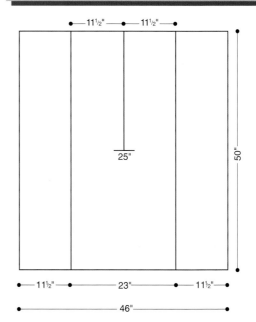

Photo: Christina L. Holmes

Chapter 5

Shore Things

Starry Crop Top

Designed by Ann E. Smith for Coats & Clark

This cropped top is a great summer look over a bikini top or tube top. Test-drive the Star Cluster stitch in your gauge swatch and you'll have a quick trip to the beach!

Sizes:

Directions are for women's sizes Extra Small (Small, Medium, Large, X-Large)
Finished Bust: 31 (35½, 39, 40, 42)"
Length: 13½ (14, 14½, 15½, 16½)"

Gauge:

Using two strands of yarn and size 13 needles, 18 sts = 5",
16 rows = 4"
To ensure the proper fit, take time to check your gauge.

Pattern Stitch:

Star Cluster (a multiple of 4 sts + 2 sts; a repeat of 4 rows)
Row 1: (RS) K1 * k2tog, (yo) twice, k2tog through the back loop of the sts (this twists the stitches); repeat from * across, ending k1.
Row 2: P2; * p1 (the first yo), p1 in the back loop of the stitch (the second yo), cluster the next 2 sts as follows (sl 2, purlwise, with yarn in back, bring yarn to front between needles, slip the same 2 sts back to left-hand needle, pass yarn to back between needles, slip the same 2 sts with the yarn in back again); repeat from * across ending p1, p1 into the back loop of the st, p2.
Row 3: K3; * k2tog, (yo) twice, k2tog in back loop of sts; repeat from * across, ending k3.
Row 4: P2; * cluster 2, p1, p1 in back loop of the st; repeat from * across, ending cluster 2, p2.

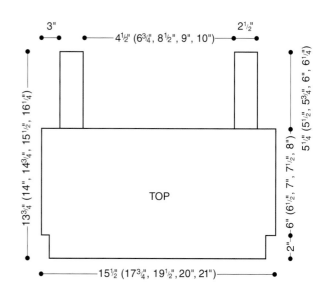

MATERIALS:

❖ Aunt Lydia's® *Denim* (cotton/acrylic, 400 yd ball)
  Red (#1003)—2 balls for all sizes

❖ Size 9/5.5mm knitting needles

❖ Size 13/9mm knitting needles, or size needed to obtain gauge

❖ Yarn or tapestry needle for finishing

❖ Size 9/I aluminum crochet hook

Instructions:

Back

Beginning at the lower edge with smaller needles and two strands of yarn held together, cast on 53 (61, 65, 69, 73) sts.

Row 1: (WS) P1, (k1, p1) across.

Row 2: K1, (p1, k1) across.

Repeat rows 1–2 to 2" from beginning, ending with a WS row and increase 1 st, 54 (62, 68, 70, 74) sts.

Change to size 13 needles and begin Star Cluster pattern, continue even to 8 (8½, 9, 9½, 10)" from beginning, ending with a RS row. Next row, p across, working p1 in first yo and p1 in back loop of st in second yo. Bind off knitwise.

Front

Work as for back.

Straps (Make two)

Using two strands of yarn and size 9 needles, cast on 9 (9, 9, 11, 11) sts. Work ribbing as for back to 10½ (11, 11½, 12, 12½)" from beginning, ending with a WS row. Bind off in ribbing.

Finishing:

Join side seams.

Bodice Edging

With RS facing and crochet hook, join two strands of yarn near one top underarm seam with a slip st. Ch 1, sc evenly around, ending with slip st in first sc; turn. Ch 1, slip st in each sc around and fasten off.

Photo: Christina L. Holmes

Straps

With WS facing, place markers 3" from each side of first side seam. Pin strap to bodice so that there is a 6" space between strap sides at the underarm. Sew strap securely to the slipped stitch row of edging. Repeat for second strap.

Bodice Tie

Using two strands of yarn and crochet hook, ch 175 (201, 225, 252, 275). Slip st in 2nd ch from hook and in each ch across. Fasten off. Insert the tie along the top edge of the bodice in last row 3 of Star Clusters, begin at the center front, weaving the tie around the top edge. Tie into a bow. Tie ends into over-hand knots. Hide ends.

Fringe Benefits Top & Miniskirt

Designed by Kathleen Sams for Coats & Clark

Head to the beach in this top and miniskirt. It's the perfect bathing suit cover-up, and you'll love how fast knitting with two strands of yarn can be. We used multi-colored pearl-finish pony beads on the fringe; you might opt for wooden beads or none.

Sizes:

Directions are for women's sizes Small (Medium, Large)
Finished chest size: 34-36 (38-40, 42-44)"
Finished skirt length: 14 (15, 16)"
Finished Hip Size: 34-36 (38-40, 42-44)"

Gauge:

In Stockinette stitch and larger needle,
    12 sts and 16 rows = 4"
To ensure proper fit, take time to check your gauge.

NOTE: Work with 2 strands held together as one throughout.

Instructions:

Skirt Back

With larger needles and two strands of yarn, cast on 48 (54, 60) sts. **Row 1 (RS):** Knit. **Row 2:** P 2, k 2, * p4, k2; repeat from * across to last 2, p2. **Rows 3-4:** Repeat last 2 rows once more. **Rows 5, 7:** Knit. **Row 6, 8:** Purl. **Row 9:** Knit. **Row 10:** P5, * k2, p5; repeat from * across. **Rows 11-12:** Repeat Rows 9 and 10. **Rows 13-16:** Repeat Rows 5-8. **Rows 17-24:** Repeat Rows 1-8.
Continue working in St st (k1 row, p1 row) to 10 (11, 12)" from beginning or desired length.

Waistband

Change to size 11 needles. Work in Rib Pattern as follows: Row 1 (RS): * K 2, p 2; repeat from * across. Repeat last row until piece measures 14 (15, 16)", or desired length, working elastic thread through last 3 rows. Bind off in rib.

MATERIALS:

❖ Red Heart® *"Soft"* (*Bounce Back®* acrylic, 5 oz/328 yd skein) Medium Blue (#7821)—4 skeins

❖ Size 11/8mm circular needles

❖ Size 13/9mm circular needles, or size to obtain gauge

❖ Elastic thread

❖ 48 pony beads (optional)

❖ Yarn or tapestry needle for finishing

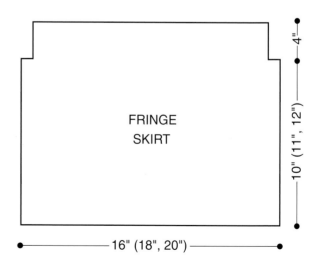

FRINGE
SKIRT

4"

10" (11", 12")

16" (18", 20")

Skirt Front
Work same as back.

Finishing:
With RS together, sew side seams. Weave in ends.

Top Back
With larger size needles and two strands of yarn, cast on 42 (48, 54) sts. K 4 rows. **Row 1 (RS):** Knit. **Row 2:** Purl. Repeat rows 1-2 to 6 (7, 8)", ending p row.

Shape Armhole
P 3, k across to last 3, purl 3. Next Row: P. Repeat last two rows until piece measures 13½ (15, 16½)" or desired length.

Shape Neck & Shoulders
Bind off 15, K across to last 3 sts, p 3. Next row, bind off 15. Put center 18 sts on a holder.

Top Front
Work same as back.

Finishing:
Roll Neck
With RS together, sew right shoulder seam. With RS facing, pick up and k 18 sts from front holder, 2 sts across seam, 18 sts from back holder. Purl next row, increase first stitch on each end—40 sts. Work in St st for 6 rows. Bind off. Sew remaining shoulder and neck seams. Sew side seams. Weave in ends.

Fringe
Cut 48, 9" lengths of yarn. Fold each strand of yarn in half, pull through bottom stitch of the hem as you would a fringe. Twist the doubled strand for the entire length, slip on one bead and knot at the end. (Make sure the knots are made at the very end so the beads hang even when worn.) Leave two stitches between each fringe.

Photo: Christina L. Holmes

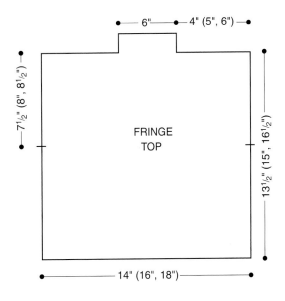

Chapter 6

Night Lights

Classic Cardigan

Designed by Elena Malo

Here's the classic cardigan jacket, sparkling with style. Holding three strands of different yarns (metallic ribbon, furry mohair and textured novelty), you'll work in Stockinette stitch on size 13 needles, and use two strands for the "fur" trim around the collar and cuffs. You'll be tempted to wear this over everything from jeans to velvet!

Sizes:

Women's sizes Small (Medium, Large, X-Large)
Finished garment at chest measures 40 (44, 48, 52)"

Gauge:

In Stockinette stitch with size 13 needles and one strand of A,B,C
    held together, 11 sts and 14 rows = 4"
To ensure proper fit, take time to check your gauge.

Instructions:

Back

Using one strand each of A, B and C, cast on 56 (60, 64, 68) sts.
Work in garter st for 5 rows. Continue in St st until piece measures
14" from start.

Shape Armholes

Bind off 4 (4, 4, 5) sts at the beginning of next 2 rows, 2 sts at the
beginning of next 2 rows, decrease 1 st each side, every other row 2
(3, 4, 4) times. 40 (42, 44, 48) sts. Work until armholes measure 8
(8½, 9, 9½)".

Shape Shoulders

Bind off 6 (7, 7, 8) sts at the beginning of next 4 (2, 4, 2) rows, 0 (6, 0, 8) at the beginning of the next 2 rows. Place remaining 16 sts on a stitch holder for back of neck.

Left Front

Cast on 32 (34, 36, 40) sts. Work 5 rows in garter st. Continue in St st, work in garter
st over last 4 sts. Keeping to pattern as established, work until piece measures 14".

Shape Armhole

Bind off 4 (5, 5, 5) sts at the beginning of next row, 2 sts at the beginning of next row,
decrease 1 st every RS row 3 (3, 4, 5) times. Continue on 23 (24, 25, 28) sts until armhole measures 6 (6½, 7, 7)" from beginning.

MATERIALS:

❖ Berroco *Optik* (cotton/acrylic/mohair/
    metallic/polyester, 87 yds, 50 gm
    hank)
    Matisse (#4902) Color A—9 (9, 10,
    10) hanks
❖ Berroco *Metallica* (rayon/metallic,
    85 yds, 25 gm hank)
    Gold (#1001) Color B—9 (9, 10, 10)
    hanks
❖ Berroco *Furz* (nylon/wool/acrylic,
    90 yds, 50 gm hank)
    Wall Street Navy (#3806) Color C—
    10 (10, 11, 11) balls

❖ 5, 1" navy coat buttons

❖ Size 13/9mm straight needles, or size
    needle to obtain gauge

❖ 3 stitch holders

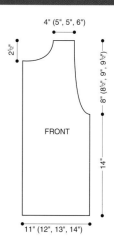

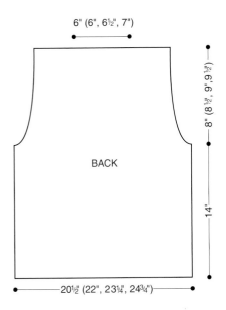

6" (6", 6½", 7")

8" (8½", 9", 9½")

BACK

14"

20½" (22", 23¼", 24¾")

Photo: Christina L. Holmes

Shape Neckline

Bind off 6 sts at the beginning of next WS row, then 2 sts once on the following WS row, decrease 1 st at neck edge every other row, 3 times.

Shape Shoulder

Bind off 6 (6, 7, 9) sts at the beginning of next RS row; bind off remaining 6 (7, 7, 8) sts. Place a marker for 5 buttonholes along front edge, evenly spaced between top of neckline and 1" from bottom edge.

Right Front

Work same as for left but reverse all shaping. Form 1 buttonhole to correspond to each marker as follows: k2tog, yo twice, slip 1, k 1, psso. Next row k1 from front, k1 from back in yo twice.

Sleeve

With 3 strands of C, cast on 32 (32, 34, 34) sts. Work in garter st for 11 rows. Change to 1 strand each of A , B and C, continue in St st, increasing 1 st each edge on first row, repeat increase every 6 (6, 4, 4) rows 7 (3, 0, 0) times, then every 4 rows, 0 (5, 8, 9) times, 48 (50, 52, 54) sts.

Shape Cap

Bind off 4 (4, 5, 5) sts at the beginning of next 2 rows, decrease 1 st each edge 14 (14, 14, 15) times, bind off remaining 12 (14, 14, 14) sts.

Finishing:

Seam shoulders. With RS facing you, and using 3 strands of C, pick up 44 sts from neckline edge, 14 sts along left front, 16 sts from the back neck, and 14 sts along right front. Work in garter st for 8 rows, bind off from WS. Seam sides, sleeve seams, sew in sleeves. Finish off all ends. Sew on buttons.

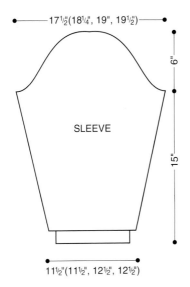

17½"(18¼", 19", 19½")

6"

SLEEVE

15"

11½"(11½", 12½", 12½")

Summer Evening Halter

Designed by Elena Malo

Take a modified halter top, add some sexy lacing across the back to adjust as much as you dare, and you've got an eye-catching evening look. Knit in one piece on size 11 needles, this design is worked with two strands of different yarns to combine sparkle and texture. (**NOTE:** although the schematic shows only one strap, there is one from each shoulder.)

Sizes:

Directions are for women's sizes Small (Medium, Large, X-Large) Finished garment at chest measures 36 (38, 40, 42)"

Gauge:

In Stockinette stitch (using 1 strand of A and 1 strand of B together) and size 11 needle, 14 sts and 22 rows = 4" To ensure the proper fit, take time to check your gauge.

Instructions:

NOTE: The halter is made in one piece with two strands of yarn held together.

Using size 11 straight needles and 1 strand of A and B held together, cast on 80 (88, 94, 102 sts). Knit for 3 rows. Work in St st until piece measures 9 (9½, 10, 11)", ending with a p row. K 68 (74, 78, 84). Place last 12 (14, 16, 18) sts on a holder. Turn, p 56 (60, 62, 66) sts, place last 12 (14, 16, 18) sts on a separate holder. Work remaining sts, decreasing 1 st each side as follows: k1, k2tog, work up to last 3 sts, slip 1, k1, psso, k1. Repeat decrease every other row 7 (8, 9, 10) more times. Work even on remaining 40 (42, 42, 44) sts until piece measures 15 (15½, 16, 17)" from start.

MATERIALS:

❖ Berroco *Optik* (cotton/acrylic/mohair/ metallic/polyester, 87 yds, 50 gm hank)
Tiffany (#4905), Color A—3 skeins
❖ Berroco *Metallica* (rayon/metallic, 85 yds, 25 gm hank)
Black/Multi (#1012), Color B— 3 skeins

❖ Size 11/8mm circular needles, 24"

❖ Size 11/8mm straight needles

❖ 3 stitch holders

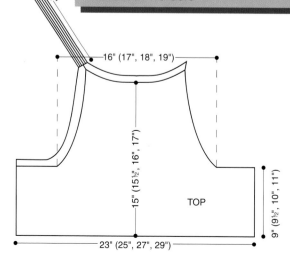

Shape Neckline

K 10 (11, 12, 13) sts, turn, slip first st, bind off slip st and next st. Repeat this decrease every other row 2 more times. (3 sts left). Next row: slip 1, k2tog, psso. Fasten off. Place center 20 sts on holder. Work on remaining 10 (11, 12, 13) sts. Shape other side of neckline to correspond to right side.

Finishing:

Pick up 10 (11, 12, 13) sts at the top of the neckline, the 20 sts from the neckline holder and 10 (11, 12, 13) sts from the other side of the top of the neckline—for a total of 40 (42, 44, 46). Work in garter st (knit all rows) for 4 rows. Bind off from WS.

⬦ From RS of armhole, with circular needle, pick up 53 (55, 57, 59) sts, including sts on holder. Cast on an additional 140 (146, 152, 160) sts for strap on right side. Work in garter st on all 193 (201, 209, 219) sts for 4 rows. Bind off from WS.

For left side: Cast on 140 (146, 152, 160) sts for strap on left side, pick up 53 (53, 57, 59) sts from left armhole, including 12 (14, 16, 18) sts on holder. Repeat as for RS. Pick up 34 (36, 38, 40) sts from each side edge of back, knit for 2 rows in garter st. Mark 4 buttonholes evenly spaced between first and last st. To make each buttonhole, bind off 2 sts. In the next row cast on 2 sts. Bind off all sts on 5th row. Slip ties through holes in a criss-cross fashion as shown in picture.

Photo: Christina L. Holmes

Harlequin Rollneck Pullover

Designed by Joyce Nordstrom for Coats & Clark

Dramatic and elegant, this pullover sweater has a few more twists and turns than other patterns in this book, but once you understand the stitch, it's not that complicated. The subtle diamond pattern is created by purling a stitch from a previous row together with a stitch from the current row on which you are knitting. Initially, the fabric will pucker, giving almost a scalloped look, but as you continue to work the pattern, the knitting will flatten out.

Sizes:

Directions are for women's sizes Extra Small (Small, Medium, Large, X-Large)
Finished bust sizes 36½ (40, 43½ , 47, 50½)"

Gauge:

In Stockinette stitch on larger needles, 7 sts = 3", 6 rows = 2"
To ensure proper fit, take time to check gauge.

NOTE: Bottom of sweater, sleeves and neck have rolled edges in Stockinette stitch rather than ribbing.

Instructions:

Back

Edge: With smaller needles and two double strands of black, cast on 38 (42, 46, 50, 54) sts. K 1 row (mark for RS), (p 1 row, k 1 row) twice; p 1 row, increase 4 sts evenly spaced, 42 (46, 50, 54, 58) sts. Fasten off black. ◈ Change to larger needles.

Pattern:

Row 1: (RS) With MC, k1, p to last st, k1.
Row 2, 4, 6: (WS) p across. Fasten off MC after row 6.
Row 3, 5: Knit across.

MATERIALS:

❖ Red Heart® *Light and Lofty*™ (acrylic, 6 oz/148 yd skein)
   Main Color (#9317 Salt & Pepper)— 10 oz
   Color A, Cloud (#9311)—6 oz
   Color B, Onyx (#9312)—6 oz
   Red Heart® *Super Saver* (acrylic, 3 oz/170 yd skein)
   Color C, Black (#312)—2 oz. (◈ used double throughout)

❖ Size 10½/6.5mm straight knitting needle

❖ Size 13/9mm circular knitting needles, 24", or size to obtain gauge

❖ Yarn or tapestry needle for finishing

Photo: Christina L. Holmes

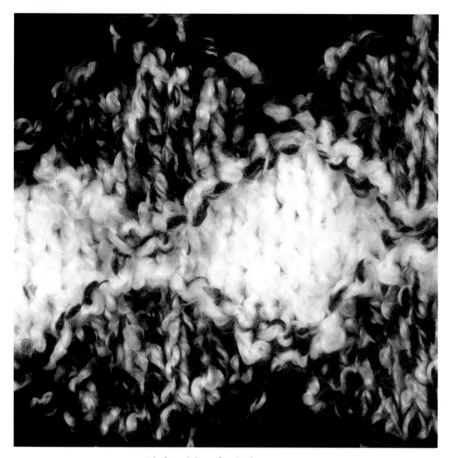

Right side of stitch pattern.

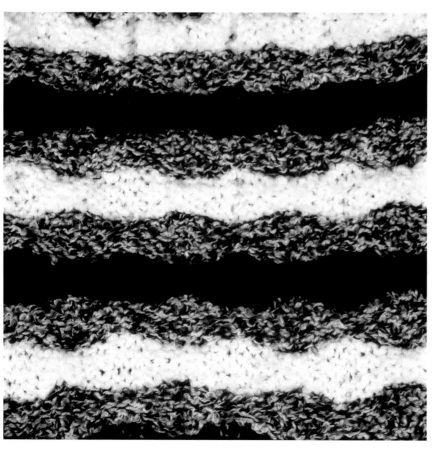

Reverse side of stitch pattern.

Row 7: 🛑(RS) With A, k1, p0 (2, 0, 2, 0); *p3, [slip next st onto right needle, drop down 6 rows directly below the next st, picking up the front loop of that st, slip both sts onto the left needle and purl them together **(p1 6 sts below)**] twice, p3. Repeat from * to last 1 (3, 1, 3, 1) sts; p0 (2, 0, 2, 0) k1.

Row 8, 10, 12: With A, p across. Fasten off A after row 12.

Row 9, 11: With A, k across

Row 13: (RS) With MC, k1, p0 (2, 0, 2, 0); *p1 6 sts below (see row 7); p6, p1 6 sts below. Repeat from * to last 1 (3, 1, 3, 1) st; p0 (2, 0, 2, 0) k1.

Row 14, 16, 18: With MC, p across. Fasten off MC after row 18.

Row 15, 17: With MC, k across.

Row 19: (RS) With B, repeat row 7.

Row 20, 22, 24: With B, p across. Fasten off B after row 24.

Row 21, 23: With B, k across.

Row 25: (RS) With MC, repeat row 13.

Repeat rows 2–25 for pattern until back measures 20 (20, 20, 22, 22)" or desired length, ending with WS row.

Shoulders

Work in established pattern across 13 (15, 16, 17, 19) sts. Bind off next 16 (18, 18, 20, 20) sts; work in pattern across remaining 13 (15, 16, 17, 19) sts. Next row (WS) bind off. Fasten off. Attach yarn to other shoulder and bind off remaining sts.

Front

Work as for back until piece measures 1½" less than back to shoulders, ending with WS row.

Front Neck

Work in established pattern across 17 (19, 20, 21, 23) sts. Bind off next 8 (10, 10, 12, 12) sts. Work in pattern across remaining 17 (19, 20, 21, 23) sts. Turn. Attaching separate yarn for left shoulder, decrease 1 st at each neck edge on 4 rows. Work even on remaining sts until front measures same as back to shoulder, ending with WS row. Bind off in pattern as for back.

Sleeves

With small needles and two strands of C, cast on 22 (23, 23, 26, 26) sts. K 1 row, (mark for RS), (p 1 row, k 1 row) twice, p 1 row, increase 4 (3, 3, 4, 4) sts evenly across last row, 26 (26, 26, 30, 30) sts. Work as for back to Row 7. Change to larger needle. **Row 7:** (RS) With A, k1, p0 (0, 0, 2, 2); * p3 **(p1 6 sts below)** twice, p3. Repeat from * to last 1 (1, 1, 3, 3) sts; p 0 (0, 0, 2, 2), k1.

Following pattern for back through row 25, then working in MC St st to end; and working new sts into established pattern, increase 1 st each side of sleeve every 4 rows 4 (4, 4, 4, 4) times; every 6 rows 5 (5, 5, 4, 5) times. When sleeve measures 17 (17½, 17½, 18, 18½)", bind off all sts.

Finishing:

Sew right shoulder seam. With the right side of the sweater facing you, with smaller needles and two strands of C, pick up and k 55 (55, 55, 61, 61) sts around the neck edge. Work in St st for 2", ending with WS row. Bind off all sts loosely. Sew left shoulder seam. Matching center sleeve to shoulder seam, sew sleeves in place. Sew underarm seams. Weave in all loose ends.

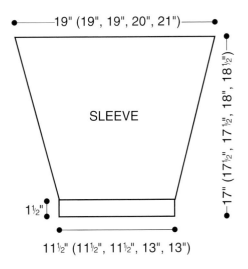

19" (19", 19", 20", 21")

SLEEVE

17" (17½", 17½", 18", 18½")

1½"

11½" (11½", 11½", 13", 13")

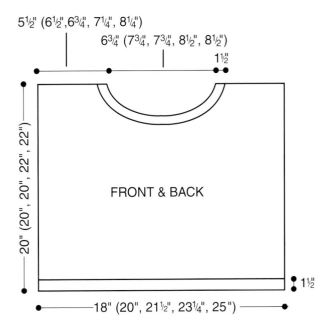

5½' (6½",6¾", 7¼", 8¼")

6¾" (7¾", 7¾", 8½", 8½")

1½"

20" (20", 20", 22", 22")

FRONT & BACK

1½"

18" (20", 21½", 23¼", 25")

Poncho With Pizzazz

Designed by Berroco Yarns

This striking evening poncho is worked in two strands of metallic ribbon. It's not super fast, but it's a straightforward Stockinette stitch and two simple rectangles. Fringe it or leave it off; you'll still have a style that will have heads turning wherever you go.

Size:

Small. Each panel of the poncho measures 26" x 13" (there are two). To increase a size, add 1" to the length and width for medium, 2" for large, 3" for extra-large and so on. Depending on size, you may need additional yarn.

Gauge:

In Stockinette stitch on size 11 needles, 3½ sts = 1"
To ensure proper fit, take time to check gauge.

Instructions:

▽ **NOTE:** Ribbon yarn may twist as you work with it—don't worry. It doesn't matter!

Make 2 pieces.
With 2 strands of *Metallica* held together, cast on 46 sts. Keeping first and last stitch in garter stitch for selvedge, work even in St st for 26". Bind off.

MATERIALS:

❖ Berroco *Metallica* (rayon/metallic, 25 gm/85 yd hank),
Silver (#1002)–11 hanks (without fringe), 12 hanks (with fringe)

❖ Size 1⅛mm needles, or size to obtain gauge

❖ Size I/9mm crochet hook

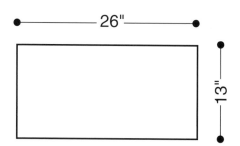

Finishing:

Steam pieces with steam iron and pressing cloth to measurements. Sew cast-on edge of one piece to the first 13" of lower right side edge of second piece. Sew bound-off edge of second piece to first 13" or right lower edge of first piece.

With crochet hook and 2 strands of *Metallica*, beginning at back point, work one row of single crochet sts around neck edge and outside edge of poncho. Work a second row around neck and outside edge in reverse single crochet. Weave in ends.

Fringe (Optional)

Cut 476, 11" lengths of *Metallica* and working with 4 strands held together and crochet hook, fold in half and draw loop through every other reverse single crochet. Pull through loop and fasten off. Trim fringe if necessary.

Photo: Christina L. Holmes

Cowl Neck Chic

Designed by Arlene Levine

This feathery, hand-dyed yarn works up quickly on size 13 needles into a cowl neck that you can pop over a ho-hum sweater and walk out with instant drama! Remember to keep your eyes on the road with this one: It's easy to set it on cruise control in a straight garter stitch, but don't look away from your stitching or you could easily drop a stitch.

Size: 9" x 24"

Gauge:

3 sts and 3 rows = 1
To ensure proper fit, take time to check your gauge.

▽ *Fluff* is a feathery yarn. To prevent tangling, it is helpful to roll the hank into a ball.
Cast on 27 sts. K each row for 24". Bind off loosely, leaving about 20" length of yarn for seaming. Thread yarn end through yarn or tapestry needle and sew ends together using an overcast stitch.

▽ Do not pull sts too tightly.

▽ If you want to adjust the sizing and knit a longer cowl, it will require a second hank of yarn. An alternative is to make the cowl narrower (7" or 8" instead of 9") which will give you more yarn for the length.

MATERIALS:

❖ Great Adirondack Yarns' *Fluff* (rayon, 82 yd hank), hand-dyed— 1 hank

❖ Size 13/9mm needles, or size to obtain gauge ▽ (We recommend using bamboo needles for this project since the stitches are less likely to slip off.)

❖ Yarn or tapestry needle for finishing

Photo: Christina L. Holmes

Beaded Evening Bag

Designed by Arnetta Kenney

With a subtle sheen to this smooth yarn and some clear "crystal" beads, you've got a great clutch bag that's a little more subdued and versatile than the usual "over-the-top" beaded evening bag. Worked in two strands on size 10 needles, the beading is done as you knit, with the beads threaded onto the yarn in advance, ready to slide forward when needed.

Size: 10" wide by 5" deep

Gauge:

15 stitches = 4".
To ensure the proper size, take time to check your gauge.

Instructions:

NOTE: The bag is knitted with 2 strands of yarn held together.

STOP With 2 strands of yarn held together, thread 24 beads onto the yarn. (Beads will be held "behind" your knitting and when you are ready to position them, you simply bring the bead up to the needle.

Cast on 38 sts. Work in garter stitch until piece measures 10".

Flap

Row 1: P
Row 2: K2tog, k to last 2 stitches, k2tog—36 sts.
Row 3: P
Row 4: K

STOP **Row 5:** P5. * Bring yarn to back of right hand needle, push 1 bead up close to work, slip the next st purlwise placing bead in front of this stitch. Bring yarn to the front of the right hand needle, purl 5*. Repeat from * to * a total of 5 times. End with p6—5 beads added.
Row 6: Repeat row 2—34 sts.
Row 7-8: Repeat rows 3 and 4.
Row 9: P2. Slip next st, adding a bead (as described in row 5), p4, add a bead on next slip st, * p5, add a bead on next slip st*. Repeat from * to * across row ending with p2—6 beads added.

Row 10: Repeat row 2—32 sts.
Rows 11 – 12: Repeat rows 3 and 4.
Row 13: P4. Add a bead on next slip st, * p5, add a bead on next slip st *. Repeat from * to * across row, ending with P3—5 beads added.
Row 14: Repeat row 2—30 sts
Rows 15 - 16: Repeat Rows 3 and 4.
Row 17: P1, add a bead to next slip st. p4, add a bead to next slip st, * p5, add a bead to next slip st*. Repeat from * to * 2 more times. P3, add a bead to next slip st, p1—6 beads added.
Rows 18 – 21: Knit.

MATERIALS:

❖ Lion Brand *Micro Spun* (microfiber acrylic, 2.5 oz/168 yd balls) Lilac (#144)—2 balls

❖ Size 10/6 mm knitting needles, or size to obtain gauge

❖ 24 size "E" beads or size with hole large enough to fit over 2 strands of *Micro Spun*

❖ 1 Large decorative button

❖ Needle for threading beads

Bind Off and Button Loop

Bind off 13 sts. With the 2 sts on the right hand needle, and while turning work, work 6 rows of garter stitch (button loop), then continue binding off across the row.

Finishing:

Place knitted fabric flat, RS facing up with loop closure at top. Fold the bottom edge up to the beginning of the flap. Sew side edges with an overcast stitch, matching garter stitch rows. Turn RS out. Fold down flap and sew decorative closure button just below the loop.

Chapter 7
Casual Routes

Classic Button-Front Vest

Designed by Lion Brand Yarn Co.

The texture is the story in this button-front vest. Very light and comfortable to wear, the basic shaping makes it a smooth road to fashion.

Sizes:

Directions are for men's sizes Small (Medium, Large, X-Large)
Finished garment at chest measures 44 (46, 48, 50)"
Finished garment length: 25½ (25½, 26, 26)"

Gauge:

In Stockinette stitch on size 10 needles, 14 sts and 20 rows = 4¼"
To ensure the proper size, be sure to check your gauge

Stitch Pattern:

Ssk = slip, slip, knit: Slip 2 sts knitwise to right hand needle one at a time, insert tip of left hand needle into fronts of these 2 sts and knit them together.

Instructions:

NOTE: All shaping decreases are done inside garter st borders.

Back

With smaller needles, cast on 72 (76, 79, 82) sts. Work in garter st (knit every row) for 6 rows. ⚠ Change to larger needles and work in St st until piece measures 14¼" from beginning, end with a RS row.

Establish Garter Armhole Borders

Next row (WS), k7, p to last 7 sts. End k7. Next row (RS): Knit. Continue to work first and last 7 sts in garter st until piece measures 15½" from beginning. End with WS row.

Armhole Shaping

Next row (RS), bind off 3 sts at beginning of row, k to end. Next row (WS), bind off 3 sts at beginning of row, k remaining armhole border sts. P to last 4 sts; end k4. Next row (RS), k4, ssk, k to last 6 sts; end k2tog, k4. 64 (68, 71, 74) sts. Continue to work 4 sts of armhole borders in garter st and rest of row in St st until piece measures 24¼ (24¼, 24¾, 24¾)" from beginning, end with a RS row. Next row (WS), k4, p14 (16, 16, 17), k28 (28, 31, 32), p14 (16, 16, 17), k4. Continue to work first and last 4 sts and center 28 (28, 31, 32) sts in garter st until piece measures 25½ (25½, 26, 26)" from beginning. Bind off all sts.

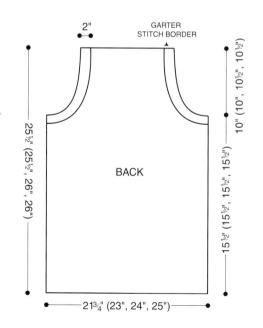

2" GARTER STITCH BORDER

25½" (25½, 26, 26")

10" (10", 10½", 10½")

15½" (15½, 15½, 15½")

BACK

21¾" (23", 24", 25")

MATERIALS:

❖ Lion Brand *Homespun* (acrylic/polyester, 6 oz/185 yd skein) Plantation (#327)—3 (4, 4, 4) balls

❖ Size 9/6mm needles

❖ Size 10/6.5mm, or size needed to obtain the correct gauge

❖ 6, ¾" buttons

❖ Stitch holders

❖ Yarn or tapestry needle for finishing

Left Front

With smaller needles, cast on 38 (40, 42, 44) sts. Work in garter st for 4 rows. 🛑 Next (buttonhole) row (RS), K to last 4 sts, k2tog, yo, k2. Continue to work buttonhole row every 16th row 5 times more and AT THE SAME TIME, work 1 more row even in garter st. Next row (RS), ◈ change to larger needles and knit row. Next row (WS), k4 (inside edge), p to end. Continue to work as established, working 4 sts of inside edge in garter st and St st over remaining sts until piece measures 14¼" from beginning, end with RS row.

Establish Garter Armhole Borders

Next row (WS), work even to last 7 sts; end k7. Continue to work in pattern established until piece measures 15½" from beginning, end with WS row.

Armhole Shaping

Next row (RS), bind off 3 sts at beginning of row, k rest of row. Next row (WS), p to last 4 sts; end k4. Next row (RS), k4, ssk, k rest of row—34 (36, 38, 40) sts. Continue to work 4 sts of armhole borders in garter st until the piece measures 18½" from beginning, end with a WS row.

Neck Shaping

Next row (RS), continue to work armhole border sts and inside edge sts in garter st. Shape neck as follows: K to last 6 sts, end with k2tog. K to end. P next row. Repeat last 2 rows 11 (11, 13, 14) times more—22 (24, 24, 25) sts. Work even until piece measures same length as back. Bind off all sts.

Right Front

With smaller needles, cast on 38 (40, 42, 44) sts. Work in garter st for 6 rows. Next row (RS), change to larger needles and knit row. Next row (WS), p to last 4 sts, end k4 (inside edge). Continue to work in pattern established, working 4 sts of inside edge in garter st and St st over remaining sts, until piece measures 14¼" from beginning, end with RS row.

Photo: Mary Colucci

Establish Garter Armhole Borders

Next row (WS), k7, p to end of row. Continue to work in pattern established until piece measures 15½" from beginning, end with a RS row. ◈ Armhole Shaping Next row (WS), bind off 3 sts at beginning of row, k remaining armhole border sts, purl to end of row. Next row (RS), knit to last 6 sts; end k2tog, k4. 34 (36, 38, 40) sts. Continue to work 4 sts of armhole borders in garter st and rest of row in St st until piece measures 18½" from beginning, end with a WS row.

Neck Shaping

Next row (RS), continue to work armhole border sts and inside edge sts in garter st, shape neck as follows. Work 4 sts, ssk, work rest of row even. Work 1 row even. Repeat last 2 rows 11 (11, 13, 14) times more—22 (24, 24, 25) sts. Work even until piece measures same length as back. Bind off all sts.

Finishing:

Sew shoulder and side seams. Block all pieces lightly. Sew buttons opposite buttonholes.

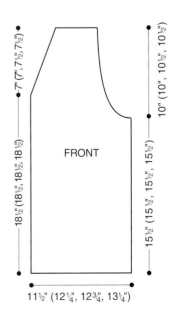

7" (7", 7½", 7½")

10" (10", 10½", 10½")

FRONT

18½" (18½", 18½", 18½")

15½" (15½", 15½", 15½")

11½" (12¼", 12¾", 13¼")

Tweedy V-Neck Vest

Designed by Lion Brand Yarn Co.

Here's a classic tweed vest that any man would enjoy wearing. Perfect for casual Fridays, the alpaca blend yarn adds a touch of luxury. Working with two strands of different colored yarns creates the tweed effect. Try it in your man's favorite color combinations.

Sizes:

Directions are for men's size Small (Medium, Large, X-Large)
Finished chest sizes 42 (44, 46, 48)"

Gauge:

In Stockinette stitch on size 10½ needles, 13 sts and 16 rows = 4"
To ensure the proper fit, take time to check your gauge.

Stitch Pattern:

Ssk = slip, slip, knit: Slip 2 sts knitwise to right hand needle one at a time, insert tip of left hand needle into fronts of these 2 sts and knit them together.

MATERIALS:

❖ Lion Brand AL•PA•KA
(wool/alpaca/acrylic, 1.75-oz/ 107 yd skein)
Black (#153), Color A—
5 (6, 6, 7) skeins
Oxford Grey (#152), Color B—
5 (6, 6, 7) skeins

❖ Size 9/5.5mm knitting needles

❖ Size 10½/6.50mm knitting needles

❖ Size 9/5.5mm 16" circular needles, or size needed to obtain gauge

❖ Stitch holders

❖ Stitch markers

❖ Yarn or tapestry needle for finishing

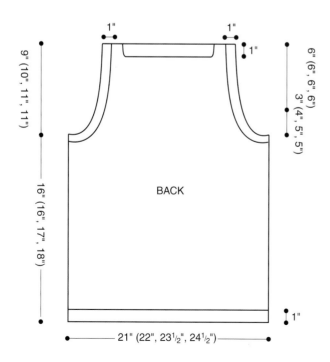

BACK

1"   1"

1"

6" (6", 6", 6")

3" (4", 5", 5")

9" (10", 11", 11")

16" (16", 17", 18")

1"

21" (22", 23½", 24½")

Instructions:

Back

NOTE: Vest is made holding 2 strands of yarn together throughout.
With size 9 needle and a strand of Color A and Color B held together, cast on 68 (72, 76, 80) sts. Work in garter st (k all rows) for 6 rows.
◆ Change to size 10 1/2 needles. Continue in St st until piece measures 16 (16, 17, 18)" from beginning, end with p row.

Armhole Shaping

Bind off 5 sts at beginning of next 2 rows. Decrease row (RS): K2, ssk, knit to last 4 sts, k2tog, k2. Repeat decreases 6 (7, 8, 9) times more—44 (46, 48, 50) sts. Work even until armhole measures 9 (10, 11, 11)". Bind off 6 sts at beginning of next 2 rows. Bind off 5 (5, 6, 6) sts at beginning of next 2 rows. Place remaining 22 (24, 24, 26) sts onto stitch holder for back neck.

Front

Work as for back until armhole measures 3 (4, 5, 5)". End with p row. Place marker in the middle of work. Continue armhole shaping and at the same time shape V-neck.

V-Neck Shaping

Knit to last 3 sts before marker, k2tog, k1. Attach two separate strands of Color A and B to other side and knit remaining sts as follows: k1, ssk, work to the end. Work both sides of the V-Neck at the same time. Next row: P. Repeat these two rows 10 (11, 11, 12) times more. When armholes measure same as back, bind off 6 sts at beginning of next 2 rows. Bind off 5 (5, 6, 6) sts at beginning of next 2 rows.

Finishing:

Neck

Sew shoulders together. With RS facing and circular needle knit across 22 (24, 24, 26) sts from back holder, pick up along left side V-Neck 3 sts from every 4 rows, 1 st from the middle, pick up along right side V-Neck 3 sts from every 4 rows, join, work in round. Next round: p, decrease 2 sts in the middle V-Neck as follows: p3tog (take 1 st from left side, 1 central st, 1 st from right side). Repeat decreases in every round. Purl 3 more rounds. Bind off purlwise.

Armbands

Sew side seams. With RS facing and circular needle pick up 4 sts from back underarm, pick up along back and front armholes 3 sts from every 4 rows, pick up 4 sts from front underarm, place marker, join, work in round. Next round: P, decrease 1 st after marker, 1 st before marker (p2tog). Repeat decreases in every round. P 3 more rounds. Bind off purlwise. Weave in loose ends. Lightly steam.

Photo: Christina L. Holmes

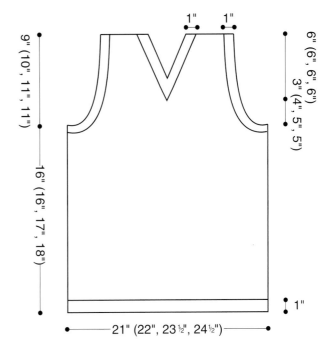

Zippy Vest

Designed by Brenda Lewis for Coats & Clark

The zippered vest is a jazzier version of an old favorite. The slip stitch pattern adds a rich texture and two strands of yarn on size 13 needles ensure that it will zip along too!

Sizes:

Directions are for men's sizes Small (Medium, Large)
Finished chest sizes 40 (44, 47)"
Finished length 25 (25½, 27½)"

Gauge:

With size 13 needles in pattern, 5 sts and 8 rows = 2"
To ensure proper fit, take time to check your gauge

Pattern Stitch:

Row 1: K1, *yarn front, slip one purlwise, yarn back, k1, rep from * to end of row.
Row 2: Purl

Instructions:

NOTE: Vest is made holding 2 strands of yarn together throughout.

Back

With size 11 needles and 2 strands A, cast on 51 (55, 59) sts. Work in ribbing as follows: **Row 1 (RS):** K1, *p1, k1; repeat from * across. **Row 2:** P1, *k1, p1; repeat from * across. Repeat rows 1 and 2 for 2½", increasing 2 sts evenly on last row, end row 2—53 (57, 61) sts. Change to larger needles and work in even pattern until 14" from beginning, ending WS row. Bind off 2 (2, 3) sts at the beginning of the next 2 rows, 49 (53, 55) sts. Decrease 1 st each end of row every RS row 2 times. Work even in established pattern until back measures 25 (25½, 27½)", ending with a WS row. If you are going to sew the shoulder seams, bind off all sts. If you are going to sew the shoulder seams, work 13 (14, 15) sts and slip to holder, bind off the next 19 (21, 21) sts for back neck, work remaining sts and slip to holder.

MATERIALS:

- Red Heart® *Super Saver* (acrylic, 8 oz/348 yd skein),
  Denim Heather (#408), Color A— 2 skeins
  Buff Fleck (# 4334), Color B— 1 skein

- Size 11/8mm knitting needles

- Size 13/9mm knitting needles, or size to obtain gauge

- Size N/15 crochet hook

- Size 14" sweater/ jacket separating zipper for small and medium; size 16" for size large

- Beige sewing thread and sewing needle

- Yarn or tapestry needle for finishing

- Stitch holders (optional)

Left Front

With size 11 needles and 2 strands A, cast on 25 (27, 29) sts. Work ribbing same as for back, including increase— 27 (29, 31). Change to size 13 needles and work even in pattern until 14", ending with WS row.

◇ Sizes small and medium only: Decrease 1 st at the neck edge next row then every other row 1 time, then every 4th row 8 (9) times. At the same time, when front measures 15", ending with a WS row bind off 2 sts at the armhole edge, then decrease 1 st at armhole edge every RS row 2 times.

Size large only: Continue in pattern until front measures 16", ending with a WS row. Bind off 3 sts at the armhole edge, decrease 1 st at the neck edge. Decrease 1 st at the neck edge every other row 1 time, then every 4th row 9 times. At the same time, decrease 1 st at the armhole edge every RS row 2 times.

Work even on 13 (14, 15) sts until front measures 25 (25½, 27½)", ending with a WS row. Bind off sts if sewing shoulders, slip sts onto holder if weaving the shoulder seams together.

Right Front

Work the same as left front, reversing neck and armhole shaping.

Finishing:

Sew together shoulder seams. Sew side seams.

Front and Neckband

With RS facing, using size N crochet hook and 2 strands of Color B, begin at the bottom edge of right front and work 1 sc into the first st, * skip the next st, 1 sc into the next st, repeat from * to bottom edge of left front. Ch 1, work 1 reverse sc into each st around. Fasten off.

Armhole Band

With RS facing, using Size N crochet hook and 2 strands of Color B, work 1 sc into the first st, * skip 1 st, work 1 sc into the next st. Join with a slip st in beginning sc. Ch 1, work 1 reverse sc into each st around. Join with a slip st.
Fasten off.
Weave in yarn ends.
Pin zipper to front bands between bottom edge and first neck shaping decrease. Sew by hand.

Photo: Christina L. Holmes

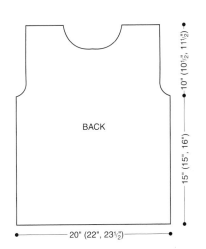

BACK

10" (10½", 11½")

15" (15", 16")

20" (22", 23½")

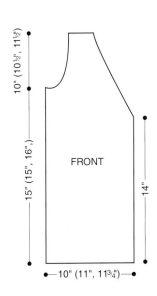

FRONT

10" (10½", 11½")

15" (15", 16")

14"

10" (11", 11¾")

Hey Baby! For The Car Seat Set

Hey Baby!
For the Car Seat Set

Salt & Pepper Sweater & Hat

Designed by Kathleen Sams for Coats & Clark

Textured, flecked yarn creates a beautiful tweedy look in this sophisticated baby cardigan with matching hat, and fun buttons like the "puppy" design shown here add a whimsical touch. The best part is that the body is knitted in one piece for minimal finishing.

Sizes:

Directions are for 3 mos (6, 9, 12, 18) mos

Gauge:

In pattern stitch on 15 needles, 8 sts and 12 rows = 4"
To ensure proper fit, take time to check your gauge.

Garter Fleck Stripe Pattern

Row 1 (RS): With A, k3, * p3, k3; repeat from * across.
Row 2: Repeat Row 1.
Row 3: With B, k3, * p3, k3; repeat from * across.
Row 4: Repeat row 3.
Repeat these 4 rows for pattern.

Instructions:

Body (Worked in one piece to underarms)

With size 13 needles and B cast on 33 (39, 45, 51, 57) sts. K 4 rows. Change to size 15 needles and work in pattern stitch until 5 (5½, 6, 6½, 7)" from beginning, end row 4.

Divide for Front and Back

Keeping continuity of stripe pattern, work across 7 (9, 11, 13, 15) sts; turn and put remaining sts on a holder. Work even on these sts until 3½ (4, 4, 4½, 4½)" above division.

Neck Shaping

Decrease 1 st at neck edge on next 2 (2, 3, 4, 5) rows. Bind off.

MATERIALS:

- Red Heart® *Light & Lofty*™ (acrylic, 6 oz/148 yd skein) Salt & Pepper (#9317), Color A— 1 (1, 2, 2, 2) skeins Onyx (#9312) Color B—1 skein

- Size 13/9mm circular knitting needles, 16"

- Size 15/10mm circular knitting needles, 16", or size to obtain gauge

- Stitch holders

- 4 or 5, ⅝" to 1" buttons

- Yarn or tapestry needle for finishing

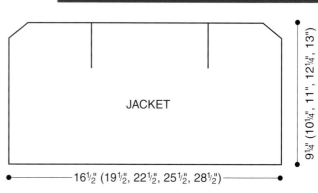

JACKET

16½" (19½", 22½", 25½", 28½")

9¼" (10¼", 11", 12¼", 13")

Back

With RS facing, join yarn to last long row and work in pattern across 19 (21, 23, 25, 27) sts. Work even in pattern stitch on these sts until back measures same as right front to shoulder. Bind off.

Left Front

With RS facing, join yarn to remaining sts. Complete to correspond to right front, reversing neck shaping.

Sleeves

With size 13 needles and B cast on 11 (11, 13, 13, 15) sts. K 4 rows. Increase 5 (5, 7, 7, 7) sts evenly spaced across next row.

▽ Change to larger needles and work in pattern stitch, shaping sides by increasing 1 st each end of 3rd row, then every other row to 23 (23, 25, 25, 27) sts. Work even until 6½ (7, 7, 7½, 8)" from beginning. Bind off.

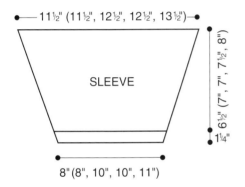

11½" (11½", 12½", 12½", 13½")

SLEEVE

6½ (7", 7", 7½", 8")

1¼"

8" (8", 10", 10", 11")

Photo: Christina L. Holmes

Finishing:

Sew shoulder seams. With RS of sweater and sleeves facing, set in sleeves and sew in armholes. Sew sleeve seams.

Neckband

With RS facing, size 13 needles and B, pick up and k4 (4, 5, 6, 6) sts across right front, 10 (12, 14, 16, 16) sts across back, 4 (4, 5, 6, 6) across left front. K4 rows. Bind off.

Front Bands

With RS facing, size 13 needles and B, pick up and k23 (25, 27, 29, 31) sts. K 4 rows. Bind off.

Sew on buttons, evenly spaced—left side for girls, right side for boys.

NOTE: There is no need to make separate buttonholes. Buttons slip easily through the bulky, textured yarn. The number of buttons you use will depend on the size sweater you make and the size button you select.

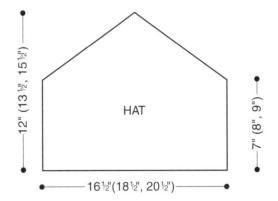

12" (13½", 15½")

HAT

7" (8", 9")

16½" (18½", 20½")

Hat

With size 13 needles and A cast on 33 (37, 41) sts. Work in pattern as for cardigan body until 7 (8, 9)" from beginning.

Shape Top

Decrease 1 st each end of every other row until 3 sts remaining. K 1 row. Cut yarn leaving a long end for sewing. Thread yarn into a yarn needle and through remaining sts. Draw up tightly and fasten securely. Sew back seam. Knot top of hat to fit.

Cable Sweat Suit

Designed by Bernat Design Studio

Racing stripes accent the grey ragg in this child's raglan-sleeved sweat suit with a buttoned shoulder and single front cable. This is one project that requires you to slow down and read through the instructions, so that you will recognize the changes that occur in shaping. It is one of the more difficult patterns in this book, but as a child's design, it's small in size! The accent colors shown are basically unisex: try a bright aqua or hot pink for a girl, and consider doing the front cable in one of the bright accents.

Sizes:

Children 6 mos (12 mos, 18 mos, 2 yrs, 4 yrs)
Finished chest sizes 20 (22, 25, 26, 29)"

Gauge:

With size 7 needles and Stockinette stitch, 19 sts and 24 rows = 4"
To ensure proper fit, take time to check your gauge.

Patterns:

Cable
Panel Pattern A (worked over 8 sts)
Row 1: (RS) P1, k6, p1.
Row 2 and even rows: K1, p6, k1.
Row 3: P1, slip next 3 sts onto a cable needle and leave at back of work, k3, then k3 from cable needle (C6B), p1.
Row 5 and 7: Same as row 1.
Row 8: Same as row 2.
Repeat rows 1-8 for panel pattern A.

Stripe
20 rows form stripe pattern:
With A, work 4 rows in St st.
With MC, work 4 rows in St st.
With B, work 4 rows in St st.
With MC, work 4 rows in St st.
With C, work 4 rows in St st.

MATERIALS:

❖ Bernat's *Berella* 4 (acrylic, 3.5 oz/ 100 gm ball)
  Grey Ragg (#10078), Main Color (MC)—3 (4, 5, 5, 6) balls
  Dark Oxford (#8893), Color A—1 (1, 1, 1, 1) ball
  Navy (#8965), Color B—1 (1, 1, 1, 1) ball
  Light Tapestry Gold (#8886), Color C—1 (1, 1, 1, 1) ball

❖ Sizes 5/3.75mm knitting needles

❖ 7/4.5mm knitting needles, or size needed to obtain tension

❖ 3, ⅝" buttons

❖ Cable needle

❖ 4 stitch holders

❖ Elastic for waist

❖ Yarn or tapestry needle for finishing

❖ Bobbins (optional)

Instructions for Suit Top:

Back

With size 5 needles and A, cast on 41 (45, 51, 55, 61) sts.

Row 1: (RS) K1. * p1, k1, repeat from * to end of row.

Row 2: P1, * k1, p1, repeat from * to end of row.

Repeat these 2 rows of (k1, p1) ribbing for 2", increasing 5 sts evenly across last row, 46 (50, 56, 60, 66) sts.

⬥ Change to MC, size 7 needles and proceed in St st until piece measures 6 (6½, 7, 8, 9)" from beginning, ending with RS row.

Shape Raglans

Bind off 2 sts at beginning of next 2 rows, 42 (46, 52, 56, 62) sts.

Next row: (RS) K1, slip 1, k1, psso. Knit to last 3 sts, k2tog. k1.

Next row: Purl.

Repeat last 2 rows 13 (15, 15, 15, 15) more times. 14 (14, 20, 24, 30) sts.

⬥ Sizes 6, and 18 months, 2 yrs and 4 yrs only: **Next row:** (RS) K1, slip 1, k1, psso. Knit to last 3 sts, k2tog, k1.

Next row: P1, p2tog, p to last 3 sts, p2tog through the back loop of the stitch, p1. Repeat last 2 rows 0 (0, 1, 1, 2) time(s) more.

All sizes: Leave remaining 10 (14,16,16,18) sts on a st holder.

Photo: Christina L. Holmes

Front

🛑 **NOTE:** When introducing a different color yarn in the middle of the row, it is helpful to use yarn bobbins or to wind small balls of the colors to be used, one for each separate area of color in the design. Start new colors at appropriate points. To change colors, bring the color you have been working with to the left on the WS and pick up the new color from under it or twist the two colors around each other where they meet, on WS, to avoid a hole.

With smaller needles and A, cast on 41 (45, 51, 55, 61) sts.

Work in (k1, p1) ribbing for 2" as given for back, increase 7 sts evenly across last row, 48 (52, 58, 62, 68) sts.

⬥ Change to size 7 needles and proceed as follows:

Row 1: (RS) With MC, k10 (14, 16, 18, 20). With A, work first row of panel pattern A (See Cable Pattern) across next 8 sts. With MC, knit to end of row.

Row 2: With MC, p 30 (30, 34, 36, 40). With A, work 2nd row of panel pattern A across next 8 sts. With MC, p to end of row. These 2 rows form pattern.

Continue in pattern until work from beginning measures same length as back before raglan shaping, ending with RS facing.

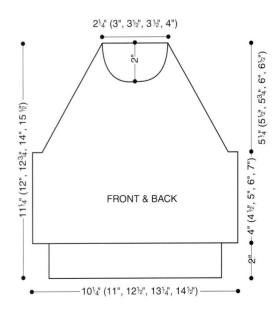

2¼" (3", 3½", 3½", 4")

2"

11¼" (12", 12¾", 14", 15 ½")

5¼" (5½", 5¾", 6", 6½")

FRONT & BACK

4" (4 ½", 5", 6", 7")

2"

10¼" (11", 12½", 13¼", 14½")

Shape Raglans

Bind off 2 sts at beginning of next 2 rows, 44 (48, 54, 58, 64) sts.

Next row: (RS) k1, slip 1, k1, psso. Continue panel pattern to last 3 sts, k2tog, k1.

Next row: Work even in pattern.

Repeat last 2 rows 7 (8, 9, 10, 11) more times. 28 (30, 34, 36, 40) sts.

Neck Shaping

Row 1: (RS) K1, slip 1, k1, psso, panel pattern across 8 sts. Turn. Leave remaining sts on a stitch holder.

Row 2: P2tog. Work panel pattern to end of row. Decrease 1 st at raglan edge on next and every other row and **at the same time** decrease 1 st at neck edge on next 3 rows.

Decrease 1 st at raglan edge as you did for the back until there are 3 sts.

Next row: (RS) Slip 1, k1, psso, k1.

Next row: P2.

Next row: Slip 1, k1, psso. Fasten off.

With RS of work facing, slip next 4 (6, 10, 12, 16) sts on a stitch holder. Join MC to remaining sts and knit to last 3 sts. K2tog, k1.

Next row: Continue panel pattern to last 2 sts, p2tog through the back loop.

Decrease 1 st at raglan edge on next and following alternate row at the same time decrease 1 st at neck edge on next 3 rows.

Decrease 1 st at raglan edge as given for back until there are 3 sts.

Next row: K1, k2tog.

Next row: P2.

Next row: K2tog, fasten off.

Sleeves

With size 5 needles and A, cast on 29 (29, 29, 35, 35) sts. Work 2" in (kl, p1) ribbing as you did for back, increase 1 st at center of last row and ending with RS facing for next row, 30 (30, 30, 36, 36) sts.

Change to size 7 needles and MC and work 2 rows in Stst increasing 1 st each end of needle on next and every other row to 32 (32, 36, 38, 38) sts.

Begin stripe pattern and increase 1 st each end of row every 2 (2, 4, 4, 4) rows, 42 (46, 50, 52, 56) sts. After completing the stripe pattern once, with MC, continue even in St st until sleeve measures 6½ (7, 7½, 8, 8½)" from beginning, ending with RS facing for next row.

Shape Raglans

Bind off 2 sts beginning next 2 rows, 38 (42, 46, 48, 52) sts.

Next row: (RS) k1, slip 1, k1, psso, knit to last 3 sts, k2tog, k1.

Next row: Purl.

Repeat last 2 rows 12 (13, 13, 15, 15) times more. 12 (14, 18, 16, 20) sts.

Next row: (RS) K1, slip 1, k1, psso, knit to last 3 sts, k2tog, k1.

Next row: P1, p2tog, purl to last 3 sts, p2tog through the back loop, p1.

Repeat last 2 rows 1 (1, 2, 1, 2) more time(s). Leave remaining 4 (6, 6, 8, 8) sts on a stitch holder.

Finishing:

Neckband

Sew raglan seams leaving back left raglan open. With RS of work facing, A and size 5 needles, K4 (6, 6, 8, 8) from left sleeve stitch holder. Pick up and knit 8 sts down left neck edge. K4 (6, 10, 12, 16) from front stitch holder. Pick up and knit 8 sts up right front neck edge. K4 (6, 6, 8, 8) from right sleeve stitch holder. K10 (14, 16, 16, 18) from back-stitch holder, decrease (k2tog) 1 st at center back, 37 (47, 55, 59, 65) sts.

Work in (k1, p1) ribbing as worked for the back for 2½", ending with RS facing for next row. Bind off loosely in ribbing. (This ribbing will later be folded over to form the collar.)

Fold neckband in half to WS and sew in position. Sew right back raglan seam leaving neckband and upper 2" of raglan seam open.

With RS of work facing, pick up and knit 13 sts along seam opening and side of neckband, working through both thickness. Work 1 row in k1, p1 ribbing as given for back.

Next row: (buttonhole row) Rib (k1, p1) 3 sts. [Bind off 2 sts. Rib 3 sts (including st after bind off)] twice.

Next row: Rib across the row (k1, p1), casting on 2 sts above bind off sts.

Next row: Work in ribbing even. Bind off in ribbing. Sew side and sleeve seams. Sew on buttons to correspond to buttonholes.

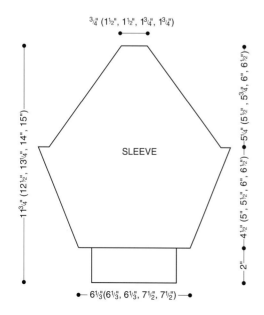

¾" (1½", 1½", 1¾", 1¾")

SLEEVE

1¾" (12½", 13¼", 14", 15")

4½" (5, 5½, 6, 6½) 5¼" (5¾, 6, 6½)

2"

6⅓" (6⅓, 6⅓, 7½, 7½)

Instructions for Sweat Pants:

Right Leg (beginning at waist)

**With size 7 needles and MC, cast on 54 (57, 60, 62, 3) sts.

Row 1: (RS) K1, *p1, k1. Repeat from * to end of row.
Row 2: P1, *k1, p1. Repeat from * to end of row.
Repeat these 2 rows (k1, p1) ribbing for 2¼" ending on a 2nd row.**

Proceed as follows:

Shape Back

Next 2 rows: K10. Turn. Slip 1 purlwise, purl to end of row.
Next 2 rows: K18. Turn. Slip 1 purlwise. Purl to end of row.
Next 2 rows: K26. Turn. Slip 1 purlwise. Purl to end of row.
Next 2 rows: K34. Turn. Slip 1 purlwise. Purl to end of row.
Next 2 rows: K42. Turn. Slip 1 purlwise. Purl to end of row.

▽ **NOTE:** To avoid a hole when knitting a slipped stitch, pick up the st below the slipped st and slip it onto left-hand needle. Knit this st together with the slip st above. Continue in St st until work from center front measures 8 (8¼, 8½, 9¼, 10)", ending with RS facing for next row.

**Shape Crotch

Continue in St st as established, increasing 1 st each end of next and following 0 (0, 0, 1, 1) every other row(s). Cast on 2 sts beginning of next 2 rows. 60 (63, 66, 70, 76) sts.
Work 2 rows even.

Shape Inseam

Continue in pattern, decreasing 1 st each end of needle on next and every other row until there are 44 (51, 56, 0, 58) sts, then on following 4th rows until there are 32 (35, 38, 40, 40) sts.
Continue even in St st until work from last cast on at crotch measures approximately 7¼ (7¾, 8¼, 9¼, 9¾)", ending with RS facing for next row.
Change to size 5 needles and A and work 6 rows in (k1, p1) ribbing. Bind off in ribbing.***

Left Leg (beginning at waist)

Work from ** to ** as for right leg.
Proceed as follows, noting that first row is WS:

Shape Back

Next 2 rows: P10. Turn. Slip 1 knitwise, knit to end of row.
Next 2 rows: P18. Turn. Slip 1 knitwise, knit to end of row.
Next 2 rows: P26. Turn. Slip 1 knitwise, knit to end of row.
Next 2 rows: P34. Turn. Slip 1 knitwise, knit to end of row.
Next 2 rows: P42. Turn. Slip 1 knitwise, knit to end of row.

▽ **NOTE:** To avoid a hole when purling a slipped st, pick up the st below the slipped st and slip it onto left-hand needle. Purl this st tog with the slipped st above.
Next row: P across all sts.
Proceed in St st until work from center front measures 8 (8¼, 8½, 9¼, 10)", ending with RS facing for next row.
Work from *** to *** as for right leg.

Finishing:

Sew inseams. Sew crotch seam. Fold waistband in half to wrong side and sew loosely in position leaving an opening to insert elastic. Cut elastic to waist measurement and insert through waistband. Sew ends of elastic together securely. Sew opening of waistband closed.

Color Block Sweater

Designed by Kathleen Sams for Coats & Clark

With three strands of yarn and large-size needles, you'll finish this colorful front-zippered cardigan so quickly you may get a ticket for speeding! That's the fun of knitting infant and children's projects—the small size makes it manageable!

Sizes:

Children's sizes Small (Medium, Large)
Finished Chest size, 26 (28, 30)"
Finished length: 14 (16, 17)"

Gauge:

In Stockinette stitch with size 15 needles and three strands of yarn held together, 10 sts and 13 rows = 4"
To ensure proper fit, take time to check your gauge.

Instructions:

NOTE: Work with 3 strands held together as one throughout.

Back

With 2 strands of B and 1 strand A, cast on 33 (35, 38) sts. K4 rows. Work in St st (k1 row, p1 row) until piece measures 13½ (15½, 16½)", ending p row.

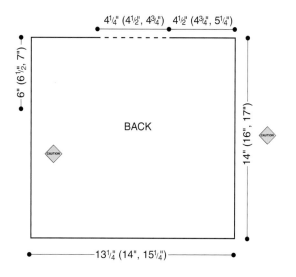

MATERIALS:

❖ Red Heart® *Kids*™ (acrylic, 5 oz/302 yd solid and 4 oz/242 yd multi-color skeins)
  Blue (#2845), Color A—3 (6, 6) skeins
  Crayon (#2930), Color B—3 (3, 3) skeins
  Green (#2677), Color C—3 (3, 3) skeins
  Red (#2390), Color D—3 skeins

❖ Size 15/10mm knitting needles or size to obtain gauge

❖ Separating zipper **NOTE:** Zipper length depends on sweater size. We used a 15" zipper length for the medium-size sweater.)

❖ Stitch holders

❖ Stitch markers

❖ Yarn or tapestry needle for finishing

Neck Shaping

Row 1: K9 (10, 11), k2tog, slip remaining sts on a holder. **Row 2:** P. Bind off.
Leave center 11 (11, 12) sts on holder. With RS facing, pick up remaining 11 (12, 13) sts. Complete to correspond to neck shaping of first side, reversing shaping.

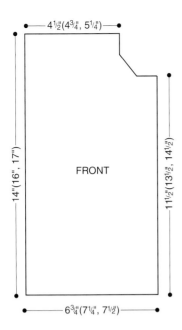

4½"(4¾", 5¼")

FRONT

14"(16", 17")

11½(13½, 14½")

6¾"(7¼", 7½")

Right Front

With 3 strands of A, cast on 15 (16, 18) sts. K4 rows. Change to 3 strands C and work in St st until piece measures 6 (7, 8)". Change to 3 strands of B and continue in St st until piece measures 11½ (13½, 14½)".

Neck Shaping

Bind off 3 sts at beginning of next row. Decrease 1 st at neck edge every right side row 2 (2, 3) times. Work even until piece measures 14 (16, 17)" ending wrong side row. Bind off.

Left Front

With 3 strands of A, cast on 15 (16, 18) sts. K 4 rows. Change to 3 strands of D and work in St st until piece measures 8 (9, 10)". Change to 3 strands of A and work even until piece measures 11½ (13½, 14½)". Complete as to correspond to first side, reversing shaping. Bind off.

Sleeves (Make 2)

Sew front and back shoulder seams. Place markers 6 (6½, 7)" below shoulder seams on front and back. With right side facing and 3 strands of A, pick up and k30 (32, 35) sts between markers. Working in garter st (k each row), decrease 1 st each end on 8th row, then every 6th row 3 times. Work even on 24 (26, 29) sts until piece measures approximately 11 (13, 14)". Bind off.

Finishing:

Neckband

With RS facing and 3 strands of A, pick up and K13 sts along the right neck edge, 11 (11, 12) sts from the back holder, and 13 sts along the left neck edge— 37 (37, 38) sts. Knit 1 row, k10 (10, 11), k2tog, k13 (13, 12), k2tog, k10 (10, 11)—35 (35, 36) sts. Knit 1 row. Bind off.
Sew side and sleeve seams. Sew zipper in place under front edge. Weave in ends.

Photo: Christina L. Holmes

12" (12¾", 14")

11" (13", 14")

SLEEVE

9½" (10½", 11½")

TIP: We recommend hand stitching the zipper. Machine sewing can warp or rip the fabric.

Girl's Tank Top

Designed by Brenda Lewis for Coats & Clark

Shoulder-tied straps give a fun touch to this child's summer tank top. The front and back are worked in one piece and finished with a single crochet trim on the neck and arms.

Sizes:

Directions are for girl's sizes Small (Medium, Large, X-Large)
Finished garment at chest measures 26½ (28½, 31, 33)"
Length: 13 (13½, 14, 15)"

Gauge:

In Stockinette stitch, using size 7 needle,
    9 sts and 12 rows = 2"
To ensure the proper fit, take time to check your gauge.

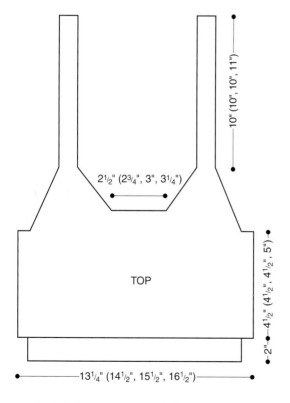

2½" (2¾", 3", 3¼")

10" (10", 10", 11")

TOP

2" — 4½" (4½", 4½", 5")

13¼" (14½", 15½", 16½")

CIRCUMFERENCE= 26½" (29", 31", 33")

MATERIALS:

❖ Aunt Lydia's® *Denim* (cotton/acrylic, 400 yd ball)
    Rose (#1026)—1 ball

❖ Size 5/3.75mm circular needles

❖ Size 7/4.5mm circular knitting needles, or size needed to obtain gauge

❖ 2 double pointed knitting needles, size 6

❖ Size H crochet hook

❖ 2 stitch holders

❖ 2 stitch markers

Instructions:

Using size 5 circular needles, cast on 120 (130, 140, 150) sts. **STOP** Spread your stitches along the length of the needle, making sure they are not twisted. Hold needle end with cast on stitches in the left hand, place marker over right hand needle point and work the first stitch on the left-hand point, pulling yarn firmly to prevent a gap. Work k1, p1 ribbing over 60 (65, 70, 75) sts, place 2nd marker on needle. Work around to the marker to complete one round. Slip the marker and continue with the next round and work k1, p1 ribbing in rounds for 2 inches, pulling yarn firmly at beginning of each round. **CAUTION** Change to size 7 needle and k in rounds until piece measures 6½ (6½, 6½, 7)".

Divide for front and back:

Next row * k to the last 4 sts before marker, bind off 4 sts before marker, remove marker and bind off next 4 sts, repeat from *. K to end of row. Slip the first 52 (57, 62, 67) sts worked onto holder for front. Working in rows on 52 (57, 62, 67) sts for back, work in St st and decrease 1 st each end of needle every right side row 3 (4, 4, 5) times. 46 (49, 54, 57) sts on needle.

Neck Shaping

Next row k17 (18, 20, 21) sts and slip onto holder for right shoulder, bind off next 12 (13, 14, 15) sts for neck back, k next 17 (18, 20, 21) sts for left shoulder. Work in St st and decrease 1 st each end of the needle every RS row 7 (7, 8, 9) times, 3 (4, 4, 3) sts on needle. P one row.

Sizes Medium and Large: only next row decrease 1 st, purl one row.

Straps

Slip 3 sts onto size 6 double pointed needle and work as follows: k3, * slip sts to opposite end of needle and holding thread firmly, k3. Repeat from * until strap measures 10 (10, 11, 11)". Bind off.

Slip sts for back right shoulder onto size 7 needle and work the same as for left shoulder. Slip sts for front onto size 7 needle and work the same as for back.

Finishing:

Underarms

With RS facing using size H crochet hook, work 1 sc into first st below strap, * skip 1 st, work 1 sc into the next st, repeat from * to the strap. Fasten off.

Neck

With right side facing, work 1 sc into the first st below strap, *skip the next st, work 1 sc into the next st, repeat from * to the strap, ch 1, work 1 reverse sc into each st across. Fasten off. Weave in yarn ends.

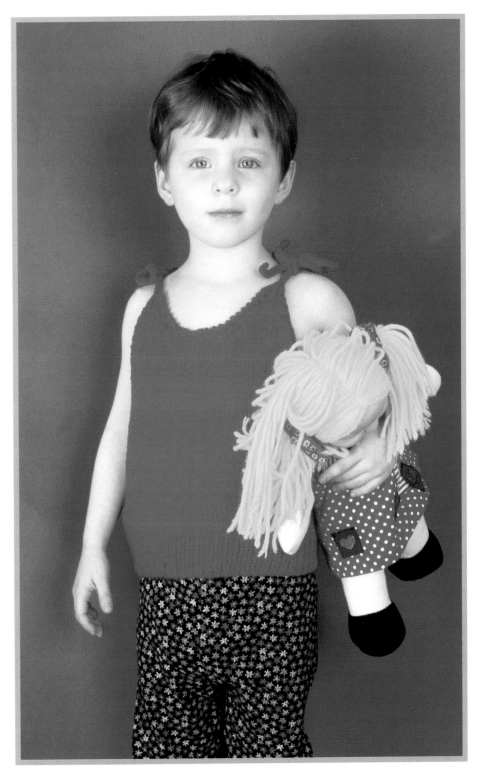

Photo: Christina L. Holmes

Broken-Cable Afghan

Designed by Bernat Design Studio

Whether in the car seat or crib, your favorite baby will be cruising to dreamland wrapped in this soft and light afghan. Once you master the broken cable pattern, you'll want to make an afghan for yourself, too!

Size:

Baby, 31 by 39"
(Adult, 43 by 57")

Gauge:

In Stockinette stitch with size 15 needle, 9 sts and 14 rows = 4"

Stitch Patterns:

C6B = slip next 3 sts onto a cable needle and leave at back of work. K3, then k3 from cable needle.

C6F = slip next 3 sts onto a cable needle and leave at front of work. K3, then k3 from cable needle.

Instructions:

Cast on 80 (110) sts.
Row 1: (WS). Knit.
Row 2: Knit.
Row 3: K, increase 18 (24) sts evenly across, 98 (134) sts.

STOP Proceed in pattern as follows:
Row 1: (RS) Knit.
Row 2 and even rows: K3, purl to last 3 sts, k3.
Row 3: K4, *C6B, k6, C6F, repeat from * to last 4 sts. K4.
Row 5, 7, and 9: Knit.
Row 11: K7, C6F, C6B, * K6, C6F, C6B. Repeat from * to last 7 sts. K7.
Row 13 and 15: Knit.
Row 16: As 2nd row.
These 16 rows form pattern.
Continue in pattern until afghan measures approximately 39 (56)", ending on a 14th row of pattern.
Next row: (RS) K, decrease 18 (24) sts evenly across, 80 (110) sts.

K 2 rows. Bind off knitwise (WS).

MATERIALS:

❖ Bernat *Breeze* (acrylic/nylon, 140 gm/178 yd balls)
 Seafoam (#106)
 Baby size—5 balls
 Full size—9 balls

❖ Size 15/10mm circular knitting needle, 24", or size to obtain gauge

❖ Cable needle

❖ Yarn or tapestry needle for finishing

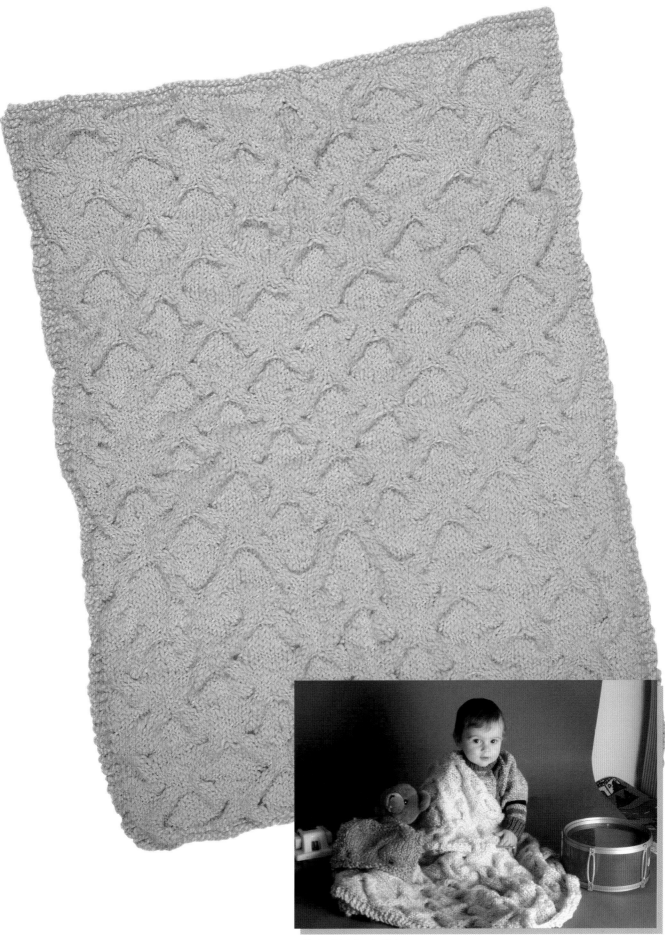

Photo: Christina L. Holmes

Grow-As-You-Go Diagonal Baby Afghan

Designed by Mary Colucci

Knitting on the diagonal is great fun. And as its name suggests, stitches have a diagonal slant. For our baby blanket, we started with a few stitches, increased until the knitted fabric was the length we liked and then we started decreasing a stitch every row, creating a square blanket. We did not have a formal pattern or gauge when we started. We simply combined yarn colors we liked and experimented with needle sizes until we got the "look" that we liked. Experiment with different yarns and sizes, too.

▽ Diagonal knitting is also a wonderful way to create shawls, and you don't have to decrease. Continue increasing until the triangle is a comfortable size for draping/wrapping around your shoulders and bind off. Also, try increasing on the first stitch instead of the second stitch of each row.

Size:

Approximately 36" square

Gauge:

With four strands of yarn and size 17 needles, 2 sts = 1"
To ensure proper size, take time to check your gauge.

Instructions:

NOTE: Blanket is knitted in stockinette stitch, holding one strand of each of the four yarn colors together at the same time.

With four strands of yarn, cast on three stitches.
Row 1: K1, increase 1 in next st, k1.
Row 2: P1, increase 1 st in 2nd st, p2.
Row 3: K1, increase 1 in next st, k3.
Row 4: P1, increase 1 in next st, p4.

MATERIALS:

❖ Caron's *Simply Soft*® (acrylic, 6 oz/300 yd skein)
Orchid (#9717)
Sage (#9705)
Bone (#9703)
Victorian Rose (#9721)
—2 skeins of each color

❖ Size 17 circular needles, 24", or size to obtain gauge

❖ Size N/9 crochet hook (optional, see Finishing)

❖ Yarn or tapestry needle for finishing

Continue alternating k rows with p rows and increasing in the second st on each row until knitting measures 36" (or the length desired) along one edge.

Maintaining St st pattern (alternating k rows with p rows), begin decreasing one st in the 2nd st of every row until only 3 sts remain. Bind off.

Finishing:

The increases in diagonal knitting form a natural chain stitch and because the blanket is knitted in Stockinette stitch the edges roll in gently. If you like the look of the edges, no further finishing is necessary; simply weave in the yarn ends. We opted to crochet rows of loose slipstitch using two strands of the same color yarn for a border. (A single crochet border also would be attractive.)

Photo: Christina L. Holmes

Grow-As-You-Go Diagonal Baby Afghan

Handy Mitten Scarf

Designed by Mary Colucci

Remember when your mother pinned your mittens to your sleeve so you wouldn't lose them? Well, here's a quick project idea that solves that age-old dilemma—the mitten scarf. Create warm "mittens" by simply turning up the ends of a scarf. Try this in your child's favorite colors or school colors. And, if you like the idea, make one for yourself, adjusting the length and amount of yarn.

Size:

Approximately 5½" wide and 52" long with 4½" "mitten" pockets

Gauge:

In garter stitch using two strands of yarn and size 13 needles,
2½ sts = 1" 9 rows = 2"
To ensure proper sizing, take time to check gauge.

Instructions:

▽ **NOTE:** The scarf is made holding two strands of yarn held together throughout. When you need two strands and are knitting with one color and one skein of yarn, pull an end from the outside of the skein and an end from the inside of the skein. (The inside end can be tricky to find, but keep poking around, pulling out small amounts of yarn, until you do.)

When changing yarn colors every two or three rows, as you will here, you do not have to cut your yarn; simply carry the strands you are not using along the side edge. If the stripes are wider, it is better to cut the yarn, leaving approximately a 6" tail, which you can later weave in, and pick up the new yarn color.

MATERIALS:

- Caron *Simply Soft*® (acrylic, 6 oz/300 yd skein)
  White (#9701), Color A—1 skein
  Red Violet (#9718), Color B—1 skein
  Royale (#9713), Color C—1 skein
  Green (#9728), Color D—1 skein

- Size 13/9mm knitting needles, or size to obtain gauge

- Size 9/N crochet hook

- Yarn or tapestry needle for finishing

Cast on 15 sts. Knit all sts, changing colors as follows:
With B, k 27 rows.
With C, k 20 rows.
With A, k 10 rows.
One strand each of C and D,
  k 2 rows.
With A, k 2 rows.
With B, k 2 rows.
With A, k 6 rows.

With C, k 6 rows.
With D, k 6 rows.
With A, k 12 rows.
With B, k 20 rows.
With A, k 2 rows.
With D, k 22 rows.
With C, k 22 rows.
With A, k 2 rows.
With B, k 20 rows.
With A, k12 rows.

With D, k 6 rows.
With C, k 6 rows.
With A, k 6 rows.
With B, k 2 rows.
With A, k 2 rows.
One strand each of C and D,
  k 2 rows.
With A, k 10 rows.
With C, k 20 rows.
With B, k 27 rows.

Photo: Christina L. Holmes

Finishing:

With the WS facing you, at either end of the scarf, fold the bottom edge of the scarf up to the end of the first Color B stripe (approximately 4½"). Sew the side edges, creating a pocket. Turn the pocket inside out so it is on the right side of the scarf. With the crochet hook and holding a strand of A, B, C, and D together, crochet the edges with a very loose slipstitch or single crochet for a neat finish.

Chapter 9

How to Stitch It (and Fix It)

Following are instructions for most of the basic stitches used throughout this book as a handy quick-reference and "refresher" guide (you can't remember everything when you're living life in the fast lane!). These instructions are given for right-handed knitters; left-handers must substitute the word "right" for "left" and vice versa, in the instructions (and if you hold the instructions up to a mirror, they will be reversed to show the "left-handed" view). **NOTE:** We've used blue for the right-hand needle and red for the left-hand needle.

Casting On

This is the foundation row for your stitches. There are different methods of "casting on," but one of the most common—and simplest—is the double cast-on, or "long-tail" cast-on method.

First, measure off a length of yarn, allotting at least 1" for each stitch you will cast on. THIS IS IMPORTANT: Many knitters find they run out of yarn before they can cast on the required number of stitches, which is a big time-waster, particularly for those of us living in the fast lane! Be generous in leaving the "long tail" when you're casting on.

First, make a slip knot by forming a pretzel shape with the yarn, then slip your needle into the right loop of the "pretzel" as shown in Diagram 1.

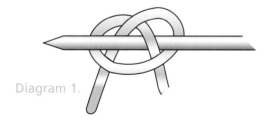

Diagram 1.

To tighten the knot, pull down on both ends of the yarn as in Diagram 2. Now you have one cast-on stitch on your needle.

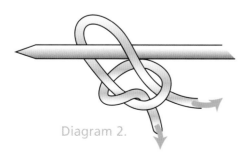

Diagram 2.

For the rest of your cast-on stitches, hold the needle with that first stitch on it in your right hand. Hold the yarn in your left hand, as shown in Diagram 3, with the short end of the yarn draped over the thumb, the yarn from the ball over your index finger, and the yarn ends held in your left palm with the other three fingers (or two fingers if it's more comfortable).

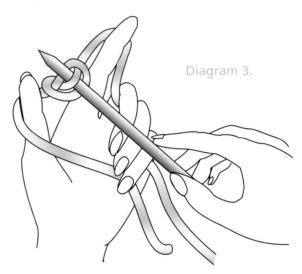

Diagram 3.

Insert the tip of your needle under the yarn on the left thumb from front to back, then over and under the strand on your left index finger, as in Diagrams 4, 5 and 6.

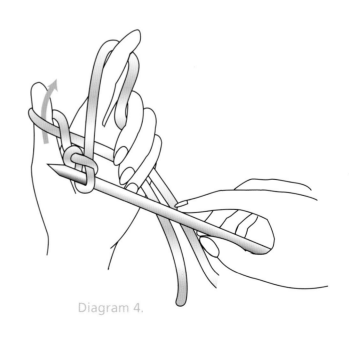

Diagram 4.

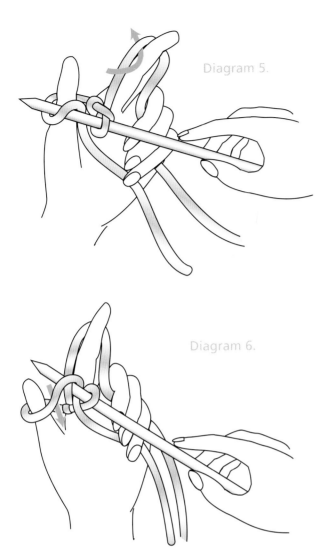

Diagram 5.

Diagram 6.

Knit Stitch (abbreviated as k)

Now you're ready to start knitting! Your left hand will hold the needle with the cast-on stitches, and your right hand will hold the yarn coming from the skein as in Diagram 8. The goal is to create an even tension with the yarn, so your stitches aren't too tight or too loose.

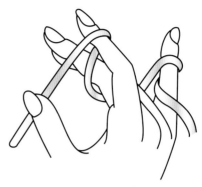

Diagram 8.

Be sure to make your stitches over the full roundness of the needle, not just the points, or your stitches will be much too tight.

Holding the needle with the cast-on stitches in your left hand, insert the right needle into the front of the first stitch, from front to back, as in Diagram 9. The right needle will be under the left one. **NOTE:** When you're doing a knit stitch, the yarn from the skein should be in BACK of the needles and your work.

Draw this loop back through the loop on your thumb, as in Diagram 7, drop the loop on your thumb and pull the short (loose) end of the yarn to tighten the new stitch on the needle.

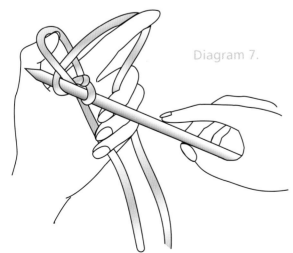

Diagram 7.

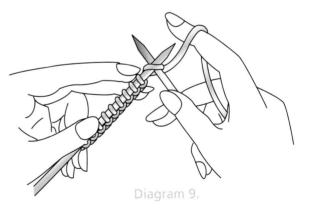

Diagram 9.

Repeat this method for each cast-on stitch required.

Bring the yarn from the skein under and over the right needle, from back to front, so it lies between the two needles, as in Diagram 10. Then bring the right needle with the yarn back through the stitch on the left needle, moving back to front, as in Diagram 11.

Now that you have the new stitch on the right needle, the next step is to slip the old stitch off the left one, by pulling it up and over the point of the left needle, as shown in Diagrams 12 and 13.

When you've repeated these steps to the end of your row, beginners should count their stitches to catch mistakes early on. Now, switch needles, so the needle full of stitches is back in your left hand, and you're ready to start another row.

To start the next row of knit stitch, insert your needle into the first stitch as shown in Diagram 14, and proceed as in Diagram 15.

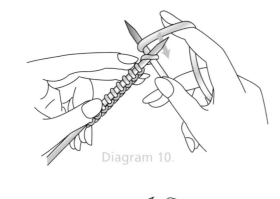

Diagram 10.

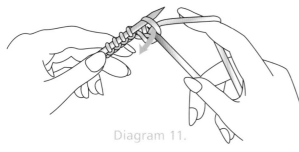

Diagram 11.

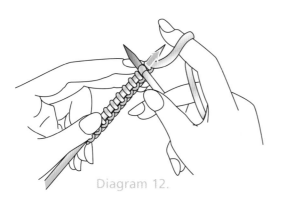

Diagram 12.

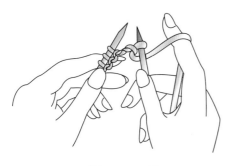

Diagram 13.

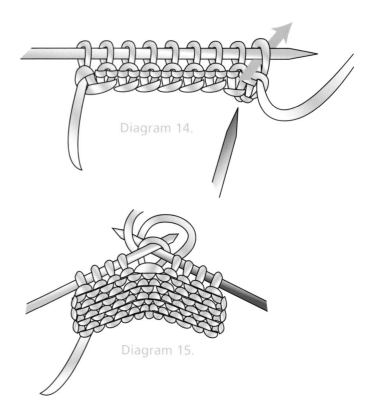

Diagram 14.

Diagram 15.

Garter Stitch (abbreviated as garter st)

When you knit every row, you're creating the garter stitch pattern, as shown in Diagram 16. The garter stitch has a bumpy texture, looks the same on both sides, and won't curl on the edges as will Stockinette stitch.

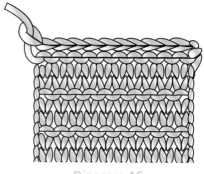

Diagram 16.

Each ridge you see in garter stitch equals two rows of knitting.

Purl Stitch (abbreviated as p)

A purl stitch is the reverse of a knit stitch—if you make a knit stitch and turn it around, the back looks like a purl stitch. The combination of knit and purl stitches is what creates the Stockinette stitch pattern (alternate rows of knit and purl) and a host of others. Remember when doing a purl stitch to keep your yarn from the skein positioned in FRONT of your needles and your work.

With your needle of cast-on stitches in your left hand, insert the right needle into the first stitch from right to left (back to front), so that your right needle is on top of the left needle, as in Diagram 17. Wrap the yarn around the right needle from right to left around the right needle, as shown in Diagram 18.

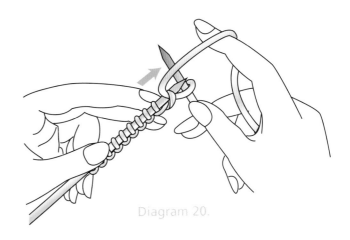

Diagram 20.

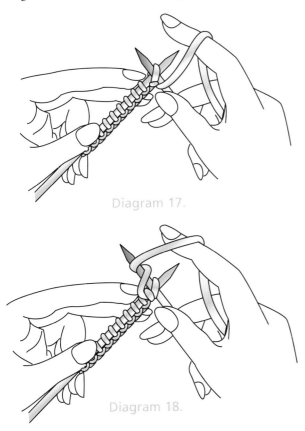

Diagram 17.

Diagram 18.

Slide the right needle with the yarn down through the stitch on the left needle, moving from front to back through the stitch, as shown in Diagram 19, then slide the old stitch off the needle, as in Diagram 20.

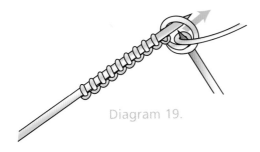

Diagram 19.

Stockinette Stitch (abbreviated as St st)

Stockinette stitch is created by knitting one row, purling the second, and continuing to alternate knit and purl rows throughout. In Stockinette stitch, you will always be knitting on a right-side row and purling on the wrong side row, so remember to bring the yarn to the back and front of your work as required. See Diagram 21.

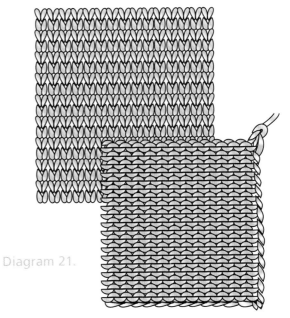

Diagram 21.

NOTE: Stockinette stitch is the stitch that will always roll at the edges. To counteract that, a pattern will often call for knitting the first one, two, or even three stitches of every purl row to create a "selvedge" (or "selvage") edge to stabilize the fabric and enable easier and neater assembly.

Reverse stockinette stitch is simply the "wrong" (purl) side of stockinette stitch used as the right side of your work.

Increasing (abbreviated as inc)

Increasing, or adding a stitch to make your piece wider, can be done by several methods, but the easiest is generally accepted to be knitting two stitches in one. To increase in a knit stitch, knit the stitch as you normally would, but DO NOT slip it off the left needle, as in Diagram 22.

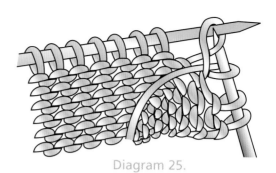

Diagram 25.

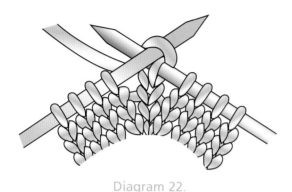

Diagram 22.

Now you will put your right needle into the stitch again, inserting it into the back of the stitch, as in Diagram 23.

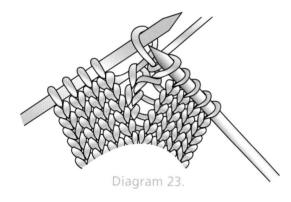

Diagram 23.

Wrap the yarn around the needle as you normally would for a knit stitch and draw through another stitch. Slip the old stitch off the left needle.

To increase in a purl stitch, purl that stitch as you normally would, but DO NOT slip it off the left needle. Then put the right needle into the BACK of the stitch, purl in that same stitch, and slip the stitch off the left needle as in Diagrams 24 and 25.

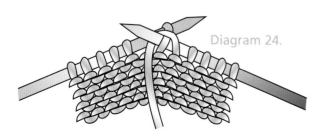

Diagram 24.

Decreasing (abbreviated as dec)

Probably the simplest way to decrease (to narrow your garment) is to knit or purl two stitches together (abbreviated as k2tog or p2tog) by inserting the needle into two stitches at the same time.

To knit two stitches together, insert the tip of the right needle into the front of the second stitch on the left needle, then through the first stitch, from left to right, as in Diagram 26, then knit the two stitches in the usual way, as if they were one stitch, as in Diagram 27.

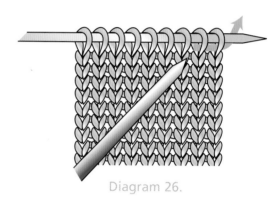

Diagram 26.

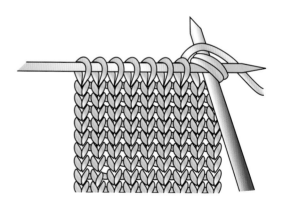

Diagram 27.

Decreasing in a purl row is done by inserting the right needle into two stitches at once, then purling them as if they were one stitch, creating a diagonal slant to the right, as in Diagram 28.

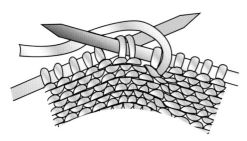

Diagram 28.

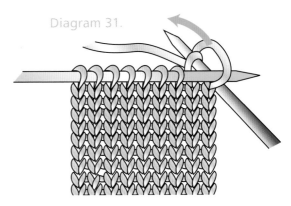

Diagram 31.

Slip, Knit and Pass Decrease Method
(abbreviated as SKP or sl 1, k 1, psso)

Depending on where a decrease is being worked on a garment, the instructions may call for this three-step method of decreasing to create a left diagonal slant.

First, slip a stitch from the left needle to the right needle knitwise, WITHOUT WORKING IT. (Just insert the right needle into the stitch and slip it off the left needle, as in Diagram 29.)

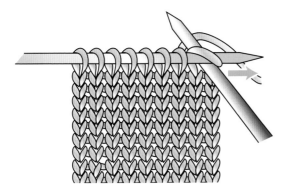

Diagram 29.

Now, knit the next stitch, so you have two stitches on the right needle, as in Diagram 30.

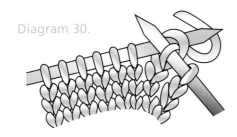

Diagram 30.

Now you'll use your left needle to "pass" the slipped stitch back over the knitted stitch and off the end of the right needle, by putting the left needle into the front of the slipped stitch and lifting it over the knitted stitch, as shown in Diagram 31. You've now decreased one stitch.

Binding Off

Patterns will sometimes tell you what method of binding off they want you to use. The following is a simple method that can be done on a knit or purl row. (Always bind off a row in the same stitch in which it was worked unless the pattern specifies otherwise.) Always bind off loosely, so the shape of the piece is not distorted and it remains flexible for ease of fit. Use larger needles for binding off if you find your bind off too tight.

Knit the first two stitches of the row. With the point of your left needle, lift up the first stitch and pull it over the second stitch as in Diagram 32, and off the right needle.

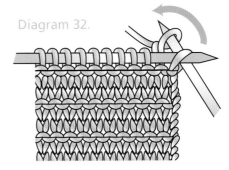

Diagram 32.

Now you'll have one stitch bound off and one stitch remaining on your right needle. Continue to work as before, knitting the next stitch and lifting the first stitch over the second and off the needle. At the end of the row, you'll be left with one stitch on your right needle. Leaving at least a 6" tail, cut the yarn and pull the end through the stitch using the tip of your right needle. Pull it tight to secure, as in Diagram 33.

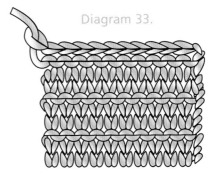

Diagram 33.

Joining Yarn

When you need to start a new skein or change colors, always do it at the beginning of a row if possible, leaving a 6" tail on the new yarn. With the new yarn, make a slip knot around the old yarn, as in Diagram 34, and continue working the next row. After a few stitches, tighten up the stitches at the beginning of the joining row and tie a temporary knot.

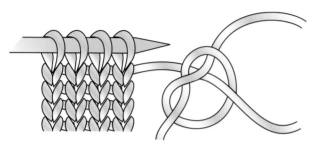

Diagram 34.

When you've finished your piece, go back and undo the knots, and weave in the ends for about 3".

There may be times when you run out of yarn in the middle of a row. If this happens, leave a 3" tail of the old yarn, wrap the new yarn around the right needle and continue working, as in Diagrams 35 and 36. Tie a knot and later weave in the ends to prevent holes and raveling. Remember, however, this is not the preferred way to join yarn.

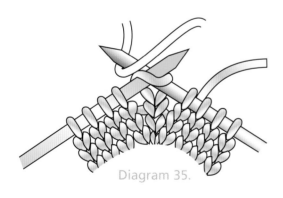

Diagram 35.

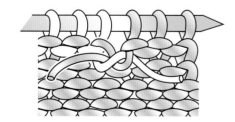

Diagram 36.

Ribbing Stitches

Several projects in this book call for ribbing on sleeves, waistbands or collars. This is simply a combination of knit and purl stitches, often just alternating knit and purl stitches across the row, as in the familiar "knit 1, purl 1" shown in Diagram 37. You'll usually find the ribbing stitch worked on a smaller needle than the body of the garment, for a snugger, but elastic fit. You'll always knit the knit stitches and purl the purl stitches on top of the ones in the row on which you're working.

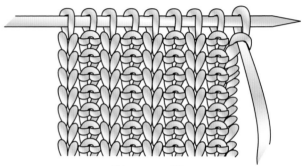

Diagram 37.

NOTE: It's important when working a ribbing stitch to remember to bring your yarn to the front when working the purl stitch and to the back when working the knit stitch.

Cables

A cable stitch is made by twisting or crossing a set of stitches over or under another group of stitches in the same row, and is accomplished with the use of a curved needle, called a cable stitch needle. You are going to put the stitches to be crossed onto the cable needle, according to the pattern instructions, knit the next group of stitches, then slip the stitches from the cable needle back onto the left needle and knit those stitches. The direction in which the cable twists depends on whether you cross the stitches in the front or back of your work. When you cross the stitches in front of your work, the cable will twist or spiral to the left; when you cross them in back of your work, you will have a "right-twist" cable.

The diagrams here show a left-twist cable:

In Diagram 38, our cable will consist of 6 stitches—3 in each half of the "twist"—twisted every few rows according to the pattern directions. First, place the stitches to be twisted on a cable needle as shown.

Then, knit the next group of stitches, as in Diagram 39.

The next step is to slip the stitches off the cable needle onto the left needle and work those stitches, as in Diagram 40.

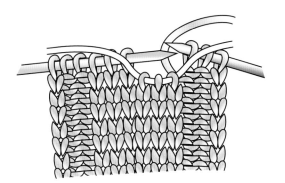

Diagram 38.

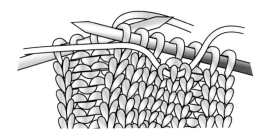

Diagram 39.

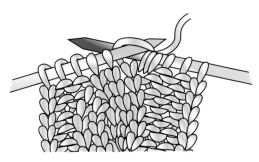

Diagram 40.

Continue as per pattern instructions to create your cable, as in Diagram 41.

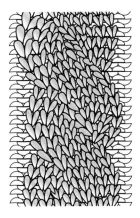

Diagram 41.

Yarn Over (abbreviated yo)

Yarn over means looping the yarn over the needle to create a "hole" or space in working lacy or decorative patterns and buttonholes.

Start by laying the yarn across the top of the needle.

These diagrams show a yarn over between knit stitches, then between purl stitches (less commonly used).

First, bring the yarn under to right needle to the front of your work, then over the right needle to the back, as in Diagram 42. Now you can knit the next stitch.

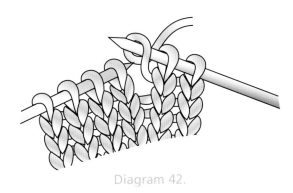

Diagram 42.

To do a yarn over between purl stitches, the yarn would be brought over the right needle to the back of the work, then under the right needle and to the front, as in Diagram 43.

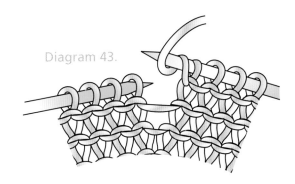

Diagram 43.

Slip Stitch (abbreviated sl st)

When a pattern says to slip a stitch, you simply transfer it from the left needle to the right needle without knitting or purling. Frequently, a pattern will say slip a stitch "knitwise" or "purlwise" which means you insert the right needle into the first stitch on the left needle as it if you were going to knit or purl and transfer it to the right needle.

Oops! Correcting Mistakes

We can't believe it—you made a mistake! Just kidding—even experienced knitters make mistakes, whether it's dropping a stitch or making an error in the number or type of stitches in a row. Here are some simple methods to help you get back on track.

A dropped stitch will look like Diagram 44, with the "bars" above it.

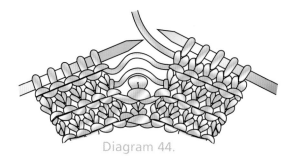

Diagram 44.

You want to pull the bar of the dropped stitch through these loops, recreating a stitch, and you want the new stitch to look just like all the others in that row.

You have two choices when you drop a stitch: unravel your knitting until you get to the dropped stitch row, as in Diagram 45; or, if there are not too many rows involved, use a crochet hook to pick it up. How you pick it up can be a little tricky, but here's an easy way to remember what to do.

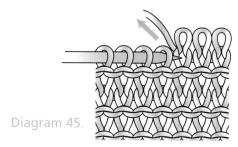

Diagram 45.

Picking Up a Dropped Stitch

First, you'll have to determine if the dropped stitch was a knit or purl stitch, then use the appropriate method to pick it up. If the stitches in the row above the dropped stitch are "flat" (knit stitches) as shown in

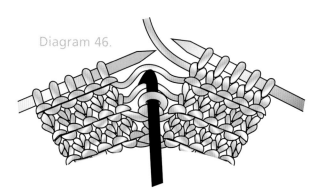

Diagram 46.

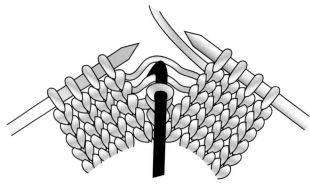

Diagram 47.

Diagram 46 or 47, pull the crochet hook into the dropped stitch from front to back (the bar will be in the back), hook onto the bar and pull the strand through the loop on the hook.

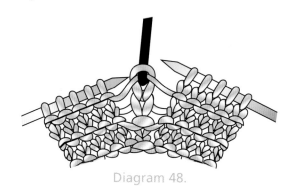

Diagram 48.

If, however, the stitches in the row above are "bumpy" (purl), as in Diagram 48, insert the crochet hook into the dropped loop from back to front, with the loose strand of the row above in FRONT of the dropped loop.

Continue until you come up to the working row, and put the stitch back on the left needle, taking care to insert the needle through the front of the stitch, so it's not twisted as you continue to work.

Correcting Twisted Stitches

Twisted stitches are especially apparent (need we say "glaring?") when you're working with bulky yarns or holding more than one strand together, as in Diagram 49, which shows twisted stitches in a knit row.

Diagram 49.

You may have inserted your needle into the back of the stitch instead of the front when you were working stockinette stitch, or put the yarn over the needles incorrectly, or picked up a stitch the wrong way.

To correct a twisted stitch in a knit row, knit it through the back loop to correct it; in a purl row, purl it through the back loop.

Correcting Extra Stitches

It's all too easy to wind up with extra stitches on your needle, particularly when working with some of the "furry" yarns and multiple strands. Other than counting stitches as you go, one of the best ways to avoid this is to remember to keep the yarn UNDER the needle when moving it to the back to knit a stitch. Diagram 50 shows the INCORRECT method, and Diagram 51 shows the correct positioning of the yarn.

INCORRECT

Diagram 50.

CORRECT

Diagram 51.

In a row of purl stitches, keep the yarn at the front of the work and below the needle, as in Diagram 52.

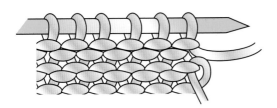

Diagram 52.

Finishing Stitches

Some patterns may specify the type of finishing stitches to use; others will let you use whatever method you're most comfortable with. Here are some common options. Whichever one you use, remember to keep it loose to allow for stretch and better fit, and always use matching yarn, unless otherwise specified.

Backstitch

A familiar stitch to embroiderers (and used in our Loop Trim Scarf to create the "border trim"), this stitch must be worked close to the edge of the pieces you are seaming together to avoid taking a deep seam that will be thick and bulky in your garment.

Place the pieces right sides together, than come up through the fabric at point A, make a stitch backwards, going down through point B, up at C, down at D, and so forth, as in Diagram 53.

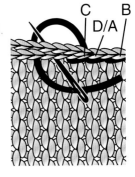

Diagram 53.

Overcast Stitch

Place right sides together and insert needle back to front, bringing the needle over the edge. Insert needle back to front again, catching only one or two strands from each edge, as in Diagram 54.

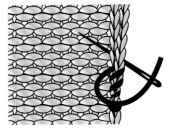

Diagram 54.

This is not considered an ideal stitch for garments, since it may not give you the smooth finish you'd like on the right side of a garment, but is good for non-wearables such as afghans or handbags.

Weaving (Invisible or "Mattress" Stitch)

Weaving is an almost invisible way to finish seams, particularly side seams. With right sides facing you and edges touching, pick up the bar between the first and second stitches on one side, then the bar between the first and second stitches on the other side. Continue working back and forth gently pulling yarn to close seam.

NOTE: Weaving is particularly good for shoulder seams and for setting in a sleeve into an armhole, as it allows you to ease and adjust for fit.

Crochet Seam Finishes

If you like to crochet, this is an easy one. Working with right sides together, matched row to row, attach a skein of yarn at the beginning of the seam. Insert the crochet hook into the outer loop of the first stitch at the top of the piece, go through to the bottom piece of fabric and pick up the corresponding outside loop. Pull your seaming yarn through the two loops of knitted fabric, for one slipstitch. You will have one loop on your hook. From this point on, you'll insert the hook into the outer loops of each of the two fabric pieces, and have three loops (one of the seaming yarn and two from the knitted pieces) on your hook. Wrap the seaming yarn over the hook and draw through all three loops as in Diagrams 56 and 57.

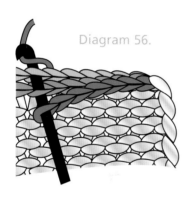

Diagram 56.

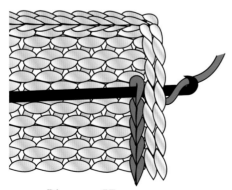

Diagram 57.

Picking Up Stitches

Several of the patterns in this book require you to "pick up stitches" as you work. Pick up stitches with the right side facing you, so the resulting ridge will be on the wrong side of your work (unless the pattern specifies otherwise).

Use the needles and yarn you are going to be continuing to work in to pick up the stitches. Insert your needle from front to back under two strands and the edge of the piece, as in Diagram 58.

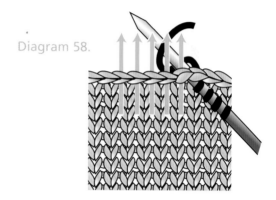

Diagram 58.

Wrap the yarn around the needle as if you were going to knit a stitch, then bring the needle back through the stitch to the right side, which will give you a stitch on the needle, as in Diagram 59.

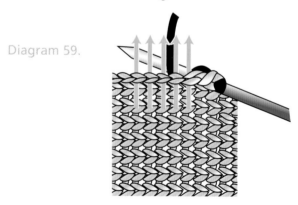

Diagram 59.

Keep working along the edge as directed.

Crochet Stitches

Some of the patterns in this book use simple crochet stitches, in particular for finishing. We've already shown the slip stitch under the finishing techniques, but here are some others you'll run across.

Chain (abbreviated as ch)

Yarn over the hook, pull through loop on hook, as in Diagram 60.

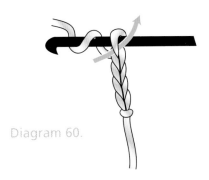

Diagram 60.

Single Crochet (abbreviated as sc)

Insert your hook in the stitch, wrap yarn over the hook, pull the yarn through the stitch, wrap the yarn over the hook again, and pull the yarn through both loops on the hook, as in Diagram 61.

Diagram 61.

Double Crochet (abbreviated as dc)

On top of your chain stitch (or along the edge of a knitted piece that serves as a foundation), wrap yarn over the hook, insert the hook from front to back into the fourth chain or stitch from the hook, as in Diagrams 62 and 63.

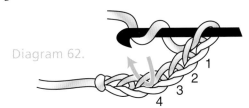

Diagram 62.

Diagram 63.

Yarn over and draw that loop through the first loop on the chain, leaving three loops on the hook, as in Diagram 64.

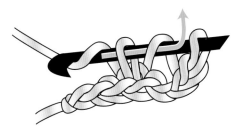

Diagram 64.

Yarn over again and draw that loop through the two loops on the hook, leaving two loops on the hook, as shown in Diagram 65.

Diagram 65.

Yarn over and pull that loop through two loops on the hook, leaving one loop on the hook, one double crochet completed, as in Diagram 66.

Diagram 66.

Reverse Single Crochet
(abbreviated as Rsc)

This stitch produces a cording effect that many knitters love. You may see it described as "crab stitch," "shrimp stitch" or "corded stitch." It's worked with the right side of the fabric facing you but in the opposite direction in which you would normally work (right handers work left to right). Pay attention to the direction in which the crochet hook points.

Beginning at the opposite end from where you'd normally start, right side facing you and one loop on the crochet hook, insert the hook head downward into the first stitch. Draw up one loop of yarn through the stitch for two loops on the hook. See Diagrams 67 and 68.

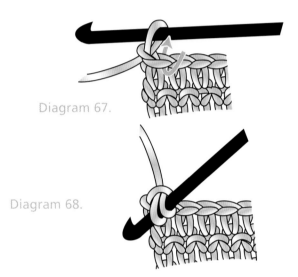

Diagram 67.

Diagram 68.

Now turn the head of the hook facing downward, wrap the yarn over the hook and pull it through the two loops on the hook (as in Diagrm 69). You have completed one reverse single crochet. Continue across row as in Diagram 70.

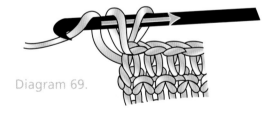

Diagram 69.

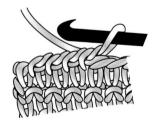

Diagram 70.

Making Fringe

Some of the items in this book call for fringe. Using a piece of cardboard cut to the desired length, wind several strands around it, secure with tie, and cut at bottom, as in Diagram 71 and 72. If you prefer, just measure out strands to twice the length of the desired fringe.

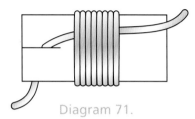

Diagram 71.

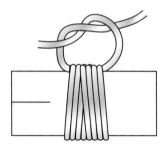

Diagram 72.

With the fringe folded in half over the crochet hook, pull the strands through the edge of your knitted piece and pull the yarn through the loop, as in Diagram 73.

Diagram 73.

Space out tassels at desired intervals as shown in Diagram 74.

Diagram 74.

Appendix

Abbreviations & Commonly Used Terms*

beg	beginning
BO	bind off
CC	contrasting color
dec	decrease
dpn	double pointed needle
EOR	every other row
inc	increase
in(s) or "	inches
k	knit
k2tog	knit two (stitches) together
MC	main color
mm	millimeter
oz(s)	ounce(s)
p	purl
psso	pass slipped stitch(es) over
p2tog	purl two stitch(es) together
RS	right side
sl	slip
ssk	slip, slip, knit
st(s)	stitch(es)
St st	stockinette stitch
WS	wrong side
yo	yarn over
* *	repeat directions between * * as many times as indicated

*We only list abbreviations used in this book. There are others commonly used in commercial patterns. Always check the pattern key before you begin your knitting.

Pattern Lingo

"work"
When reading patterns in this book and other resources, "work," "work even," "work across," or "work up" are commonly used terms. "Work" is just another way of saying, "keep on knitting." For instance, if the pattern says, "work across," continue following the pattern established and complete the row.

"knitwise" or "purlwise"
When you see these terms, they mean to insert your right needle into the next stitch on the left needle as if you were going to knit or purl. For instance, a pattern might say, "Slip the next stitch purlwise," which mean slip the next stitch as if you were going to purl that stitch but you don't.

"back loop"
Knitting into the back loop of a stitch, sometimes abbreviated "tbl" (through the back loop), twists the stitch. If you are knitting, instead of putting the right needle through the front loop of the stitch on the left needle, insert it into the back loop as you normally would from the front to back and complete the new stitch as usual, drawing a loop through. To purl through the back loop, which is done in the "Cable Sweat Suit" in the *Hey Baby Chapter*, bring the right needle from the back to the front through the back loop of the stitch on the left needle and complete the stitch as usual.

Fast FAQs

I don't understand what the pattern is telling me to do.

Just don't understand pattern instructions? Here's what Evie always tells us and it works much of the time: "It's always easier with your knitting in front of you." Take out your needles and yarn and then try following the pattern instructions, one step at a time.

Why aren't the edges of my knitting straight?

Having trouble keeping the edges of your knitting straight? It can be tricky, especially when you use textured or dark-colored yarns, because stitches are difficult to see clearly. One of the most common errors is picking up an extra stitch at the end of the row. This usually happens when you bring the yarn over the needle. Check out the illustration in the Stitch Instructions, Diagrams 50 and 51. Count your stitches frequently. If you have added stitches, unravel your knitting to the row where the problem started.

Where did those extra stitches come from?

You counted your stitches and you have more than you should have. The edges look straight. Where did they come from? Another common mistake that adds unwanted stitches to your knitting is forgetting to drop the "old" stitch from the left needle after you have pulled up the loop of yarn forming the new stitch, or picking up the yarn between stitches and knitting it, creating a new stitch.

Fitting stitches on the needles: How much is too many?

There are no hard and fast rules about the length needle you should use, but you want your stitches to fit on the needle and slide easily without "popping off." When knitting bulky sweaters, using multiple strands of yarn or making afghans, you might want to consider using circular needles. Just like straight knitting needles, circulars come in different lengths.

When do you use circulars?

In addition to large projects, circulars are frequently used in this book for finishing necklines, where you are picking up stitches in a circle and which would be awkward to do with straight needles.

How do you work with circular needles?

You can use circular needles just like straight needles, knitting back and forth, or you can knit in the round, creating a tubular piece of knitting. To use circular needles like straight needles, you knit your stitches from the left needle to the right. At the end of the row, you turn your work so that the yarn end is in your left hand. If you don't turn your work at the end of the row, and just keep going, you'll knit a tube. When knitting in the round, the right side of fabric always faces you. Accordingly, when working a Stockinette stitch, knit all the stitches on every round. When working a garter stitch, alternate knit and purl rows.

Working with two or more strands of yarn sounds complicated.

There's nothing complicated in multiple-strand knitting. When a pattern says to knit using two or more strands of yarn, hold them together and knit them as if they were one strand. You do not want to wind the different colors or yarns into one ball; simply pull a thread from each skein or ball. Occasionally, you will have to untwist the yarns to keep them flat and untangled. There are more tips on working with multiple strands of yarn in the "Tips on working with textured yarns" section in this chapter.

Do the same needle sizes differ?

Yes, there are subtle differences in needle sizing between manufacturers, which is another reason to always check your gauge.

Are the same knitting abbreviations used around the world?

No, there are variations. Always consider the source of your project pattern and check the abbreviation key.

How do I start a new skein of yarn in the middle of a project?

Oops! You ran out of yarn and have to start a new skein. It's best to start a new skein at the beginning of a row because it is easier to work in the ends when you finish the project. See Stitch Instructions, Diagrams 34-36. Simply drop the yarn you had been working with and start knitting with yarn from the new skein. Some people find it is easier to tie a loose knot with the yarn ends. When they finish the project, they untie the knot and work in the ends.

I want to change the size of a pattern. Can I do it?

If you want to make a sweater larger or smaller than the sizes provided, we really recommend that you ask an expert knitter to assist you. Adjusting the shaping can be done but it's complicated and some patterns just cannot be changed. Your best bet is always to find a pattern that is written in your size range.

Knots: Why can't I make them?

The experts say, "No knots," for three very good reasons:

1. Knots inevitably "pop" through to the front of your project,
2. They leave bumps in your knitting, and
3. They come out!

How do I change yarn color for horizontal stripe patterns?

When you are changing yarn colors to create a horizontal stripe pattern, you will often cut off one yarn color, leaving a 6" end, and pick up the new color and continue knitting. If a yarn color is repeated every other row or every two rows, you can "carry" the yarn color not being used along the side of your work. When you finish the stripe of one color, simply pick up the strand of the other color and begin knitting.

Why are there holes in my knitting?

You might have dropped a stitch, in which case, you should check out Diagrams 44-48 in the Stitch Instructions, which show how to pick up dropped stitches.

Can I pull the yarn end from the center of the skein?

It's preferable to pull yarn from the inside of the yarn skein or ball rather than use the outside end. The skein stays neater and the yarn is less likely to get tangled. However, finding that inside end can be tricky. There are instructions on some skeins but on others you just have to stick two fingers into the center of the skein and fish around. Usually, you'll pull out a wad of yarn but eventually you'll find the end.

My stitches are tight stitches. I can hardly move them across the needle.

If your stitches are barely moving along the needle, you need to loosen up and not pull the yarn so tight. As you become more comfortable holding the needles, your tension will loosen up. If you tighten your stitch on the shaft of the needle rather than on the point, it will help to ease your tight tension. Tight tension can be a special problem when you cast on because you want that row to be stretchy and flexible. You'll probably find that you will have to switch to a larger-size needle to obtain the necessary gauge for your project (see section on Gauge in this chapter).

My stitches are too loose. What can I do to make them look even?

If your stitches are too loose, you need to focus on pulling the yarn tighter as you are making your stitches. Sometimes it is easy to "stretch" your stitches, which makes them look larger and misshapen. To prevent stretching, position the stitches as close to the edge of your needle as possible so you do not have to pull the yarn. Practice making the stitch loops uniform on the needle. Practice is the best thing.

Help! The edges of my knitting are curling.

Certain stitches, such as stockinette (alternately knitting one row and purling one row), almost always will curl in, which can be an attractive edging. However, if you hate that look, consider adding two knit stitches at the beginning and end of every row. If you have already completed your project, you can crochet a border. It will help to flatten the knitting, but you'll have to do several rows to really straighten it out and it might not flatten out completely.

What's a "ridge" in garter stitch?

Two rows of knitting make a ridge. For more details on garter stitch, see the Stitch Instructions.

Cast on: How much yarn will I need for my tail so I don't run out before I finish casting on?

If you use the double cast-on or long tail method, figure on one inch of yarn for every one stitch as a general rule, however, bulky yarns or multi-stranded work may require more. Be generous!

The yarn I'm using is in a hank and I'm finding it difficult to work with.

Several of the yarns mentioned in this book come in hanks. To prevent tangles, it is helpful to wind the hank into a ball before you start your project. Untwist the hank and find one end. (It's helpful to have someone hold the hank while you wind it or slip it over the back of a chair.) Wind the yarn around your fingers several times, then slip the yarn off your fingers, turn slightly and roll several more times over your fingers and continue until all the yarn is wound. This process prevents you from pulling the yarn too tightly and stretching it.

Here's a general rule for picking up stitches that are not on a holder. If you are picking up along a horizontal or bound off edge, pick up one stitch in each stitch. For stitches along a vertical edge, pick up 3 stitches for every four rows. And for a diagonal, pick up one stitch per stitch or row. But when all is said and done, it's really what looks best to you that's the rule. It's ok to pick up fewer stitches if you are pleased with the finished look.

Resource List

Following is a list of suppliers of yarns used in this book.

Bernat Yarns
P.O. Box 40
Listowell, Ont.
Canada, N4W 3H3
P.O. Box 435
Lockport, NY 14094
www.bernat.com

Berroco, Inc.
14 Elmdale Rd.
Uxbridge, MA 01569-0367
www.berroco.com

Caron International
1481 W. 2nd St.
P.O. Box 222
Washington, NC 27889
www.caron.com

Coats & Clark
(Red Heart Yarns)
8 Shelter Drive
Greer, SC 29650
www.coatsandclark.com

The Great Adirondack Yarn Co.
950 Co. Hwy. 125
Amsterdam, NY 12010

Lion Brand Yarn Co.
34 W. 15th St.
New York, NY 10011
www.lionbrand.com

Muench Yarns
(distributors of Horstia)
285 Bel Marin Keys Blvd.
Unit J
Novato, CA 94949-5724

Reynolds Yarns
Division of JCA, Inc.
35 Scales Lane
Townsend, MA 01469

Skacel Collection **(Mondial Yarns)**
P.O. Box 88110
Seattle, WA 98138-2110
www.skacelknitting.com

Unique Kolours
(Colinette Hand Dyed Yarns)
1428 Oak Lane
Downingtown, PA 19335
www.uniquekolours.com

For information on learning how to knit or crochet, Warm Up America!, special events, guilds, or just connecting with other knitters, log on to **www.knitandcrochet.com** at the Craft Yarn Council of America Web site.

Design&Knit
the *Sweater*
of Your
Dreams

J. Marsha Michler

DESIGN AND KNIT THE SWEATER OF YOUR DREAMS

DEDICATION

To mom the artist, pianist, seamstress, knitter, designer of houses and gardens, raiser of five kids, spinner, dyer, weaver who had the foresight to give me the tools at an early age and to allow the creative use of them is, ever was, and always will be my inspiration and role model.

ACKNOWLEDGMENTS

A great many thanks to my agent, Sandy Taylor, and the wonderful people at Krause who helped to make this book a reality. Thanks to my editor, Christine Townsend, and layout artist Jamie Martin. Many thanks also to Ross Hubbard for photographing the sweaters, and my deepest appreciation to the lovely models, Tracy Schmidt, Amy Tincher-Durik, Jean Stockwell, Alicia LaCanne, Tracy Radies, Tricia Kertzman, and Katherine Stephani. My thanks also to the proprietors of the Green Fountain Inn in Waupaca, Wisconsin, for their hospitality.

The software used to create the graphs is Stitch Crafts Gold©, Version 5, by Compucrafts, P.O. Box 6326, Lincoln Center, Massachusetts. Illustrations were accomplished using Adobe® Illustrator® 8.

Most of the yarns used in this book are from Webs, Division of Valley Fibers Corporation, P.O. Box 147, Northampton, Massachusetts, supplier of Webs' branded yarns, and mill ends. Thanks to Barbara for her invaluable assistance and for graciously supplying yarns.

TABLE OF CONTENTS

PREFACE

This book, for me, represents a lifetime of knitting experience. Early on, I taught myself how to hold the needles and form the stitches into the shape of a garment. Later, when teaching knitting to others, I had the pleasure of re-learning my own beginnings of this craft! It is truly a joy to be writing about something that has been with me for so many years.

As much as I loved to knit, the ability to make a sweater that I could enjoy wearing eluded me for a long time. Commercial patterns gave no guidelines for getting a sweater to fit right—sleeves were often too constricting, necklines didn't feel right, or instructions were incorrect or incomprehensible, and so on. In short, I made many sweaters that have since been donated to worthy causes, or ripped out and the yarn reused.

In all of my pattern following, there didn't seem to be a remedy for getting a sweater to fit right. The yarn I believed in when I purchased it, and still did even after making a sweater that I couldn't wear. I realized that my difficulties had nothing to do with the yarn, but did have everything to do with the fit of the finished garment.

The revelation came when I first tried to design a sweater. I began by determining the basic shape of a sweater, and then applied my own adaptations to that shape. This was a challenge because I had no set of directives telling me how to proceed, and the sweater patterns of the time were in written form only. There were no diagrams to show the shapes and sizes of the individual parts.

The **Russian Jacket** was my first original creation. It was knitted after I did sketches and diagrams of my ideas using existing sweaters to check fit and size, and swatches of stitch patterns to find a suitable one for the yarn. Much to my surprise, the sweater turned out perfectly, and is one I still wear. After that first sweater, I have made only original sweaters using the same designing methods; I am truly happy with them, and wear them all regularly.

That very same design process is the one presented in this book, along with the simple tools I have developed to make sweater designing easier. Now you can knit from scratch, or just be more knowledgeable in following patterns to knit sweaters that will give you long-lasting pleasure and pride.

Planning a sweater begins with making swatches to find a suitable pattern stitch.

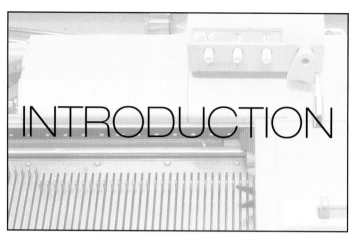

INTRODUCTION

The three main categories for making the sweater of your dreams are:

- Yarn, gauges, and swatches
- Stitch and color patternings
- Instructions for shaping and fitting a sweater

Choose a beautiful yarn; purchase a sufficient quantity—and then what? You are now at a point of beginning, and one of no return. So many really beautiful yarns are available to us, that yarn shopping can seem like going to heaven. Getting the yarn to take the shape of a garment that is equally luscious to wear can be a challenge that keeps knitters from progressing with confidence in their skills. But no more! There are ways to design a garment that include finding the appropriate fit and style, and ways of working with sweater shapes that will result in the sweater of your dreams.

Making a swatch is sometimes the *last* thing we want to do before diving into a new yarn and sweater pattern or idea … but it is the most important thing to do. Swatches teach us about the yarn, and are necessary in obtaining a gauge, and finding the correct needle size. In learning to do designs of your own, you will make many swatches in your exploration of pattern stitches, and in "trying out" new yarns and knitting fibers.

Watching patternings form out of a very few basic stitches is fascinating; there is limitless variety in what can be done with stitches. Learning to "read" patterns from the knitting itself is a simple skill requiring a little observation. After reading through this book and practicing, you will be able to understand how stitch patterns work, and then design your own.

Fitting a sweater has everything to do with what, in terms of clothing, makes you feel most comfortable. The historical use of a sweater has been to provide insulation, to keep warm in the face of plummeting temperatures and chilling winds.

Now, sweaters are an integral component of fashion, fitting into any occasion from casual to evening wear, and for all seasons. Regardless of the purpose of the sweater, however, we still need to be comfortable. Getting a sweater to fit well takes only a little planning, and is easy to do.

This book is for all knitters, from beginner to experienced. If you are a beginner, this book will help you to better understand knitting patterns, and gives instructions for basic sweater types. The experienced knitter who wants to be less dependent upon patterns, or do entirely original ideas, is here given direction in doing just that. How to fit and shape a sweater, how to make and evaluate a swatch, and how stitches are made into patterns are the three essential aspects of sweater design. It's easy to get started with any of these.

What to Look for in a Design

Here are a few things to consider as you think about designing a beautiful sweater.

Color

Using a mirror, hold your choice of yarn up to your face. Is it a color you can wear? Does it complement and highlight your skin tones and hair color? Will it fit in with your wardrobe? Is the color in line with most of the clothing colors you already have?

Or, if it is wildly different, are you willing to make that difference in your life? In other words, only bring home the most radiant of the yarn colors from the store if you know that you can and will step out your door in the finished garment. You may consider buying only one skein of that wonderfully brilliant shade, and the remainder in a color you know you are definitely going to wear. Then, use the bright skein sparingly in a color-worked pattern in the sweater.

Texture

Yarn textures vary widely from silky smooth, to coarser, traditional knitting wools and cottons, to fanciful "fuzzies" and chenilles. Fancy pattern stitches show up best in smooth yarns. More textured yarns thrive on simple stitches such as stockinette, reverse stockinette, or garter stitch.

Different weights of yarn affect the appearance of a sweater. In general, heavier yarns such as worsted and bulky weights tend to make a casual sweater with more body and less drape. Finer yarns make a thinner fabric with more drape and less body.

Style

Do you want to knit a traditional style of sweater, or are you looking for something different? The easy way to begin working with styles is to start with the form of a traditional sweater, and work variations into it. You can choose among sleeve styles, ease, types of neckline, pullover versus cardigan, hem treatments, and so on.

At the same time, be willing to experiment, seeking combinations that are interesting, offbeat—or even flashy—whatever it is that reflects who you are.

Comfort

Being comfortable in a sweater has to do with the amount of ease allowed, and the lengths of the different parts of the sweater. The best way to be sure you are making the proper fit for your needs is to find an existing sweater or sweatshirt that fits the way you like it to, measure it, and apply the measurements to your new project.

You may find that as soon as you've finished one sweater that you really love to wear, you'll have an idea for the fit of the next one. You may want to try one that is longer, shorter, wider, or narrower.

Using a Knitting Machine

I sometimes like to make a sweater in a very fine gauge. Hand knitting a fine-gauged sweater is very time-consuming, so I often prefer to use a knitting machine. This way it is possible to start and finish a sweater in as little as one weekend.

Machine knitting is distinctly different from hand knitting. The machine stitch tends to be firmer and very even. The yarns are on cones instead of skeins. The machine itself can appear daunting to a beginner, can take some time to learn, and is far more costly than a set of hand knitting needles.

Although there are no "machine knitting" instructions in this book, the procedure is the same. Make a gauge swatch according to instructions with your machine. Do the *Measuring for Fit* worksheet in this book (page 179), fill the dimensions into the worksheet for the type of sweater you want to knit, and then use the gauge swatch to determine the number of stitches to use. Machine knit the pieces of the sweater, and then sew them together.

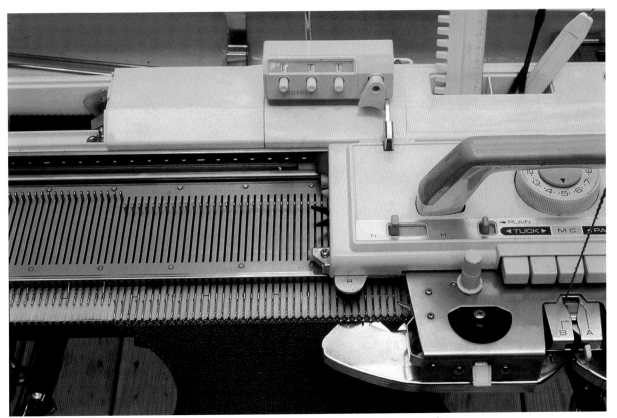

A knitting machine adds to the range of possibilities in creating knitwear.

Using a Spinning Wheel

I enjoy creating my own yarns, and this means either actually spinning raw wool, or just plying two or more existing yarns together. I often take two or three fine yarns that were coned for machine knitting, and spin them into a heavier yarn for hand knitting. In this way it is possible to combine textures and colors for many different effects.

Yarns can also be held together while they are knitted. Spinning them results in a more even blending of the fibers that is easier to knit with.

The ideas in this book are readily applicable to hand-spun yarns. Just follow the instructions to create a sweater as unique as the yarn you've spun!

Fine machine knitting yarns can be plied into one heavier yarn by using a spinning wheel or by simply holding them together.

Enjoy the tactile experience of knitting by trying different types of yarns and fibers.

TOOLS

It is a real plus to have a set of knitting needles in all sizes (especially sizes 4 through 10-1/2) in 14" lengths; that way, you can readily change to a different size if you need to. Purchase circulars as needed, (unless you buy them as a set). Circulars are necessary for knitting wide sweaters such as the dolman style, and may be used for neckline ribbings. A large, dull sewing needle is needed for sewing the sweater together. You will need a scissors or trimmers for cutting the yarn.

Have plenty of needles on hand so you always have the size needed.

Other things you will need are:

Tape Measure

Questions of size are resolved by measuring. Always have a tape measure handy, keeping it with your knitting.

Ruler

Important for accurate measuring of gauge swatches.

Calculator

An excellent tool for the minimal number crunching to be done.

Pencil and Eraser

Graph Paper

Regular graph paper, or knitter's graph paper—see Appendix (page 273) or a cross-stitch or knitting computer program. This is for plotting stitch and color patterns, raglan, and other sweater shapings.

Notebook

With lined or unlined paper. Use this for sketching your sweater ideas, and for logging the dimensions, gauges, and stitch patterns of each sweater you knit.

CHAPTER 1

THE YARN OF YOUR CHOICE

The most I can do here is to give some very general information about fibers, as fibers and yarns really are hands-on types-of-things that you need to experience by, and for, yourself: Try the different types of yarns available, make lots of swatches in different stitch patterns, play, experiment, mix different fibers together to get to know their characteristics. Fibers, most especially the natural ones, are wonderful, beautiful things, and they are what knitting is all about. Explore them and luxuriate in them. Learn about them with the awareness that there is always more to be learned.

There are many different types of yarns available that are derived from several basic fibers. These yarns are smooth or textured, nubby, loopy, or shaggy, and yet others are woven ribbons or chenilles. In some yarns the fiber is barely spun, in others it is tightly spun. Some yarns are one-ply; others are two- or more plies (a "ply" is one spun strand of yarn).

Discover the characteristics of the yarn by knitting it. Make swatches of it in stockinette stitch and various pattern stitches. Evaluate the swatches. Check for drape by holding a swatch up by one corner and then laying it over your arm—will it cascade in soft folds, or is it firmer? Try knitting a knit/purl ribbing stitch to find out if a ribbing will have resiliency. Imagine the yarn as a sweater: what type of design will best enhance the yarn and the pattern stitch?

When making swatches, make each large enough so you can get a good idea of how the sweater fabric will look, act, and feel. Knit them at least 4" square (although larger swatch sizes, between 6" and 8", are preferable).

KNITTING FIBERS

Wool

Wool is a classic, time-honored sweater fiber, and the most resilient of the knitting fibers. Individual strands of wool vary in length and curl from one breed of sheep to another … some are coarse, others fine and soft. The breed differences result in yarns that carry those same characteristics, but are not always as evident to the hand knitter as they are to the spinner who works directly with the fleece. Wool is an insulator, so is perfect for winter or any cool-weather wear. Wool loves to be washed, and should always be washed before storing, or moths can be attracted.

By knitting swatches, a pattern stitch can be found that is appropriate for the yarn. The two yarns here are a yellow alpaca and a multi-colored cotton.

Cotton and Linen

Cotton and linen are both plant fibers, but they are processed in ways that are very different from each other. Cotton grows on the plant as a ball of fluff that is then picked, processed, and spun. Linen is spun from strands of fiber that are taken from the stem of the flax plant after a long process ("retting") that rots away the unusable parts of it. Both fibers lack resiliency, but are excellent for summer knitwear, and are washable in any water temperature.

Rayon

Rayon is a machine-made fiber derived from wood or cottonseed, kind of a hybrid of both "natural" and "synthetic." Rayon can be slippery-smooth and highly lustrous, but can also be made to have a matte finish. Like cottons, rayons are not resilient. Weightier than wool, the knitted fabric is often very drapey, and is wonderful for making elegant sweaters. Rayon is washable in cool water, but the fiber weakens when wet so it should be washed with care (it firms up when dried).

Silk

Silk is made from silkworm cocoons that are either unraveled, or carded and spun. Many of its qualities are similar to rayon, except it is the lightest-weight of fibers. Pure silk has a dry, crunchy feel, distinguishing it from synthetics. Silk can be both warm and elegant, has excellent drape, and is wonderful when blended with fibers such as wool or cotton. Wash silks gently in cool to lukewarm water.

Acrylic

Acrylics are washable, synthetic wool-substitutes that are excellent for children's wear, or for those who are allergic to wool.

Angora/Cashmere/Mohair/Alpaca

These are specialty fibers. Angora is from the Angora rabbit, and makes a very soft and lightly fuzzy yarn. Mohair comes from a goat, and makes a very fuzzy, or fuzzy and loopy, yarn that is coarser than angora. Cashmere is a smooth goat fiber, making a luxuriously soft yarn. Alpaca is made from the wool of a South American mammal that is related to llamas. Alpaca is similar to wool, but is softer and very warm.

Synthetics

In addition to acrylics, there are the synthetics that sometimes make up the entire yarn, but are often used in addition to natural fibers in blended yarns. These can be of any description—smooth, fuzzy, loopy, metallic and so on. Follow the care instructions that come with these yarns.

YARN SIZES, APPROXIMATE GAUGES, AND NEEDLE SIZES

Yarns, whatever the fiber, are classified by how thick they are, and these sizes are called "weights," as you can see in the chart. There are also in-between sizes. Most skeined yarns are labeled with a suggested needle size and the stitch gauge that can be expected. The stitch gauge refers to stockinette stitch; the same yarn used in a fancy pattern stitch is likely to have a very different gauge.

You can see that a yarn that obtains a gauge of three stitches to the inch requires fewer stitches to be knitted than, say, a yarn that knits to eight stitches per inch. The heavier yarns make heavier sweaters that are quicker to knit. The lighter-weight yarns make softer, drapier sweaters that take longer to knit.

From bottom to top: fingering weight yarn on size 4 needles, sport weight yarn on 6's, worsted weight yarn on 8's, and bulky weight on 10-1/2's.

Fingering weight	7–8 sts	= 1"	Needles 2–4
Sport weight	6–7 sts	= 1"	Needles 5–7
Worsted weight	4–5.5 sts	= 1"	Needles 7–9
Bulky weight	3–3.75 sts	= 1"	Needles 10–11

CHOOSING THE CORRECT NEEDLE SIZE

If you have chosen a yarn that is not labeled with an appropriate needle size, or if you have spun or plied to create your own yarn, you will need to find the needle size on your own. Choose a needle size—guess at what is close to a correct size—and knit a swatch perhaps 4" (10 cm) square. You may need to knit several swatches using different size needles each time, then compare them.

Evaluate the swatch. Look for the knitting to be springy but not baggy, and firm but not constricted. If the knitting turns out baggy, the sweater will not hold its shape. If the knitting is constricted, the sweater may feel stiff and unpliable, and will take longer to knit than if you "up" the needle size. Look for additional characteristics that will affect how the sweater will feel when it is worn. Fuzzy mohairs, for instance, can be too warm and dense if knitted tightly.

KNITTING A GAUGE SWATCH

Knit a swatch at least 4" (10 cm) square (or larger, if necessary) to include a full repeat of any pattern stitch used. Bind off, and lay it out flat. If it curls, pin the edges to an ironing board or other pin-able surface.

Using a ruler, find the number of inches that give a whole number, such as 2" over nine stitches. You will then need to divide to find the exact number of stitches per inch. Nine divided by two inches = 4-1/2 stitches per inch. I always re-measure in another area, and measure the width of the swatch itself, and then compare the results to check for accuracy.

If the per-inch gauge is fractional, use that exact number (it can be rounded to a number plus two decimals) in figuring how many stitches to knit.

Find the row gauge by measuring vertically and counting the rows per inch.

If the sweater will be blocked (see Blocking, page 147), block the gauge swatch and measure for the gauge after blocking.

PREPARING A SWATCH WHEN USING CONED YARNS

Yarns that are skeined for hand knitting do not require any pre-treatment. I frequently use yarns that are coned for machine knitting. These yarns are often wound on the cones rather firmly and may change after washing as the yarn relaxes. Knit the gauge swatch, then wash, dry, and block the swatch exactly as will be done with the finished sweater, then measure for the gauge. Wash, dry, and block the sweater pieces before sewing them together.

ESTIMATING YARDAGE

Most yarn labels include the weight of the yarn, and the yardage of the skein. The weights of yarn vary widely, since weight depends on type of fiber, number of plies, and how tightly or loosely the yarn is spun. Unless we are using only one brand and style of yarn, the weight of the yarn cannot be used to determine how much is needed.

Using the yardage is a more accurate way of determining the amount needed. Yarn shops can often give an estimate of the yardage needed to make a sweater of a particular size. If, however, your idea includes extra length and width, or a yarn-consuming pattern stitch, it will be necessary to do your own calculations. (Note: if using metrics, use meters instead of yards.)

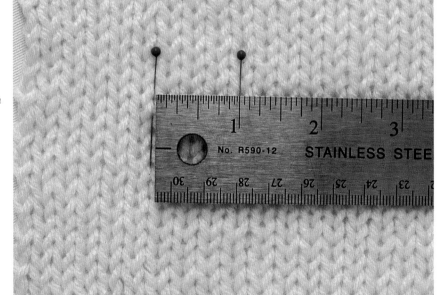

Using a couple of pins make it easy to discern the number of stitches per inch.

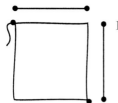

1. Knit a swatch 4" (10cm) to 8" (20cm) square or larger, as needed, to encompass any pattern stitches used. On paper, make a note of the size of the swatch. Now rip it out.

2. Lay a tape measure out flat. Without stretching the yarn, measure the yarn from the ripped-out swatch (one yard is 36"). Jot down the number of yards, then find the yardage per square inch as follows:

Yardage divided by square inches = yards per square inch.
Example:
Yardage swatch of 4" square = 16 square inches.
Ripped out yardage = 10.5 yards.
10.5 divided by 16 = .66 yards per square inch.

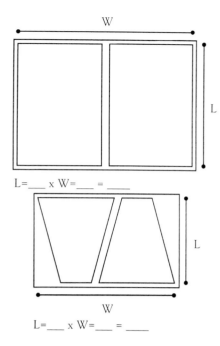

L=___ x W=___ = ____

L=___ x W=___ = ____

3. Sketch the pieces of your sweater design so they are laid inside of rectangular areas. Write in the lengths and widths of the rectangles. Multiply the length times the width of each of the areas and add them together (you will need to estimate somewhat). Now, multiply the total square inches of the sweater pieces by the yards per square inch obtained in Step 2, above. This gives the approximate number of yards needed to knit the sweater. Add a little extra to cover the ribbings, and do buy an extra skein just in case. Unused skeins can usually be returned, but you can also keep them, and use small amounts in color-worked designs.

RIPPING OUT

The nature of designing is that it is a trial-and-error process. There will be a need to rip out sections, and even whole pieces, of your knitting. It's always best to take it out if it isn't right. After you've ripped out a few times, you get used to doing it, and accept it as part of knitting.

While we are on the subject, begin ripping out the sweaters you have made but haven't worn. Prepare the yarn for re-knitting by winding it into loose skeins and washing it. Allow the yarn to dry—you may need to weight it to get the kinks out—then wind it into loose balls. Think about what you would rather make out of the yarn, and sketch some ideas. My own policy is that if I haven't worn a sweater once in a full year, there must be something I don't like about it. Time to rip!

Pick up stitches from the row below so none are lost.

Tip:

Sometimes you will need to rip out a section of your knitting to correct a mistake or make a change. Here is an accurate method of picking up the stitches so they do not become twisted or lost. Rip out all of the rows that need to be removed except one. A stitch at a time, carefully tug on the unraveling yarn and, as the stitch is about to pop loose, pick it up on a knitting needle without twisting the stitch.

If you are only taking out one row, keep the stitches on the needle and hold it in your left hand (reverse for left-handedness). Insert the other needle into the stitch below the unwanted row on the left-hand needle, slide the stitch off the left needle, pull out the unwanted stitch, and continue across the row. This is especially useful if you are knitting a fancy pattern stitch and need to keep the integrity of the stitches. Yarn-overs and other stitches can easily become lost in ripping out.

WASHING

Always check yarn labels before washing or blocking. Some yarns must be dry cleaned, and some should not be blocked.

Any washable yarn can be washed according to these guidelines for washing wool. You will notice there is no agitation in this recipe—do not agitate your wool sweater or it will "felt." Felting tends to erase the lines between individual stitches of the knitting, making the surface into a smooth, fuzzy blur. Fibers other than wool can be moved about in the water, although it really isn't necessary if you use this soaking technique. Also, wool shrinks if subjected to differing water temperatures, and if heated while drying.

Use cool water, staying with the same temperature throughout the process if you are washing wool. Fill a basin with water and add a mild soap. Place the sweater into the water. Allow it to soak for awhile (I leave mine for several hours because I tend to forget it's there). Pull the plug and let the water drain. Again, walk away so it can continue to drain as water runs out of the sweater.

Now begin the rinsing. Refill the basin with water (let it fill so the water runs in next to, not on to, the sweater) and let it soak for a few minutes to a few hours depending on your schedule. Pull the plug and let it drain again.

Repeat the rinsing until the rinse water runs clear. Squeeze the sweater very gently to remove any water, then lay it on a bath towel. Wrap the towel around the sweater, and add another towel if needed. Leave it to lie until the towels are soggy; you can repeat this step using dry towels if needed.

Now the sweater can be draped over a drying rack or several clotheslines so it is well supported. Dry it away from heat or sun. The best time to launder sweaters is on a cool, breezy day when they can be dried in the shade outdoors. You will find that once dried, the sweater will have regained its original shape and it will smell like fresh wool.

BLOCKING

I have found blocking to be mostly unnecessary. Blocking can be used to correct the sizes of sweater pieces if they were knitted incorrectly, or if they somehow stretched out in knitting (neither of these things should happen). Be sure to check first with the label of the yarn, because some yarns should not be blocked.

Some knitters love to block, so if this is your forte, here is how. The easiest way is to pin the sweater piece out flat and then lightly mist with water, and leave it alone until it is completely dried. When pinning, measure to check that lengths and widths are as intended.

Blocking can also be achieved by steaming. Pin the piece, cover it with a bath towel, and move a steam iron in circles over the towel (without touching it). Remove the towel and leave the knitted piece to dry.

Use any pin-able surface that won't be damaged by water. I use a large, well-stuffed floor pillow made of velveteen.

I use a velvet floor pillow for blocking—whatever works!

CHAPTER 2

THE
PATTERNS
OF
STITCHES

The idea of this chapter is not to provide a stitch dictionary, but to show how stitch patterns can be created. By following along with the order of the patterns (they grow in complexity), and by knitting them, you should begin to see how to design your own. Use the pattern examples as jumping off points for your own ideas, and think up ways to work variations on them.

You can also do what I've done here: make same-size swatches of all of the stitch patterns and sew them together into an afghan. The afghan can then serve as a visual "dictionary" of stitches.

Observe your knitting as you work the stitch patterns. Learn to "read" the knitting so you can always see where you are in a pattern, and you will then be able to follow the pattern in that way. This is also important if you wish to devise your own stitch patterns, and in combining several patterns into one sweater. After knitting a swatch, turn it over and look at the back of it—you may be looking at yet another stitch pattern idea.

Make same-size swatches of the stitch patterns and sew them together to make an afghan. This is a good exercise in establishing gauges—you will need to find the gauge for each stitch pattern in order to make the swatch a particular size. The blocks in this afghan are 6-1/2" square.

Tips:
In following some stitch patterns, keeping track of which is the right side of the knitting can be difficult. When you begin knitting, on a right-side row, observe where the "tail" is (the beginning of the yarn), either to the left or the right of the knitting. If you remember where it is, then you will always know you are working on the right or wrong side of the knitting.

If you set your knitting down in the middle of a row, it is easy to find which way to continue. Look for where the yarn is coming from. That's where you knitted last, and now you need to continue the yarn onto the other needle.

The swatches shown on the following pages were knitted in worsted weight yarn on size 9 needles. Other weights and types of yarns, and choice of needle size, may give a different appearance from what is seen in the photos.

Stitch patterns are affected by the type of yarn that is used. Some yarns will show a pattern distinctly, while others will blur pattern textures to varying degrees. "Ya never know 'til ya try it," is the axiom I go by. The only way to discover what works best is by making lots of swatches trying different patterns. Here are some suggestions for different types of yarns:

- Smooth yarns—try the knit/purl combinations or any stitch pattern.
- Light to medium textured yarns—try any pattern stitch, use what works best.
- Heavily textured yarns—plain stitches such as stockinette, reverse stockinette, or garter stitch.
- Mohair—bold cables or other bold patterns.
- Smooth, lightweight yarns—lace, or intricate patterns.
- Bulky yarns—cables or bold patterns that use simple stitches.

READING GRAPHED STITCH PATTERNS

Begin reading a graphed pattern at the bottom of the graph. Row 1 is (usually) the right side (RS) of the knitting, and is read from right to left. Row 2 is the wrong side (WS), and is read from left to right. Repeat the rows in the same sequence.

Each square represents one stitch of one row. Refer to the Symbol Definitions on the inside covers of the book to be sure how to work each stitch.

Graphed designs are more than representations of stitches to follow; they also give a "picture" of the design. In knit/purl, color, lace, and cable designs you can see from the graph how the stitches will appear in the knitting. In knit/purl patterns, as well as color patterns, by drawing on graph paper several repeats of a pattern you can see what the effect will be on a sweater. In lace patterns, the placement of the YO's shows where the holes will appear. In cables, you can see where, and how often, the cabling occurs.

DESIGNING AND GRAPHING STITCH PATTERNS

Once you've learned to read a graphed design, the next step is to learn to design your own stitch and color patterns. Designs can be invented by doodling on graph paper. Use the symbols that have the most meaning for you (symbols are often different from one designer to another).

When I graph stitch pattern ideas, I try to keep the design as simple as possible. For instance, in knit/purl patterns, it is easiest to knit a design in which the reverse side row repeats the stitches of the right side row (knit a stitch on the right side, purl it on the wrong side). In patterns featuring several cables, having all of the cables cross in the same row makes it easy to keep track of when to cable. In lace patterns, it is easiest to work all of the "lace-making" stitches on the right side, and to purl the entire reverse side row. It isn't always possible to simplify as much as this, but thinking of ways to make the knitting easier, quicker, or more intuitive is well worth doing.

Ordinary graph paper does not accurately represent knitting. In knitting, there are often more rows than stitches to the inch. Take this into consideration by adding an extra row here and there, making the pattern appear elongated vertically. You can also use knitter's graph paper—the squares are wider than they are long. By knitting a swatch of the design, you will be able to see if any adjustments need to be made. See page 273 for knitter's graph paper

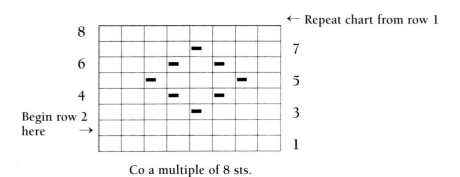

Co a multiple of 8 sts.

MULTIPLES AND STITCH GAUGES

A "multiple" is the basis of a stitch or color pattern. If the "base" stitches are repeated across a row, the design is continuous.

Cast on a number that divides to the multiple in order to have an even number of repeats of the pattern. For instance, a multiple of 4 requires a number of stitches evenly divisible by 4: 8, 16, 20, 24, 28, 32, and so on.

A multiple applies to one stitch or color pattern. Two or more pattern repeats can be combined to form one multiple. For instance, one design may be a repeat of two stitches, and another consists of four stitches repeating. The multiple to use is four, because it encompasses both designs (add the repeats together). Most of the stitch patterns are presented as "multiples," with the graph showing only one repeat. For instance, if the same three stitches are repeated, the multiple is three. Base your sweater on the stitch multiple. Make the back and front pieces a number of stitches that divide to that number, and begin the sleeves using it. That way, the design will run continuously around the body

of the sweater, and will be centered on the sleeves.

Use the multiple and the stitch gauge in combination to determine the number of stitches to knit a sweater. For example: Your stitch gauge tells you to use 86 stitches for each of the front and back pieces for the size of sweater you want to knit. The stitch pattern that you've chosen has a multiple of five stitches. 86 divided by 5 = 17.2. You need a whole number, so round the answer down to 17, or up to 18 repeats of the design. 17 x 5 = 85 sts. 18 x 5 = 90 sts. Use either 85 or 90 stitches to knit the sweater.

In working with copies of a design, try as many different arrangements as you can think of, spacing the foreground objects closer together or farther apart, or stacking them, and observe how they relate to each other and how the background changes in relation to the design. I call this process "taking a design through its paces," and find it to be a necessary step in discovering the best way a design will work.

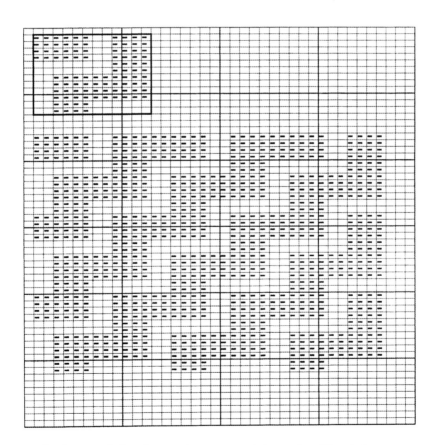

This design, in the boxed area at the top, was copied a number of times both horizontally and vertically to see how it would look on a sweater.

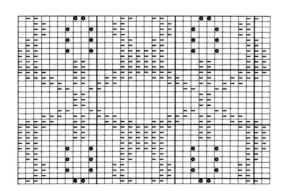

Here, a floral design was mirrored, then copied six times. Note how the background creates a secondary design. Focus your eyes on the spaces between the floral shapes to see this.

The same floral design, in different arrangements.

Tip:

A computer program is quicker, neater, and easier to use than graph paper. The cross-stitch program I use has plenty of symbols that can be used as is (or edited), and the graph can be modified to reflect a greater number of rows-to-the-inch than stitches. Knitting programs work much the same way. Here are the advantages to using a computer program:

Erasing is clean and instantaneous (erasing is an inevitable part of designing).

A design can be copied, and the copy can be worked on so as to keep the original intact.

Designs can be mirrored both vertically and horizontally (see the floral design on facing page).

A design can be copied and pasted to make enough repeats to show how it will look on a sweater.

A design can be printed in the size needed. Very complicated designs are easier to read if enlarged, and simple designs, in which only a few set-up rows are needed, can be printed in a smaller size.

Although the software makes all of these things both quick and simple to do, I also often do a preliminary sketch on plain or graph paper. Find what works best for you by trying the different ways.

KNIT AND PURL PATTERNS

Knit/purl pattern stitches make use of the "bump" of the purl stitch on a stockinette stitch background, or the reverse—the lack of bumps on a reverse stockinette stitch ground. Note how the variations of the patterns change the texture of the knitted fabric. It sometimes only takes a slight variation to create an entirely different effect.

Directions for the variations are not written out, but can be followed in the graphs. Multiples for the variations are shown by the number of stitches enclosed in the box around the graph.

In the written instructions, the asterisks (*) show the part of the design that is repeated. *Repeat between the *'s until the end of the row unless directed otherwise.* Where the instruction simply says "K" or "P," knit or purls the entire row. Where parts of an instruction appear in (parentheses) do that part the number of times indicated, then move on: "(C4F) twice, K4" means to cable over 4 stitches two times, then K4.

Repeat the sequence of rows in order unless directed otherwise.

The Three Most Basic Stitches Used for Knitting Sweaters

Garter Stitch

Notice this fabric is thicker than that of stockinette stitch, and that the edges do not curl, making it good for sweater edges. It makes a dense fabric that is thicker than stockinette stitch.
Row 1 K
Row 2 K

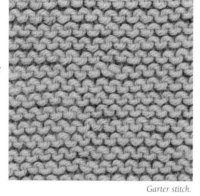

Garter stitch.

Stockinette Stitch

This is the most-used stitch in sweater-knitting.
Row 1 K
Row 2 P

Stockinette stitch.

Reverse Stockinette

This is also the reverse side of the stockinette stitch.
Row 1: P
Row 2: K

Reverse stockinette.

Seed Stitch

mult of 2

Variations: Space the "seeds" farther apart, and/or add more plain rows in between.
Row 1: * K1, P1 *
Row 2: P
Row 3: * P1, K1 *
Row 4: P

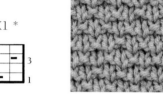

Seed stitch.

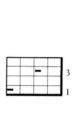

Seed stitch.

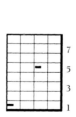

Seed stitch.

 K on RS, P on WS   — P on RS, K on WS

Moss Stitch

mult of 2

    This pattern comes out
the same on front and back.
Variation: make a "thicker"
moss by doubling up on
the stitches.
Row 1: * K1, P1 *
Row 2: * P1, K1 *

Moss stitch.

Moss stitch.

Diamond Pattern

mult of 5

    Seed stitches are placed
to form diamond-like
shapes.

    Variations: make the
diamond shapes larger or
more pronounced.
Row 1: K
Rows 2 and 6: P
Row 3: * K2, P1, K2 *
Row 4: * (P1, K1) twice,
    P1 *
Row 5: same as Row 3
Rep rows 1 - 6

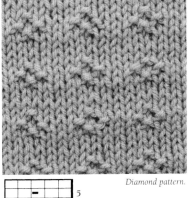

Diamond pattern.

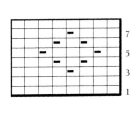

Diamond pattern.

Diamond pattern.

Diamond pattern.

☐ **K on RS, P on WS**   — **P on RS, K on WS**

Diagonal Pattern

mult of 5

Variations: reverse the diagonal at intervals to make a zigzag pattern, or make the pattern more pronounced.

Row 1: * K4, P1 *
Row 2: * P1, K1, P3 *
Row 3: * K2, P1, K2 *
Row 4: * P3, K1, P1 *
Row 5: * K1, P4 *

Continue as established, moving the P stitch one stitch over on the right side, and moving the K stitch one stitch over on the wrong side rows.

Diagonal pattern.

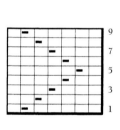

Diagonal pattern.

Diagonal pattern.

Block Pattern

mult of 8

Variations: make the blocks larger or smaller, or in varied sizes. Rows 1 and 3: * K4, P4 *
Rows 2 and all WS rows: P the knit, and K the purl stitches of previous row.
Rows 5 and 7: * P4, K4 *
Rep rows 1 - 8

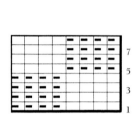

Block pattern.

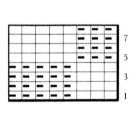

Block pattern.

Triangle Blocks

mult of 6
Row 1: * K5, P1 *
Row 2: * P2, K4 *
Row 3: * K3, P3 *
Row 4: * P4, K2 *
Row 5: * K1, P5 *
Row 6: K

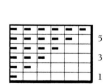

Triangle blocks.

☐ **K on RS, P on WS**   ⊟ **P on RS, K on WS**

Geometric Designs

Geometric patterns are easy to design on graph paper. The diagram shows only one repeat of the design shown. Knit the design by following the graph.

Geometric designs.

Tip:

The knit and purl pattern graphs can also be used for color-worked patterns.

Non-geometric Designs

Floral and other forms can be worked into knit/purl patterns. Look around you for ideas to graph, then try them by knitting them. The possibilities are endless. I prefer floral forms, but all around us are numerous shapes that can be tried. Larger designs such as these are easiest to knit by following the graph. Writing out the patterns would be arduous.

Non-geometric designs.

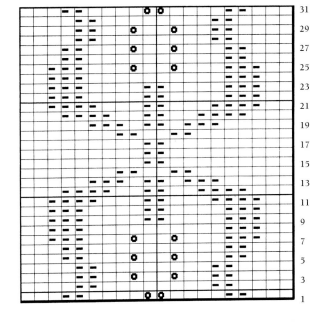

 **K on RS, P on**   **P on RS, K on WS**   **O Bobble**

RIBBINGS

Any stitch pattern that creates a narrow column-like effect can be classified as a ribbing. Most often used along the edges of knitwear, ribbings form sturdy edges that don't curl. Often ribbings are used to "draw in" the sweater so it fits snugly around your hips, wrists, and neck. The stretchiest type of ribbing for this purpose is the knit/purl rib, in its various combinations of 1 x 1 (Knit 1, Purl 1), 2 x 1, 2 x 2, and so on.

The fiber used also has an effect on the ribbing. Wool gives the most springiness in combination with a knit/purl rib. The same ribbing worked in cotton, for instance, will have less stretch because the cotton fiber lacks elasticity.

Experiment with various combinations of knit and purl stitches, trying other combinations than those given here such as 3 x 2, 4 x 2, 5 x 2, 5 x 3, and so on.

1 x 1 Ribbing

mult of 2
Row 1: * K1, P1 *
Row 2: same as row 1

1 x 1 ribbing, multiple of two.

4 x 3 Ribbing

mult of 7
Row 1: * K4, P3 *
Row 2: * K3, P4 *

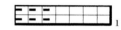

4 x 3 ribbing, multiple of seven.

2 x 2 Ribbing

mult of 4
Row 1: * K2, P2 *
Row 2: same as row 1

2 x 2 ribbing, multiple of four.

Crossed 2 x 2 Ribbing

mult of 4
Row 1: * C2F, P2 *
Row 2: * K2, P2 *

Crossed 2 x 2 ribbing, multiple of four.

2 x 1 Ribbing

mult of 3
Row 1: * K2, P1 *
Row 2: * K1, P2 *

2 x 1 ribbing, multiple of three.

Crossed 2 x 1 Ribbing

mult of 3
Row 1: * C2B, P1 *
Row 2: * K1, P2 *

Crossed 2 x 1 ribbing, multiple of three.

 K on RS, P on WS   P on RS, K on WS   C2F   C2B

Broken Ribbing

mult of 3
Row 1: K
Row 2: * K2, P1 *

Broken ribbing, multiple of three.

Twisted Ribs

There are two ways to do a twisted rib. The twisted stitches can be worked on the right side only. Or, the twisted stitch is twisted on the right side, and again on the wrong side. Twisting on the right side only creates a textured stitch, while twisting on both sides makes a firmer stitch.

Twisted 1 x 1 Ribbing

mult of 2
Row 1: * K1B, P1 *
Row 2: * K1, P1 (or P1B) *

Twisted 1 x 1 ribbing, multiple of two.

Twisted 2 x 1 Ribbing

mult of 3
Row 1: * K1B (twice),
    P1 *
Row 2: K1, P2 (or P1B
    twice) *

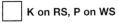

Twisted 2 x 1 ribbing, multiple of three.

Chunky 1 x 1 Ribbing

mult of 2
Knitting into the stitch below the one on the needle creates a thicker, larger stitch.
Rows 1, 2, and 4: * K1, P1 *
Row 3: * K1 into stitch below, P1 *
Rep rows 3 and 4

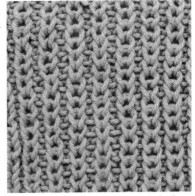

Chunky 1 x 1 ribbing, multiple of two.

Garter and Rib

mult of 9
Note that this stitch gives a shaped edge to the knitting.
Row 1: * K3, (P1, K1) 3 times *
Row 2: * (P1, K1) 3 times, K3 *

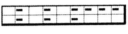

Garter and rib.

Moss and Rib

mult of 8
Row 1: * K1, P1 *
Row 2: * P1, K1, (K1, P1) 3 times *

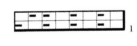

Moss and rib.

Cable Ribbing

mult of 9
Row 1: * K1, P1, K4, P1, K1, P1 *
Row 2: * K1, P1, K1, P4, K1, P1 *
Row 3: * K1, P1, C4B, P1, K1, P1 *
Row 4: same as row 2
Rep rows 1 - 4

Cable rib.

☐ **K on RS, P on WS**   — **P on RS, K on WS**   ◺ **K1B on RS, P1B on WS** | **K into st below**   ◹◺ **C4B**

Colorful ribbings: the two at the top of the photograph are corrugated ribbings—work the K sts in one color, and the P stitches in a second color stranding the unused color across the back. The bottom two are worked two or more rows in one color, then two or more rows in a second color.

CABLES

The principle of cabling is simple: The designated stitches are crossed over each other, the procedure being completed within one row of knitting. You will need a cable needle (or any similar device—I often use a hairpin or a paper clip unfolded into the shape of a hairpin) to temporarily hold the few stitches that are being cabled.

There are four basic types of cables: Rope, double, uncrossed, and traveling. In rope cables, the stitches are crossed over each other in one direction only—either to the right or the left. Double cables have the crossings made in both directions. In uncrossed cables, the cabled stitches do not cross behind other stitches, staying instead on the surface of the knitted fabric. In traveling cables, the cable stitches are moved one stitch at a time to either direction, and are either crossed or not.

Tips for cabling:

Placing the cabled stitches to the back of the work crosses the cable to the right. Bringing the cabled stitches to the front crosses to the left.

Do not twist the cabled stitches as they are placed back onto the needle—keep them in the same order they were already in.

When combining cables in a sweater design, try to match the row repeats so all the cabling is done on the same row. This makes it easy to know when to cable.

Cables worked on a background of stockinette stitch give a different effect than placing purl stitches alongside.

 K on RS, P on WS   C4B

Ways to Vary Cables

- Increase or decrease the number of stitches cabled—you can cable 2 (C2F, C2B), 4 (C4F, C4B), 6 (C6F, C6B), 8 (C8F, C8B), and more stitches. The more stitches cabled, the more your garment will be "drawn in." Larger cables decrease the stitch gauge.
- Increase the distance between cable rows by any even number of rows, elongating the cable.
- Work cables with or without purl stitches alongside. Cables can be worked on a background of stockinette or any pattern stitch.
- Rope cables are traditionally made using an even number of stitches, but can be done on uneven stitch counts. (To cable five sts, place two on cn, hold to front or back of work, K3, K2 from cable needle, for example.)
- The open center of traveling cables can be filled with moss, bobbles, or other pattern stitches.
- The cable itself can be worked in other stitches besides the stockinette; try cabling in ribbing and other pattern stitches.

Multiples for the following cables are given only where cables are used in combination with other pattern stitches. Most are given as individual cables, which are often used within other stitch patterns. Often, cables are set apart from the rest of the knitting by placing one or more purl stitches on either side.

Rope Cable 1

worked over 4 sts
Row 1: K4
Row 2 and all WS rows: P
Row 3: C4B
Rep rows 1 - 4

Rope Cable 2

worked over 4 sts
Rows 1 and 5: K4
Row 2 and all WS rows: P
Row 3: C4B
Rep rows 1 - 6.

Rope Cable 2.

Rope Cable 3

Variations can be done simply by deciding on which row to cable.

Rope Cable 3.

Isolated Cable

worked over 8 sts
Small sections of cables can be inserted anywhere in your knitting.
Rows 1 and 5: P2, K4, P2
Rows 2, 4, 6, and 8: P the knit, and K the purl sts of previous row
Rows 3 and 7: P2, C4B, P2

Isolated cable.

Edging Cable

A cable can be knitted all by itself and then used as an edging. C.o. 8 stitches and cable on the fifth row and every eighth row (C8B) after that. After working to the length needed, bind off. On the sample shown here, stitches were picked up along the cable's edge and knitted in stockinette stitch. The cable could also have been sewn on to the edge of a sweater.

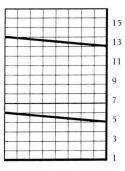

Edging cable.

Rope Cable With Moss

mult of 8
Rows 1 and 5: * (K1, P1) twice, K4 *
Row 2 and all WS rows: * P4, (P1, K1) twice *
Row 3: * (K1, P1) twice, C4B *
Rep rows 1 - 6

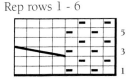

Rope cable with moss.

Rope Cable with Moss Block Pattern

mult of 8

Cables interspersed with blocks of moss stitch create a pattern with a distinctly diagonal feel.
Rows 1, 3, and 7: * (K1, P1) twice, K4 *
Rows 2, 4, and 6: * P4, (P1, K1) twice *
Row 5: * (K1, P1) twice, C4B *
Rows 9, 11 and 15: * K4, (K1, P1) twice *
Rows 10, 12, 14, and 16: * (P1, K1) twice, P4 *
Row13: * C4B, (K1, P1) twice *
Rep rows 1 - 16

Cable and rib.

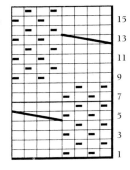

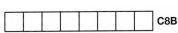

☐ K on RS, P on WS   — P on RS, K on WS   ◨ C4B   ▭ C8B

Cable and Ribbing

mult of 15

Similar to the cable and rib pattern earlier, this is the same on a larger scale. While the other was intended for a ribbed edging, this is suitable for a sweater body.

Row 1 and 3: * K6, (P1, K1) 4 times, P1 *

Row 2: and all WS rows: P the knit, and K the purl stitches of previous row.

Row 5: * C6B, (P1, K1) 4 times, P1 *

Rep rows 1 - 6

Cable and Ribbing

Multiple Plaited Cable

worked over 18 sts

Change the width by adding or subtracting a multiple of 4 stitches. Use as a panel amongst other stitch patterns.

Rows 1 and 5: K18

Row 2 and all WS rows: P

Row 3: (C4F) 4 times, K2

Row 7: K2, (C4B) 4 times

Rep rows 1 - 8

Multiple Plaited Cable

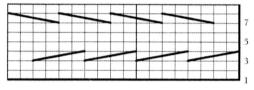

Plaited Cable

worked over 9 sts

A double cable in which the crossings alternate.

Rows 1 and 5: K9

Row 2 and all WS rows: P

Row 3: C6F, K3

Row 7: K3, C6B

Rep rows 1 – 8

Plaited Cable

Wishbone Cable

worked over 12 sts

Note in this double cable how the direction of the cables is different from the plaited cable, going outward from the center instead of intertwining.

Rows 1 and 3: K12

Row 2 and all WS rows: P

Row 5: C6B, C6F

Rep rows 1 - 6

Wishbone Cable

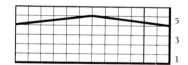

Plaited Cable Reversed

Vary the plaited cable by working C6B in place of C6F, and C6F in place of C6B. To see what this looks like, simply turn the above swatch upside down.

Horseshoe Cable

Worked the same as the wishbone cable but the cables are reversed. Work C6F, C6B instead of C6B, C6F. To see what it looks like, turn the wishbone cable upside down.

Wave Cable

worked over 4 sts

Cabling creates a sinuous, wavy pattern without crossings.

Rows 1 and 5: K4
Row 2 and all WS rows: P
Row 3: C4B
Row 7: C4F
Rep rows 1 - 8

Wave Cable

Honeycomb Cable

mult of 8 sts

This is the same idea as the wave cable, placing the cables side by side and alternating the direction of every other cable.

Rows 1 and 5: K
Row 2 and all WS rows: P
Row 3: C4B, C4F
Row 7: C4F, C4B
Rep rows 1- 8

Honeycomb Cable

XO Cable

worked over 8 sts

Rows 1, 5, 9, and 13: K8
Row 2 and all WS rows:
  P the knit, and K the purl sts of previous row.
Rows 3 and 7: C4B, C4F
Rows 11, and 15: C4F, C4B
Rep rows 1 - 16

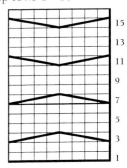

XO Cable

Honeycomb with Rope Cable

mult of 8 + 4

As an example of experimenting with cables, two different types of cable were combined, alternating with each other to create a new and different stitch pattern. Rows 3 and 11 are the two cable rows of honeycomb, and rows 7 and 15 are rope cable.

Rows 1, 5, 9, and 13: K
Row 2 and all WS rows: P
Row 3: K2, * (C4B, C4F,) * end with K2
Row 7: C4B, * (K4, C4B) *
Row 11: K2, * (C4F, C4B) * K2
Row 15: K4, * (C4B, K4) *
Rep rows 1 - 16

Honeycomb with Rope Cable

No diagram provided; follow the written instructions.

Tips:
Panels Versus Continuous Stitch Patterns

Some designs will result in a half of a part of the design at the sides of the swatch; for instance, the two "knit" stitches in row 3, above, represent half of the four-stitch cable. This design will work fine if the sweater is knitted "in the round," thereby eliminating the half-stitch pattern, or if the pattern stitch is used in a panel surrounded by other pattern stitches. However, if used for an entire sweater front and back, it will show up as an unworked area when the side seams are sewn together.

 **K on RS, P on WS**   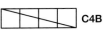 C4B   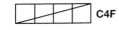 C4F

Traveling Cable

worked over 12 sts
Row 1: P3, T3B, T3F, P3
Row 2 and all wrong side
    rows: purl the knit, and
    knit the purl stitches of
    previous row.
Row 3: P2, T3B, P2, T3F,
    P2
Row 5: P1, T3B, P4, T3F,
    P1
Row 7: T3B, P6, T3F
Row 9: T3F, P6, T3B
Row 11: P1, T3F, P4, T3B,
    P1
Row 13: P2, T3F, P2, T3B,
    P2
Row 15: P3, T3F, T3B, P3
Row 17: P4, C4B, P4
Rep rows 1 - 18

Traveling Cable

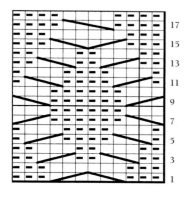

    If you get the
impression after working
up this swatch that you
can get cables to "wander"
all over your knitting,
you are right. Begin with
a greater number of stitches and establish several cables on a
background of reverse stockinette. "Wander" them creatively.

Traveling with Rope Cable

worked over 8 sts
    This cable begins on a
WS row.
Rows 1: (WS) K2, P4, K2
Rows 2 and 6: (rs) P2, C4B,
    P2
Row 3 and all WS rows: K
    the purl, and P the knit
    sts of previous row.
Row 4: P2, K4, P2
Row 8: P1, T3B, T3F, P1
Row 10: T3B, P2, T3F
Row 12: K3, P2, K3
Row 14: T3F, P2, T3B
Row 16: P1, T3F, T3B, P1
Rep rows 2 - 17

Traveling with Rope Cable

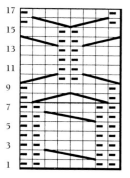

LACE

    Lacy-textured fabrics can be created by experimenting with different arrangements of yarn-overs combined with decrease stitches as in laces 1, 2, and 7. Flat laces are a simple matter of creating holes in the knitted fabric by using yarn-overs (see Laces 3 and 4). Other laces are more sculptural and require more thought, ingenuity, and experimentation to design. Compare the following graphs to the knitted pieces, and knit a swatch of each while observing the knitting to see how the stitches form lace.

    Use lace as all-over sweater fabrics, or as panels within other stitch patterns.

    Some of the patterns require an extra stitch at the beginning or end of rows that is not part of the multiple. And some patterns have a different number of stitches from one row to the next—so for the purpose of graphing, where there is no stitch, the square is blocked out.

Lace 1

mult: an even number of
    stitches
    Compare laces 1 and 2
to see how YO's and K2togs
can be used to create
various patterns.
Row 1: K1, *YO, K2tog, *
    end with K1
Row 2: P1, *YO, P2 tog, *
    end with P1

Lace 1

Lace 2

mult: an uneven number of
    stitches
    This pattern staggers
the stitches just enough to
create a slight zigzag effect.
Row 1: K1, * YO, K2 tog *
Row 2 and all WS rows: P
Row 3: * K2 tog, YO * end
    with K1
Rep rows 1 - 4

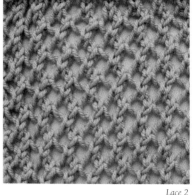

Lace 2

☐ K on RS, P on WS   — P on RS, K on WS   ◺ T3B   ◹ T3F   ◹ C4B   ⊢ Yarn Over   ╱ K2tog on RS, P2 tog on WS

Lace 3

mult: an uneven number of stitches

Laces 3 and 4 are flat laces consisting of holes made on a stockinette stitch background. Flat laces are easy to design on graph paper. Each hole is created by a yarn-over. On the graph paper, place the YO's (an increase), where you want them, then add a K2tog (a decrease) for each YO.

Row 1: K
Row 2 and all WS rows: P
Row 3: K1, * YO, K2 tog *
Rep rows 1 - 4

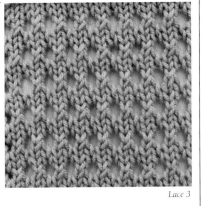
Lace 3

Lace 4

C.o. 22 stitches

This lace was designed as a panel to be used amongst other stitch patterns. Follow the graph.

Lace 4

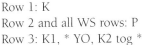

Lace 5

mult of 4, beginning with at least 8 sts

Doubling up on the YO's makes larger holes in the fabric.

Row 1: (WS) * K2tog, (YO) twice, K2 tog, *
Row 2: (RS) * K1, (K1, P1) into double YO, K1 *
Row 3: K2, * K2 tog, (YO) twice, K2 tog, * end with K2
Row 4: K2, * K1 (K1, P1) into double YO, K1, * end with K2

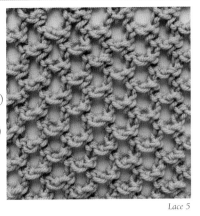
Lace 5

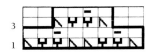

Lace 6

mult of 12 + 1

This lace demonstrates how the knitted fabric itself can be shaped by the use of YO's and K2tog's. Note the scalloped edges at top and bottom. This pattern is based on the "Old Shale" pattern commonly used for shawls or afghans.

Row 1: * K1, (K2tog) twice, (YO, K1) three times, K1, (K2tog) twice, * end with K1
Rows 2 and 3: K
Row 4: P

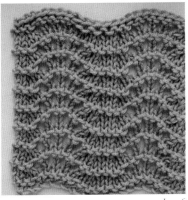
Lace 6

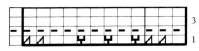

Lace 7

mult of 6
Row 1: * K1, YO, K2tog tbl, P1, K2tog, YO *
Row 2: P

Lace 7

 **K on RS, P on WS**   **P on RS, K on WS**   **Yarn Over**   **K2tog on RS, P2 tog on WS**   **ssk**   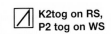 **K2 tog. tbl on RS, P2 tog. tbl on WS**

Laces 8 through 10 incorporate decreases that accentuate the YO's. Different decreases have different effects:

K2tog—leans to the right, and is more pronounced if used before the YO (K2tog, YO)

ssk—leans to the left, and is more pronounced if used after the YO (YO, ssk)

SKpsso—leans to the left, and is more pronounced if used after a YO (SKpsso, YO)

K2tog tbl—leans to the left

Lace 8

mult of 7
Row 1: * K1, YO, K2 tog, K4 *
Row 2 and all WS rows: P.
Row 3: * K2, YO, K2 tog, K3 *
Row 5: * K3, YO, K2 tog, K2 *
Row 7: * K4, YO, K2 tog, K1 *
Row 9: * K3, K2tog tbl, YO, K2 *
Row 11: * K2, K2 tog tbl, YO, K3 *
Row 13: * K1, K2 tog tbl, YO, K4 *
Row 15: * K2 tog tbl, YO, K5 *
Rep rows 1 - 16

Lace 8

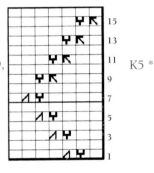

Lace 9

mult of 9 sts
Row 1: * K1, YO, K2 tog tbl, K3, K2 tog, YO, K1 *
Row 2 and all WS rows: P.
Row 3: * K2, YO, K2 tog tbl, K1, K2 tog, YO, K2 *
Row 5: * K3, YO, Sl 1, K2 tog, psso, YO, K3 *
Row 7: K
Rep rows 1-8

Lace 9

Lace 10

mult of 12
Note how the YO and decreases change places from the lower to the upper part of the diamond shape. This was done to retain the outlining. Decorative bobbles are added to this lace pattern.
Row 1: *P1, YO, ssk, K5, K2tog, YO, P1, K1 *
Row 2 and all WS rows: P.
Row 3: * P1, K1, YO, ssk, K3, K2tog, YO, K1, P1, K1 *
Row 5: * P1, K2, YO, ssk, K1, K2tog, YO, K2, P1, K1 *
Row 7: *P1, K4, B, K4, P1, K1 *
Row 9: * P1, K2, K2tog, YO, K1, YO, ssk, K2, P1, K1 *
Row 11: * P1, K1, K2tog, YO, K3, YO, ssk, K1, P1, K1 *
Row 13: * P1, K2tog, YO, K5, YO, ssk, P1, K1 *
Row 15: same as row 7
Rep rows 1 - 16

Lace 10

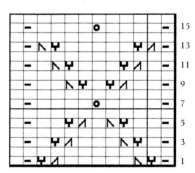

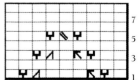 K on RS, P on

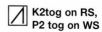 P on RS, K on WS

Yarn Over

K2tog on RS, P2 tog on WS

K2 tog. tbl on RS, P2 tog. tbl on WS

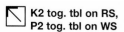 ssk

 Bobble

Lace 11

This is an example of creating an original design using the principles given so far. To knit this pattern, follow the graph. Then, devise a design of your own.

Lace 11

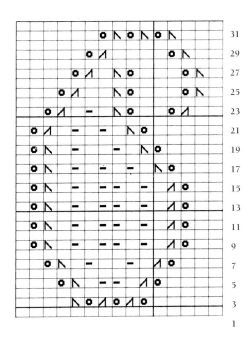

Laces 13 through 15 are yet more intricate than those above. In these patterns, stitches are placed in ways that "pull" the lines of the stockinette stitch into diagonal directions. This type of lace takes a great deal of ingenuity to design because it is necessary to think sculpturally. The rows may not have the same number of stitches because a YO may occur in one row, and a corresponding decrease may happen a row or more later. Note how in Lace 13 the increases work to make each "leaf" dimensional.

Lace 13

mult of 9
Row 1: * P2, K1, YO, K3tog, YO, K1, P2 *
Row 2 and all WS rows: K the P sts, and P all remaining sts
Row 3: * P2, K1, YO, K3, YO, K1, P2 *
Row 5: * P2, K1, YO, K5, YO, K1, P2 *
Row 7: * P2, K1, YO, K2tog tbl, K3tog, K2tog, YO, K1, P2 *
Row 9: * P2, K1, K2tog tbl, K1, K2tog, K1, P2 *
Rep rows 1 - 10

Lace 13

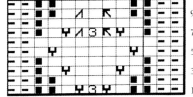

Lace 12

mult of 8

Cables are added to a lace pattern.
Row 1: * K2tog, YO, K4, YO, ssk *
Row 2 and all WS rows: P
Row 3: * K2tog, YO, C4B, YO, ssk *
Continue as established, working the cable on every sixth row.

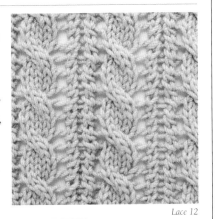

Lace 12

| | K on RS, P on WS | — | P on RS, K on | $\diagdown$ | ssk | O | Bobble | $\curlyvee$ | Yarn Over | ■ | no stitch | $\diagup$ | K2tog on RS, P2 tog on | **3** | K3tog. | $\diagdown$ | K2 tog. tbl on RS, P2 tog. tbl on WS |

Lace 14

mult of 8 + 4

An old pattern called "Traveling Vine."

Row 1: K2, * YO, K1B, YO, K2tog tbl, K5, * end with K2

Row 2: P2, * P4, P2 tog tbl, P3, * end with P2

Row 3: K2, * YO, K1B, YO, K2, K2tog tbl, K3 * end with K2

Row 4: P2, * P2, P2 tog tbl, P5, * end with P2

Row 5: K2, * K1B, YO, K4, K2tog tbl, K1, YO, * end with K2.

Row 6: P2, * P1, P2tog tbl, P6, * end with P2

Row 7: K2, * K5, K2tog, YO, K1B, YO, * end with K2

Row 8: P2, * P3, P2tog, P4, * end with P2

Row 9: K2, * K3, K2tog, K2, YO, K1B, YO, * end with K2

Row 10: P2, * P5, P2tog, P2, * end with P2

Row 11: K2, * YO, K1, K2tog, K4, YO, K1B, * end with K2

Row 12: P2, * P6, P2tog, P1, * end with P2

Lace 14

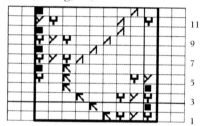

Lace 15

mult of 12 + 1

This is an adaptation of an old lace pattern. One way to learn about laces is to try to adapt an existing pattern.

Row 1, 21, and 23: * P1, K2tog, K3, YO, P1, YO, K3, K2tog tbl * end with P1

Row 2 and all WS rows: P

Row 3: * P1, K2tog, K2, YO, K1, P1, K1, YO, K2, K2tog tbl * end with P1

Row 5: * P1, K2tog, K1, YO, K2, P1, K2, YO, K1, K2tog tbl * end with P1

Row 7: * P1, K2tog, YO, K3, P1, K3, YO, K2tog tbl * end with P1

Rows 9, 11, and 13: * P1, YO, K3, K2tog tbl, P1, K2tog, K3, YO * end with P1

Row 15: * P1, K1, YO, K2, K2tog tbl, P1, K2tog, K2, YO, K1 * end with P1

Row 17: * P1, K2, YO, K1, K2tog tbl, P1, K2tog, K1, YO, K2 * end with P1

Row 19: * P1, K3, YO, K2tog tbl, P1, K2tog, YO, K3 * end with P1

Rep rows 1 - 24

| | K on RS, P on WS | | − | P on RS, K on WS | ■ | no stitch | Yarn Over | | K2 tog. tbl on RS, P2 tog. tbl | | K2tog on RS, P2 tog on | | K1B |

Textures and Special Effects

Note the different textural effects created by twisting, dropping, increasing and decreasing, slipping, and wrapping stitches. Graphs are not given for these stitch patterns. You can graph them by choosing a symbol for each of the specialty stitches.

Slipped Stitches

mult of 2
Slipping a stitch on the RS row and working it on the WS creates an elongated stitch.
Row 1: * K1, sl 1 purlwise *
Row 2: P

Slipped Stitches

K or P into the back loop of each stitch.

Row 1: * K1B *
Row 2: * P1B *

K or P into the back loop of each stitch.

Dec on one row, inc on the next.

mult of 2
Row 1: * K2tog *
Row 2: * K into front and back of stitch *

Decrease on one row, increase on the next.

Triple Stitch

mult of 4
Row 1 and all RS rows: P
Row 2: * (K, P, K into next st), P3tog *
Row 4: * P3tog, (K, P, K into next st) *

Triple Stitch

Dropped Stitch

Drop a stitch off the needle and ravel it to the bottom of the knitting.

Dropped Stitch

Wrapped Stitches

To wrap the next four sts, insert needle between fourth and fifth sts on left-hand needle from front to back, pick up yarn and pull through, then K2tog, K2.

Wrapped Stitches

Right Twist

mult of 2

Row 1: from the front, knit through the back loop of the second stitch, then K the first st and slide both off the needle.

Row 2: P

Right Twist

Popcorn

Into the next stitch, (K into front of loop, K into back of loop) three times and slide st off needle. Then bring second, third, and fourth, fifth, and sixth sts over the first.

Popcorn

Bobble

Into the next stitch, (K into front of loop, K into back of loop) three times and slide st off needle. [Turn the knitting and P the 6 sts. Turn, and K the sts]. Then bring second, third, and fourth, fifth, and sixth sts over the first. For a larger bobble, repeat the instructions in the parentheses.

Bobble

Elongated Stitches

Wrap the yarn around the needle twice, and in the following row, drop off the two extra loops. The "block" effect in this swatch was done the same as the Bobble: turn the knitting and work stockinette stitch until three extra rows are created.

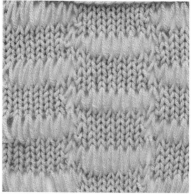

Elongated Stitches

CHAPTER 3

THE SHAPE
OF THINGS
TO COME

The most important defining characteristic of a sweater is its sleeve type. Sleeve types influence the shape of the entire sweater. For instance, the straight sleeve fits square with the sweater back and front pieces with no shaping done to the armhole area. The rounded form of the cap sleeve also takes a shaped armhole, and the raglan style is formed of a steady slope of sleeve and body pieces all the way up to the neckline. The dolman style presented in this book is made all-in-one with the sweater body (dolman sleeves can also be made separately).

Other, more secondary, characteristics include length of sweater body and sleeves, cardigan versus pullover, neckline treatment, cuffs or edgings, and other details that can be applied to a sweater of any of the sleeve styles. Let this chapter suggest some of the options in putting together a style that you may like to knit. Make sketches of your ideas.

SLEEVE STYLES

Straight Sleeve

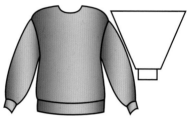

(See page 185 for the worksheet *Straight Sleeve Sweater*). The majority of the sweaters in this book are of the straight sleeve type, a style that is sometimes called "dropped shoulder." The sleeve top is bound off straight across with no armhole shaping done to the sweater body pieces. Because of its simple form, it is ideal for making elaborate stitch-patterned and color-worked sweaters, and also for beginning knitters.

Make the top of the sleeve wide enough for comfort. It should be a minimum of 6" (15cm) wider than the measurement of your upper arm. There is no maximum width, so go where your sense of style takes you!

If you like, the sleeve can be knitted directly onto the sweater front and back pieces thus eliminating a seam. See the "Pick Up and Knit Technique" on page 257.

The sleeve can be set-in slightly by knitting indents into the armhole area of the sweater front and back pieces, with a similar shaping to the upper sleeve. For examples, see **Autumn Tones** on page 254, and **Polar Bear** on page 260.

Cap Sleeve

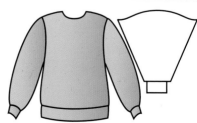

(See page 206 for the worksheet *Cap Sleeve Sweater*.) A cap sleeve consists of a rounded sleeve top that is fitted into a shaped armhole.

If you stand sideways in front of a mirror, you can see the rounded shape of your upper arm where it attaches to your shoulder. The cap sleeve is designed to follow this shape. The armhole of the sweater is indented and slightly shaped, with a corresponding indent to the sleeve top.

The traditional fit for a cap sleeve is to have the seam at the very top of the arm where it meets the shoulder, with a small amount of ease in the upper sleeve. If the upper sleeve is close-fitted, the sleeve cap will also be narrowly shaped.

The sleeve also adapts well to the oversized look. If the upper sleeve is designed with plenty of ease, the top of the cap will fit lower on the upper arm, creating a "dropped shoulder" and the sleeve cap will be shaped wide.

A cap sleeve can also be knitted wider than the armhole and sewn in gathers to the armhole to make a puffy sleeve top, a style that fashionably emerges now and then.

Raglan Sleeve

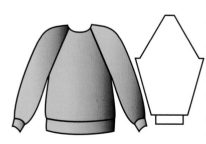

(See page 226 for the worksheet *Raglan Sleeve Sweater*.) The raglan sleeve style brings the top of the sleeve all the way to the neckline. After a slight initial bind-off, the upper sleeve incorporates steady shaping, as do the sweater's upper front and back pieces.

The row gauge (see Gauge Swatch on page 144) must be accurate; if it is off (even only slightly), the depth of the armhole will be too short, or longer than expected.

Using graph paper, it is easy determine the necessary shaping of both sweater body and sleeve pieces.

Decreases for Raglan and V-Neck Shaping

"Fully-fashioned" shaping places the decrease stitches in from the edge. The decrease stitches can be placed one, two, or three stitches in from the edge of the knitting.

To decrease:
- at the beginning of a RS (knit) row: K1, ssk, complete row.
- at the end of a RS row: knit up to last 3 stitches, K2 tog, K1.
- at the beginning of WS (purl) row: P1, P2 tog, completerow.
- at the end of WS row: work up to last 3 stitches, P2 tog tbl, P1.

Dolman Sleeves

Although dolman sleeves can be made separately, see the worksheet *One-Piece Dolman Sweater* on page 216, in which they are treated as one with the sweater.

Width of Upper Sleeves

It is important to fit this part of the sweater carefully, because this area has much to do with both the style and the comfort of the sweater. See the sweater, **Elegance in Cotton** on page 190 for the stylish effect of a wide upper sleeve. When you measure to fit the sweater, you will make this determination by checking various widths before a mirror.

Narrow sleeves are best in the cap or raglan styles due to the sleeve and armhole shaping that helps to reduce bulk in the underarm area.

I prefer generously-wide upper sleeves, both for freedom of movement and to avoid trapping heat. Any of the sleeve styles can accommodate as much width as you wish to add.

You will need to find your own upper arm comfort zone. One of the best ways to do this is to compare sweatshirts and sweaters in your wardrobe, and use the upper arm measurement of the garment that fits most comfortably. Also check with the Basic Dimensions chart in the Appendix.

Sleeve Increases

Sleeves begin narrow at the wrist and are increased up to the armhole (unless you have a different shape in mind). Here are some different ways the increases can be done:

a. Spread the increases evenly over the length of the sleeve.
b. Work the increases on every right-side row until the sleeve is the width desired, then knit the remainder of the sleeve straight up.
c. Work the increases so there are more at the beginning, and fewer at the upper parts of the sleeve, creating a greater slope at the beginning and less further along.
d. To make a "blousy" lower sleeve, work increases in the row above the cuff adding most or all of the stitches needed.

SWEATER BODY AND SLEEVE LENGTHS

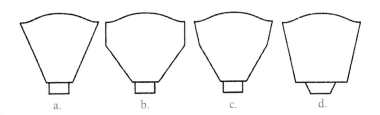

a.   b.   c.   d.

There are four more or less standard sweater lengths for the body of the sweater. These include (from left to right in the illustration) waist, hip, crotch, and below crotch (tunic). These are traditional sweater lengths only, and you should feel free to also knit knee, mid-calf, above-waist, or any length you wish.

Long sleeves can be knitted to fit at the wrist, upper hand, or knuckles. Short sleeves can be made anywhere between the elbow and the upper arm. You can also make 3/4-length or 7/8-length sleeves that fit anywhere between the elbow and the wrist.

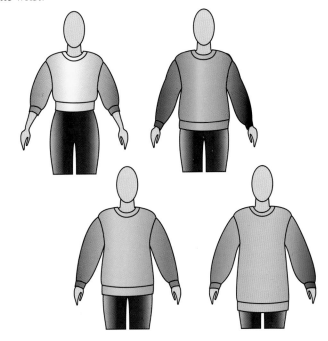

CUFFS OR EDGINGS

Ribbings are the most common way of finishing the edges of a sweater. Cuffs or edgings can be used to create a close fit such as a stretchy K/P ribbing worked in wool. Or, to merely stabilize the edges of the knitting and prevent curling and distortion, a non-elastic pattern stitch can be used. See pages 158-159 for some elastic and non-elastic ribbings.

Cuffs for the sleeves and bottom of the sweater can be any length you prefer—from a mere 1/2" to several inches. Sleeve cuffs can be made extra long with thumb holes, see page 210.

Use needles that are at least two sizes smaller than those used to obtain the stitch gauge for the sweater to make a firmer stitch, and if desired, use fewer stitches for the edging to draw it in a little more.

A simple formula for how many stitches to use for the body ribbing is to use 90 percent of the sweater body stitches.

Using a calculator:

Number of sweater body stitches minus 10 percent

Round up or down to the nearest even number if knitting a 1 x 1 rib, or use your pattern stitch multiple. For the sleeves:

Number of stitches at lower sleeve minus 20 percent

Some additional ways to finish the edges of a sweater:

Knit a hem. Knit about 1" in stockinette stitch that is later turned to the inside and sewn in place.

Knit several rows in garter stitch, or any firm pattern stitch.

Make a curled edge by knitting in stockinette stitch for an inch or more.

Tip:

If you are not sure how many stitches to use for the ribbing, knit it last by picking up stitches on the sweater body or sleeves. That way, if it isn't right, it can be ripped out and easily re-knitted.

NECKLINE STYLES

The basic neckline shapes are Boat, Round, V, and Square. These can be finished with ribbing or another suitable pattern stitch.

The back neck of the sweater is often knitted straight across but, if you like, it can be shaped similarly to the front but making it only about 1" (2.5cm) deep (except for the boat neck).

Boat Neck

The upper edge of the front and back parts of the sweater are knitted straight across, and the shoulders are sewn leaving an opening for the neck. The length of the shoulder seams is found by trying the sweater on.

To obtain a firm edge, use needles about two sizes smaller than those used for the sweater for the final 1" of sweater front and back pieces. A ribbing stitch can be used, or garter stitch, or any stitch that prevents curling. To make a hemmed boat neck, knit in stockinette stitch for an extra 1" (2.5cm);

turn this amount to the inside and sew loosely in place. Then, when sewing the shoulders, sew into the fold of the hem (see **Cotton Tunic** on page 192). See **Elegance in Cotton** on page 190 for a variation in which the boat neck edge is sewn into a slight curve.

Round

A versatile style, this neck shaping is used to make a crewneck, mock turtle, or a turtleneck. Other variations can include making a wide neck opening for an off-the-shoulder look, and making a cowl or draped turtleneck by enlarging the opening or by making the turtleneck wider and longer.

Take care that the opening will accommodate the size of your head if you are making a pullover. You can roughly calculate the size of an opening before knitting it by adding together the widths and depths of the neck opening and then comparing with the size of your head. The opening can usually be a little smaller than your head because knitting stretches.

Shape the front neck opening as follows:

Width of neck opening = _____"(cm) x stitch gauge = _____ sts.

If you are making a crewneck, allow for the width of the ribbing (if the ribbing will be 1" wide, add an extra 2" to the width of the neck opening).

Bind off approximately 4/5 of the stitches (or put them on a holder). Attach a second ball of yarn so that both sides of the neck can be worked at the same time. Decrease one stitch at each side of the neck opening until all decreases are made. Work even to the total length of the sweater.

Square

Calculate the stitches the same as for the round neck, but bind off (or put on a holder) all stitches at once. Knit the sides of the neck straight up.

V-Shaped

Calculate the shaping of the V-neck as follows:

Width of neck opening = _____ x stitch gauge = _____ sts. Divide the result by 2 to find the number of stitches to decrease at each side of the V. Allow for the width of the ribbing (if the ribbing will be 1" wide, add an extra 2" to the width of the neck opening).

Determine the depth of the V, allowing for the ribbing: Depth x row gauge = _____ rows.

This gives the number of rows over which the decreases are worked. Compare with the number of stitches to be decreased, and spread them equally along the edge of the V. The decreases can be arranged so that the upper 1" to 2" of the V is worked even to the top of the sweater. If you have difficulty figuring out how to distribute the decreases, plot them on graph paper, then use the graph as your knitting pattern.

To begin the shaping, first see that the sweater is an uneven number of stitches; if necessary CO one stitch at the beginning edge. Knit up to two stitches before the center stitch, work the first decrease, bind off the center stitch, and continue to shape the V, attaching a second ball of yarn to work both sides at once. See Decreases for V-Neck Shaping on page 173.

For a variation on the v-neck, see **Purple Tango** on page 200, for which the neckline shaping is made to accommodate a simple shawl collar.

Knitting the Neckband

To knit a neckband on two needles, first sew up one shoulder seam. If you are using a circular needle, sew both shoulder seams. Begin picking up stitches at one unsewn shoulder if using two needles, and at either shoulder if using a circular needle.

To figure out how many stitches to pick up, use a tape measure to carefully measure around the neck opening. Multiply by the sweater body stitch gauge, then subtract 5 percent to 10 percent of the stitches.

Neck opening = _____ x sweater stitch gauge = _____ - (minus) _____ percent = _____sts.

More often than any other area of the sweater, the neckband may require adjustment after knitting. If you find after knitting it that it is either too loose or too snug, rip out and pick up a more appropriate number of stitches and re-knit the band. It should be comfortable to wear, and not distort the neck area of the sweater by either stretching or pulling on it.

Round Neckband

Using needles one to two sizes smaller than those for the sweater, pick up the stitches evenly along the entire edge. When you get to the bound-off stitches at the front neck, pick up one for each. Knit to the length desired, and then bind off loosely in the same pattern stitch. Sew the remaining shoulder and the neckband seam.

For a hemmed crewneck, knit twice the length desired, bind off loosely. Loosely sew the bound-off edge to the pick-up row.

V- and Square Neckbands

Using needles one-to-two sizes smaller than those for the sweater, pick up the stitches evenly along the entire edge. At the center front of the V-neck, pick up one where the stitch was bound off earlier. If needed, place a safety pin through it so it is easy to see.

At the center front of the V-neck and at the corners of the square neck, work shaping as follows. On right side rows, K2tog tbl, knit the center stitch, K2. On the wrong side, K2 tog, purl the center stitch, K2 tog tbl.

Front Openings

This topic is covered on page 249.

SHOULDER SEAM

The shoulder seam is important because it stabilizes the bound-off stitches of the upper front and back pieces. If you are tempted to knit the front and back pieces as one unit, keep in mind that the weight of the sweater can stretch the shoulder area out of shape.

If you like, the shoulders can be shaped. Stand before a mirror and determine the amount of slope your shoulder takes. Work two to four bind offs, making them the same for each shoulder, to approximate the shape of your shoulders. If you have relatively square shoulders, use only two bind-offs, or none at all.

QUICKIE SWEATERS

If you are new to sweater-knitting, you may be eager to see a finished product, and sometimes it is just plain fun to make a sweater that finishes quickly. Here are some suggestions for a design that will go more quickly than most:

- Use a plain pattern stitch such as stockinette, or reverse stockinette.
- Use "fat" yarn, a heavy worsted or bulky (keeping in mind that bulky yarns make warm sweaters, especially if they're wool).
- Have less to knit by choosing a smaller size, shorter body and sleeve lengths, large neck opening.
- Make a vest, a short sleeved, or sleeveless sweater.

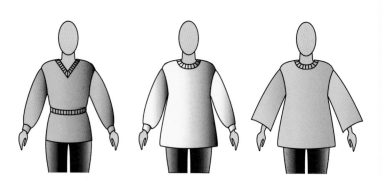

Ideas

Although the classic sweater style is knitted straight up to the armhole, there are other ways that sweaters can be shaped.

- As shown by the dolman style on page 215, fit a short sweater at the waist and increase up to the armhole.
- Decrease up to a fitted waist then increase up to the armhole.
- Flare the bottom of the sweater and decrease up to the armhole. Flare the sleeves also, or not.

SWEATERS IN TWO PIECES

The classic sweater set consists of a sleeveless fitted top worn under a buttoned cardigan.

The two-piece idea can also consist of a vest worn over a long-sleeve sweater (see **Trompe L'Oeil** on page 258 for an adaptation of this).

Figure Flattery

Here are a few hints on how best to enhance your figure.

For a slimming profile, choose an overall stitch pattern that creates a vertical "line" such as cables and wide ribbings, also use V-necks and front openings.

Thinner fabrics (fingering and sport weight yarns) are more slenderizing than heavier (worsted and bulky weights) ones.

Short, close-fitting styles tend to enhance a good figure or a person with short stature.

Bulky fabrics, horizontal stripes, and rounded necklines are wonderful on thin people.

Dropped shoulders, wide upper sleeves, hip- and tunic-lengths, bulky yarn weights, and large, dramatic stitch and color patterns are beneficial to tall people.

CHAPTER 4

FITTING
THE
SWEATER

it is the backbone of garment design, and is the key to comfort, itself. Fit is also a very personal thing. A style that fits one person may be too big, too small, too short, or too long for the next. Personally, I like my sweaters to be roomy, and my winter ones to have extra-long sleeve cuffs and high turtlenecks. I think the reason for this is that my creative work makes me want to be free and unrestricted, and I know what keeps me warm. Our individual preferences regarding fit are important.

For this chapter you will need a tape measure, a mirror (full-length is best), a pencil, and paper.

Try to understand what type of fit you like and why. How do you like your clothes to make you feel? Do you prefer a "second skin," or would you rather be enveloped in sensuous drape? Do you like the reassurance of a garment's weight, or do you prefer to feel you are wearing nothing at all?

Try sketching a sweater that fulfills your idea of what a good "fit" means. What type of yarn will you use? Pattern stitch? Color?

For the worksheets for the *Straight, Cap, Dolman,* and *Raglan Sleeve Sweaters* (*see pages 184, 206, 216, 226*), actual body measurements are used to determine the size of the sweater to be knitted. In other words, in one step you will be measuring yourself while also planning the size and shape of the sweater. The resulting dimensions are then easily translated into the number of stitches or rows to knit.

Do the *Measuring for Fit* worksheet on the facing page (see also page 270) for each sweater you knit, unless you are going to make each sweater exactly the same. If you are knitting a sweater for someone else, take his or her measurements, use the Standard Dimensions chart in the Appendix, or use the dimensions of an existing garment (sweater or sweatshirt).

Using a tape measure, stand before a mirror to be sure you are measuring correctly. Wear lightweight clothing for accuracy. After measuring, you may like to compare the measurements taken with those of a sweater that fits really well.

For convenience an extra copy of the Measuring for Fit Worksheet appears in the appendix

One way to fit a sweater is to knit according to the dimensions of an existing garment that fits comfortably.

EASE

Ease is the extra space inside the body and sleeves of a sweater. Ease is added so the garment can be put on and taken off easily, to provide the comfort of roominess, and for style. A sweater worn alone can be made more snug than one worn over another garment, and a pullover must have sufficient ease for getting in and out of. Plentiful ease can be more appropriate for sweaters made of finer yarns, with less ease needed with heavier yarns. "Stretchability" can take the place of ease. You will need to determine your own ease requirements for what makes you feel comfortable and is best for your appearance. My advice is to experiment with ease—use a little more or a little less with each sweater you knit.

Guidelines for amount of ease to allow in the body of the sweater:

Tightly-fitted	allow 0"
Close-fitting	allow 2"
Loose-fitting	allow 4"-6"
Oversized	allow 8"-10" or more

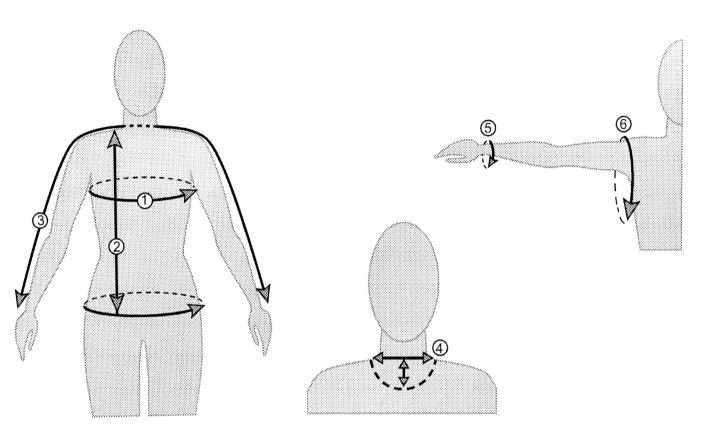

MEASURING FOR FIT WORKSHEET

1.) Measure around the widest part of your chest/bust area. Add ease to this measurement, according to the chart on page 178; also, check how the bottom of the sweater will fit, and make any necessary adjustments. The result is then divided in half for the front and back pieces of the sweater.

Chest/bust measurement = _____"(cm)
Add ease of ___"(cm) for a total of _____"(cm)
Total divided by 2 = _____"(cm) ①

2.) Measure from top of shoulder (the highest point along a normal shoulder seam), to exactly where you want the sweater to end. Do this standing before a mirror with the tape measure draped from your shoulder.

Shoulder to bottom of sweater = _____ "(cm) ②

3.) Measure from sleeve end to sleeve end. It is best to do this with arms at sides. It may be easier to measure from the nape of your neck to one sleeve end, and then multiply by two.

Sleeve end to sleeve end = _____"(cm) ③

4.) For the neck opening, measure the distance from the shoulder seam down to where the collar will end. For v or lower necklines, this is where you want the lowest point of the v (not including the ribbing). Measure to obtain the width of the neck opening. Because it is difficult to obtain these accurately, you may want to refer to the Standard Dimensions chart on page 274, or compare your results with an existing sweater.

Depth of neck opening = ____"(cm) ④
Width of neck opening = ____"(cm) ④

5.) Measure and add the amount of ease desired for the part of the sleeve just above the cuff. Loop the tape measure around your arm or wrist to find a comfortable circumference.

Width of lower sleeve = ____"(cm) ⑤

6.) Determine the fullness of the widest part of the sleeve by draping the tape measure around your upper arm. Allow ease. (See Information on Sleeves on page 40. One-half of ⑥ will be the depth of the armhole of the sweater.)

Width of upper sleeve = ____"(cm) ⑥

SPECIAL FITTING NEEDS

- *Pregnancy.* I personally balk at the idea of making a maternity sweater that is worn for several months and then put aside. Instead, make an oversized sweater that can be worn afterwards when you have those days where you feel like wrapping yourself in something big and cozy. Or, make a sweater for someone bigger than you, wear it while you need it, then hand it on.

- *Large hips and narrow chest.* To make a sweater that is hip-length or longer, measure around your hips and add ease. Measure your chest/bust and add ease. Multiply each by the stitch gauge, then subtract to find the number of stitches to be decreased from the bottom of the sweater to the armhole area. Divide by 2 to find the number of decrease rows—decreasing one stitch each end of a row. Decrease evenly between bottom and armhole of the sweater front and back.

- *Narrow hips and large chest.* These adjustments are the same as for large hips and narrow chest, but calculate the increases needed, instead of decreases.

Tips

You can work on the design of a sweater as you are knitting it. For an example of how this works, read through the instructions for the sweater, *Damask Block* on page 186.

Keep notes on each sweater you knit. Some designs you will likely use again, and others you may want to make with variations. I keep my notes in a small spiral notebook that stays in my knitting basket. For each sweater design I sketch a diagram of the pieces to be knitted, note dimensions, write out stitch patterns, and include a yarn description, needle sizes, gauge, and numbers of stitches to be knitted.

When following a purchased sweater pattern, compare the dimensions of the design to those you've determined using your measurements and desired amount of ease. This will give an indication of how the garment will fit.

Keep a notebook to jot down the particulars of each sweater you knit, and to sketch out ideas for future projects.

CHECKING FIT AS YOU KNIT

Although measurements provide crucial information for achieving an accurate fit, it is still a good idea to check the fit as you proceed. Here is how to do this for the individual sweater pieces.

Back/Front

Knit halfway across a row, spread the knitting out along both needles, then hold the piece up to yourself while standing before a mirror. Check that width and length will be as intended.

Sleeves

Spread the stitches out along both needles and drape the piece over your outstretched arm. Check length and width, and the fit of the cuff.

Neckline

After you've begun the neckline ribbing, check that you have the appropriate number of stitches by slipping the stitches onto a long, circular needle. Try on the sweater. If knitting a turtleneck, try on to check the length of the neck ribbing.

CHAPTER 5

SOME
SWEATERS
TO KNIT

This section includes worksheets for making four sweater styles: Straight Sleeve, Cap Sleeve, Dolman, and Raglan. Find a style that you will be comfortable knitting and wearing, or experiment with all of them. Sweater designs are given as examples—refer to them for ideas and for specific knitting instructions. If you are not yet comfortable with designing a sweater on your own, several sizes are given for most of the sweaters. For any of them, try adapting lengths and widths to suit your own fitting needs. Further on in the chapter are additional ideas to work with—how to plan for a front opening, designing a sweater in sections, and other creative ideas. Begin anywhere you like, but do try something that challenges your creative impulses.

Note also the blended yarns used for the sweaters in this chapter. In **Damask Block**, two similar wool yarns blend their colors. In **Elegance in Cotton, Cotton Tunic,** and **Cotton Cover-Up,** two soft and slightly textured cottons were plied for interesting colorings in a soft, drapey fabric. **Fuchsia Takes a Ribbing** consists of wool blended with cotton to make a fabric that blends the qualities of both. **Purple Tango** is comprised of two cottons and a chenille to result in a luxuriously textured, velvety soft fabric. Experiment with combinations of your own to create a unique yarn.

Note: Yardages are given for some of the sweaters, and these are to be considered approximate only. It is best that you make a yardage swatch of your yarn, and compare it with the dimensions of the sweater that you wish to knit (see "Estimating Yardage" on page 144). Where yardages are not given, it is assumed that you are using leftover yarns, or that you will be changing the design to suit your own ideas.

DESIGNING A STRAIGHT-SLEEVE SWEATER

To knit a sweater using this worksheet, first do *Measuring for Fit* (page 179) to determine sweater sleeve and body lengths and widths, and neckline shaping (neck shaping is optional—see **Damask Block** on page 186, and **Elegance in Cotton** on page 190).

The diagram shows the four main pieces of the sweater, and how they fit together. (The sweater back

is shown upside down—it is actually knitted from the bottom up.) The numbers from *Measuring for Fit* (page 179) correspond to the diagram with ① resulting in the number of stitches to knit for front and back pieces of the sweater. ② is the length to knit the sweater, and so on.

Follow the directions accompanying the worksheet to knit a sweater.

STRAIGHT SLEEVE SWEATER WORKSHEET

Procedure:
    Do the worksheet Measuring for Fit (page 179)
    Choose a yarn and find gauges
Stitch gauge = _____
Row gauge = _____

① x stitch gauge = _____ stitches to knit for each of back and front.
Subtract 10 percent = _____ stitches for ribbing. . . . .

② = _____"(cm): length to knit for each of front and back. . .

② minus ④ (depth) = _____"(cm): begin neck bind offs. . .

④ (width) x stitch gauge = _____ stitches to bind off for neck.

⑤ x stitch gauge = _____ stitches for beginning of sleeve above ribbing. . . . .

Subtract 20 percent = ___ stitches for ribbing.
- _____ - _____ - _____

③ minus ① = _____ "(cm).
Divide the result by 2 = _____ "(cm): Length of sleeve.

⑥ x stitch gauge = _____ stitches at top of sleeve.

⑤ x stitch gauge = _____ stitches above ribbing.
Subtract to = _____ stitches to be increased. Divide by
        2 = _____ total increase rows.

Subtract length of ribbing from sleeve length = _____ "(cm)
x row gauge = _____ total rows.

    Divide by 2 = _____ total RS rows.

Instructions

Needle size for body of sweater _____
Needle size for ribbing _____

Back

→ Cast on this number of stitches using the smaller needle size. Work desired length of ribbing. Change to larger needles, increase to the number of stitches to knit for the back.

→ Knit the back to this length and bind off.

Front

→ Knit the front same as the back up to here. Shape the neckline according to the instructions for your preferred neck style (page 174). Work to same length as back and bind off all stitches.

Sleeves

→ Cast on this number of stitches using the smaller needle size. Work desired length of ribbing. Change to larger needles, and increase to the number of stitches to knit for the sleeve.

    Compare the increase rows with the total RS rows, and distribute increases evenly on RS rows to top of sleeve, or see sleeve-increase methods on page 173. Bind off all stitches. Make second sleeve the same. See page 175 for finishing the neck. Sew the pieces of the sweater together.

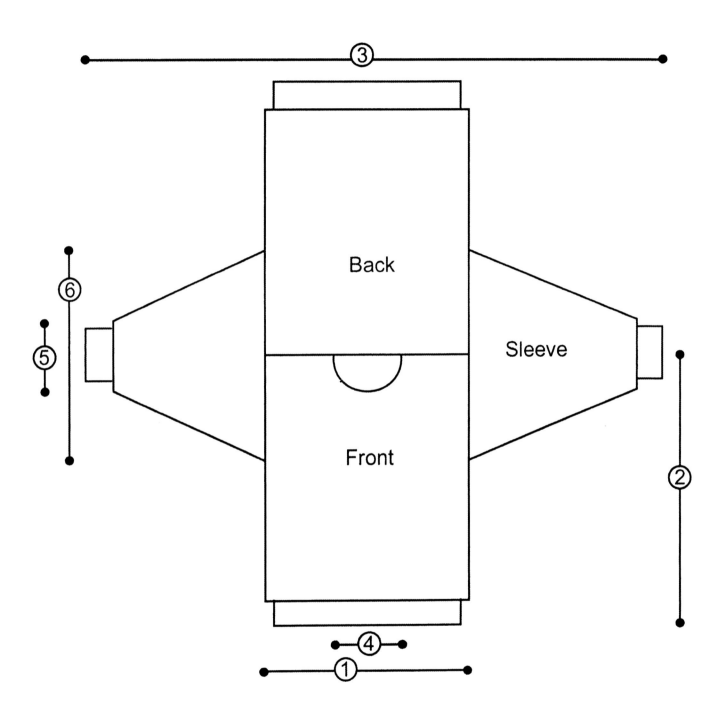

DAMASK
BLOCK

ead through the following instructions or, better yet, *knit* this sweater! This easy-to-knit sweater is presented in a way that is different from other sweaters in this book. The idea is to help you understand the process involved in designing a sweater, how decisions are made, and how the sweater comes together. At each point where I made a decision, you may make one of your own, varying the design to suit your own ideas or needs. The instructions refer to the worksheet *Measuring for Fit* on page 179, and the worksheet for *Straight Sleeve Sweaters* on page 184.

Sizes

Directions are for size Medium with a finished circumference of 44"/112cm. (Sizes Small 40"/101.5cm, and Large 48"/122cm, are in parentheses.)

Yarn

For an easy sweater, a worsted weight yarn also makes a quicker project than a lightweight yarn, so, from my stash of wool yarns I decided to ply two sport weights by holding them together as I knitted. (You can use a single strand of worsted weight yarn instead, if you wish.) I tried different color combinations and knitted several color swatches, and discovered that purple with rust met with my liking. The yarns are a smooth texture, so a pattern stitch will show up well.

Yardage

1580 (1420, 1750) yards of each color.

Needles

Size 8 needles are appropriate for the yarn (I also tried 7's and 9's), with size 6 needles for the edgings.

Pattern Stitch

It was my objective to design an easy-to-knit sweater, but one that also had an interesting pattern stitch. I decided on a combination of stockinette and garter stitch, using plain garter for the cuffs. After knitting a number of swatches and thinking about what combination would make an interesting pattern stitch, the idea of making garter stitch "blocks" arrived.

Garter Block Pattern Stitch

(Cast on a multiple of 10 sts. Note: the garter stitch is worked by purling on every row.)

Row 1: * K5, P5 *
Row 2: Purl
Rep these two rows for a total of eight rows (the garter stitch sections will have four ridges)
Row 9: * P5, K5 *
Row 10: Purl
Repeat these two rows for a total of eight rows. Repeat rows 1–16 for pattern.

Swatch and Gauge

To be sure of the combination of pattern stitch and yarn choice, and to establish the gauge, I knit a swatch of the pattern stitch. Wanting the swatch to be at least 4" square, I used 20 sts, or 2 multiples of the stitch pattern, and knit for about 4".

Gauge on size 8 needles
4 sts and 6 rows = 1"/2.5cm.

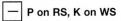

▢ K on RS, P on WS   ▬ P on RS, K on WS

Here are a couple of pattern stitch variations on this sweater that you may like to consider.

Variation 1. Make the cuffs in garter stitch as the sweater shown here, and the body and sleeves in stockinette stitch. This eliminates the pattern stitch, but retains the basic style of the sweater.

Variation 2. Work the garter and stockinette sections in stripes instead of blocks. (Repeat rows 1 and 2 of the pattern stitch throughout.)

Look for ways to vary stitch pattern ideas and try to visualize how the finished sweater will look in them.

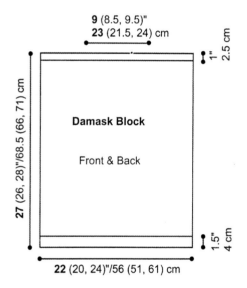

9 (8.5, 9.5)"
23 (21.5, 24) cm

1" / 2.5 cm

27 (26, 28)"/68.5 (66, 71) cm

Damask Block

Front & Back

1.5" / 4 cm

22 (20, 24)"/56 (51, 61) cm

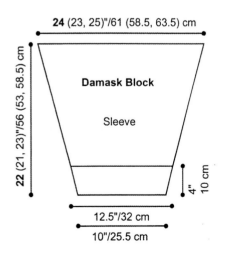

24 (23, 25)"/61 (58.5, 63.5) cm

22 (21, 23)"/56 (53, 58.5) cm

Damask Block

Sleeve

4" / 10 cm

12.5"/32 cm

10"/25.5 cm

To begin knitting, all I need is to find the width of front and back pieces. I will think about the neck treatment and the sleeve styles as I knit.

Beginning with ① of *Measuring for Fit* (page 179), I determine the width of the sweater. A 44"/112cm circumference gives me about 10"/25.5cm of ease, about what I like. 44"/112cm divided by two gives a 22"/56cm width for each of the back and front pieces. And now we apply the gauge to the width: 22"/56cm x 4 sts per inch/2.5cm = 88, and this is rounded to the nearest multiple of 10 (necessary because the pattern stitch requires a multiple of 10) to equal 90 stitches.

I then decide on the length of the sweater (② of *Measuring for Fit*). I would like this sweater long for casual wear, and go for a total length of 27 (26, 28)"/68.5 (66, 71)cm.

In my notebook, I begin to sketch a diagram showing the general shape of the sweater, filling in the dimensions and numbers of stitches used. I make sure to write down the pattern stitch, the gauge, and needle size information.

Begin to Knit

Now we can begin to knit the back piece of the sweater. For the bottom edge of the sweater, I used needles two sizes smaller than for the remainder of the sweater. So, on size 6 needles, I cast on 90 (80, 100) stitches. Knitting in garter stitch I stop at 1-1/4"/3cm, which appears to be a suitable length for the edging. Changing to size 8 needles, I proceed to knit the back of the sweater beginning with row 1 of the Garter Block pattern stitch.

Planning the Neckline

While knitting, I'm thinking about the neck treatment. A garter stitch boat neck will work well, because it will match the garter stitch edging at the bottom of the sweater. So I plan to end the pattern stitch 1"/2.5cm short of the top of the sweater, and then to work in garter stitch using size 6 needles for 1"/2.5cm. I finish the back of the sweater this way, also noting the boat neck decision in my notebook.

The front of the sweater is knitted exactly the same as the back, because the neckline is the same on both front and back. (For a different type of neckline, I would calculate where to stop in order to begin the neckline shaping.)

Planning the Sleeves

While knitting, I think about the sleeves, and find I am torn between two ideas. I could make 3/4 length sleeves with a 1-1/4"/3cm garter stitch edging at the bottom edge. Or, I could make a fold-back garter stitch cuff (about 4"/10cm total length) on a full-length sleeve. I like both ideas, but since I need to choose one, I go for the full-length sleeve.

Using ⑤ and ⑥ of *Measuring for Fit*, I choose 10"/25.5cm for a lower sleeve circumference to make a loose-fitting cuff. Liking roomy upper sleeves, I drape the tape measure and decide on 24"/61cm for the sleeve top.

Using ③ of *Measuring for Fit*, I subtracted the 22"/56cm width of my sweater and determined that each sleeve will be 22 (21, 23)"/53 (51, 58.5)cm long. Of this, the cuff will take 2"/5cm (it is a 4"/10cm fold-back cuff), leaving 18 (17, 19)"/46 (43, 48)cm that will be knitted in pattern stitch with increases. With this information, I begin one sleeve.

I cast on to size 6 needles 40 stitches and knit in garter stitch (knit every row) for a total of 4"/10cm. Then I increase 10 sts (for a total of 50) as additional assurance that the cuff will fit more closely than the lower sleeve. This is done on the WS, so the pattern stitch can begin on the RS on the following row.

It is now necessary to calculate the sleeve increases. The sleeve begins with 50 sts and will end at 24 (23, 25)"/61 (58.5, 63.5)cm wide with 96 (92, 100) sts. 96 – 50 = 46 total increases, divided by two = 23 increase rows (since two stitches are increased per row).

The sleeve will be 18"/46cm long from above the cuff. 18" x 6 rows to the inch = 108 rows, divided by two = 54 RS rows. Comparing 23 inc rows with 54 RS rows tells me that the sleeve can be increased evenly almost to the top by working two increases on every other RS row (23 x 2 = 46), with a few rows left over. Therefore, increases will be made every fourth row (every other RS row) until there

are 96 (92, 100) sts, then the sleeve is worked straight to a total of 22 (21, 23)"/56 (53, 58.5)cm.

After one sleeve is knitted, I sew up the shoulder seams of the front and back pieces, then sew on the sleeve. I check the fit of the sleeve, and the length of the sweater. If there are any changes to be made, I take out the seams and make them, then knit the second sleeve.

Finishing

All parts for this sweater are finished and can be sewn together. Sew the shoulder seams, trying on the sweater to find the right size for the neck opening. The sleeves are sewn on next. Then sew the sleeve seams, and finally the side seams.

I check that the sleeve information and any changes are jotted into my notebook. If you knitted along, you now have a finished sweater and a completed pattern. If you think about this, it is done in a different order than the way you may have been taught—to buy a pattern, find a matching yarn, and to knit the sweater. Here, we have found a yarn, and then knitted the sweater and drafted the pattern at the same time.

THREE COTTON SWEATERS

The following three sweaters were machine knitted. Each is made of two fine, lightly slubbed cotton yarns that were plied into one strand on a spinning wheel. The designs can be hand knitted to the dimensions given, or, to achieve your own fit, use the worksheet, *Measuring for Fit* (page 179) and the worksheet *Straight Sleeve Sweater* (page 184). See instructions for the individual sweaters.

Yarn

Use the yarn of your choice (suggestions are given with each sweater), and find the yardage needed as per instructions on page 144.

Needles and Gauge

See page 144 to find the correct needle size, and to establish the gauge. You will also need to have needles that are two sizes smaller for knitting the hems.

Pattern Stitch

Choose a plain stitch such as stockinette for a textured yarn, or a pattern stitch for a plain yarn.

ELEGANCE
IN COTTON

D rape is important to this elegant and yet simply shaped sweater. Draped garments fall gracefully along the lines of the figure, and move with the motions of the wearer. There are certain additional features that bring this sweater out of the realm of the ordinary. The lower sleeve is made with an ease of only 3/4"/2cm so that the sleeve can be pulled up on the forearm and remain in place. The wide upper sleeve gives the sweater a graceful, elegant look. A softly curved neckline, created by turning the upper edge to the inside and hemming it, and using hems instead of ribbings give it a "couture" rather than a "sweater" look. To hand knit this sweater, choose a drapey fiber such as a soft cotton, silk, rayon yarn, or knitting ribbon.

Sizes

Small (Medium, Large), with finished circumferences of 42 (46, 50)"/106 (117, 127)cm.

Back and Front

C.o. using needles two sizes smaller than those used to obtain the gauge. Knit for 2"/5cm (1"/2.5cm of this will be hemmed to the back later). Change to the larger needles. Knit to the top and b.o. all sts. Knit the front the same.

Sleeves

C.o. with the smaller needles and knit for 2"/5cm (1"/2.5cm of this will be turned to the back later). Change to the larger needles and increase evenly to the top of the sleeve, then b.o. all sts.

Finishing

Sew the shoulders. Sew the sleeves on. Sew side and underarm seams. Turn in hems of sleeves, front and back 1"/2.5cm and sew loosely. To form a curved neckline, turn in the upper edge about 2"/5cm in the center tapering to almost nothing at the shoulder seams. Turn in the back neckline a small amount. Sew these loosely.

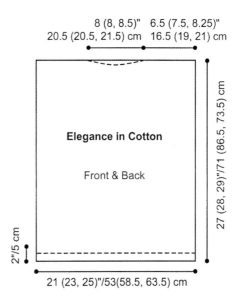

8 (8, 8.5)"   6.5 (7.5, 8.25)"
20.5 (20.5, 21.5) cm   16.5 (19, 21) cm

27 (28, 29)"/71 (86.5, 73.5) cm

Elegance in Cotton

Front & Back

2"/5 cm

21 (23, 25)"/53(58.5, 63.5) cm

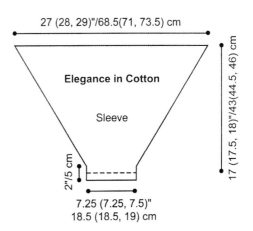

27 (28, 29)"/68.5(71, 73.5) cm

Elegance in Cotton

Sleeve

17 (17.5, 18)"/43(44.5, 46) cm

2"/5 cm

7.25 (7.25, 7.5)"
18.5 (18.5, 19) cm

Hems are a durable edge-finish.

COTTON
TUNIC

This tunic-length boat neck sweater is fashioned with wide sleeves that can be worn folded up if desired. The simple style, like **Elegance in Cotton** (page 190), can be knitted of a plain cotton, or a wool yarn for a casual look, or a silk or rayon yarn for a dressier appearance.

Sizes

Small (Medium, Large), with finished circumferences of 40 (44, 48)"/101.5 (112, 122)cm.

Back and Front

C.o. using needles two sizes smaller than those used to obtain the gauge. Knit for 2"/5cm (1"/2.5cm of this will be turned to the back later). Change to larger needles and knit up to 1"/2.5cm of the desired length of the sweater. Change to the smaller needles and knit for 2"/5cm. Make the front the same.

Sleeves

C.o. using the smaller needles, knit for 2"/5cm (1"/2.5cm of this will be turned to the back later). Change to the larger needles and increase evenly to the top of the sleeve. B.o. all sts.

Finishing

Hem the upper edges of front and back pieces by turning 1"/2.5cm to the back and stitching in place. Sew the shoulders at the fold of the hem, allowing sufficient neck opening to get the sweater on and off. Sew the sleeves on. Sew side and underarm seams. Turn in hems of sleeves and sweater body 1"/2.5cm and sew loosely.

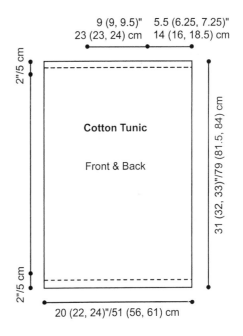

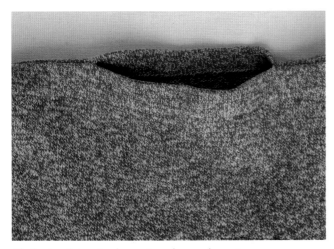

The boat neck is a simple way to make a neck opening.

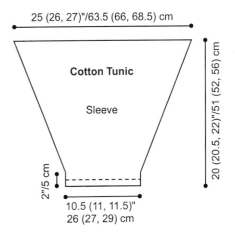

COTTON
COVER-UP

A stand-up collar and roomy sleeves give distinction to this casual zip-front sweater that can be tossed on over a bathing suit or a t-shirt and jeans. Make it in cotton for cool, comfortable summer wear.

A zip-front sweater is easy to design because there is no front band to plan for. Begin with a 30"/76cm separating zipper, and plan the length of the front of the sweater including the collar, to match the zipper length.

The sleeve used for the sweater shown is the same as that for **Elegance in Cotton** (page 190). You can instead use the **Cotton Tunic** (page 192) sleeve if you prefer. Refer to the diagram to see how the parts of the sweater are fitted together.

Sizes

Small (Medium, Large), with finished circumferences of 40 (44, 48)"/101.5 (112, 122)cm.

Knit the back and sleeves the same as for **Cotton Elegance** (page 190). Knit each front 1/2 the width of the back, shaping the neck edges. See neckline shaping for a round neck on page 174. Sew the shoulder seams.

Collar

Measure the neck opening. Multiply by the stitch gauge. Cast on and knit 4"/10cm. Sew one long edge to the neck opening.

Zipper

Lay the sweater out flat. Baste the zipper to the fronts using sewing thread and placing the zipper 2"/5cm above the neck seam. Fold the collar in half lengthwise and secure it with pins. Enclose the zipper tapes into the open short ends of the collar and pin, then finish the tape ends

by folding them to the back and stitching in place. Sew the long edge of the collar to the neck seam using yarn. Sew the zipper tapes in place using sewing thread. Thread a large needle with the sweater yarn and work a row of running stitch along each zipper tape through all layers.

Finishing

Sew the sleeves on. Sew sleeve and side seams. Sew hems of the body and sleeves.

A running stitch is a decorative way to finish a zipper.

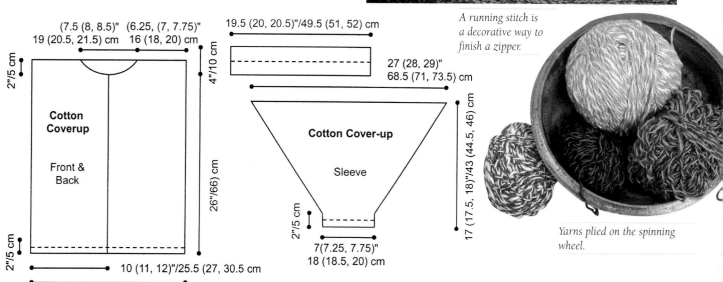

Yarns plied on the spinning wheel.

FUCHSIA
TAKES A
RIBBING

The interesting neck treatment of this sweater is its partially sewn-up turtleneck.

Ribbed sweaters follow the lines of the body. If you want to make a sweater that fits closely without feeling tight, choose a ribbed pattern stitch.

Two gauges are used for a ribbed, stretchy pattern stitch. This allows a comparison of the knitting when it is both in a relaxed state, and slightly stretched, and gives a better idea of how the sweater will fit than if only one gauge were used.

The sweater is made of two yarns, a wool in fuchsia and a cotton in dark multi-shades, blended by knitting them together. Wool and cotton meld nicely—you can feel both the wool and the cotton in the blend. The cotton adds softness, and the wool contributes to the springiness of the ribbed pattern stitch. The yarns give the right weight for a spring or fall season sweater … not too warm, and yet warm enough.

Sizes

Small (Medium, Large), with finished circumferences of 36"/91.5cm unstretched—40"/101.5cm slightly stretched (40-45, 44-50)"/(101.5-112, 112-127)cm.

Yarn

One strand of sport weight yarn is held together with a strand of fine cotton machine knitting yarn throughout (see Instructions for Using Coned Yarns on page 144). To substitute one yarn for the two, choose a heavy sport weight, or a light worsted weight that gets the same gauge.

Yardage

1300 (1500, 1650) yards of each color.

Needles

Sizes 7 and 5.

Gauge

5 sts unstretched or 4 sts slightly stretched, and 6 rows = 1"/2.5cm over Wide Ribbing pat st using size 7 needles.

Wide Ribbing

(mult of 4 sts)

Row 1: K3, P1

Row 2: K1, P3

Rep rows 1 and 2 for pat

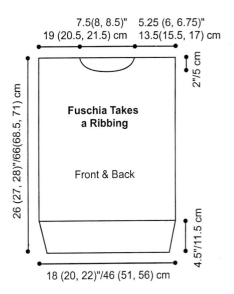

7.5(8, 8.5)" 5.25 (6, 6.75)"
19 (20.5, 21.5) cm   13.5(15.5, 17) cm

2"/5 cm

Fuschia Takes a Ribbing

Front & Back

26 (27, 28)"/66(68.5, 71) cm

4.5"/11.5 cm

18 (20, 22)"/46 (51, 56) cm

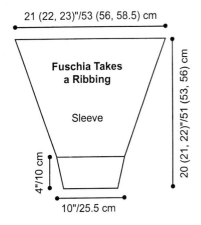

21 (22, 23)"/53 (56, 58.5) cm

Fuschia Takes a Ribbing

Sleeve

20 (21, 22)"/51 (53, 56) cm

4"/10 cm

10"/25.5 cm

☐ K on RS, P on WS   ⊟ P on RS, K on WS

Instructions

Back

With smaller needles, c.o. 80 (90, 100) sts. Work in 1 x 1 rib for 4 1/2"/11.5cm ending on a RS row. Next row (WS), P and inc 10 sts evenly spaced across row–90 (100, 110) sts. Change to larger needles and work in pat st until piece meas 26 (27, 28)"/66 (68.5, 71)cm from beg, then b.o. in ribbing.

Front

Work same as back. When piece measures 24 (25, 26)"/61 (63.5, 66)cm, shape neck: Work 30 (34, 38) sts, join a second ball of yarn and b.o. center 30 (32, 34) sts, work to end. Working both sides at once, b.o. 1 st at each neck edge every other row four times, until 26 (30, 34) sts rem at each shoulder. When piece meas same as back, b.o. all sts.

Sleeves

With smaller needles, c.o. 42 sts. Work in 1 x 1 rib for 4"/10cm ending on a RS row. Next row (WS), P and inc 18 sts evenly spaced across row–60 sts. Change to larger needles and work in pat st, inc one st each end every other row until 126 (130, 130) sts. When piece measures 20 (21, 22)"/51 (53, 56)cm from beg, b.o. all sts in ribbing.

Finishing

Sew right-hand shoulder seam. With smaller needles, pick up 94 (100, 106) sts evenly around neckline. Work in 1 x 1 rib for 9"/23cm. B.o. loosely in ribbing. Sew remaining shoulder seam. Starting at the base of the neck, sew up 4"/10cm of the turtleneck and fasten off securely. Sew on sleeves. Sew sleeve and side seams.

Blending cotton with wool creates a sweater fabric that has characteristics of both.

PURPLE TANGO

This sweater is yummy to wear, and so luxuriously soft. Strands of three different yarns were held together throughout to create the yarn for this sweater, and not one of them is intended for hand knitting: a purple rayon chenille, a weaving yarn that knits into a fabric too flimsy to make a sweater even on very fine needles, and two fine, slubbed cottons made for machine knitting, one blue, and the other multi-colored. This combination knits to a bulky gauge, but the resulting fabric does not feel bulky, and has excellent drape.

The neckline treatment consists of a simple way to fashion a shawl collar. The collar is knitted directly onto the sloped edge of the neckline with its bottom edges overlapped and sewn in place.

Sizes

Small (Medium, Large), with finished circumferences of 38 (42, 46)"/96.5 (106, 117)cm.

Yarn

Three fine yarns including a rayon chenille, and two cottons for machine knitting (see Instructions for Using Coned Yarns on page 144) held together throughout. To substitute, use any combination of yarns held together, or one bulky-weight yarn to give the same gauge.

Yardage

850 (960, 1070) yards of each color.

Buttons

1/2"/1.25cm, 3.

Needles

Sizes 9 and 7, 16"/40.5cm circular needle in size 7.

Gauge

3-1/4 sts and five rows = 1"/2.5cm over St st using size 9 needles.

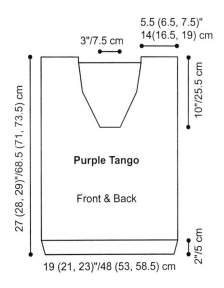

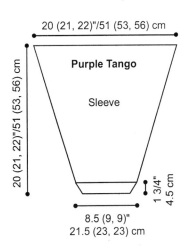

Instructions

Back

With smaller needles c.o. 62 (68, 74) sts. Work in 1 x 1 rib for 2"/5cm. Change to larger needles and work in St st. until piece meas 26 (27, 28)"/66 (68.5, 71)cm from beg.

Shape neck

Work 18 (21, 24) sts, join a second ball of yarn and b.o. center 26 sts, work to end. Working both sides at once, work even for 1"/2.5cm more, then b.o. each shoulder.

Front

Work same as back. When piece meas 17 (18, 19)"/43 (46, 48) cm shape neck: Work 25 (28, 31) sts, join a second ball of yarn and b.o. center 12 sts, work to end. Working both sides at once, b.o. one st at neck edge every fourth row 7 times until 18 (21, 24) sts remain at each shoulder. When piece meas the same as the back, b.o. all sts.

Sleeves

With smaller needles, c.o. 28 (30, 30) sts. Work in 1 x 1 rib for 1-3/4"/4.5cm. Change to larger needles and work in St st, inc one st each end of every row until 42 sts. Then, inc one st each end of every other row until 66 (68, 72) sts. When piece meas 20 (21, 22)"/51 (53, 56)cm, b.o. all sts.

Shawl Collar

Sew both shoulder seams. With circular needle, beg at lower edge of one side of neck opening, pick up 52 sts along side neck, 26 at back neck, and 52 along other side neck, but none along lower front edge–130 sts in all. Work in 1 x 1 rib for 4"/10cm, b.o. in ribbing. Overlap the two ends and sew to the sweater front.

Finishing

Sew on sleeves. Sew sleeve and side seams. Sew on the buttons placing them about 1"/2.5cm apart at the lower part of the collar. Make thread loops on the loose edge of the collar.

This blend of yarns including rayon chenille is a luxurious mix.

The shaped sleeve cap is not as difficult to design as it may appear; in fact, it is very easy to design a sleeve cap that will fit the sweater's armhole. A little extra planning will be needed to get the sweater to fit the way you want it to, so read through the instructions below, and for the two sweaters that follow—**Winter in Maine** and **Larkspur.**

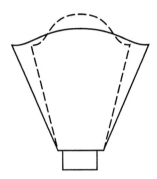

The shape of the sleeve cap is dependent upon the width of the upper sleeve (as demonstrated in the diagram here). A narrow upper sleeve results in a narrow, elongated cap. A wide upper sleeve makes a shorter and wider cap.

The cap of the sleeve is a different shape than the armhole. The armhole is indicated by the dashed line on the diagram accompanying the worksheet (page 207). The very uppermost part of the cap will fit the curve where arm meets shoulder, and the outer sections will be pulled into the curve of the shaped armhole of the sweater front and back pieces. The gaps (seen on the worksheet diagram between armhole and sleeve) show how bulk is reduced in the underarm area as compared to the straight sleeve sweater style.

Shaping the Armhole

The armholes of the front and back pieces of the sweater are indented anywhere from as little as 1" to as much as 3-1/2". Normally, one major decrease is followed by smaller ones to give the indent a rounded shape.

In planning the sweater, be aware of the measurement across the yoke area of the sweater. Stand with your arm at your side and observe the vertical line formed between your body and your arm. Continuing this line up to the shoulder gives the placement of the armhole seam. Measure across from one seam placement to the other, and you will have the width of the yoke. Multiply by the stitch gauge to find the number of stitches across the yoke, and make the armhole decreases accordingly.

Measurement x stitch gauge = number of stitches to knit for upper part of front and back pieces.

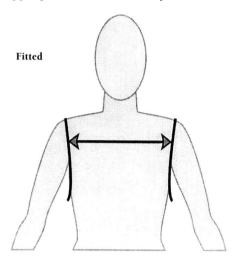

Fitted

Measure to find the width of the upper front and back pieces (yoke area) of the sweater. Sleeves can be fitted closely (above) or loosely (below).

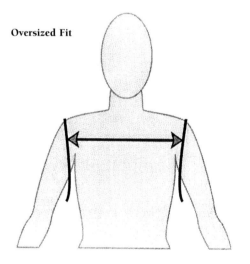

Oversized Fit

Shaping the sleeve cap:

1. You will need tape measure, paper, pencil, and scissors. The paper is for making a pattern; a sheet of newspaper will do, or tape sheets of paper together. First, knit the front and back pieces of the sweater.
2. Sew one shoulder seam and lay the sweater out flat.

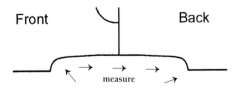

Front   Back

measure

Measure the entire armhole with the tape measure, then add about 1" extra, to make the sleeve cap just slightly larger than the armhole. A small amount of ease should be added to the cap, and when the cap is sewn to the armhole the ease is taken up into the seam.

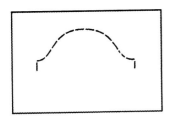

3. Using ⑥ of Measuring for Fit, indicate with the pencil on the paper the width of the upper sleeve. Take the tape measure and arrange it on its side to indicate the shape of a sleeve cap using the same length as determined in Step 2, above. Note how the cap follows a horizontal line at each end, and is rounded at the top. (This can also be done with a piece of string the same length as the measurement determined above. Arrange it as evenly as possible). Using a pencil, sketch along the string or tape measure.
4. Cut out the paper pattern then fold the pattern in half lengthwise to check that the sleeve cap is even from one side to the other. It's not likely to be, so take the scissors and trim it. Re-measure the cap. If you've

trimmed away too much, lay the pattern on another sheet of paper and sketch a new line that evenly adds the amount needed. Cut out the pattern.

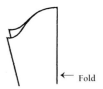

← Fold

5. Knit one sleeve up to the armhole, then shape the sleeve cap following the outline of the paper pattern. * Lay the knitting out flat on the pattern every few rows and bind off stitches as needed to follow the shape. Be sure to make bind offs evenly on both sides of the sleeve (a bind off made at the beginning of a RS row must be followed by an equal one made on the following WS row). B.o. the final sts. Write down the number and frequency of the bind offs, then follow your notes when knitting the second sleeve, OR graph the sleeve cap shaping, then make the second sleeve according to the graph.

When sewing the pieces of the sweater together, ease the sleeve cap into the armhole before sewing sleeve and side seams.

*Note: Since the length of the sleeve cap varies according to the width of the upper sleeve, it may be necessary to check that the length of the sleeve will be as intended. Sew both shoulder seams of sweater front and back, and put it on. Measure from the edge of the shoulder seam down to where the sleeve will end. Measure the sleeve up to the armhole, add the length of the cap and compare. Make any adjustments to the sleeve up to the armhole, then knit the cap.

CAP SLEEVE SWEATER WORKSHEET

Procedure:
    Do the worksheet Measuring for Fit (page 179)
    Choose a yarn and find gauges

stitch gauge = _____

row gauge = _____

① x stitch gauge = _____ stitches to knit for each of back and front.
Subtract 10 percent = _____ stitches for ribbing . . . .

⑥ divided by 2 = _____ "(cm). . . . .
Subtract the result from ② = _____ "(cm).

② minus ④ (depth) = _____ "(cm): Begin neck bind-offs . .

④ (width) x stitch gauge = _____ total of stitches to bind off for neck.

⑤ x stitch gauge = _____ stitches for beginning of sleeve above ribbing. . . . .
Subtract 20 percent = _____ stitches for ribbing.

③ minus ① = _____ "(cm).
Divide the result by 2 = _____ "(cm): Length of sleeve to armhole.

— —— - —— - ——

⑥ x stitch gauge = _____ stitches at armhole.

⑤ x stitch gauge = _____ stitches above ribbing.

Subtract to =   _____ stitches to be increased. Divide by 2 to = _____ total increase rows.

Subtract length of ribbing from sleeve length = _____ x row gauge = _____ total rows.

Divide by 2 = _____ RS rows.

Instructions

needle size for ribbing _____

needle size for body of sweater _____

Back

Cast on this number of stitches using the smaller needle size. Work desired length of ribbing. Change to larger needles, increase to the number of stitches to knit for the back.
Knit this length up to armhole. Work armhole decreases, then knit back to total length of sweater. Bind off all stitches.

Front

Knit the front same as for the back to here. Shape the neckline according to the instructions for your preferred neck style (pages 174 - 175). Work to same length as back and bind off all stitches.

Sleeves

Cast on this number of stitches using the smaller needle size. Work desired length of ribbing. Change to larger needles, increase to the number of stitches to knit for the sleeve.

Compare the increase rows with the total RS rows, and distribute increases evenly on RS rows to top of sleeve, or see Sleeve-increase Methods on page 173. Shape sleeve cap according to instructions on page 204. Make second sleeve the same. See page 175 for finishing the neck. Sew the pieces of the sweater together.

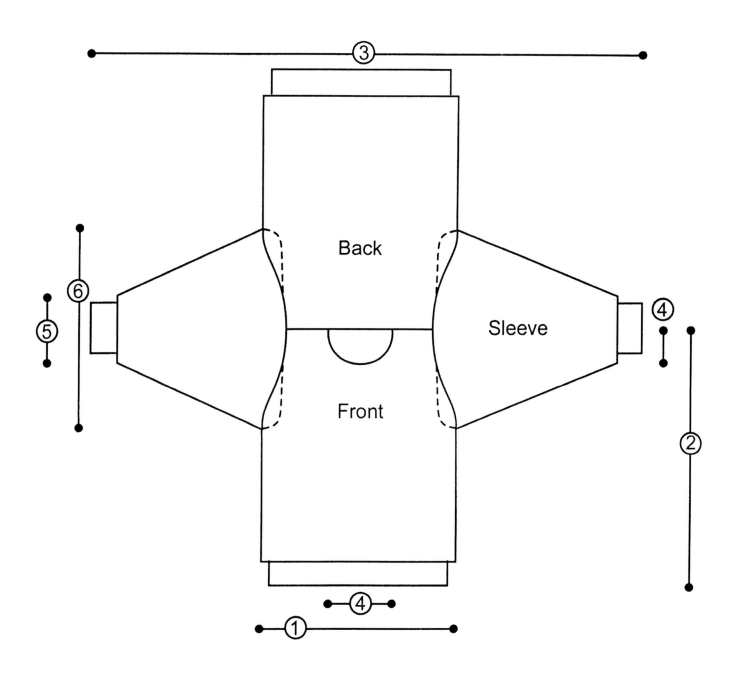

Back

Sleeve

Front

WINTER IN
MAINE

One of my winter bundle-ups, I chose to make this sweater extra roomy (about 16" of ease in the circumference) with extra-long turtleneck and sleeve cuffs. The sleeve cuffs each have a thumb hole. The cap and upper sleeve are wide to have plenty of room to wear a shirt or two underneath. This one is good to wear while shoveling snow!

One way to repeat a color pattern is to mirror the design. Here, the design is mirrored from the bottom of the sweater to the upper area, with a slight variation used in the yoke. A touch of moss stitch occasionally used gives texture to the sweater. A stitch multiple of four is maintained throughout.

Sizes

Small (Medium, Large), with finished circumferences of 46 (50, 54)"/117 (127, 137)cm.

Yarn

Smooth, worsted weight wool in three colors: Cranberry, deep green, and taupe. Substitute with worsted weight wool yarns that obtain the same gauge.

Yardage

Approximately 1500 (1600, 1700) divided between three colors, with a little extra for the ribbing color.

Needles

Sizes 8 and 6.

Gauge

4-3/4 sts and 5-1/2 rows = 1"/2.5 cm over color and st pats using size 8 needles.

This cuff can be worn down over the hand, or folded up to the wrist.

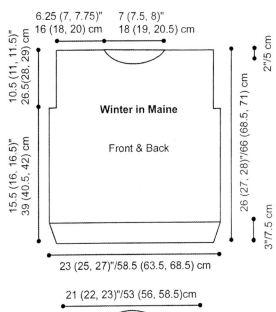

Winter in Maine

Front & Back

6.25 (7, 7.75)" 16 (18, 20) cm

7 (7.5, 8)" 18 (19, 20.5) cm

10.5 (11, 11.5)" 26.5(28, 29) cm

15.5 (16, 16.5)" 39 (40.5, 42) cm

2"/5 cm

26 (27, 28)"/66 (68.5, 71) cm

3"/7.5 cm

23 (25, 27)"/58.5 (63.5, 68.5) cm

21 (22, 23)"/53 (56, 58.5)cm

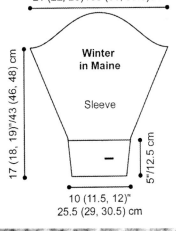

Winter in Maine

Sleeve

17 (18, 19)"/43 (46, 48) cm

5"/12.5 cm

10 (11.5, 12)" 25.5 (29, 30.5) cm

Color and Stitch Key

◢ Dark Red

✖ Dark Green

• Taupe

⊙ P on RS, K on WS

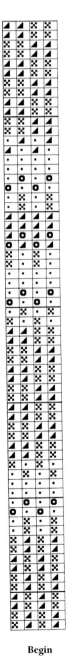

Begin

End

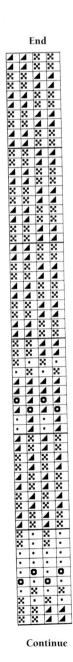

Continue

Instructions

Back

With smaller needles c.o. 98 (106, 114) sts. Work in 1 x 1 rib for 3"/7.5cm. Inc 12 (14, 14) sts evenly across last row—110 (120, 128) sts. Change to larger needles and begin color pat as charted, until 15-1/2 (16, 16-1/2)"/39 (40.5, 42)cm from beg. Shape armhole: (B.o. 4 sts at the beg of next two rows) twice, b.o. one st at the beg of next two rows–92 (102, 110) sts. Work in color pat without incs until piece meas 26 (27, 28)"/66 (68.5, 71) cm, then b.o. all sts.

Front

Work same as back. When piece meas 24 (25, 26)"/61 (63.5, 66)cm, shape neck: Work 33 (37, 41) sts, join a second ball of yarn, b.o. center 26 (28, 28) sts, work to end. Working both sides at once, dec one st at neck edge every row 3 (4, 4) times until 30 (33, 37) sts rem for each shoulder. When piece meas the same as the back, b.o. shoulder sts.

Right Sleeve

With smaller needles c.o. 36 (42, 46) sts. Work in 1 x 1 rib for 2-1/2"/6.5cm. To make thumb hole: On the RS, work 8 sts, b.o. the next four, work to end of row. Next row (WS), work up to bound off sts, c.o. four sts and work to end of row. Work even until cuff meas 5"/12.5cm. Inc 12 sts evenly across last row–48 (54, 58) sts. Change to larger needles and follow chart for color and stitch pats. At the same time inc one st each side of every RS row until 100 (104, 110) sts. Shape sleeve cap following the graph, following the shaping as given for all sizes (larger sizes will have a greater number of stitches to bind off at the top). Work second sleeve the same, but placing the thumb hole at the opposite side of the cuff.

Finishing

Sew one shoulder seam. Pick up 78 (82, 82) sts around neck and work in 1 x 1 rib for 8-1/2"/21.5cm, then b.o. in ribbing. Sew neck and remaining shoulder seam. Sew sleeve caps into armholes. Sew side and sleeve seams.

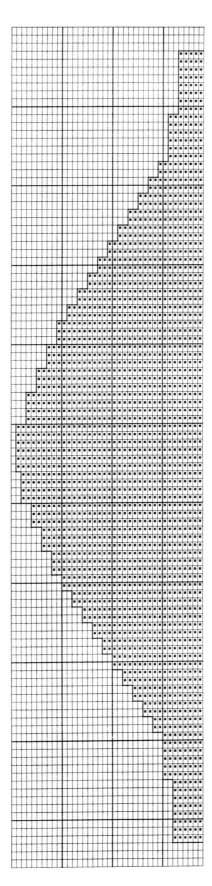

Sleeve cap for Winter in Maine

LARKSPUR

attern stitches show up sculpturally when they are worked in a plain wool yarn, especially when contrasted against the plain surface of the stockinette stitch. The cables, popcorn, and moss stitch panels making up the yoke of this sweater were designed by plotting on graph paper (see Combining Stitch Patterns on page 259). The pattern stitches make for a gauge of fewer stitches per inch than stockinette stitch, so, instead of adjusting the gauge of the pattern stitch yoke, it was used to "draw in" the yoke area, making the cap of the sleeve fit closer to the shoulder than it otherwise would have. The patterned yoke appears on both front and back of the sweater. The deep ribbings of the sweater bottom and sleeves are subtly increased by using three sizes of needles.

Size

Medium only, with a finished circumference of 44"/112cm. To make this sweater in a different size than that given, read through the instructions, then make your adaptations by using the worksheet *Cap Sleeve Sweater* (page 206).

To customize the size of this sweater design, first determine the width of the front/back pieces. Multiply by your stitch gauge, then fit this number of stitches to a ribbing multiple. The bottom ribbing used here is a multiple of 19 stitches. To adjust the width of the ribbing, change the number of ribbed stitches between the cables, thereby changing the multiple. Re-graph the pattern stitches for the yoke to fit the size needed.

Yarn

Smooth worsted weight wool, light blue heather. Substitute with worsted weight wool yarn that obtains the same gauge.

Yardage

1500.

Needles

Sizes 6, 7, and 8.

Gauge

4-1/4 sts and 5-1/2 rows = 1"/2.5cm over St st using size 8 needles.

Ribbing Stitch Pattern

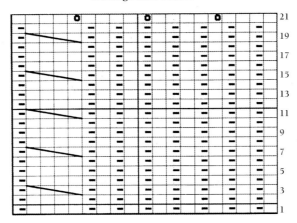

Cable and Bobble Stitch Pattern
rep 8 rows

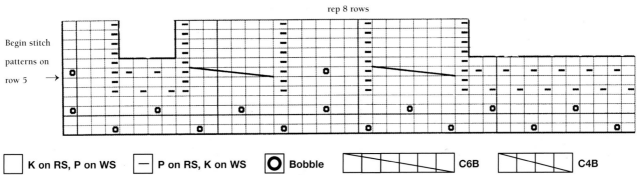

| K on RS, P on WS | — P on RS, K on WS | O Bobble | C6B | C4B |

Instructions

Back

With size 6 needles, c.o. 95 sts. Follow Ribbing st pattern. When ribbing meas 2"/5cm, change to size 7 needles. At 4"/10cm, change to size 8 needles. At 6"/15.5cm and on RS, knit across row making a PC every fifth stitch. P the following row. Work even in St st until piece measures 16"/40.5cm.

Armhole shaping

B.o. four sts at beg of next two rows, then one st at each end of every row three times—81 sts. Next RS row: Begin Cable and Bobble st pat according to graph. Work even in st pat until piece meas 27"/68.5cm, then b.o. all sts.

Front

Work same as back. When piece meas 24-1/2"/62cm, shape neck: Work 27 sts, join a second ball of yarn and b.o. center 27 sts, work to end. Working both sides at once, b.o. one st at each neck edge every other row three times, until 24 sts rem for each shoulder. When piece meas same as back, b.o. all sts.

Sleeves

With size 6 needles, c.o. 44 sts, work in K1 P1 ribbing for 2" (5 cm). Change to size 7 needles and inc one st at beg of row. Inc one st every 1"/2.5cm four more times at alternating ends of rows. At 4"/10cm, change to size 8 needles and work in pat to 6"/15.5cm—48 sts. On the next RS row change to St st and PC every sixth st. Inc one st each end of every RS row until 80 sts. Then inc one st each side of every other RS row until 94 sts. Work even until piece meas 18"/46cm. Follow the graph to knit the sleeve cap.

Finishing

Sew one shoulder seam. Using size 6 needles, pick up 72 sts around neck. Work in 1 x 1 rib for 7"/18cm. B.o. loosely in ribbing. Sew remaining shoulder and neck seam. Sew sleeve caps into armholes. Sew sleeve and side seams.

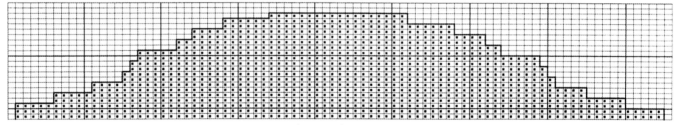

Sleeve cap for Larkspur.

DESIGNING A ONE-PIECE DOLMAN SWEATER

The dolman style is especially suitable for making short-sleeve, waist-length sweaters, while also lending itself to long-sleeve, longer sweaters. The one thing to keep in mind regarding the size of the sweater is that there are no shoulder seams to stabilize the shoulder area, so it could become stretched out of shape if the yarn is too heavy or the sleeves too large and heavy. And, because the fit of the sweater has more to do with drape than with seams following the lines of the body, consider yarns that will enhance the drape—lightweight wools, fine cottons, silks, and mohair are excellent possibilities.

The one-piece format of this style lends itself to many interesting treatments, such as those used in the following two sweaters. Both use mixed gauges, demonstrating how design areas can be incorporated into parts of a sweater. To knit a simple, basic dolman sweater, follow the *One-Piece Dolman Sweater* worksheet (page 216).

There are two ways to design a dolman sweater. One is to do all of the calculations and then knit according to the numbers. The other is to make a paper pattern using the basic dimensions, and then knit to follow the shape of the pattern. Do whichever is easiest for you after reading through the instructions below. Once you've made one, you will be able to refer to the sweater itself, and use it as a pattern for a next sweater.

To make a paper pattern, use newspaper or tape sheets together and, using pencil and a ruler or yardstick, make the pattern according to the dimensions derived from *Measuring for Fit* (page 179) and the worksheet below.

When doing *Measuring for Fit*, ignore ⑥. For ①, use your body circumference at the bottom of the sweater adding a desired amount of ease.

Use the same number of stitches for the ribbing as for the beginning of the body of the sweater, especially for the front of the sweater. Increasing in this area (in addition to the side increases) can create an unwanted bulge.

When planning the increases along each side of the sweater, and to distribute them evenly, compare the number of RS rows with the stitches to be increased (see the worksheet). These two figures indicate how the increases will be spread over the distance. If the numbers come out equal (for instance 36 increase rows over 36 RS rows), simply increase one stitch at each end of every RS row. Or, if there are 36 increase rows and 72 RS rows, you will work increases on every other RS row.

If the numbers do not come out even, you can look for ways to make them even, such as by making the sweater body shorter or longer, or the widest part of the sweater narrower or wider. You can also work the increases unevenly by skipping an increase row here and there.

If the sleeves are long, there will be many stitches across the full width of the sweater. Use a long, circular needle. You will also need a short circular needle (16"/40.5 cm) to pick up and knit the neckline stitches afterwards.

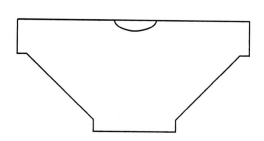
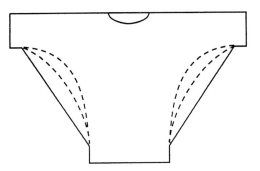

The diagram on the left shows the dolman shape given in the worksheet on the following page. That on the right shows how the length of the sweater and the shapes of the sleeves can be changed to create different styles.

ONE-PIECE DOLMAN SWEATER WORKSHEET

Procedure:
    Do the worksheet Measuring for Fit (page 179)
    Choose a yarn and find gauges

Stitch gauge = _____

Row gauge = _____

Note: To make it easier to calculate the main part of the sweater, body and sleeve ribbings are not included in the calculations below. Use the dimensions inside of the ribbing (keeping the ribbing in mind as part of the total dimensions).

① x stitch gauge = _____ stitches to begin front. ....

② minus 1/2 of ⑤ = _____ "(cm): Sweater length up to beginning of sleeve opening.

Multiply by row gauge = _____ number of rows along which increases will be distributed. Divide by 2 = _____ RS rows.

③ x stitch gauge = _____ stitches at widest part of sweater.

Stitches at ③ minus stitches at ① = _____ stitches to be increased.

Divide by 2 = _____ sts to be increased at each side of sweater. ....

② minus ④ (depth) = _____ "(cm)....................................

④ x stitch gauge = _____ bind offs for neck.

When sweater = ②: At back of neck CO the same number of stitches that were bound off (④ x stitch gauge).

⑤ x stitch gauge = _____ stitches for sleeve ribbing. ....

Instructions

Needle size for body of sweater _____

Needle size for ribbing _____

Front

Cast on this number of stitches using the smaller needle size. Work desired length of ribbing. Change to larger needles.

Knit up to the sleeve opening, distributing increases evenly (see page 173).

Work even up to neck shaping. Shape the neckline according to the instructions for your preferred neck style (pages 174 - 175).

Work even to end of sleeve opening, then begin decreasing to match the increases made for the front of the sweater.

Pick up and knit this number of stitches for the sleeve ribbings. See page 175 for finishing the neck. Sew up the side seams.

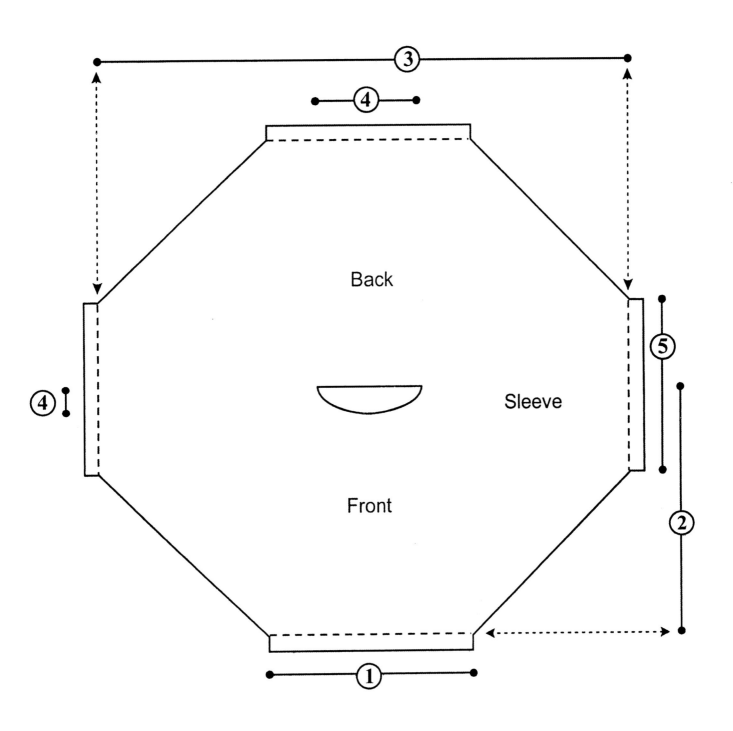

Back

Sleeve

Front

TEA PARTY

The lace panel in this sweater is a simple stitch pattern. The challenge of designing this sweater was in combining stitch patterns that have two different gauges. To do a similar design, make your calculations as best you can—and be prepared to fudge a little when necessary!

The dolman style is readily adaptable to making small sweaters—waist-length and short-sleeved—that are very comfortable to wear. This top fits to about 2"/5cm below the waist. Although here made in wool, try the design in other fibers as well, such as cotton or linen for summer wear, or rayon or silk for dressy occasions.

Size

Medium only, with a finished waistline circumference of 30"/76cm, and length from shoulder of 20"/51cm. To make other sizes, do *Measuring for Fit* (page 179) and the worksheet *One-Piece Dolman Sweater* (page 216). Make the length about 2" below waist, and the sleeve openings the size of your choice. Draw the width of the lace panel onto the worksheet diagram, then figure out how many stitches to knit according to the gauges of the lace stitch and stockinette stitch.

Yarn

A plain sport weight wool in purple. (Feel free to substitute with any sport weight yarn that obtains the same gauge.)

Yardage

860.

Needles

Sizes 6 and 4, 16"/40.5 cm circular needle size 4.

Gauge

4.4 sts and 6-1/2 rows = 1"/2.5 cm over St st, and 4 sts = 1"/2.5cm over lace panel using size 6 needles.

Lace Pattern

(mult of 2)

Row 1: YO, K2 tog.

Row 2: P.

Row 3: K.

Row 4: P. Rep these four rows for pat.

K on RS, P on WS   K 2tog   Yarn Over

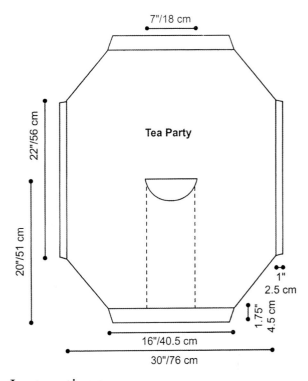

Tea Party

7"/18 cm

22"/56 cm

20"/51 cm

16"/40.5 cm

30"/76 cm

1"
2.5 cm

1.75"
4.5 cm

Instructions

Front

With smaller needles, c.o. 70 sts and work in 1 x 1 rib for 1-3/4"/4.5cm, decreasing two sts within the last WS row–68 sts. On the RS, change to larger needles and set up the pat: 20 sts in St st, lace pattern over 28 sts, 20 sts in St st. P next row. Continue in st pat and inc 1 st each end every RS row–124 sts. Work even for 8"/20.5cm.

Neck shaping

Next row (RS): Work 50 sts, join a second ball of yarn, b.o. center 24 sts, and work in pat to end. Working both sides at once, dec 1 st at neck edge every row 5 times until 45 sts rem for each shoulder. Work even until piece meas 20"/51cm from beg.

Back

C.o. 45 sts at back of neck–135, and work in St st for entire back of sweater. Work shaping as for front, but decreasing instead of increasing. End with 79 sts. Dec nine sts evenly spaced across next row–70 sts. Change to smaller needles and work in 1 x 1 rib for 1-3/4"/4.5cm. B.o. loosely in ribbing.

Finishing

With smaller needles, pick up 98 sts along each sleeve edge and work in 1 x 1 rib for 1"/2.5cm. With circular needles pick up 104 sts evenly around neck opening and work in 1 x 1 rib for 2"/5cm. Fold neck ribbing 1"/2.5cm to the inside and stitch in place loosely. Sew side seams.

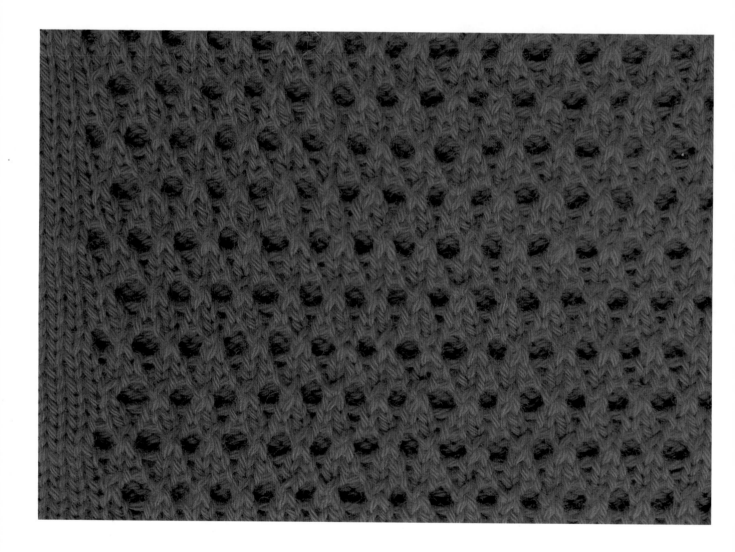

CABLES & DIAMONDS

ot for the faint-hearted, this was a challenging sweater to design for two reasons. First, two different gauges are used, and second, a color pattern is inserted within the stitch pattern in the shoulder area. The color pattern and the stitch pattern each have a different gauge and a different multiple.

Let a project such as this one challenge your knitting knowledge and instincts. The pattern is not written out for this sweater, because you will need to use your own dimensions for the sizing you require, fitting the different parts to it. The diagram of the sweater shown is given here, and you can form your own conclusions from it.

The front and back of the sweater are knitted in one piece that does not include the color pattern sections of the sleeves. Stitches are picked up along the sleeve edges and the color pattern is then worked, centering the design across the number of sts used.

There are several ways to accomplish a similar sweater:

1. Make very careful calculations, paying close attention to gauges and multiples.
2. Make a paper pattern, sketch in the different pattern areas, then knit to fit.
3. Make the sweater in separate pieces and sew them together at the end.

Begin by doing *Measuring for Fit* (page 179) and the worksheet *One-piece Dolman Sweater* (page 216), sketching the color pattern areas into the diagram. Decide how to tackle the project (see 1 through 3, above), and then proceed.

The yarn used here is a worsted weight mohair in pink (A) and rose (B). Needles in size 10 were used for the main parts of the sweater; size 8's were used for the ribbings. The gauges are 4 sts and 7 rows = 1"/2.5cm over the color pattern, and 5 sts and 5-1/2 rows = 1"/2.5cm over the cable pattern on the size 10 needles. The patterns and graphs for the cable and color patterns are given here.

Size

Medium only, with a finished waistline circumference of 32"/81.5cm, and length from shoulder of 20"/51cm.

. . . .

Cable Pattern

(mult of 15)

The cable pattern consists of 9-st plaited cables on a background of St st

Rows 1: and 5: K

Row 2 and all WS rows: P

Row 3: K3, * C6F, K3, K6, * end with K3

Row 7: K3, * C6B, K6, * end with K3

Rep rows 1–8

. . . .

Color Key

⬥ Dark Rose

■ Pink

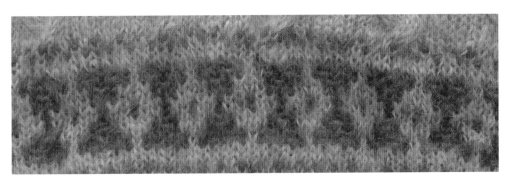

☐ K on RS, P on WS   ⬭ C6F   ⬭ C6B

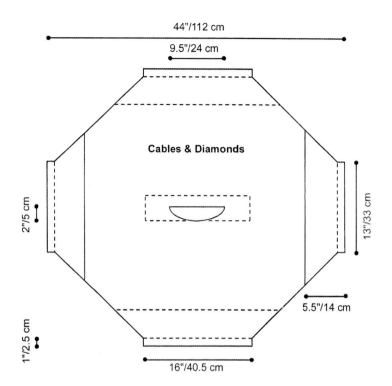

44"/112 cm

9.5"/24 cm

Cables & Diamonds

13"/33 cm

2"/5 cm

5.5"/14 cm

1"/2.5 cm

16"/40.5 cm

Designing a a Raglan Sleeve Sweater

Designing a raglan-sleeved sweater consists of making a sloping upper sleeve fit with the sloping armhole of the sweater body. It is easiest to do this by charting the pieces of the sweater on graph paper. The graph then becomes the pattern to follow as you knit. Refer to the diagram and graph for the **Woolly Bear** sweater on page 228 as an example as you plot your own graph.

Begin by selecting a yarn. Do a gauge swatch and determine needle size(s). Carefully measure for the gauges—both stitch and row gauges must be accurate for the success of the sweater. Do *Measuring for Fit* (page 179), then follow instructions below to graph the sweater pieces.

Use graph paper, or a computer cross-stitch or knitting program. If using graph paper, tape sheets together large enough for the rows (length) and stitches (width) of the back of the sweater. Other pieces, front and sleeves, can be plotted directly onto the graphed back of the sweater.

One square of the graph paper is equal to one stitch, and a row of squares is equal to one row of knitting.

Follow directions given on the worksheet *Raglan Sleeve Sweater* (page 226) to plot the individual parts of the sweater. Make an initial bind-off of 1/2"/1.25cm–1"/2.5cm to both upper sleeve and the beginning of the sweater armhole.

Two major determinants of the fit and style of the raglan sweater are the width of the upper sleeve and the depth of the armhole. The sleeve width is determined by ⑥. To find the depth of the armhole measure up from the bottom of the sweater to where you want the armhole to begin—the armhole can be quite low for an oversize sweater, or up near the armpit for a fitted sweater.

Different slopes fit together because the row count for each piece is the same.

You can design a wide sleeve for a narrow sweater body, or a narrow sleeve for a wide sweater. In other words, the slope of the upper sleeve can be different from that of the sweater body. What is important is that the same number of rows be used for each, as they are sewn together row by row. In the swatches shown here, one slope was made by decreasing on every row, and the other by decreasing on every other row: different slopes, same number of rows, and they fit together perfectly.

Adding a color pattern to the sweater is as easy as adding the design onto the existing graph. Choose a design with a multiple that fits the body of the sweater, or adjust the number of stitches to fit the multiple.

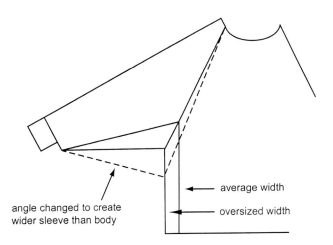

angle changed to create
wider sleeve than body

average width

oversized width

Raglan Sleeve Sweater Worksheet

Procedure:
    Do the worksheet Measuring for Fit (page 179)
    Choose a yarn and find gauges

Stitch gauge = _____

Row gauge = _____

① x stitch gauge = _____ stitches to knit for each of back and front. ....
② minus 1/2 of ④ (depth) = _____ "(cm) x row gauge = _____ rows. ....
④ (width) = _____ "(cm) x stitch gauge = _____ sts at top of sweater. ....
Measure up from the bottom of the sweater to the point where you want the armhole to begin = _____ "(cm) x row gauge = _____ rows. ....
⑥ x stitch gauge = _____ = stitches at widest part of sleeve.

⑤ x stitch gauge = _____ = stitches for beginning of sleeve above ribbing.
③ minus ④ = _____ "(cm) divided by 2 = _____ "(cm):
Length of sleeve up to armhole x row gauge = _____ rows. Subtract, and begin graphing just above the ribbing.

To Knit the Sweater

Follow the graph adding ribbed cuffs: Use 10 percent fewer stitches for back and front ribbings, and 20 percent fewer for sleeve cuffs. Knit the four pieces, then sew sleeves to body leaving one seam unsewn. Pick up stitches around neckline and rib to the length desired. B.o. loosely. Sew all remaining seams.

You will need: graph paper (tape sheets together) or a cross-stitch or knitter's computer program.
    Note: ④ (depth) is the width of the top of the sleeve only, not to the bottom of the neck opening.
Needle size for body of sweater _____

Needle size for ribbing _____

Using the worksheet to graph a sweater

Back

→ Determine the width of the body of the sweater on the graph beginning above the ribbing.
→ Use the row gauge to indicate total length of sweater on the graph.
→ Center the stitches for the top of the sweater on the graph.
→ Graph the slope between beginning of armhole and top of sweater beginning with an initial bind off of about 1/2" to 1".

Front

Determine the shape of the front neck opening, and graph the neck opening onto the graph for the back.

Sleeve

Begin plotting the sleeve on the same graph.
    Center the stitches for ④ (depth) at top of graph.
    The length from armhole to top is the same number of rows as the front and back of the sweater.
    Plot the increases between sleeve bottom and armhole, and the slope of the upper sleeve using the same initial b.o. as for the sweater front and back.

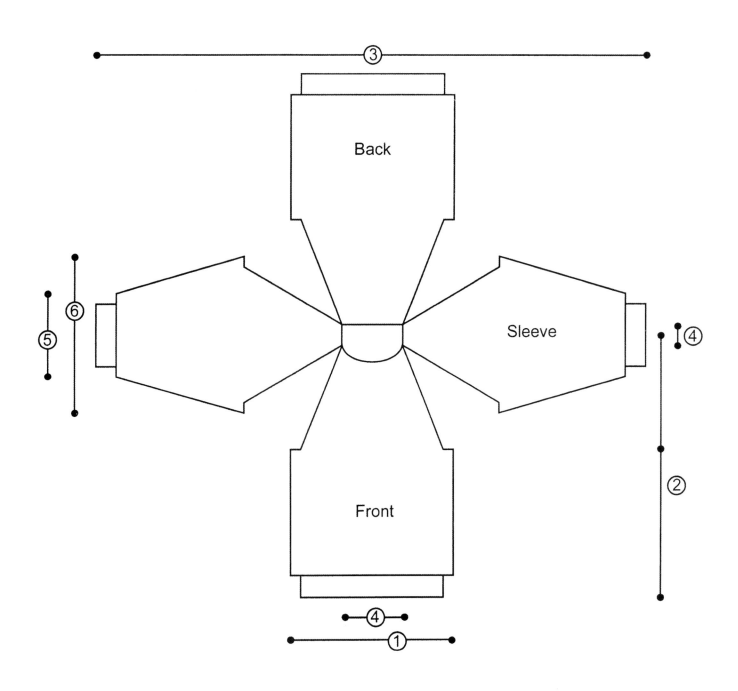

WOOLY
BEAR

This sweater apparently looks as cuddly as it feels, because when I wear it people seem to want to touch it! A variegated mohair yarn makes an interesting background for a subtle color pattern confined to the upper and lower parts of this sweater. The color pattern came about by doodling on graph paper.

Size

Medium only, with a finished circumference of 46"/117cm.

Yarn

Bulky weight mohair, brown variegated, and small amount of denim. Substitute with mohair yarns that obtain the same gauge.

Yardage

850 of main color (MC), small amount of second color (SC).

Needles

Sizes 10 and 8.

Gauge

3-1/2 sts and 4-1/2 rows = 1"/2.5cm over St st using size 10 needles.

Color pattern is a multiple of 6.

Use Raglan Shaping as given on page 173.

Work all selvedge sts, and RS decrease sts in MC.

Instructions

Back

With smaller needles and MC, c.o. 70 sts. Work in 1 x 1 rib for 1-3/4"/4cm ending on a WS row. Next row (RS): Change to larger needles and work in St st and SC, and inc 8 sts evenly spaced across row—78 sts. Begin color pat on following RS row according to chart. Complete color pat then work even until piece measures 13-1/2"/34cm, then follow graph working raglan shaping and color pat to top. B.o. all remaining sts.

Front

Work same as back until piece measures 24-1/4"/61.5cm. Shape neck: work up to b.o.'s on graph, b.o. center sts, fasten on a second ball of yarn for each color, then work to end of row. Working both sides at once,

follow the graph for shaping and color pat. B.o. remaining sts.

Sleeves

With smaller needles and MC c.o. 26 sts. Work in 1 x 1 rib for 2-1/2"/6.5cm ending with a WS row. Next row (RS), change to larger needles and St st and SC, increasing 2 sts evenly spaced—28 sts. Begin color pat on following RS row. Follow chart working color pattern and sleeve shaping to top of sleeve. B.o. remaining sts.

Finishing

Sew 3 of the 4 raglan seams. Using smaller needles, pick up 76 sts around neckline and work in 1 x 1 rib for 3". Bind off loosely. Sew remaining raglan seam and neck seam. Fold neck 1-1/2"/4cm to the inside and stitch loosely. Sew sleeve and side seams.

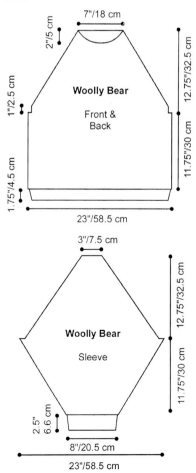

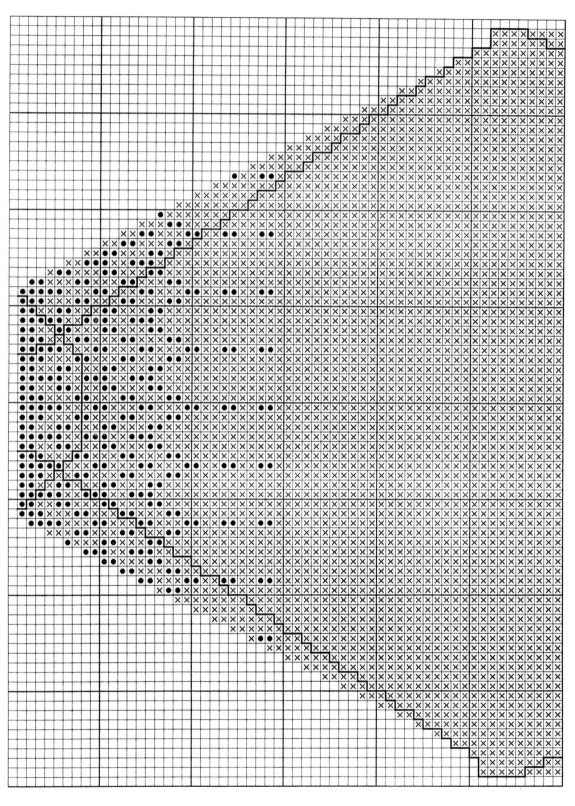

(Continuation of pattern on page 231; attach here)

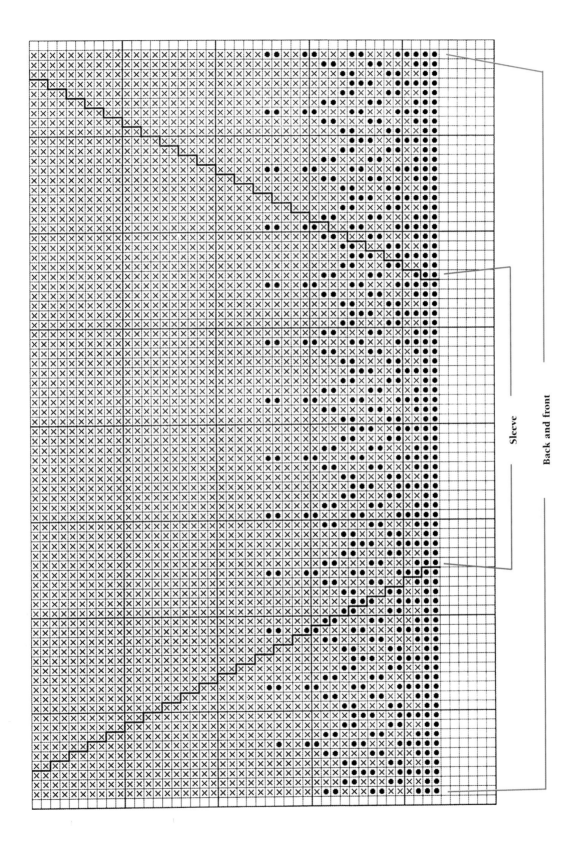

Sleeve

Back and front

DESIGNING FOR COLOR-WORKING

Fair Isle is a method of knitting with two or more colors in which yarns not in use are carried along the back of the work. Normally, only two colors are used in one row, and both hands are used to carry the yarns so the knitting can proceed quickly. It is easy to develop simple, geometric color patterns, either in the knitting, or on graph paper. This is a great way to use up leftover yarns. Yarns should be of similar gauges, but can be a mix of types. Experiment by making swatches using some of the color patterns given with the following sweaters. Then try devising some of your own.

Designing for Fair Isle Knitting

Begin with simple geometrics, such as squares, rectangles, and triangles. See the following sweaters for some examples. Designs can be created in the knitting, by doodling on graph paper, or by using a cross-stitch or knitter's computer program.

In each row, keep color areas to a maximum of five stitches per color to avoid long floats.

When planning a sweater, establish a multiple (see Multiples and Stitch Gauges on page 151).

Knit swatches of your ideas in various color combinations to see how the patterns look in different colors. See the following sweaters for some simple pattern ideas to begin with. Assemble several compatible colors and begin to knit a sweater!

Here are some Fair Isle techniques:

• The technique for handling the two yarns consists of holding the main color over the right-hand forefinger, and the secondary color over the left-hand forefinger (reverse for left-handedness). As you knit or purl along, use the appropriate color as needed. Picking up the left-hand yarn with the needle is kind of a "scooping" action, unlike the right forefinger, which wraps the yarn around the needle. Although this technique is a bit of an exercise to learn, once you do learn it, it is possible to knit quickly.

• The color not being knitted is carried along the back of the work and is called a "float." Keep the floats a bit loose—if pulled tight, they will cause the knitted piece to pucker. Keeping the stitches spread out on the needle just after they are knitted can prevent puckering. Knit a few stitches, spread them out, and repeat. (Or, on the other hand, *use* the puckering to create a unique sweater fabric!)

• If floats are long, they can be woven into the knitting. As you knit, hold the next stitch back (away from yourself), and bring the float in front of it, then knit the stitch over the float. Floats should not strand over more than five stitches, or they will make a loopy mess of the back of your knitting and will catch on things when you wear the sweater.

• Where colors are sharply contrasting, it is best to plan that lighter colors only are woven in. Woven-in floats have a tendency to show through.

TWO STEP

A sweater like this one is a good place to begin if you are new to two-color knitting. I've graphed the patterns, but suggest that you try your own creative color changing using two colors and looking for ways to vary the design. Try doing this "in the knitting," rather than on graph paper so you can watch the design develop in the colors.

In making this sweater, I worked out the color patterns while knitting, inventing as I went along. After establishing two sets of color pattern rows (see "Color Pattern 1" and "Color Pattern 2" on the graph), the goal became to see how many different ways they could be used.

Once the patterns are determined they may be mixed, matched, and repeated in various ways. One variation is implicit—substituting color A for color B in each of the color patterns. No matter what you do, you are likely to end up with a harmonious design for your sweater because the basic elements do not change.

Throughout the sweater, after two 2-color rows are worked, two plain rows follow. If you are a beginner to two-color knitting, you will find that using plain rows in a design has its advantages. Working them allows correcting of any mis-gauges that may have occurred in handling the two colors, and gives a brief respite in learning to work with two colors, which of course makes the sweater go faster.

Sizes

Small (Medium, Large), with finished circumferences of 36 (40, 44)".

Yarn

This sweater is made of two specialty yarns, both knitting ribbons. One is a cream-colored cotton/rayon blend, and the other is a blue, 100-percent rayon. Both are worsted weight. Substitute with any two worsted weight yarns that obtain the same gauge.

Yardage

988 (1097, 1208) divided between two colors.

Needles

Sizes 8 and 4.

Gauge

5 sts and 5-1/2 rows = 1"/2.5cm over color pattern and St st using size 8 needles.

Color pattern is a multiple of four.

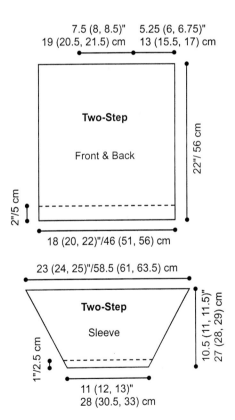

7.5 (8, 8.5)" 5.25 (6, 6.75)"
19 (20.5, 21.5) cm 13 (15.5, 17) cm

Two-Step

Front & Back

22"/ 56 cm

2"/5 cm

18 (20, 22)"/46 (51, 56) cm

23 (24, 25)"/58.5 (61, 63.5) cm

Two-Step

Sleeve

10.5 (11, 11.5)"
27 (28, 29) cm

1"/2.5 cm

11 (12, 13)"
28 (30.5, 33) cm

Instructions

Back

With smaller needles and the lighter color, c.o. 92 (100, 112) sts and work in St st for 2"/5cm ending with a WS row. Change to larger needles and work color pat following chart to top or until 22". B.o. all sts. Make the front same as the back.

Sleeves

With smaller needles and MC, c.o. 56 (60, 64) sts and work in St st for 1"/2.5cm ending with a WS row. Change to larger needles and work color pat following chart. At the same time inc one st each end every RS row until 116 (120, 124) sts. Work even in color pattern until the piece meas 10-1/2 (11, 11-1/2)"/26.5 (28, 29)cm, then b.o. all sts.

Finishing

Sew shoulders. To clean finish edge of neck opening, turn the edge to the inside approx 1/4"/.75cm at center and tapering to nothing at shoulders, stitch in place. Sew on sleeves. Sew sleeve and side seams. Turn 1"/2.5cm of lower edge of back and front to inside and stitch in place loosely. Turn 1/2"/1.25cm of lower edge of sleeves to inside and stitch.

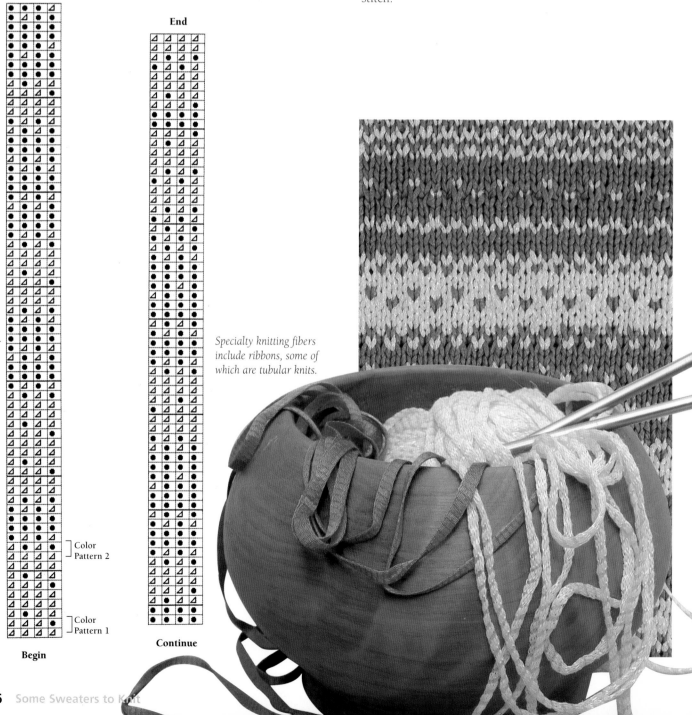

Specialty knitting fibers include ribbons, some of which are tubular knits.

SCRAP
BAG
MEDLEY

esigned in the knitting, my objective was to not repeat any of the color-working. I was happy to get to the top of the sweater because I found myself running out of ideas! This sweater is made of plain knitting wools plus a blue mohair. It is a scrap bag sweater (made of leftover yarns), and a favorite because it fits comfortably. I like how the design and the colors—teal, burgundy, blue, and taupe—came together.

The color pattern, too, is a "scrap bag" of multiples. As it was designed while knitting, I did not become concerned about how many different multiples surfaced. If the color pattern had been graphed first, the design would have been adjusted to fit one or two. Allow yourself a sense of artistic license in knitting a similar sweater. You can try re-graphing this color pattern, or try ad-libbing one of your own in the knitting.

Yarn

Use any worsted weight wool yarns that obtain the same gauge (one can be mohair), four colors.

Tip:

Save your leftovers from knitting projects. Small bits of colors can be used in color-worked designs as accents with larger amounts making up the bulk of the colors. Select colors that work well with each other.

Size

Medium only, with a finished circumference of 45"/112cm.

Needles

Sizes 8 and 6.

Gauge

Four sts and five rows = 1"/2.5cm over color pattern and St st using size 8 needles.

Color Key

◣	Cranberry
✚	Blue
⬚	Taupe
■	Teal

Instructions

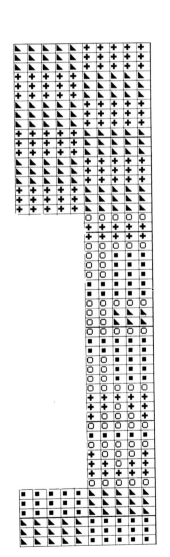

Begin

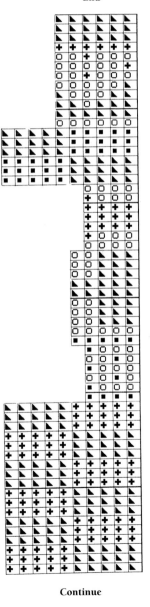

End

Continue

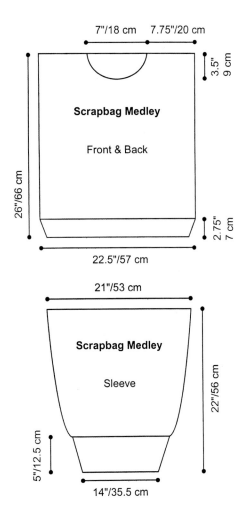

7"/18 cm   7.75"/20 cm

3.5"/9 cm

Scrapbag Medley

Front & Back

26"/66 cm

2.75"/7 cm

22.5"/57 cm

21"/53 cm

Scrapbag Medley

Sleeve

22"/56 cm

5"/12.5 cm

14"/35.5 cm

Back

With smaller needles, c.o. 82 sts. Work in 1 x 1 rib for 2-3/4"/7cm. On the last row, inc eight sts evenly spaced across row–90 sts. Change to larger needles and begin color pat from chart on the next RS row. Work until the piece meas 26"/66cm, then b.o. all sts.

Front

Work same as back. When the piece meas 22-1/2"/57cm, shape neck: Work 34 sts, join a second ball of yarn for each color and b.o. center 22 sts, work to end. Working both sides at once, b.o. 1 st at neck edge every other row three times, until 31 sts remain for each shoulder. When the piece measures the same as for the back, b.o. shoulder sts.

Sleeves

With smaller needles, c.o. 38 sts. Work in 1 x 1 rib for 5"/12.5cm. On the last row, inc 18 sts evenly spaced across row–56 sts. Change to larger needles and begin color pat from chart on the next RS row. At the same time, inc one st each end every fourth row until 84 sts. Work even until the piece meas 22"/56cm, then b.o. all sts.

Finishing

Sew one shoulder. Using size 6 needles, pick up 72 sts evenly around neckline and work in 1 x 1 rib for 8-1/2"/21.5cm, then b.o. loosely in ribbing. Sew rem shoulder and neck seam. Sew on sleeves. Sew sleeve and side seams.

CHECKERED STRIPES

This color patterning is very similar to **Two-Step** (page 234), except that more colors are used. The patternings were designed in the knitting, and are based on a multiple of four.

From the bottom of the sweater to the top, the design does not repeat, and note that the sleeves are not a repeat of the sweater body design. Because the "motif" is simple (1 and 1, 2 and 2, with an occasional plain row), and the colors blend with each other, the sweater as a whole appears neither "busy" nor incoherent.

The accompanying chart gives some, but not all, of the color patterns used. It is best if you make your own decisions regarding which patterns and colors to use. Then you will be able to knit a four-stitch color pattern without needing to carefully follow a chart. It's wonderful to watch a pattern grow as you knit, especially if that pattern is your own.

Yarn

A smooth, sport weight wool in five colors of your choice (taupe, denim, rose, burgundy, light blue are the colors used for the sweater shown) that obtains the same gauge.

Sizes

Small (Medium, Large), with finished circumferences of 34 (38, 42)"/86 (96.5, 106)cm.

Needles

Sizes 6 and 4.

Gauge

5-1/2 sts and rows = 1"/2.5cm over color pat and St st using size 6 needles.

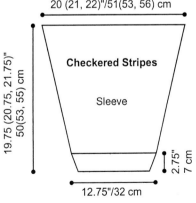

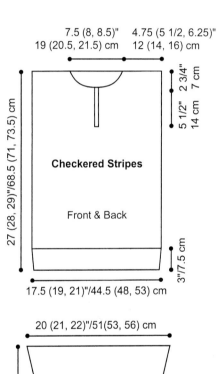

7.5 (8, 8.5)"   4.75 (5 1/2, 6.25)"
19 (20.5, 21.5) cm   12 (14, 16) cm

2 3/4"   7 cm

5 1/2"   14 cm

Checkered Stripes

Front & Back

27 (28, 29)"/68.5 (71, 73.5) cm

3"/7.5 cm

17.5 (19, 21)"/44.5 (48, 53) cm

20 (21, 22)"/51(53, 56) cm

Checkered Stripes

Sleeve

19.75 (20.75, 21.75)"/50(53, 55) cm

2.75"   7 cm

12.75"/32 cm

Color Key

- ☒ Taupe
- ⊙ Cranberry
- ◣ Denim
- · Lt. Blue
- ☐ Rose

End

Continue

Begin

Back

With smaller needles c.o. 86 (94, 104) sts and work in 1 x 1 rib for 3"/7.5cm. Change to larger needles and St st, work one plain row, and inc 10 (10, 12) sts evenly spaced across row–96 (104, 116) sts. On the following row begin working the color pats from chart. Work even in pat until piece meas 27 (28, 29)"/68.5 (71, 73.5)cm, then b.o. all sts.

Front

Work same as back. When the piece measures 18-3/4 (19-3/4, 20-3/4)"/47.5 (50, 53)cm, beg front opening: Work 47 (51, 57) sts, join a second ball of yarn for each color and b.o. center two sts, work to end. Working both sides at once, work even until piece meas 24-1/4 (25-1/4, 26-1/4)"/61.5 (64, 67)cm, then shape neck: B.o. 16 (16, 18) sts at each neck edge, then one st each row five times until 26 (30, 34) sts remain for each shoulder. When the piece meas the same as the back, b.o. shoulder sts.

Sleeves

With smaller needles c.o. 40 sts and work 1 x 1 rib for 2-3/4"/7cm, then change to larger needles and increase 30 sts evenly spaced across the row–70 sts. On the next RS row begin color pat from chart. At the same time, inc one st each end of every fourth row until 110 (116, 122) sts. Work even until sleeve is 19-3/4 (20-3/4, 21-3/4)"/50 (53, 55)cm, then b.o. all sts.

Finishing

Sew both shoulders. Using smaller needles, pick up 100 (100, 104) sts around neck beg and ending at front opening. Work in 1 x 1 rib for 2-1/4"/6cm, then b.o. loosely in ribbing. To finish front opening, work three rows of single crochet around the entire opening, dec at bottom point so sts lie flat. *Or* pick up sts along entire opening, and work in 1 x 1 rib for 3/8"/1cm, dec at the bottom point so sts lie flat, then b.o. in ribbing. Sew on two metal clasps.

FIESTA

A wide-shaped neckline, short front opening which is more decorative than functional, and wide sleeves are the distinguishing details of this sweater—in addition to its bright, happy color patterning. A fancy silver pin somehow seems right for its closure.

The color patterning is repetitive from bottom to top of the sweater, but the colors change with each repeat, and the sleeves repeat a section of the sweater body design. As it was designed in the knitting—and I took my usual artistic license (see **Scrap Bag Medley** on page 238)—the pattern for the actual sweater is slightly different than that given in the chart. The charted one is a multiple of five throughout.

Yarn

Smooth sport weight wool in the colors of your choice (rust, fuchsia, purple, gray, and loden green are the colors used for the sweater shown) that obtain the same gauge.

Sizes

Small (Medium, Large), with finished circumferences of 42 (46, 50)".

Needles

Sizes 5 and 3.

Gauge

Six sts and seven rows = 1"/5cm over color pat and St st on size 5 needles.

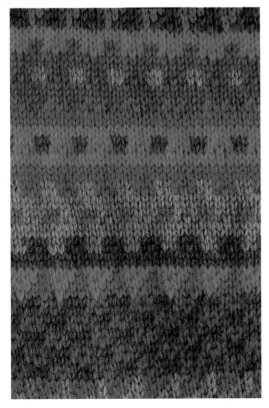

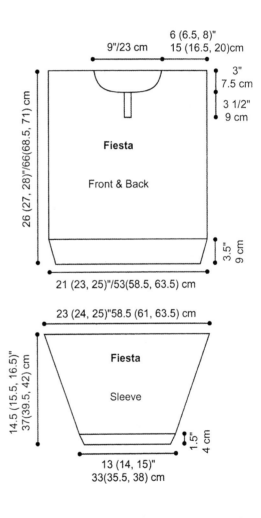

Color Key

◣ Moss

◆ Purple

☐ Fuschia

▨ Rust

▪ Grey

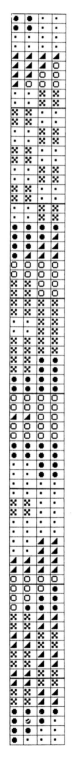

Begin

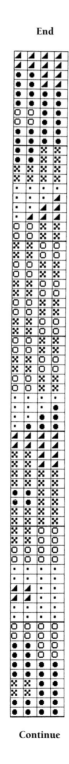

End

Continue

Instructions

Back

With smaller needles, c.o. 112 (120, 135) sts. Work in 1 x 1 rib for 3-1/2"/9cm. On the last row, inc 13 (15, 15) sts evenly spaced across row–125 (135, 150) sts. Change to larger needles and begin color pat from chart. Work even until the piece meas 26 (27, 28)"/66 (68.5, 71)cm, then b.o. all sts.

Front

Work same as back. When the piece meas 19-1/2 (20-1/2, 21-1/2)"/49.5 (52, 54.5)cm, beg front opening: Work 59 (64, 71) sts, join a second ball of yarn for each color, and b.o. 7 (7, 8) sts, work to end. Working both sides at once, work even until the piece meas 23 (24, 25)"/58.5 (61, 63.5)cm. At beg of next row inc 0 (0, 1) sts, and beg neck shaping: B.o. 6 sts at each side of neck opening every other row four times, until 35 (40, 48) sts rem for each shoulder. Work even until the piece measures same as back, then b.o. shoulder sts.

Sleeves

With smaller needles, c.o. 70 (76, 80) sts. Work in 1 x 1 rib for 1-1/2"/4cm. On the last row, inc 10 sts evenly spaced across row–78 (84, 90) sts. Change to larger needles and begin color pat from chart and at same time inc one st each end every other row for 3"/7.5cm, then every fourth row until 138 (144, 150) sts. When the piece meas 14-1/2 (15-1/2, 16-1/2)"/37 (39, 42)cm, b.o. all sts.

Finishing

With smaller needles, along one side of front opening pick up 21 sts and work in 1 x 1 rib for 1"/2.5cm, then b.o. in ribbing. Rep for other side of opening. Fold ribbing to inside and loosely stitch in place. Stitch bottom edges in place.

Neckband

Pick up 144 sts around neck opening including upper edges of opening ribs. Work in 1 x 1 rib for 1"/2.5cm, then b.o. loosely. Fold to back and hem in place. Sew on a metal clasp, or use a fancy pin to close the opening.

PLANNING A FRONT OPENING

It's sometimes nice to have a sweater that opens—if you are getting too warm, for instance, or to wear it partly open—or not "on" at all, but as a shoulder wrap.

A front opening can be added to any style of sweater.

A front opening can be centered or not, full-length or partial (placket). Decide where on the front you want it, then apportion the front sts accordingly.

The convention for a man's sweater is to put the buttonholes on the left, and for a woman's on the right—but this is *only* a tradition; I pay no attention to it and do most of my buttoned sweaters with the buttons on the "man's" side.

Button bands are commonly worked in K/P ribbing, but bands can also be made in garter, seed, or other stitches. Use needles two sizes smaller than those used for the main parts of the sweater to help ensure a firmer edge.

Here are three ways to add a band to a sweater:

- Knit the bands separately and sew them on. Cast on the number of stitches needed for the width of the band, and knit to the length required. The bands can be sewn on as they are being knitted (see **Autumn Tones** on page 254).
- Knit the bands onto the sweater by picking up and knitting along the sweater's edge. Use a long circular needle if necessary. Knit to the width of the band, then bind off loosely.
- Knit the band along with the fronts of the sweater. This method uses the same needle size as for the body of the sweater and will lack the firmness that it would have if knitted on a smaller needle size.

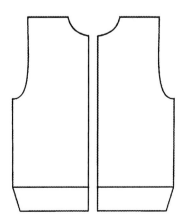

The calculations for the width of the button band in planning a sweater are as follows. You need to know the width of the sweater (①) of *Measuring for Fit*).

Decide on the width of the button band.

① minus width of band = _____ "(cm) x stitch gauge for the sweater = _____ stitches.

Distribute the stitches evenly on either side of the opening.

Make the button band first. If it is made separately, sew it onto the sweater front. Sew the buttons onto the band. Then knit the buttonhole band, making the buttonholes to match the placements of the buttons.

Before beginning the buttonhole band, have the buttons handy. Make a swatch of the band and work a buttonhole in it to find the right size opening. Depending on the size of the button, bind off the center one, two or three stitches, and work to the end. On the next row cast on the same number of stitches above those bound off, and continue to knit the band.

Here are some ideas to consider if you wish to try using button bands creatively. To design bands such as these it may be easiest to either graph the sweater or make a paper pattern to follow as you knit. Since these bands may be purely decorative, make sure the neckline allows the sweater to be put on and off over the head. (The centered band is on the back of the sweater.)

RUSSIAN
JACKET

The opening of this sweater was moved over to one side of the neck. The turtleneck can be worn open as a collar, or buttoned up. Sleeves knitted plainly in stockinette stitch contrast with the pattern stitch of the body of the sweater.

This is the first sweater I ever designed. It is made of a beautiful worsted weight wool yarn that began as a natural color, and was hand-dyed by my mother who, at the time, was beginning her exploration of spinning, dyeing, and weaving.

I had knitted a natural-colored wool sweater to be used as a store model at the yarn shop where I was employed. Like most sweaters that derived from commercial patterns of the time, the sleeves were way too tight, making the sweater uncomfortable and unwearable. The sweater nevertheless spent some time on display, after which I took it home, promptly ripped it out, and then sent the yarn to mom. When she sent it back, I was overjoyed to see the beautiful color it had become. Inspired to do something sensational with it, I soon abandoned my collection of knitting patterns, and began swatching to find a stitch pattern. With a vague idea in mind of making a side-buttoned sweater, the stitch pattern of choice soon made itself known, and the sweater came together with only a few rip-outs along the way. It has been one of my favorites ever since. Like a true classic, it never goes out of style.

With a stitch pattern like this one, the size of the sweater must be adapted to fit the repeats (instead of having the repeats adapt to a shape and size). Establish the number of repeats for the back. For the fronts, subtract one repeat for the button bands, and divide the remainder across the front.

Size

Medium only, with a finished circumference of 44-1/2"/113cm.

Yarn

A smooth worsted weight, high quality, resilient wool that obtains the same gauge.

Yardage

1800.

Buttons

9 buttons, 3/4"/2cm.

Needles

Sizes 8 and 6; cable needle.

Gauge

4-1/2 sts and 5-1/2 rows = 1"/2.5cm over St st, and 11 sts = 1-3/4"/4.5cm over 1 rep of pat st using size 8 needles.

The sweater back is 13 repeats of the pat, the right front is eight, the left front is four.

Instructions

Back

With smaller needles, c.o. 128 sts. Work in 1 x 1 rib for 2-1/2"/6.5cm, ending with a RS row. Next row (WS), change to larger needles, P, and inc 15 sts evenly spaced across row–143 sts. On next row begin the pat st and work even until the piece meas 20"/51 cm, then b.o. all sts.

Right Front

With smaller needles, c.o. 80 sts. Work same as Back, inc eight sts when changing to larger needles–88 sts. Work even until piece meas 8"/20.5cm. Shape neck: On a RS row (neck edge), b.o. 22 sts, then one st every row eight times until 44 sts rem for shoulder. Work even until the piece meas 20"/51cm, then b.o. all sts.

Left Front

With smaller needles, c.o. 40 sts. Work same as Back, increasing four sts when changing to larger needles–44 sts. Work even until the piece meas 20"/51cm, then b.o. all sts.

Sleeves

With smaller needles, c.o. 36 sts. Work in 1 x 1 rib for 2-1/2"/6.5cm, ending with a RS row. Next row (WS) change to larger needles, P, and inc four sts evenly spaced across row–40 sts. Working in St st, inc one st each end every third row until 98 sts. When the piece measures 19"/48cm, b.o. all sts

Turtleneck

Sew both shoulder seams. With smaller needles, pick up 92 sts evenly spaced around neckline including 1-1/2"/4cm along upper edge of left front. Work in 1 x 1 rib for 6-1/2"/16.5cm, then b.o. loosely in ribbing. Sew on sleeves, and sew sleeve and side seams.

Button Bands

With size 6 needles, c.o. eight sts and work in 1 x 1 rib for length of left front opening. Sew the band on. Sew on buttons beginning 3/4"/2cm from lower edge, the next one even with the top of the ribbed cuff, and the top button 3-1/2"/9cm down from the top, the next one 5-1/2"/14cm down, and the remainder evenly-spaced. Knit the second band, placing a buttonhole at each button placement. To knit the buttonhole, b.o. off the center two sts, and on the following row c.o. two at the center. Sew band to right front.

AUTUMN
TONES

Have you ever wanted a casual cardigan to toss on as you walk out the door? This easy-going style features a deep v-neck and fold-back sleeve cuffs. The narrow stripe in the ribbed cuffs is a decorative touch. Knitted in stockinette stitch with its colors used in wide stripes makes for a design that is easy to knit. It is a straight-sleeve style in which the sleeves are set into a slightly indented armhole.

This sweater was made of a palette of colors brought together by a common thread. Two different yarns are held together throughout, one is a sport weight in five shades, and the other a fingering weight in dark red. The finer, dark red yarn has the effect of deepening and enriching the colors of the sport weight yarns, while it blends the whole palette together. One of the blended colors was chosen for the sleeves of the sweater.

Try doing a similar sweater using colors of your own choice, blended throughout with one common color.

Sizes

Small (Medium, Large), with finished circumferences of 46 (50, 54)"/117 (127, 137)cm.

Yarn

One strand of wool sport weight yarn (in gray, purple, fuchsia, rust, and dark green) held together with one strand of wool fingering weight yarn in dark red. Substitute with five colors of a sport weight and a fingering weight wool yarn that together obtain the same gauge (the colors of your choice).

Yardage

1235 (1400, 1480) of dark red, plus same amount divided between five colors.

Buttons

1/2"/1.25cm wooden buttons, 6.

Needles

Sizes 7 and 5.

Gauge: 4-1/2 sts and 6-1/2 rows = 1"/2.5cm over St st on size 7 needles.

Color Pat for Ribbings

1 x 1 rib with four rows per color in the following sequence: gray, purple, fuchsia, rust, dark green.

Color Pat for Back and Front

10 rows per color following the same sequence as ribbing.

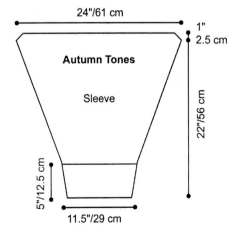

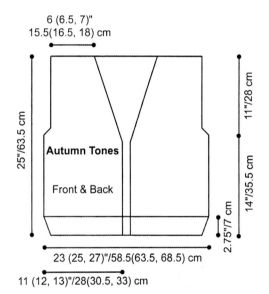

Note: At top of sweater back and fronts, end by knitting only five rows of the final color.

Five colors are each blended with a dark red, creating unity and harmony amongst the colors.

Instructions

Back

With smaller needles, c.o. 94 (100, 110) sts. Work in 1 x 1 rib following color pat for the ribbings, and inc 10 (12, 12) sts across the last row–104 (112, 122) sts. Next row (RS), change to larger needles, St st, and first color of color pat for back and front. Work even until the piece meas 14"/35.5cm.

Armhole Decreases

Dec one st each end of every row six times until 92 (100, 110) sts rem. Work even until piece measures 25"/63.5cm. B.o. all sts.

Fronts

With smaller needles, c.o. 46 (50, 54) sts. Work in 1 x 1 rib following color pat for the ribbings, and inc four sts across the last row 50 (54, 58) sts. Next row (RS), change to larger needles, St st, and first color of color pat for back and front. Work even until piece meas 13-1/2"/34cm. Beg neckline shaping: Dec one st at end of every fourth row. At the same time: When piece measures 14"/35.5 cm, beg armhole shaping: dec one st beg of every row six times. When 27 (29, 31) sts remain, work even until piece meas 25"/63.5cm. B.o. all sts. Work remaining front reversing the shapings.

Sleeves

With smaller needles, c.o. 46 sts. Work in 1 x 1 rib following color pat for the ribbings twice (making sleeve cuffs twice as long as for sweater body), and inc six sts across the last row–52 sts. Next row (RS), change to larger needles, St st, and sleeve color. Inc one st each end of every fourth row until 108 sts. Work even until piece meas 22"/56cm, then beg armhole shaping: Dec one st each end every row six times (12 sts decreased). When piece meas 23"/58.5cm, b.o. all sts.

Finishing

Sew shoulder seams. Sew on sleeves. Sew side seams.

Button band

With smaller needles, c.o. 8 sts. Work in 1 x 1 rib for about 10"/25.5cm. Leave sts on needle and begin sewing the ribbing to the sweater beginning at one lower front edge. For a woman's sweater, begin sewing to the left front. For a man's sweater, begin sewing to the right front. Continue to knit and sew, stretching the rib slightly at the back neck. Sew the buttons onto the band, placing the bottom button 3/4"/2cm up from lower edge, and the top button at beg of neckline shaping, and spacing remaining buttons between. Make buttonholes to match button placements while continuing to knit and sew on the ribbing. To make buttonholes, b.o. center two sts on one row, and c.o. two at the center of following row.

PICK UP AND KNIT

With this technique, you can add new knitting to an existing knitted piece. It is most often used for adding neckbands, turtlenecks, other neckline treatments, and button bands. Once you get to know it, you will find it marvelously flexible for other uses as well. Here are some ways this technique can come in handy:

- If you are unsure about how many stitches to use for the bottom and sleeve cuffs of a sweater, leave them for last. Before the sweater is sewn together, pick up and knit the ribbings. Then, if the cuffs are not right, they can easily be taken out and done over.
- Like the sweater, **Trompe L'Oeil**, following, it is easy to add sleeves to a short sleeved sweater. In the same way, you can add to the bottom of a sweater to achieve the look of a shorter sweater worn over a longer one. Pick up and knit to the length and shape desired.
- If you are making a straight sleeve sweater, the sleeves can be knitted directly onto the sweater. Knit the front and the back pieces, then sew both shoulder seams. (If you are working the neckband on two needles, sew one shoulder, pick up and knit the neckband, then sew the remaining shoulder.) Pick up the number of stitches needed for the upper sleeve, then knit from the top of the sleeve down to the cuff, reversing all shapings.

Other creative uses may also be found; for instance, try picking up and knitting stitches anywhere on a sweater for any special effects that you can imagine.

Directions for Picking Up Stitches

Measure the edge or area where stitches will be picked up, multiply by the stitch gauge, and pick up that number of stitches. If picking up to knit a ribbing, use the smaller needles as required for the sweater.

Note: Reverse the following directions if you are left-handed.

Working from right to left and using one knitting needle, insert the needle through the knitting, wrap the yarn around the needle and pull through. Repeat to pick up the number of stitches needed. Normally, the needle is inserted through two loops at the edge of the knitting.

When picking up for neckbands and other edgings, have the right side of the work facing you so you can easily see how and where to pick up a loop. The first row of knitting, then, will be a wrong side row.

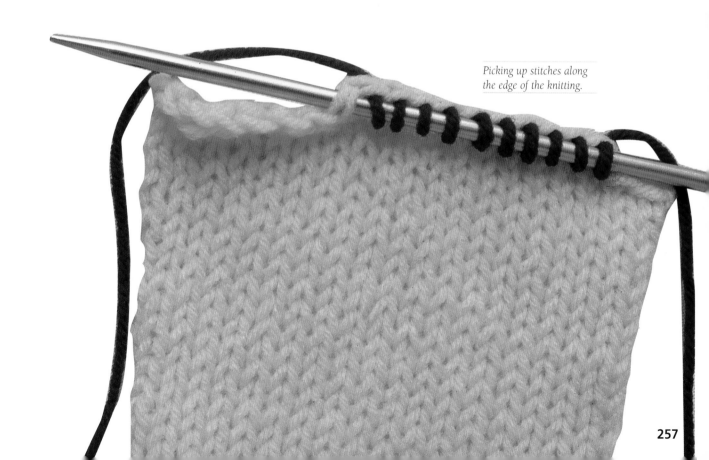

Picking up stitches along the edge of the knitting.

TROMPE
L'OEIL

The technique of pick-up-and-knit is used here to create the look of one sweater worn over another when it is actually all one piece. This sweater is the same as **Tea Party** on page 218, with long sleeves added. My original idea was to create a sweater set consisting of a short-sleeved, lace-panel dolman top to be worn under a straight-sleeve cardigan. After knitting the one-piece top, I wondered if it would make sense to simply add sleeves to it, saving the knitting of the front and back pieces. So I picked up and knitted one sleeve, sewed the seams and tried it on. It worked out so well I did the second sleeve, and added a mock turtleneck to the sweater.

Working on the wrong side of the sweater, stitches were picked up along the base of the ribbing (where it attaches to the sweater). The side and sleeve seams of the sweater were first taken out so the piece could lie flat.

Yarn, needles, and gauge are the same as for Tea Party, page 218. You'll need approximately 450 yards of yarn.

Sleeve

Pick up 86 stitches on size 6 needles along the base of the sleeve ribbing. Work even for 3/4"/2cm, then dec one st each end every fourth row until 60 sts remain. At 14-3/4", change to size 4 needles and dec 14 sts evenly spaced across row–46 sts. Work in 1 x 1 rib for 2-3/4"/7cm, then b.o. loosely in ribbing. Rep for second sleeve. Sew sleeve and side seams.

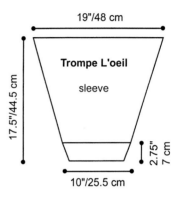

Stitches for the sleeve are picked up at the base of the ribbing so the ribbing stays loose.

COMBINING STITCH PATTERNS

Magical worlds open up once you start working with either stitch patterns or color-working—or both. A kind of language begins to develop among the yarn, yourself, and the stitches. You learn the intricacies of the character of the yarn, and as your knowledge of stitch patterns grows, sometimes you can kind of sense what the yarn wants to do, and will do well. A broad horizon of possibilities opens up as you begin to realize that each combination of yarn, stitch pattern, and sweater shape can be unique and different.

Take your yarn of choice through its paces by trying different patterns in it. Stitch patterns, if chosen well, bring out the best qualities of the yarn. Every yarn shows off patterns differently. Experimenting like this is the only way to find combinations that speak to each other, to the yarn, and to you. Make swatches! The ones you don't use can be taken out and the yarn reused.

First, do *Measuring for Fit* (page 179) and choose a sweater style.

After you have swatched and found several stitch patterns to combine, begin to fit the patterns together. Do this by sketching the shape of the sweater, indicating the placements of the patterns on the sketch. Then determine the width of each of the patterns, adding or subtracting stitches to fit the size of the sweater. You may need to find a separate gauge for each stitch pattern; then work with the gauges to fit the width of the sweater.

It is often easiest to graph the patterns as they will be used on the sweater, adding any neckline and sleeve shaping to the graph. Then, the graph can be used as your pattern for the sweater. If your stitch patterns are intricate, it will be much easier to follow the design if it is graphed.

POLAR
BEAR

B ecause of this sweater, I no longer own a coat. This sweater, with a windbreaker over it, is all I need on the coldest winter days outdoors. Bulky wool yarns make a thick, warm sweater, and a bulky wool sweater is not for the indoors (unless your heating system fails). If you have trouble staying warm in winter, this is the type of sweater to have—wool is an excellent insulator.

Smooth, bulky wool yarns are wonderful for showing off stitch patterns—especially since the stitches are much larger than in finer yarns. A simple cable has a dramatic effect.

Sizes

Small (Medium, Large), with finished circumferences of 44 (48, 52)"/112 (122, 132)cm.

Yarn

A bulky-weight wool with low twist that obtains the same gauge.

Yardage

1100 (1200, 1300).

Buttons

8 metal buttons, 7/8"/2cm, 1 metal clasp.

Needles

Sizes 10-1/2 and 9.

Gauge

Three sts and four rows = 1"/2.5cm over St st and Moss sts, cable panel = 5-3/4"/14.5cm wide using size 10-1/2 needles.

Moss Stitch

Row 1: (multiple of 2) * K1, P1 *

Row 2: * P1, K1 *

Rep these two rows

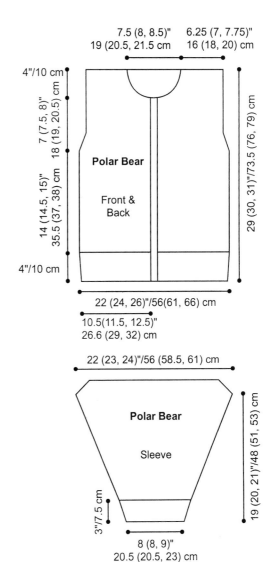

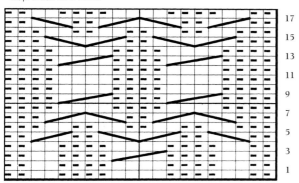

Cable Panel (see graph, left)

(worked on 22 sts)

Row 1: K1, P2, K2, P4, K4, P4, K2, P2, K1

Row 2 and all WS rows: Purl the knit, and knit the purl sts of previous row

Rows 3 and 19: K1, P2, K2, P4, C4B, P4, K2, P2, K1

Row 5: K1, P2, T3F, P2, T3B, T3F, P2, T3B, P2, K1

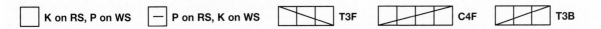

☐ K on RS, P on WS   ⊟ P on RS, K on WS   ⊠ T3F   ▱ C4F   ▱ T3B

Row 7: K1, P3, T3F, T3B, P2, T3F, T3B, P3, K1
Rows 9 and 13: K1, P4, C4B, P4, C4B, P4, K1
Row 11: K1, P4, K4, P4, K4, P4, K1
Row 15: K1, P3, T3B, T3F, P2, T3B, T3F, P3, K1
Row 17: K1, P2, T3B, P2, T3F, T3B, P2, T3F, P2, K1.
Rep rows 1–20

....

Instructions

Back

With smaller needles, c.o. 72 (76, 80) sts. Work in 1 x 1 rib for 4"/10cm, ending with a WS row. Next row (RS), change to larger needles and set up pats as follows: Moss Stitch over 6 (6, 8) sts, Cable Panel over 22 sts, Moss Stitch over 16 (20, 20) sts, Cable Panel over 22 sts, and Moss Stitch over 6 (6, 8) sts. Work even in pats until piece meas 18 (18-1/2, 19)"/46 (47, 48)cm.

Shape Armhole

Dec one st every other row each side four times–68 sts. Work even until piece meas 29 (30, 31)"/73.5 (76, 79)cm, then b.o. all sts.

Left Front

With smaller needles, c.o. 34 (36, 38) sts. Work in 1 x 1 rib for 4"/10 cm, ending with a WS row. Next row (RS): Change to larger needles and set up pats as follows: Moss Stitch over 6 (6, 8) sts, Cable Panel over 22 sts, Moss Stitch over 6 (6, 8) sts. Work even in pats until piece measures 18 (18-1/2, 19)"/46 (47, 48)cm.

Shape Armhole

Dec one st beg of every RS row four times. Work even in pats until piece measures 24"/61cm.

Shape Neck

At the beg of the next WS row, b.o. 5 (5, 7) sts, then dec one st at the beg of each WS row three times. Work even in pats until piece meas 29 (30, 31)"/73.5(76, 79)cm, then b.o. all sts.

Right Front

Make the same as left front, reversing all shapings.

Sleeves

With smaller needles, c.o. 24 (24, 27) sts. Work in 1 x 1 rib for 3"/7.5cm. Change to larger needles and inc each side of every other row until 66 (70, 72) sts. Work even until piece meas 19 (20, 21)"/48 (51, 53)cm.

Shape Armhole

Dec each side of every other row four times–58 (62, 64) sts, then b.o. all stitches.

Button Band

With smaller needles, c.o. six sts. Work in 1 x 1 rib for length of front opening, then b.o. all sts. For a woman's sweater, sew button band to left front of sweater (right front for a man's sweater). Sew on eight buttons, having bottom button 1-1/2"/4cm from bottom of band, and top button 1"/2.5cm from top of band. Space others equally apart.

Buttonhole Band

With smaller needles c.o. six sts. Work in 1 x 1 rib, making a buttonhole at each button placement. To make buttonhole: B.o. center two sts, work to end. On the next row c.o. two sts at center. Sew band to sweater.

Neck

Sew both shoulders. With smaller needles, pick up 60 (60, 64) sts evenly spaced around neck. Work in 1-x-1 rib for 4"/10cm, then b.o. loosely. Fold neck 2"/5cm to the inside and sew loosely. Sew sleeves into armholes. Sew sleeve and side seams. Sew metal clasp to neck of sweater.

Sweaters entered the fashion world but are still practical garments.

DESIGNING A SWEATER IN SECTIONS

Separately knitted, vertical sections can be sewn together to form a sweater. This is an easy way to combine stitch patterns. Simply knit the widths needed to fit within the size limitations of the sweater design.

It is also a good way to use up leftover yarns. Make swatches of yarns of different colors and textures, then sew them together to see how they work together.

Although it is not essential that all gauges be the same, the yarns used should be *similar* in gauge. This is so the sweater fabric will be somewhat coherent.

Unite the scheme by choosing one yarn for all of the ribbings or edgings. Although any of the sweater styles can be used, the straight-sleeve style is easiest because less shaping is needed.

Instructions for Combining Sections

1. After doing Measuring for Fit, sketch a diagram of the sweater shape. The sweater can be made in one large piece as **Cozy Cables** (page 264). Or, you can make separate front and back pieces.

2. Pick a strategy for making sure all the parts will fit together. A full-size paper pattern is one way. Using newspaper, make a pattern the size indicated by your diagram. Another way is to measure, and keep measuring as you make the pieces. Either way, you will need to lay the pieces out on a flat surface as they are knitted to see how they will go together.

3. Make swatches of the pattern stitches you want to use, and plan the widths of the different sections of the sweater to fit together within the diagram or pattern.

4. Knit the pieces to make up the front and back of the sweater. When knitting the front sections, remember to do the neck shaping. (See Neckline Styles on pages 174 - 175.)

5. When the front and back pieces are completed, sew the pieces together at the shoulders and try it on to check the fit. Make any necessary adjustments.

6. Knit the sleeves by combining sections as for the sweater body, or use a plain stitch such as stockinette, knitting each as one piece. Sew on the sleeves.

7. Pick up and knit where ribbings are needed: bottom, sleeves, front openings, and neckline, making the ribbings the length desired. Sew any remaining seams.

Work up swatches of different patterns to find several that will work together.

COZY
CABLES

This is my winter computing sweater, designed for sitting at the computer when I'm not active enough to stay warm. There are thumb holes in the extra-long sleeve cuffs so I can type (almost like gloves without the fingers). The turtleneck is also made extra long so when it is unrolled it covers up to my eyes keeping my nose warm. The sweater is long, and is buttoned so it can be opened in stages as I slowly warm up on a chilly day.

This is a "creative project," so specific instructions are not given except for the diagram. Follow instructions for designing a sweater in sections, adapting the design to your own needs and ideas.

The sweater shown here consists of four cable panels and five bobble insertions. The sleeves are in plain stockinette stitch. Ribbings are made a little more snugly than usual, are extra long, and contain thumb holes in the sleeve cuffs (for thumb hole instructions, see **Winter in Maine** on page 208). Two worsted weight yarns are used, a heather wool for the cable panels, and a navy wool for the bobble insertions and ribbings. Thirteen 3/4" buttons were needed.

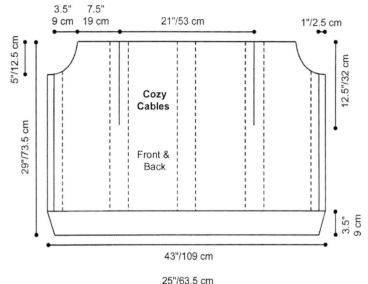

Bobble Insertion.

(CO 5 sts.)

Row 1: P2, B, P2

Row 2: K

Row 3: P

Row 4: K

Rep these 4 rows for pat

Cable Panel (see below)

CO 44 sts.

Row 1: K2, P2, C2B, P1, K4, P1, C2B, P2, K12, P2, C2B, P1, K4, P1, C2B, P2, K2

Row 2 and all WS rows: P the K, and K the P sts of prev row

Row 3: K2, P2, C2B, P1, C4F, P1, C2B, P2, C6F, C6B, P2, C2B, P1, C4F, P1, C2B, P2, K2

Rep these four rows for pat

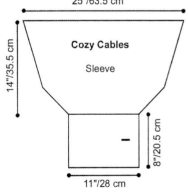

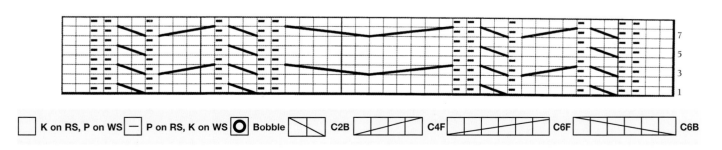

DESIGNS FOR VESTS AND TOPS

A vest in its simplest form is a sweater without sleeves. Like a sweater, a vest can be made to fit closely or loosely. The cap-sleeve sweater style is the one to use to make a fitted vest because of the shaped armhole. Use the straight-sleeve sweater style to make an extended shoulder vest or a short-sleeve top. The dolman style is ideal for short-sleeve summer tops.

The armhole of a vest should be generous enough for a shirt to be worn underneath, but that of a top should be more closely fitted. Allow for any edge finish that will be added to the armhole—a ribbing or other edge stitch will extend the shoulder line and "shrink" the size of the armhole opening. Make these adjustments when doing the *Measuring for Fit* worksheet (page 179).

To Knit a Vest or Top

Knit the back and front pieces. Sew one shoulder. Pick up stitches along the neckline to knit the neck edging in ribbing or the stitch of your choice. Sew the remaining shoulder seam and neck edging. Pick up stitches along one armhole and knit the edging. Repeat for the second armhole. Sew the side seams.

As you would for a sweater, make the following decisions:

- Choose a neckline style:
  Boat neck
  Rounded
  Square
  V-shaped

- Use any armhole shaping from:
  None
  To deeply-shaped

- Have a front opening:
  Or not

- Finish edges with:
  Ribbing, stockinette stitch (curled),
  Garter or other non-curling stitch,
  Hems

- Make the vest:
  Long (tunic),
  Short (waist or shorter)
  Or in-between

- Use a yarn that is:
  Fancy and textured, plain
  Or your creation

- Choose from:
  A pattern stitch,
  Color-working,
  Or plain stitch.

BOUCLE VEST

A vest in a plain style—in this case an oversized pullover with scooped neckline—makes a quick and easy project. It is knitted of a stylish, loopy mohair yarn (also called "boucle"), so textured it would be nearly impossible to follow the stitches if anything other than a plain stitch pattern were used. The reverse stockinette stitch was chosen because it has the effect of enhancing the loopiness of the yarn, with stockinette stitch to make the curled edgings.

Sizes

Small (Medium, Large), with finished circumferences of 38 (42, 46)"/96.5 (106, 117)cm.

Yarn

Loopy mohair (boucle) yarn in a worsted gauge.

Yardage

550 (650, 750).

Needles

Sizes 8 and 5.

Gauge

Four sts = 1"/2.5cm over St st using size 8 needles.

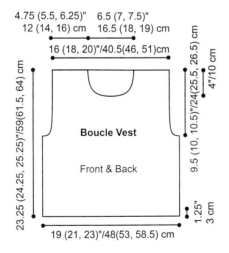

4.75 (5.5, 6.25)" 6.5 (7, 7.5)"
12 (14, 16) cm 16.5 (18, 19) cm

16 (18, 20)"/40.5(46, 51)cm

9.5 (10, 10.5)"/24(25.5, 26.5) cm

4"/10 cm

23.25 (24.25, 25.25)"/59(61.5, 64) cm

Boucle Vest

Front & Back

1.25"
3 cm

19 (21, 23)"/48(53, 58.5) cm

Back

With smaller needles, loosely c.o. 68 (76, 82) sts. Work in St st for 1-1/4"/3cm. Change to larger needles, begin RS and inc 8 (8, 10) sts evenly spaced across row–76 (84, 92) sts. Work even until piece meas 12-1/2 (13, 13-1/2)"/32 (33, 34)cm, then work armhole bind offs: B.o. four sts at the beg of next two rows, then one st each side every other row–64 (72, 80) sts remain. Work even until piece meas 23-1/4 (24-1/4, 25-1/4)"/59 (61.5, 64)cm, then and b.o. all sts.

Front

Work same as back until piece meas 19-1/4 (20-1/4, 21-1/4)"/49(51.5, 54)cm. Shape neck: Work 29 (33, 37) sts, join a second ball of yarn and b.o. center 18 sts, work to end. Working both sides at once, b.o. one st at neck edge every other row until 19 (22, 25) sts remain for each shoulder. When piece meas same as back, b.o. shoulder sts.

Finishing

Sew one shoulder seam. With smaller needles, pick up 74 (80, 84) sts around neck: 26 (32, 36) along the back neck, 15 along each side, and 18 along the front. Work 1-1/2"/4cm in St st, then b.o. loosely. Sew remaining shoulder seam. With smaller needles pick up 76 (80, 84) sts along one armhole. Work in St st for 1-1/4"/3cm, then b.o. Rep for other armhole. Sew side seams.

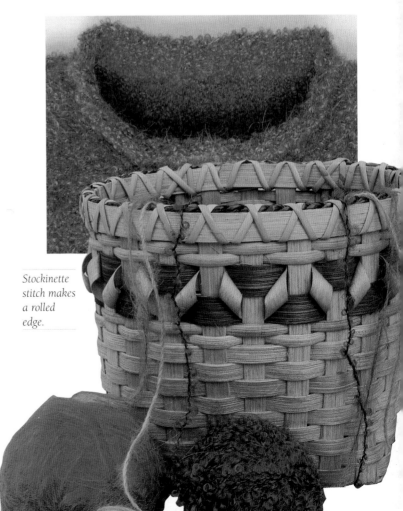

Stockinette stitch makes a rolled edge.

APPENDIX

MEASURING FOR FIT WORKSHEET

Fill out the information on this form for each sweater you design. Widths, lengths, and ease may vary for different styles. For more information on fitting a sweater, see pages 177 - 181.

The circled numbers correspond to those used on the worksheets for the individual sweater types.

Chest/bust measurement = _____ "(cm)

Amount of ease_____ "(cm)

Total_____ "(cm)

Total divided by 2 = _____ "(cm) ①

Shoulder to bottom of sweater = _____ "(cm) ②
Sleeve end to sleeve end = _____ "(cm) ③
Width of neck opening = _____ "(cm) ④
Depth of neck opening = _____ "(cm) ④
Lower sleeve circumference = _____ "(cm) ⑤
Upper sleeve circumference = _____ "(cm) ⑥

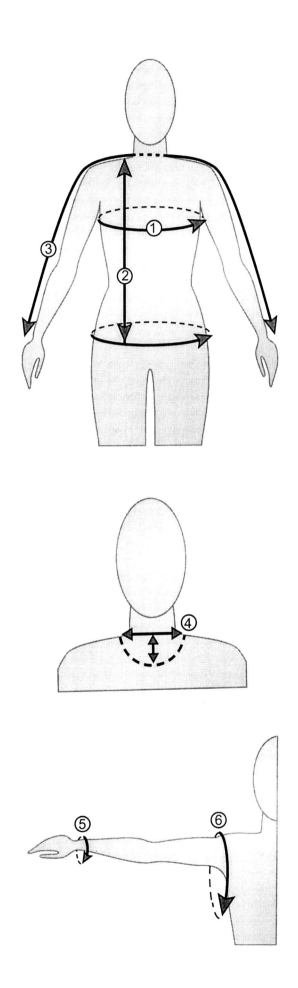

FINISHING A SWEATER

Careful finishing works wonders in obtaining a professional-looking garment. First, use a dull needle to darn in the yarn ends. Weave the ends horizontally through the backs of the stitches. Cut the ends leaving a short end so it doesn't work its way through to the front. If the sweater pieces require blocking, see page 147. Sew the remaining seams, matching any stitch and color patterns. First, align the seams to be joined and tie them loosely with a loop of yarn at intervals. Thread a blunt needle with the same yarn as the sweater—unless the yarn is a specialty type that will not sew easily. In that case, use a same-colored smooth wool yarn.

When sewing up the ribbings, join the edges of the stitches. When sewing up stockinette stitch areas, use the following technique.

Working just in from the edge stitch and working vertically, pick up two loops of two rows and pull through. Do the same on the other piece and continue. This makes an invisible joining.

To join a sleeve top to an armhole, work in a similar fashion, picking up two loops of two rows on one piece, and two loops of one row on the other.

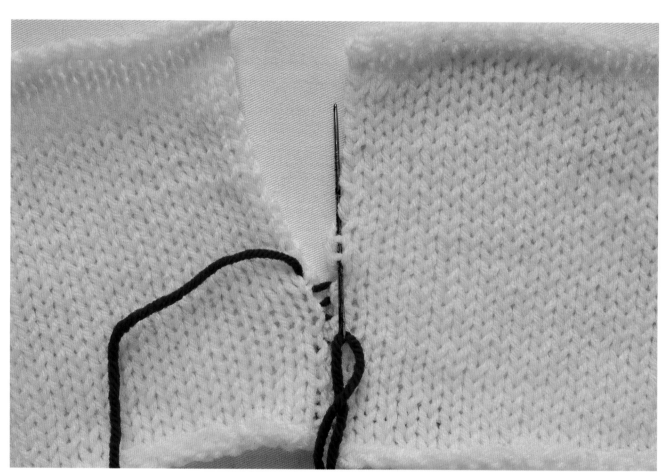

Seams are invisible with this technique.

Knitter's graph paper
Photocopy as needed.

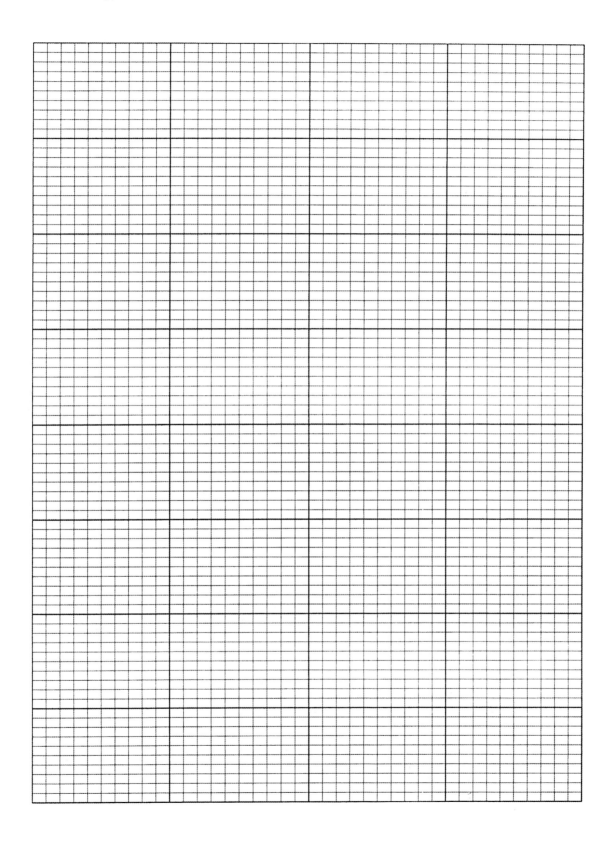

BASIC SWEATER DIMENSIONS

The table below is a compilation that is "averaged" from hundreds of sweater patterns published in book, magazine, and pamphlet form. Variations exist on all of the dimensions given. They represent a generic fit and do not include the ease required for wide sleeves, enlarged neck openings, or variations in body length.

You can knit a straight sleeve sweater directly from the chart. For other sleeve styles and variations, refer to the text.

The table gives a "standard fit" with an ease of 2".
To knit a fitted sweater: knit one size smaller.
To knit a loose-fitting sweater: knit 2 - 3 sizes larger.
To knit an oversized sweater: knit 4 - 6 sizes larger than the chest/bust size below.

Women's sizes are given in the unshaded columns, and men's in the shaded columns.

Other Standard Dimensions
Lengths to knit ribbings:
Bottom of sweater: About 2-1/2" for women's, and 3" for men's.
Sleeve cuffs: About 2-1/2".
Crewneck: Rib for 2", turn 1" to inside, and hem.
Mock turtleneck: 4" or longer.
Turtleneck: 6" or longer.

Depth of neckline: 2" – 3".

Size:	34 "/86 cm		36"/91.5 cm		38"/96.5 cm		40"/101.5 cm		42 "/106.5 cm		44"/112 cm		46"/117 cm		48"/122		To Knit a straight-sleeve sweater
Front/back width (circumference)	18" (36") 46 cm (91.5 cm)	18" (36") 46 cm (91.5 cm)	19" (38") 48 cm (96.5 cm)	19" (38") 48 cm (96.5 cm)	20" (40") 51 cm (101.5 cm)	20" (40") 51 cm (101.5 cm)	21" (42") 53 cm (106.5 cm)	21" (42") 53 cm (106.5 cm)	22" (44") 56 cm 112cm	22" (44") 56 cm 112cm	23" (46") 58.5 cm 117cm	23" (46") 58.5 cm 117cm	24" (48") 61 cm 122cm	24" (48") 61 cm 122cm	25" (50") 63.5 cm 127cm	25" (50") 63.5cm 127cm	Multiply x stitch gauge for # of stitches to knit. Calculate ribbing.
Sweater length	20" 51 cm	24.5" 62 cm	21" 53 cm	25.5" 65 cm	22" 56 cm	26" 66 cm	22.5" 57 cm	26.5" 67 cm	23" 58.5cm	27" 68.5cm	25" 63.5cm	27" 68.5cm	25" 63.5cm	28" 71 cm	25" 63.5cm	29" 73.5cm	Knit back to this length. Front: do neck shaping as desired.
Sleeve end to sleeve end	54" 137 cm	54" 137 cm	55" 139 cm	56" 142 cm	56" 142 cm	57" 145 cm	57" 145 cm	61" 155 cm	58" 147cm	62" 157.5cm	60" 152cm	62" 157.5cm	61" 155cm	66.75" 169.5cm	64" 162.5cm	68" 173cm	Use to calculate sleeve lengths.
Total width of neckline opening	6.5" 16.5 cm	6.5" 16.5 cm	6.5" 16.5 cm	7" 18 cm	6.75" 17 cm	7" 18 cm	7" 18 cm	7.5" 19 cm	7" 18 cm	8" 20 cm	7.5" 19 cm	8.5" 21.5cm	7.75" 20 cm	8.5" 21.5cm	8" 20 cm	8.75" 22 cm	Multiply by stitch gauge for total stitches for neck bind-offs.
Lower sleeve circumference	7.5" 19 cm	7.5" 19 cm	8" 20 cm	8" 20 cm	8.5" 21.5 cm	8.5" 21.5 cm	9" 23 cm	9.5" 24 cm	9" 23 cm	10" 25.5cm	9" 23 cm	10" 25.5cm	9.25" 23.5cm	11" 28 cm	9.5" 24 cm	11.5" 29 cm	Multiply by stitch gauge to begin sleeve. Calculate ribbing.
Upper sleeve width	15" 38 cm	18" 46 cm	16" 40.5 cm	19" 48 cm	18" 46 cm	19" 48 cm	19" 48 cm	20" 51 cm	20" 51 cm	20.75" 53 cm"	21" 53 cm	21" 53 cm	21" 53 cm	22.25" 56.5cm	21.5" 55 cm	23" 58.5cm	Increase sleeve to this width.

THE BEST OF *WORKBASKET*® MAGAZINE

VINTAGE to VOGUE

35

Knit and Crochet Classics

Introduction

A great needlecraft magazine joins premiere yarn companies in recreating classic fashions from its last seven decades

When we first approached leading yarn companies with our concept for this book, they were intrigued. We had just purchased seventy years of archives from the world's once largest needlecraft magazine, *Workbasket*. As we perused its pages from as far back as the 1930s, we imagined how fun it would be to do a book revisiting some of its classic fashions and invite the world's most prestigious yarn companies to recreate the fashions. The yarn companies we approached were as excited as we were about the idea.

At its apex in the '90s, *Workbasket* was the largest needlecraft magazine in the world. First launched in 1935 during the Depression, it began as a modest little newsprint pamphlet called, endearingly, *Aunt Martha's Workbasket*. As its tagline "For Pleasure and Profit" implied, it provided readers not only leisure but a means to supplement their meager family budgets during those lean times. The diminutive digest became relied upon and loved by armies of avid needlecrafters over the decades. By the time *Workbasket* ceased publication in 1996, it had garnered a modern readership of many millions, and its end was mourned by generations.

To peruse the pages of *Workbasket* magazine's past seven decades is to experience time capsules in history. There were the jaunty hats and suits of the 1930s, and the bold, broad-shouldered 1940s fashions for women during World War II, when so many *Workbasket* readers were working in factories welding and riveting for the war effort. The 1950s brought new prosperity and prim fashions to go with it. The '60s and '70s brought Baby Boomer fashions that—surprise!—are the very styles being revived everywhere in retail stores today. Whatever the decade, timeless classics abound in the pages of *Workbasket* and underscore the adage, "everything old is new again." Thus, our title, *Vintage to Vogue*.

One aspect of fashion, however, *has* changed dramatically—the incredible array of textiles offered by today's yarn companies. The variety of colors, textures, weights, and styles available to needlecrafters today is nothing less than mind-boggling. No wonder needlecrafting is so popular again! We invited these premiere companies—Coats & Clark, Lion Brand, Berroco, Cascade, Tahki Stacy Charles, and Handy Hands, a leader in tatting—to participate in this book, with spectacular results!

Vintage to Vogue is packed with 35 projects of many styles, yarn types, and skill levels, all with complete, easy-to-follow directions. We've also provided a section of How-to Basics in Knitting, Crocheting, and Tatting, as well as a Resource section, containing product information, informative Web sites, and sources for free patterns, all for *your* pleasure! Aunt Martha would be proud...

1930s

1940s

1950s

1960s

1970s

1980s

1990s

VINTAGE to VOGUE

TABLE OF CONTENTS

Chi-Chi Shag

Workbasket's 1984 whisper-soft pullover is transformed into a sumptuous shag that shouts sensation! The contemporary sweater is knit in Tahki Stacy Charles' textural and irresistibly tony Casca yarn.

■ **PROJECT**
Sage Shag Pullover, by Tahki Stacy Charles

■ **SKILL LEVEL:**
Beginner

■ **SIZE**
Small (Medium, Large)
Directions for Small with larger sizes in parentheses.
If there is only one figure, it applies to all sizes.

■ **MATERIALS**
TAHKI STACY CHARLES Austermann Casca
13 balls (50 g balls, each approx 55 yds), in #05 Green

■ **NEEDLES**
Size 15 knitting needles
Size 10½ crochet needles

■ **GAUGE**
7 sts and 11 rows = 4" over Rev St st.
TAKE TIME TO CHECK GAUGE.

1984 Workbasket

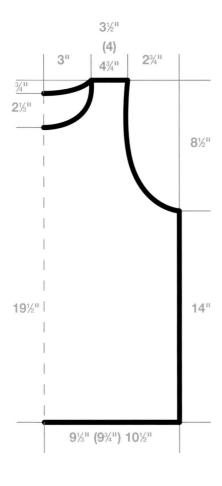

ABBREVIATIONS:

beg = begin, beginning; **bet** = between; **BO** = bind off; **CO** = Cast on; **dec** = decreas(e)(s)(ing); **inc** = increase(e)(s)(ing); **pat** = pattern; **rnd** = round; **rem** = remaining; **RS** = right side; **sc** = single crochet; **st(s)** = stitch(es); **St st** = Stockinette stitch; **tog** = together.

DIRECTIONS

BACK

Cast on 34 (36, 40) sts and work in St st until piece measures 14" from beg.

Shape Armholes: Bind off 2 sts at beg of next 2 rows, dec 1 st each side every 2nd row 3 times = 24 (26, 30) sts. Work even until pieces measures 22" from beg.

Shape Neck: Bind off center 8 sts and working both sides at once, bind off 2 sts from each neck edge once. Work even until piece measures 23" from beg. Bind off rem sts each side for shoulders.

FRONT

Work same as back until piece measures 19¾" from beg.

Shape Neck: Bind off center 4 sts and working both sides at once, bind off from each neck edge 2 sts once and 1 st twice. Work even until piece measures 23" from beg. Bind off rem sts each side for shoulders.

SLEEVES

Cast on 17 sts and work in St st, inc 1 st each side every 7th row once, then every 11th (9th, 9th) row 3 (4, 4) times = 25 (27, 27) sts. Work even until piece measures 16½" from beg.

Shape Cap: Bind off 3 sts at beg of next 2 rows, 2 sts at beg of next 2 rows, dec 1 st each side every 2nd row 4 times, bind off 2 sts at beg of next 2 rows. Bind off rem sts.

FINISHING

Block pieces to finished measurements. Sew shoulder seams. Set in sleeves. Sew side and sleeve seams. With RS facing and crochet hook, work 1 rnd sc evenly around neck edge.

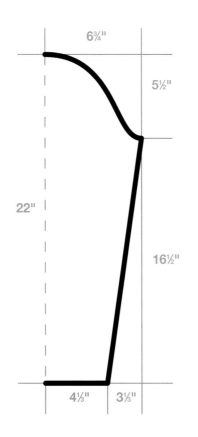

Timeless Tee

A classic stands the test of time. The basic tee has certainly done that! It's been a staple of American fashion for decades. This **Workbasket** *1935 tee is revisited in Berroco's simple-to-knit top, richly rendered in Monet yarn.*

■ **PROJECT**
Knit Tee, by Berroco

■ **SKILL LEVEL**
Intermediate

■ **SIZES**
X-Small (Small, Medium, Large, X-Large, XX-Large)
Directions for X-Small with larger sizes in parentheses.
If there is only one figure, it applies to all sizes.

■ **FINISHED MEASUREMENTS**
Bust: 34 (36, 40, 44, 48, 54)"
Length: 21 (21, 21½, 22, 22½, 23)"

■ **MATERIALS**
BERROCO MONET (50 g balls), 9 (10, 11, 12, 13, 14) hanks, Water Lilies. Note: Please see tips on working with Monet before starting to knit. 1 St Marker. Small amt. of smooth yarn in matching color for seaming.

■ **NEEDLES**
Size 10 straight knitting needles OR SIZE TO OBTAIN GAUGE. Size 10 circular knitting needles, 16" length

■ **GAUGE**
7 sts = 2"; 12 rows = 2" in Reverse St st. In order to ensure correct finished measurements, accurate stitch and row gauges must be achieved. TAKE TIME TO CHECK GAUGE.

1935 Workbasket

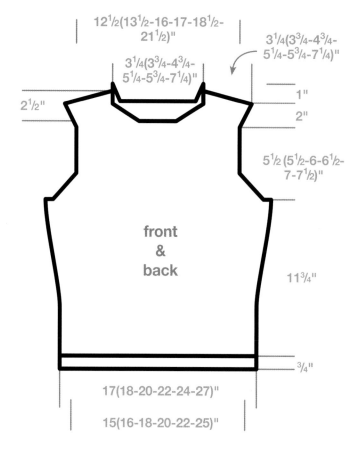

12½(13½-16-17-18½-21½)"

3¼(3¾-4¾-5¼-5¾-7¼)"

3¼(3¾-4¾-5¼-5¾-7¼)"

1"

2½"

2"

5½ (5½-6-6½-7-7½)"

front
&
back

11¾"

¾"

17(18-20-22-24-27)"

15(16-18-20-22-25)"

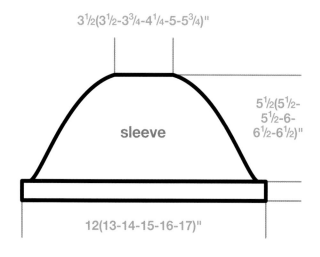

3½(3½-3¾-4¼-5-5¾)"

5½(5½-5½-6-6½-6½)"

sleeve

12(13-14-15-16-17)"

■ TO CHECK GAUGE

Cast on at least 20 sts, using the yarn and needles specified in the instructions. Work pattern for 3". Bind off all sts. Using a ruler as a guide, count the number of sts and rows over 2". (Do not include selvage stitches or cast on and bind off rows.) Divide by 2. If this number is MORE than given in the instructions, try a size larger needle and again check your gauge. If the number is LESS than given in the instructions, try a size smaller and check your gauge. The needle size you use does not matter as long as the stitch and row gauge is accurate.

ABBREVIATIONS

beg = begin(ning); **ch** = chain; **dc** = double crochet; **dec** = decrease; **inc** = increase; **k** = knit; **M1p** = Pickup horizontal strand between st just worked and next st, place on LH needle, p this st (inc 1); **p** = purl; **pat(s)** = pattern(s); **rep** = repeat; **RH** = right hand; **RS** = right side; **rnd(s)** = round(s); **st(s)** = stitch(es); **tog** = together; **WS** = wrong side; **yo** = yarn over; **end on WS** = end having just completed a WS row; **end on RS** = end having just completed a RS row.

GLOSSARY

Stockinette Stitch (St st): K 1 row, p 1 row alternately when working on straight needles. K EVERY round when working on a circular needle.

Garter Stitch: Knit EVERY row when working on

straight needles. K 1 round, p 1 round when working on a circular needle.

Binding Off Across Cables: To dec when binding off across the top of a cable, k2 tog then bind off this st—this counts as 2 sts bound off. This is done to keep the cable from flaring out on the bind-off row and helps keep the shoulders and neck from stretching.

Steam: Lay the piece WS down on a padded surface and cover with a pressing cloth. Press lightly with a steam iron. Set iron down carefully; do not drag as this will stretch the piece. This method will allow you to manipulate fabric and achieve greater length or width, if desired. It will also set stitches and even out the stitch quality for a more professional look.

Steam Lightly: Lay the piece WS down on a padded surface and move steam iron slowly back and forth 1" above piece. Do not allow iron to touch knitted fabric. Steam will allow knitted fabric to blossom. Selvages and ribbings will lay flat. This method may not allow you to block pieces larger or smaller.

TIPS FOR WORKING WITH MONET

1. When working with Monet, it is advisable to keep track of the number of rows worked. This ensures that your back and front will be exactly the same lenth.

2. Keep track of rows and sts when knitting your gauge swatch. Measure your gauge over the entire swatch. Due to the nature of the yarn, it is difficult to count sts and rows.

3. Sew seams with smooth yarn in a similar color.

DIRECTIONS

BACK

With straight needles, cast on 52 (56, 62, 69, 76, 87) sts. Knit 4 rows. Work even in Reverse St st until piece measures 4½" from beg, end on WS. Inc 1 st each end of next row. Rep this inc every 2¼" 3 times more. Work even on 60 (64, 70, 77, 84, 95) sts until piece measures 12½" from beg, end on WS.

Shape Armholes: Bind off 2 sts at beg of the next 2 rows.

Dec Row (RS): P2, P2 tog, p to last 4 sts, p2 tog, p2. Rep this dec every RS row 5 (5, 4, 6, 7, 7) times more. Work even on 44 (48, 56, 59, 64, 75) sts until armholes measure 5½ (5½, 6, 6½, 7, 7½)", end on WS.

Next Row (RS): P2, M1p, p to last 2 sts, M1p, p2. Rep this inc every 1" once more. Work even on 48

(52, 60, 63, 68, 79) sts until armholes measure 7½ (7½, 8, 8½, 9, 9½)", end on WS.

Shape Shoulders and Neck: Next Row (RS): Bind off 3 (5, 5, 6, 6, 9) sts, p until there are 10 (10, 14, 14, 16, 18) sts on RH needle, join another hank of yarn and bind off center 22 (22, 22, 23, 24, 25) sts, p to end. Working both sides at once, bind off 3 (5, 5, 6, 6, 9) sts at beg of the next row, then 4 (4, 6, 6, 7, 8) sts at beg of the next 4 rows. AT THE SAME TIME, dec 1 st at each neck edge EVERY row twice.

FRONT

Work same as for back until armholes measure 5½ (5½, 6, 6½, 7, 7½)", end on WS.

Shape Neck: Next Row (RS): P2, M1p, p until there are 18 (20, 24, 25, 27, 32) sts on RH needle, join another hank of yarn and bind off center 10 (10, 10, 11, 12, 13) sts, p to last 2 sts, M1p, p2. Continue to work incs at each side same as for back and AT THE SAME TIME, bind off 2 sts at each neck edge twice, then dec 1 st at each neck edge every RS row 4 times. When armholes measure 7½ (7½, 8, 8½, 9, 9½)", bind off 3 (5, 5, 6, 6, 9) sts at each armhole edge once, then 4 (4, 6, 6, 7, 8) sts twice for shoulders.

SLEEVES

With straight needles, cast on 42 (46, 49, 53, 56, 60) sts. Knit 4 rows.

Shape Cap: Bind off 2 sts at beg of the next 2 rows.

Dec Row (RS): P2, p2 tog, p to last 4 sts, p2 tog, p2. Rep this dec every RS row 4 (8, 10, 9, 8, 10) times more, then every other RS row 6 (4, 3, 5, 6, 5) times, end on WS. Bind off 2 sts at beg of the next 2 rows. Bind off remaining 12 (12, 13, 15, 18, 20) sts.

FINISHING

Block pieces flat with steam iron and pressing cloth. Sew shoulder seams.

Neckband: With RS facing, using circular needle, beg at center back neck, pick up and k13 (13, 13, 13, 14, 14) sts to left shoulder, 13 sts along left front neck edge, 10 (10, 10, 11, 12, 13) sts across front neck edge, 13 sts along right front neck edge, then 13 (13, 13, 14, 14, 15) sts across remaining back neck edge 62 (62, 62, 64, 66, 68) sts. Mark for beg of rnd and carry marker up. P 1 rnd, k 1 rnd, p 1 rnd. Bind off all sts knitwise. Sew in sleeves. Sew side and sleeve seams.

Divine Duster

Svelte, soft and sumptuous, this classic wine duster in Coats & Clark's Red Heart Light & Lofty yarn can rise to most any occasion, formal or casual.

■ **PROJECT**
Light & Lofty Duster, by Coats & Clark

■ **SKILL Level:**
Intermediate

■ **SIZE**
One Size to Fit Bust 36-38"

■ **MATERIALS**
COATS & CLARK RED HEART® "Light & Lofty™" yarn
8 skeins (each skein 6 oz), Wine

■ **NEEDLES**
Size N-15 (10mm) crochet hook or size to obtain guage

■ **GAUGE**
In sc = 8 rows = 4", 8 sts = 4"
TAKE TIME TO CHECK GAUGE.

beg = begin(ning); **ch** = chain; **mm** = millimeters; **rem** = remain(ning); **rep** = repeat; **sl** = slip; **sc** = single crochet; **st(s)** = stitch(es); **tog** = together; * = repeat whatever follows the * as indicated.

DIRECTIONS:

BACK

Ch 43. **Row 1:** Sc in 2nd ch from hook and in each ch across; turn—42 sc. **Row 2:** Ch 1, sc in each sc across; turn. Rep Row 2 until 30" from beg.

Shape Raglan: Row 1: Sl st in first sc, sc across next 40 sc; turn (DO NOT WORK LAST SC). **Row 2:** Ch 1, sc in each sc across; turn—40 sc. **Row 3:** Ch 1, sc2tog, sc in each sc across to last 2 sc, sc2tog; turn—38 sc. **Row 4:** Ch 1, sc in each sc across; turn. Rep last 2 rows until 14 sc rem. Fasten off.

RIGHT FRONT

Ch 23. **Row 1:** Sc in 2nd ch from hook and in each ch across; turn—22 sc. **Row 2:** Ch 1, sc in each sc across; turn. Rep Row 2 until 30" from beg.

Shape Raglan: Row 1: Ch 1, sc across 21 sc; turn. **Row 2:** Ch 1, sc in each sc across—21 sc. **Row 3:** Ch 1, sc in each sc across to last 2 sc, sc2tog; turn—20 sc. **Row 4:** Ch 1, sc in each sc across; turn. Rep last 2 rows 6 more times—14sc. **Next Row:** Ch 1, sc 2tog, sc in each sc across to last 2 sc; sc2tog; turn—12 sc. **Next Row:** Ch 1, sc in each sc across; turn—12 sc. Rep last 2 rows until 4 sts rem.

LEFT FRONT

Work same as for Right Front, reverse raglan shaping.

SLEEVES (Make 2)

Ch 21. **Row 1:** Sc in 2nd ch from hook and in each ch across; turn—20 sc. **Row 2:** Ch 1, sc in each sc across; turn. Rep last row until 3" from beg, end wrong side row. Inc 1 sc each end of next row, then every 6th row until 32 sts. Work even in sc 3 more rows.

Shape Raglan: Row 1: Sl 1 st, sc in next 30 sc; turn—30 sc. **Row 2:** Ch 1, sc in each sc across;

turn—30 sc. **Row 3:** Ch 1, sc2tog, sc to last 2 sc, sc2tog; turn—28 sc. **Row 4:** Ch 1, sc in each sc across; turn. Rep last 2 rows until 6 sts rem. Fasten off.

With right sides together, pin raglans in place on front and back pieces of coat and stitch in place.

Border: With right side facing, join yarn at top neck, ch 1, 35 sc across neck and raglan tops; turn. **Row 2:** Ch 1, sc in each sc across—35 sc. **Row 3:** Ch 1, sc in each sc across—DO NOT TURN but turn work and continue working along front edge, sc evenly spaced around working 2 sc in each corner. Fasten off. Sew side and sleeve seams. Weave in ends.

Vintage design.

Artistic License

∎ ∎ ∎

Workbasket's 1966 jacket, inspired by the geometric art of Piet Mondrian, is pure '60s in color! Lion Brand has artfully revived this smart jacket in Cotton Ease yarn, drawing from Mondrian's palette of primary colors. Oh, what a difference color makes!

■ **PROJECT**
Mondrian Cardigan, by Lion Brand

■ **SKILL LEVEL**
Intermediate

■ **SIZES**
Small (Medium, Large, X-Large)
Directions for Small with larger sizes in parentheses.
If there is only one figure, it applies to all sizes.

■ **FINISHED MEASUREMENTS**
Finished chest: 36 (40, 44, 48)"

■ **MATERIALS**
LION BRAND Cotton Ease
A—3 (4, 4, 5) skeins Vanilla
B—1 (1, 2, 2) skeins Licorice
C—1 (1, 1, 1) skein Cherry red

■ **NEEDLES**
Sizes 7 and 8 knitting needles
1 st. holder

■ **BUTTONS**
Seven ¾" buttons of your choice

■ **GAUGE**
With n. 8 needles in stock st 4" square = 17 sts
and 22 rows
TAKE TIME TO CHECK GAUGE.

1966 Workbasket

beg = begin(ning); **k =** knit; **p** = purl; **RS** = right side; **WS** = wrong side; **dec** = decrease; **sts** = stitches; **beg** = beginning; **ssk** = slip, slip, knit; **sssk** = slip, slip, slip, knit (slip the first, second, and/or third stitch knit-wise one at a time, then insert the tip of left-hand needle into the back of these 2 or 3 sts and knit them together.)

DIRECTIONS

BACK

With B and needle n. 7 cast on 83 (91, 101, 109) sts. Work in seed st as follows: k1, * p1, k 1; for 8 rows. Fasten off B. Join A with needles n. 8 work in stock st until piece measures 14" from start, ending with a p row.

Shape Armholes: Bind off 5 (6, 6, 7) sts at the beg of next 2 rows, dec 1 st each side inside first and last st every 2nd row 4 (4, 6, 6) times; Work dec row as follows: k1, k 2 tog, knit up to last 3 sts, ssk, k1. Work even on 65 (71, 79, 85) sts until armholes measure 7½ (8, 8½, 9)" from beg, ending with a p row.

Shape Shoulders: Bind off 7 (8, 9, 10) sts at beg of next 4 rows, 6 (7, 8, 9) sts at beg of next 2 rows. Leave remaining 25 (25, 27, 27) sts on a st holder for back of neck.

RIGHT FRONT

With needles n. 7 and B cast on 41 (45, 53, 57) sts. Work seed st border as for back. Fasten off B. With A and needles n. 8 work in stock st until 4" above border, and with k row. Fasten off A. With needles n. 7 and B p 1 row. Work in seed st for 7 rows. Fasten off B. With A and needle n. 8 work in stock st until piece measures same length as back to underarm. End with a p row.

Shape Armhole: Work same as right side of back armhole. Work on rem sts for 9 rows counting first armhole row as row 1. End on WS. Fasten off A. With B and needles n. 7 k 1 row. Continue shaping according to directions and only for L and XL sizes, work in seed st for 7 rows. Fasten off B. With C and needles n. 8 work in stock st until 5½ (6, 6, 6½)" above underarm. End with a WS row.

Shape Neckline: (RS)—bind off 7 (7, 8, 8) sts at beg of 1st row, 2 sts at beg of next 2 RS rows. Dec 1 st inside first st every 2nd RS row 3 (3, 4, 4) times. Work on rem 20 (23, 26, 29) sts until armhole measures same as back in length. End with RS row.

Shape Shoulder: Row 1: p and bind off 7 (8, 9, 10) sts at the beg of row, p to end. **Row 2:** knit. **Row 3:** p and bind off 7 (8, 9, 10) sts, p to end. **Row 4:** knit. **Row 5:** p and bind off rem 5 (6, 7, 8) sts. Fasten off last st.

LEFT FRONT

Begin same as right front. Work seed st stripe with B. Fasten off B. With needles n. 8 and C work in stock st until 6" above border. End with a p row. Fasten off C. With B and needles n. 7 k 1 row. Work in seed st for 7 rows. Fasten off B. With needles n. 8 and A work in stock st until same length as back to underarm. End with a p row.

Shape Armhole: Bind off 5 (6, 6, 7) sts, work to end of row. Fasten off A. With needles n. 7 and B p 1 row. Work in seed st for 7 rows, shaping armhole as for back. End on RS. Fasten off B. With needles n. 8 and C p 1 row. Work in stock st and continue shaping armhole for larger sizes for 8 rows, end on RS. Fasten off C. With B and needles n. 7 p 1 row. Work in seed st for 7 more rows, end on RS. Fasten off B. With A and needles n. 8 work in stock st. Shape neckline and shoulder to match right front, but with reverse shaping.

Vintage design.

SLEEVES

With B and needles n. 7 cast on 47 (49, 51, 53) sts. Work in seed st as for back. Fasten off B. With C and needles n. 8 work in stock st for 8 rows. Fasten off C. With B and needles n. 7 k 1 row. Work in seed st for 7 rows. Fasten off B. With A and needles n. 8 work in stock st inc 1 st inside first and last st every 8 rows 8 times 63 (65, 67, 69) sts. Work even until sleeve measures 16" or desired length to underarm.

Sleevecap: Bind off 5 sts at the beg of next 2 rows, dec 1 st each side inside first and last st every 2nd row 14 (15, 16, 17). Dec 2 sts (k 1, k 3 tog—work up to last 4 sts, sssk, k1) every 2nd row twice. Bind off rem 17 sts.

FINISHING AND BORDER

Block pieces to measurements. Sew shoulder seams.

Neck Border: Join B on neck edge of right front. With needles n. 7 pick up and knit 25 (26, 27, 28) sts up to shoulder seam, pick up and knit 25 (25, 27, 27) sts from holder, pick up 25 (26, 27, 28) sts from next shoulder seam to left neck edge. Work on 75 (77, 81, 83) sts in seed st for 8 rows. Next row: (WS) purl and bind off firmly.

Left Front Border: Join B on top edge at corner of neck border. Pick up and knit 84 (86, 88, 90) sts. Work in seed st for 8 rows, bind off with a p row from WS. Place a marker for 7 buttonholes evenly spaced between 3¼" from top and bottom edge, counting 2 sts for each buttonhole.

Right Side Border: In same manner work right side border until 3rd row in seed st is completed. Buttonhole row: Work in pattern. Form 1 buttonhole to correspond to each marker on left edge as follows: Bind off first st, sl last st worked to left needle, k 2 tog. Next row, cast on 2 sts over each buttonhole. Work 3 more rows in seed st, bind off with a purl row on WS.

Sew sides, sew sleeves, set in sleeves. Sew on buttons. Finish off all ends. Steam lightly.

Ravishing in Red

Workbasket's April 1969 crochet shell in marvelous magenta becomes sultry and sophisticated in Tahki Stacy Charles' luscious contemporary version created in sensuous, scarlet Casca yarn.

■ **PROJECT**
Scarlet Shag Shell, by Tahki Stacy Charles

■ **SKILL LEVEL:**
Beginner

■ **SIZE**
Small

■ **FINISHED MEASUREMENTS**
Finished Chest: 36
Length: 20½"

■ **MATERIALS**
TAHKI STACY CHARLES Austermann Casca Red
5 balls (50g balls)

■ **NEEDLES**
Size 10½ knitting needles
OR SIZE TO OBTAIN GAUGE.

■ **GAUGE**
Gauge 13 sts and 18 rows = 4" over St st.
TAKE TIME TO CHECK GAUGE.

ABBREVIATIONS:

beg = Begin(ning); **BO** = bind off; **dec** = decreas(e)(s)(ing); **st(s)** = stitch(es); **rem** = remaining; **St st** = Stockinette stitch; **tog** = together.

DIRECTIONS

BACK

Cast on 57 sts and work in St st until piece meaures 10¼" from beg.

Shape Armholes: Bind off center 3 sts at beg of next 2 rows, then dec 1 st each side every 2nd row 4 times and every 4th row 9 times. Work even until piece measures 19" from beg.

Shape Neckline: Bind off center 9 sts and working

both sides at once, bind off from each neck edge 3 sts once, 2 sts once, and 1 st once. Work even until piece measures 20¼" from beg. Bind off rem 2 sts each side for shoulder.

FRONT

Work same as for back until piece measures 17¾" from beg.

Shape Neckline: Bind off center 5 sts and working both sides at once, bind off from each neck edge 2 sts twice and 1 st 4 times.

FINISHING

Block pieces to measurements. Sew shoulders and side seams.

Magnum Opus

■■■

Workbasket's *1966 cardigan combines casual chic with fashionable function. But Cascade Yarns ups the ante with their contemporary cardigan of Magnum wool in five stunning hues and rich textures . Definitely a magnum opus!*

■ **PROJECT**
Multicolor Bulky Cardigan, by Cascade

■ **SKILL LEVEL**
Intermediate

■ **SIZES**
Small (Medium, Large)
Directions for Small with larger sizes in parentheses.
If there is only one figure, it applies to all sizes.

■ **FINISHED MEASUREMENTS**
Finished Chest: 37½ (48, 58½)"

■ **MATERIALS**
CASCADE's Magnum yarn in five colors:
MC A—4 balls brown
MC B—2 balls gray
CC 1—1 ball blue
CC 2—1 ball red
CC 3—1 ball green
14 buttons with shanks

■ **NEEDLES**
Sizes 13 and 15 long circular needles
OR SIZE TO OBTAIN GAUGE

■ **GAUGE**
15 sts and 15 rows equal 10" across and
5" high in pattern using larger needles.
TAKE TIME TO CHECK GAUGE.

1966 Workbasket

ABBREVIATIONS

beg = Begin, beginning; **bet** = between; **BO** = bind off; **CC** = contrasting color; **ch** = chain; **CO** = Cast on; **dc** = double crochet; **dec** = decreas(e)(s)(ing); **eor** = every other row; **inc** = increase(e)(s)(ing); **k** = knit; **lp** = loop; **MC** = main color; **p** = purl; **pat** = pattern; **pm** = place marker; **rem** = remaining; **RS** = right side; **sk** = skip; **st(s)** = stitch(es); **tog** = together; **WS** = wrong side; **yo** = yarn over.

DIRECTIONS

NOTE 1: Garment is made in one piece to underarms.

NOTE 2: Needle size will most greatly effect row gauge and you should obtain at least as many rows per inch that are called for in gauge listed.

NOTE 3: Color sequencing as follows: CC 1, 2, and 3 in that order. MC A & B alternate changing on row 3 after having completed CC 3.

PATTERN STITCH:

Rows 1 and 2: With CC * purl 1, knit 1, purl 1, slip next st holding yarn to back of work * across ending purl 1, knit 1, purl 1.

Rows 3, 4, and 5: With MC * purl 1, knit 1 * across ending purl 1.

BODY

With MC A CO 59 (75, 91) sts.

Row 1: With smaller needles rib row, *k1, p1* across ending K1.

Row 2: *p1, k1* across ending p1. Continue ribbing as set for a total of 4" = 9 rows.

Change to larger needles and CC1 begin pattern st. Work even in pattern for 16 (15, 14)" ODL.

ARMHOLES

Next row divide for armholes by working across 13 (17, 21) sts, BO 1 st, place sts just worked on a holder for right front, work across 31 (39, 47) sts, BO 1 st, place sts just worked on holder for back, work across remaining 13 (17, 21) sts. Work on left front's sts until garment measures 21" from CO edge and a RS row has just been completed.

NECK

BO 3 sts, then 1 eor 2 times. Work even until garment measures 25" from CO edge and shape shoulders by SZ 1 working to 4 sts before armhole edge, wrapping 4th st, turn, work to neck edge, turn working all sts, making sure to pick up wrapped sts.

Place all sts on holder. SZ 2 working to 4 sts before armhole edge. Wrap 4th sts, turn work across, turn, work to 8th st before armhole edge, wrap 8th st. Turn. Work across. Turn. Work across all stitches, picking up wrapped stitches.

Place sts on a holder. SZ 3 work to 5 sts before armhole edge. Wrap 5th st. Turn work to neck edge. Turn work to 10th st before armhole and wrap 10th st. Turn work to neck edge. Turn work to end, picking up all wrapped sts.

Place all sts on holder. Transfer back sts to needle and work in pat as established until garment measures 25" from CO edge. Work across 9 (13, 17) sts, BO center 11 (13, 13) sts, work across to 4 (4, 5) sts before armhole edge. Wrap and turn. BO 1 st at neck edge, turn and work across to 0 (8, 10) sts before armhole. Wrap and turn. Work across to neck edge. Turn work to armhole edge, picking up all wrapped stitches.

Place sts on a holder. Rejoin yarn to neck edge and work to 4 (4, 5) sts before armhole edge. Wrap and turn. BO 1 st at neck edge. Turn and work to 0 (8, 10) sts before armhole edge. Wrap and turn. Work to neck edge, turn, and work across all sts, picking up wrapped sts.

SHOULDERS

Place shoulder sts on a holder. Rejoin yarn at armhole edge of right front and work even until garment measures 21" from CO edge, having just completed a WS row. BO 3 sts, then 1 eor 2 times. Work on remaining sts until garment measures 25" and shape shoulders as before.

Place shoulder sts on holder. Turn garment inside out, and place right front shoulder sts on a needle. Place corresponding back shoulder's sts on another needle. Place these 2 needles parallel with RS of garment facing each other and knit tog 1 st from each needle. Knit tog another st from each needle and pass 1st new st over 2nd. Continue in this manner until all sts are bound off.

Repeat for other shoulder.

RIBBING FRONT AND BOTTOM

Turn garment right side out and with smaller needles and MC A pick up and knit 1 st for every 3 out of 4 rows along left edge, making sure that you have an odd number of sts. Work rib as for bottom boarder for 4" = 9 rows. BO all sts in rib.

BUTTONHOLES

Mark right front edge at 7 different points for buttonholes. The top buttonhole should be about ¼" from neck edge. Then pick up and knit same num-

Vintage design.

ber of sts with MC A and work as rib, making buttonholes at predetermined places by YO, k2tog on 4th and 8th rows. BO all sts.

SHAWL COLLAR

With right side facing, smaller needles and MC A, pick up and knit 1 st for each bound off st and 3 out of every 4 rows along straight edge of neckhole, making sure there is an odd number of sts. Rib 1 row, then begin shaping shawl collar by short rowing 4 less sts at each edge until center portion meaures 8" and you have worked an equal number of short rows on both sides of collar. Knit across to neckline edge, picking up all wrapped sts. Turn. Work to opposite neck edge, picking up all wrapped sts. BO all sts in rib.

SLEEVES

With MC A CO 15 (19, 23) sts. With smaller needles rib as set for sweater border for 4". Change to larger needles and CC 1. Work in patt for 17", increasing 1 st at each edge EO 4th row 7 (6, 6) times—29 (31, 35) sts. BO all sts. With matching yarn, sew in sleeve top to armhole opening, leaving edge st unattached. Sew up side seams.

FINISHING

Turn garment inside out and weave in all yarn ends. Sew on buttons to correspond to buttonholes.

Granny Squares Galore!

■ ■ ■

In fashion, everything old is new again. Styles of the '60s and '70s are hot and Granny Squares are climbing the charts! Lion Brand has revised Workbasket's 1975 Granny Squares ensemble with Wool Ease yarn in 10 smashing colors.

■ **PROJECT**
Granny Squares Cardigan & Shell, by Lion Brand

■ **SKILL LEVEL:**
Beginner

■ **SIZES**
Sizes 10 – 12

■ **MATERIALS**
LION BRAND Wool Ease yarns
Black (2 skeins)
One skein each of the following Wool Ease yarns
(or your choice of colors):

Magenta	Turquoise
Yellow	Orange
Lime	Lilac
Purple	Gray
Coral	Apricot

■ **NEEDLES**
Size H crochet hook

■ **GAUGE**
Each square measures approx. 4"
TAKE TIME TO CHECK GAUGE.

1975 Workbasket

cardigan

ABBREVIATIONS

beg = begin(ning); **bet** = between; **BO** = bind off;
CC = contrasting color; **ch** = chain; **CO** = Cast on;
dc = double crochet; **dec** = decreas(e)(s)(ing) **eor**
= every other row; **hdc** = half double crochet; **inc** =
increase(e)(s)(ing); **k** = knit; **lp** = loop; **MC** = main
color; **p** = purl; **pat** = pattern; **pm** = place marker;
rnd = round; **rem** = remaining; **RS** = right side; **sc**
= single crochet; **seq** = sequence; **sl st** = slip stitch;
sk = skip; **sp** = space; **st(s)** = stitch(es); **St st** =
Stockinette stitch; **wyif** = with yarn in front; **wyib** =
with yarn in back; **WS** = wrong side; **yo** = yarn over.

DIRECTIONS

GRANNY SQUARES

With a CC, ch 4, join with sl st to form ring.

Rnd 1: Ch 3, 2 dc in ring, * ch 1, 3 dc shell in ring,
repeat from * twice, ch 1, join in top of ch 3, fasten
off.

Rnd 2: Join another CC in any ch 1 sp, ch 3
(counts as 1 dc), (2 dc, ch 1, 3 dc) in same sp, * (3
dc, ch 1, 3 dc) in next ch 1 sp—corner shell made,
repeat from * twice, join, fasten off.

Rnd 3: Join a third CC in any corner sp, ch 3, (2
dc, ch 1, 3 dc) in same sp, * 3 dc in sp between
corners, (3 dc, ch 1, 3 dc) shell in corner sp, repeat
from * twice, 3 dc between shells, join, fasten.

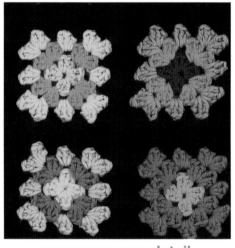

granny square detail

Rnd 4: Join black and any corner sp, ch 3 (2 dc, ch
1, 3 dc) in same sp, * (3 dc in next sp) twice, (3 dc,
ch 1, 3 dc) in corner sp, repeat from * twice, 3 dc
between each of 2 side shells, join, fasten off.

HALF SQUARES

With a CC, ch 5.

Row 1: (3 dc, ch 1, 3 dc) shell in 5th ch from hook,
ch 1, dc in same ch as shell, fasten off, do not turn.

Row 2: Join another CC in third ch of beginning ch,
ch 4, 3 dc in first sp, shell in ch 1 sp of shell, 3 dc

shell

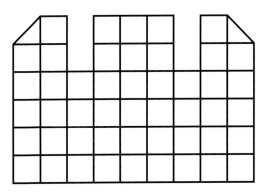

cardigan body
chart I

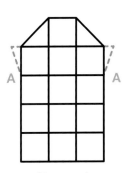

cardigan sleeve
chart II

in last ch 1 sp, ch 1, dc in dc, fasten off.

Row 3: Join another CC in third ch of ch 4 at beginning of last row, ch 4, 3 dc in each of next 2 sps, shell in shell, 3 dc in each of next 2 sps, ch 1, dc in dc, fasten off.

Row 4: Join black in third ch of ch 4 at beginning of last row, ch 4, 3 dc in each of next 3 sps, shell in shell, 3 dc in each of next 3 sps, ch 1, dc in dc, fasten off.

CARDIGAN

Make 74 squares and 6 half squares, alternating colors as desired on first three rnds.

Front and Back: Sew squares together, following Chart I.

Sleeves: Sew squares together, following Chart II. Work crochet gussets by joining black at A on chart. Sc in each of next 3 sts, hdc in each of next 3 sts, dc to underarm, ch 3, turn. Dc to last 6 dc, hdc in each of next 3 dc, sc in each of last 3 dc, fasten off. Sew shoulder and sleeve seams. Sew sleeves into armholes.

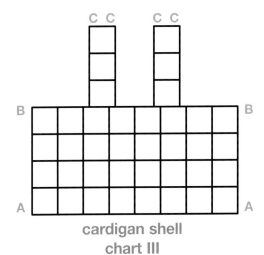

cardigan shell
chart III

SHELL

Make 38 squares of your choice of varying color combinations. Sew together, following Chart III. Sew seams, back matching As and Bs. This seam will be down middle of back. Then sew sleeve seams CC to back of shell.

FINISHING

Sc around all edges.

Ivory Elegance

Simplicity and elegance are basic ingredients of a classic and this ribbed turtleneck certainly qualifies. The contemporary version is from Cascade's Italian Lana D' Oro line.

■ **PROJECT**
Ivory Turtleneck, by Cascade

■ **SKILL LEVEL**
Beginner

■ **SIZES**
Small (Medium, Large)
Directions for Small with larger sizes in parentheses.
If there is only one figure, it applies to all sizes.

■ **FINISHED MEASUREMENTS**
Finished Bust Size: 46 (49, 52)"

■ **MATERIALS**
CASCADE'S Lana D'Oro Cascade Yarn
Your choice of color, 20 (21, 22) skeins

■ **NEEDLES**
Sizes 3 and 6 knitting needles

■ **GAUGE**
Tension: Using #6 needle and in rib pattern slightly
stretched, 8 sts = 1"
TAKE TIME TO CHECK GUAGE.

ABBREVIATIONS

beg = begin(ning); **ch** = chain; **dc** = double crochet; **rep** = repeat(s); **rev** = revers(e)(ing); **st(s)** =
stitch(es); **t-ch** = turning chain; **WS** = wrong side

DIRECTIONS

BACK

With #3 needle cast on 182 (198, 208) sts and work in knit 2, purl 2 rib ending the row with knit 2 for 17 (18, 19)".

Shape Armholes: Keeping pattern correct, bind off 3 sts at the beginning of the next 2 rows, then 1 st at the beginning of the next 2 rows, then 1 st at the beginning of the next 2 rows. 170 (186, 196) sts remaining. Continue straight until armhole measures 10".

Shape Back, Neck, and Shoulders: Keeping pattern correct, bind off 24 (28, 31) sts, pattern 24 (28, 30) sts, turn and leave remaining sts on hold for later. Work 1 row back, turn, bind off 24 (28, 30) sts Rejoin yarn and bind off the center 74 sts loosely and pattern to end. Bind off 24 (28, 31) sts pattern to end. Turn and work to end. Bind off remaining 24 (28, 30) sts.

FRONT

Work as for back until piece measures 6½" above armhole shaping.

Shape Front Neck and Shoulders: Pattern 75 (83, 88) sts, turn and work back, leaving remaining sts on hold for later. Working on left front only, *at neck edge only*, bind off 8 sts 1 time, 4 sts 2 times, 3 sts 1 time, 2 sts 1 time and 1 st 6 times. 48 (56, 61) sts remaining. When armhole measures 10" shape shoulders as follows: on outside edge only, bind off 24 (28, 31) sts. Pattern to end, turn and pattern back. Bind off remaining sts. Rejoin yarn and bind off center 20 sts and pattern to end. Work right shoulder as for left side.

SLEEVES

With #3 needles cast on 86 sts and work in k2, p2 rib as for back for 2". Change to #6 needles and continue until sleeve measures 4". Start increases: continuing in rib pattern increase 1 st at each edge on this row and every following 3rd row to 164 sts. When sleeve measures 24", shape sleeve top. Bind off 12 sts at the beginning of the next 2 rows, then 9 sts at the beginning of the next 8 rows. Bind off 14 sts at the beginning of the next 2 rows, then bind off remaining 40 sts.

Photo: Courtesy of Cascade Yarns.

COLLAR

Collar is worked alone and sewn on sideways. With #3 needle, cast on 86 sts and work in k2, p2 rib for 25" and bind off. Sew together bind off and cast on edges. Sew collar to neck of sweater with the seam facing the outside. Sew shoulder seams and side seams. Set in sleeves. Roll back a 4" cuff.

Crimson Tide

■ ■ ■

The waves of fashion are sometimes fleeting, but tropical is always in! Try this simple, loosely knit pullover by Tahki Stacy Charles, done in red-hot Austermann Zoom yarn. But cool as a sea breeze!

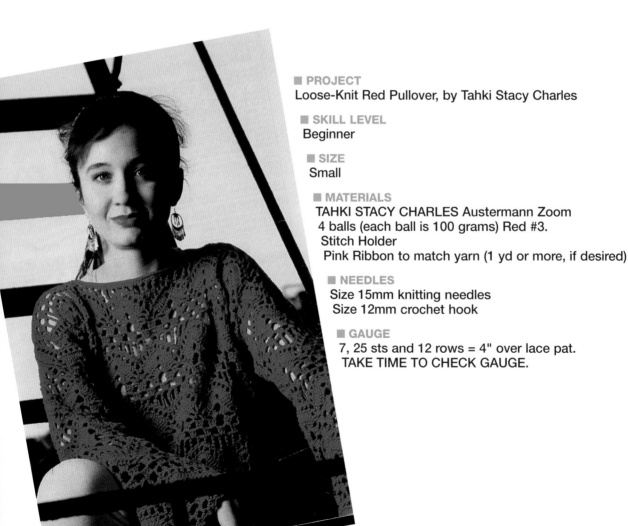

■ **PROJECT**
Loose-Knit Red Pullover, by Tahki Stacy Charles

■ **SKILL LEVEL**
Beginner

■ **SIZE**
Small

■ **MATERIALS**
TAHKI STACY CHARLES Austermann Zoom
4 balls (each ball is 100 grams) Red #3.
Stitch Holder
Pink Ribbon to match yarn (1 yd or more, if desired)

■ **NEEDLES**
Size 15mm knitting needles
Size 12mm crochet hook

■ **GAUGE**
7, 25 sts and 12 rows = 4" over lace pat.
TAKE TIME TO CHECK GAUGE.

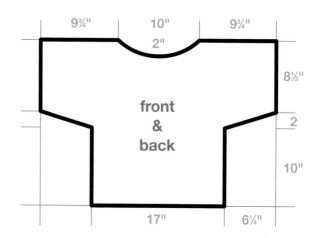

Workbasket magazine often featured celebrities as models or as needlecraft designers. Here, movie and theater actress, Anne Bobby, ("Born on the Fourth of July," "Burden of Proof") models a crocheted sweater featured in *Workbasket's* April 1992 issue. Anne is also an accomplished needle artist whose works have appeared in the Metropolitan Museum of Modern Art.

ABBREVIATIONS

Beg = Begin(ning); **bet** = between; **BO** = bind off; **CC** = contrasting color; **ch** = chain; **CO** = cast on; **dc** = double crochet; **dec** = decreas(e)(s)(ing); **eor** = every other row; **inc** = increase(e)(s)(ing); **k** = knit; **lp** = loop; **MC** = main color; **p** = purl; **pat** = pattern; **pm** = place marker; **rem** = remaining; **RS** = right side; **sc** = single crochet; **seq** = sequence; **sk** = skip; **ssk** = slip, slip, knit; **sssk** = slip, slip, slip, knit (slip the first, second, and/or third stitch knitwise one at a time, then insert the tip of left-hand needle into the back of these 2 or 3 sts and knit them together); **st(s)** = stitch(es); **St st** = Stockinette stitch; **tog** = together; **wyif** = with yarn in front; **wyib** = with yarn in back; **WS** = wrong side; **yo** = yarn over.

DIRECTIONS

LACE PATTERN

Worked over a multiple of 4 sts + 2 selvage sts.

Row 1: 1 selvage st, P2, * yo, P4 tog; rep from *, end P2, 1 slevage st.

Row 2: 1 selvage st, K2, * K1, in next yo work K1, P1 and K1; rep from *, end K2, 1 selvage st.

Row 3: 1 selvage st, P1, *yo, P4 tog; rep from *, end P3, 1 selvage st.

Row 4: 1 selvage st, K3, *K1, in next yo work K1, P1 and K1; rep from *, end K1, 1 selvage st.

Rep rows 1-4 for lace pat.

BACK

Cast on 34 sts and work in garter st for 2 rows. Work in lace pat for 10".

SLEEVES

Cast on 4 sts at beg of next 6 rows = 58 sts. Work 6½" more. Work even until piece measures 18½" from beg.

NECK

Shape Neck: Bind off center 12 sts and working both sides at once, bind off from each neck edge 3 sts once. Work even until piece measures 20½" from beg. Place remaining 20 sts on a holder.

FRONT

Work same as back.

FINISHING

Block pieces to measurements. Weave (or k) shoulders tog. Sew side seams. For neckband, with RS facing and crochet hook, work 1 rnd sc (54 sts) and 1 rnd backwards sc (from left to right) evenly around neck edge. Work in same way around lower edge of sleeves (working 22 sts). Weave ribbon through neck and tie at center front.

With All the Trimmings!

■ ■ ■

This fluff-trimmed cardigan from the 1960s becomes sumptuous and seductive in Berroco's glorious Optik yarn trimmed with Zap and sparkling paillettes of Lazer FX.

■ PROJECT
Button-front Cardigan with Fluff Collar & Cuffs, by Berroco

■ SKILL LEVEL
Intermediate

■ SIZES
Women's X-Small (Small, Medium, Large, X-Large, XX-Large)
Directions for X-Small with larger sizes in parentheses.
If there is only one figure, it applies to all sizes.

■ FINISHED MEASUREMENTS
Bust (butttoned): 36 (38, 40, 42, 44, 46)"
Length: 22 (22½, 23, 23½, 24, 24½)"

■ MATERIALS
A—BERROCO OPTIK (50 g) 9 (9, 10, 10, 11, 11) hanks Van Gogh
B—BERROCO LAZER FX (10 g) 3 (3, 3, 3, 3, 4) balls Gold/Black
C—Optional: BERROCO ZAP (50 g), 1 hank Olive
Seven ¾" buttons

■ NEEDLES
Sizes 7 or 8 straight knitting needles
OR SIZE TO OBTAIN GAUGE.
Size 6 mm (J) crochet hook for Zap trim.

■ GAUGE
16 sts = 4"; 24 rows = 4" in St st on size 8 needles
TAKE TIME TO CHECK GAUGE.

1964 Workbasket

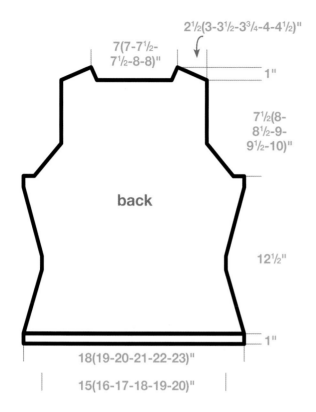

7(7-7½-7½-8-8)"

2½(3-3½-3¾-4-4½)"

1"

7½(8-8½-9-9½-10)"

back

12½"

1"

18(19-20-21-22-23)"

15(16-17-18-19-20)"

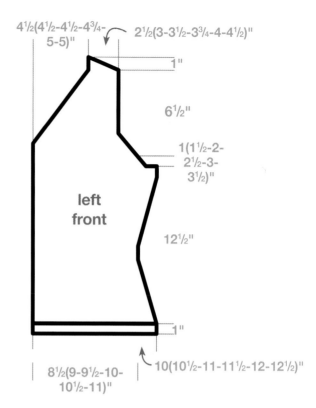

4½(4½-4½-4¾-5-5)"

2½(3-3½-3¾-4-4½)"

1"

6½"

1(1½-2-2½-3-3½)"

left front

12½"

1"

8½(9-9½-10-10½-11)"

10(10½-11-11½-12-12½)"

ABBREVIATIONS

beg = begin(ning); **CC** = contrasting color; **ch** = chain; **dc** = double crochet; **dec** = decrease; **inc** = increase; **k** = knit; **KSP** = K1, then sl st back to LH needle, lift 2nd st on LH needle back over returned st and replace returned st on RH needle (1 st dec'd); **K2SP** = K2 tog, then sl st back to LH needle, lift 2nd st on LH needle back over returned st and replace returned st on RH needle (2 sts dec'd); **lp(s)** = loop(s); **MC** = main color; **M1k** = pickup horizontal strand between st worked and next st, place on LH needle, k this st (inc 1); **M1p** = pickup horizontal strand between st just worked and next st, place on LH needle, p this st (inc 1); **p** = purl; **psso** = pass sl st over k st; **pat(s)** = pattern(s); **rep** = repeat; **RH** = right hand; **RS** = right side; **rnd(s)** = round(s); **sc** = single crochet; **SKP** = sl 1, k 1, psso; **sl** = slip; **SSK** = Sl 2 sts knitwise, insert point of LH needle through FRONTS of these 2 sts and k 2 tog; **st(s)** = stitch(es); **TBL** = through back lp(s); **tog** = together; **WS** = wrong side; **wyib** = with yarn in back; **wyif** = with yarn in front; **yo** = yarn over; **end on WS** = end having just completed a WS row; **end on RS** = end having just completed a RS row.

TIPS FOR WORKING WITH (optional) ZAP

1. Cast on and bind off loosely or with larger needles.

2. Take a strand of Zap and pull it through your fingers. Note the directions of the fringe. The strands should flow away from you as you work. Knitting this way will enhance the fullness of Zap garments.

3. From time to time, with tip of needle, pull loops formed by Zap ends gently through to release yarn and create greater fullness.

4. Use purl side for RS of work.

DIRECTIONS

NOTE 1: After ribbing has been completed, B should be added to A every 5th row. Work with both yarns held tog on that row.

NOTE 2: When B is not in use, it may be carried loosely up the side of work, making sure to wrap both yarns tog every other row to eliminate long loops.

BACK

With smaller needle, using A, cast on 73 (77, 81, 85, 89, 93) sts.

Row 1 (RS): K1, * pl, k1, rep from * across.

Row 2: P1, * k1, p1, rep from * across. Rep these 2 rows until piece measures 1" from beg, end on WS, dec 1 st at end of last row—72 (76, 80, 84, 88, 92) sts. Change to larger needles and work in St st, adding B as in note, dec 1 st each side every ¾" 4 times, then every 1" twice—60 (64, 68, 72, 76, 80) sts. Work even until piece measures 7" from beg, end on WS. Inc 1 st each end of next row, then every 1" 5 times more—72 (76, 80, 84, 88, 92) sts. Work even until piece measures 13½" from beg, end on WS.

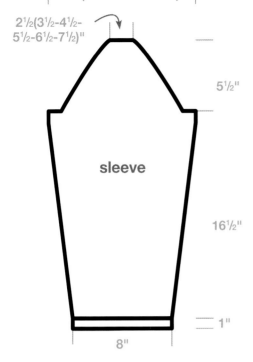

12(13-14-15-16-17)"

2½(3½-4½-5½-6½-7½)"

5½"

sleeve

16½"

1"

8"

Shape Armholes: Bind off 4 sts at beg of the next 2 rows. Dec 1 each side every RS row 8 times—48 (52, 56, 60, 64, 68) sts. Work even until armholes measures 7½ (8, 8½, 9, 9½, 10)", end on WS.

Shape Shoulders and Neck: Next Row (RS): Bind off 4 (4, 5, 5, 6, 6) sts, k until there are 7 (9, 9, 11, 11, 13) sts on RH needle, join another hank of A and bind off center 26 (26, 28, 28, 30, 30) sts, k to end. Working both sides at once, bind off 4 (4, 5, 5, 6, 6) sts at beg of the next row, then 3 (4, 4, 5, 5, 6) sts at beg of the next 4 rows. AT THE SAME TIME, dec 1 st at each neck edge every RS row once.

LEFT FRONT

With smaller needle, using A, cast on 41 (43, 45, 47, 49, 51) sts.

Row 1 (RS): K1, * p1, k1, rep from * to last 2 sts, end k2.

Row 2: K2, p1, * k1, p1, rep from * across. Rep these 2 rows until piece measures 1" from beg, end on WS, dec 1 st at end of last row—40 (42, 44, 46, 48, 50) sts. Change to larger needles. Keeping 2 sts at front edge in Garter St and remaining sts in St st, add B as in note. Dec 1 st at armhole edge every ¾" 4 times, then every 1" twice—34 (36, 38, 40, 42, 44) sts. Work even until piece measures 7" from beg, end on WS. Inc 1 st at beg of the next row, then every 1" 5 times more—40 (42, 44, 46, 48, 50) sts. Work even until piece measures 13½" from beg, end on WS.

Shape Armholes: Bind off 4 sts at beg of the next row. Dec 1 st at armhole edge every RS row 8 times. AT THE SAME TIME, when armhole measures 1½", end on WS.

Shape V-Neck: New Row (RS): Continuing to shape armhole, work to last 4 sts, k2tog, k2. Rep this dec every RS row 15 (14, 14, 12, 13, 12) times more, then every other RS row 2 (3, 4, 6, 6, 7) times—10 (12, 13, 15, 16, 18) sts. When armhole measures 7½ (8 , 8½, 9, 9½, 10)", end on WS. Bind off 4 (4, 5, 5, 6, 6) sts at armhole edge once, then 3 (4, 4, 5, 5, 6) sts twice for shoulder. Mark the position of 7 buttons evenly spaced along front edge, with the first at top of ribbing, the last ½" below start of neck shaping and the other 5 spaced evenly between.

RIGHT FRONT

Work to correspond to left front, reversing all shaping and working next decs as k2, SSK. Make buttonholes on RS rows opposite markers as k2, k2 tog, yo, k to end.

SLEEVES

With smaller needles, using A, cast on 33 sts. Work in ribbing same as for back for 1", end on WS, dec 1 st at end of last row—32 sts. Change to larger needles and work in St st, adding B as in note, inc 1 st each side every 4th row 0 (0, 0, 0, 1, 7) times, every 6th row 0 (0, 1, 9, 15, 11) times, then every 8th row 0 (3, 11, 5, 0, 0) times, then every 10th row 1 (7, 0, 0, 0, 0) times, then every 12th row 7 (0, 0, 0, 0, 0) times—48 (52, 56, 60, 64, 68) sts. Work even until sleeve measures 17½" from beg, end on WS.

Shape Cap: Bind off 4 sts at beg of the next 2 rows. Dec 1 st each side every RS row 13 times, then every other RS row twice. Bind off remaining 10 (14, 18, 22, 26, 30) sts.

FINISHING

Sew shoulder seams. Sew in sleeves. Sew side and sleeve seams.

Neck Edging (Optional): With RS facing, using crochet hook and C, beg at right front edge, work 1 row sc around entire neck edge. Fasten off. Rejoin yarn in first sc and, with RS facing, work 1 sc in each sc around. Fasten off.

Sleeve Edging (Optional): With RS facing, using crochet hook and C, beg at sleeve seam, work 1 rnd sc around lower edge of sleeve, join with sl st in first sc. Ch1, then work 1 sc in each sc around, join with sl st in first sc. Fasten off. Sew on buttons.

Needlework Nouveau

■ ■ ■

Tatting is making a comeback in the most unlikely places—in teen fashions as chokers, earrings, and even belts! But you don't have to be a teen to wear this tasteful beaded ensemble by Handy Hands, inspired from a 1954 Workbasket *issue.*

■ **PROJECT**
Tatted Choker & Earrings, by Handy Hands

■ **SKILL LEVEL**
Beginner

■ **MATERIALS**
Flora Size 10 thread, color of your choice
Approx. 30 seed beads for 12" choker, 9 each for earrings
Pierced earring wires

■ **NEEDLES**
Shuttle or tatting needle

ABBREVIATIONS

Rw = Row; **Ch** = Chain(s); **Cl** = Close ring.

CHOKER DIRECTIONS

Note: *See How-To Tat Basics beginning on page 120 for more information and Diagrams.*

To do a +b, slide a bead on a small crochet hook, hook the picot, slide the bead on the picot and join as normal.

Pre-string 30 beads. (You may want to string more if you want the choker longer. Figure 2½. beads per inch.)

1954 Workbasket

Ch 1-3-4-4-4-4 +b (join to first picot of this chain). Rw.

Ch 4-4-4-4-4-4 +b (join to first picot of this chain). Rw

Repeat from * to * for desired length.

Join to the beginning. Tie/Hide/Cut.

FOR END TIES: Thread 12" length of thread through each picot end of choker so there are two 6" lengths and knot securely. Tie small bow or loose knot at nape of the neck to secure.

EARRINGS DIRECTIONS

Pre-string 9 beads for each earring.

Ch 1-1 Rw.

Ch 6-2 Rw.

Ch +b (to 1st picot made) 6-2 Rw.

Ch +b (to 2nd picot made) 8-2 Rw.

Ch +b (to 3rd picot made) 8-2 Rw.

Ch +b (to 4th picot made) 10-2 Rw.

Ch +b (to 5th picot made) 10-2 Rw.

Ch +b (to 6th picot made) 8-2 Rw.

Ch +b (to 7th picot made) 8, pull up bead for picot, 2 Rw.

Ch +b (to 8th picot made) 1. Tie/Hide/Cut.

Thread pierced earring wires on each smaller picot end.

Town & Country Cardigan

■■■

*When it comes to style **and** practicality, button-front cardigans make all kinds of horse sense. This beautiful textured sweater with wooden buttons designed by Coats & Clark is rendered in rustic Red Heart Tweed. Perfect for a walk—**or ride**—in the country!*

■ PROJECT
Tweed Cardigan, by Coats & Clark

■ SKILL LEVEL
Intermediate

■ SIZES
Small (Medium, Large, X-Large)
Directions for Small with larger sizes in parentheses.
If there is only one figure, it applies to all sizes.

■ MATERIALS
COATS & CLARK Red Heart® "Tweed™" yarn
8 (9, 10, 10) skeins Cranberry
Five ¾" buttons

■ NEEDLES
Size F and H crochet hook
Yarn needle
Sewing needle
Thread to match

■ GAUGE
16 sts and 13 rows = 4" in pattern st using
size H needle
18 sts and 20 rows = 4" in sc using size F needle
TAKE TIME TO CHECK GAUGE.

1990 Workbasket

ABBREVIATIONS

beg = begin(ning); **ch** = chain; **dc =** double crochet; **dec =** decrease; **ea** = each; **est** = established; **mm** = millimeters; **pat** = pattern; **rem** = remain(ning); **rep** = repeat; **sl** = slip; **sc** = single crochet; **st(s)** = stitch(es); **tog** = together; ***** = repeat whatever follows the * as indicated: **yo** = yarn over.

PATTERN STITCH

Note: (Multiple of 3 plus 2).

Base row: (Right side) ch3 (counts as 1 dc), 1 dc in the 2nd st, 1 dc in ea st across.

Row 1: ch1, 1 sc into ea st across, 1 sc into the top of the turning ch.

Row 2: ch3, 1dc into the 2nd st. * tr/rf of dc below next st, skip 1 st, 1dc into ea of the next 2 sts, repeat from * across.

DIRECTIONS

RIBBING

Using size F needle, ch 13.

Row 1: 1 sc into the 2nd from needle, 1 sc into the next 11 ch, turn.

Row 2: Ch 1, 1 sc into the back of ea st across, turn. Repeat row 2 and work until ribbing measures 17½ (19½, 20½, 21½)".

Using size H needle (right side) work 74 (83, 86, 92) dc along long edge of ribbing. Work in pattern st beginning with row 1 until back measures 23½ (24½, 25, 26)" ending with a wrong side row. Fasten off.

POCKET LININGS (Make 2)

Using size H needle ch 20.

Row 1: 1 dc into the 3rd ch from needle and ea of the next 16 chs, turn.

Row 2: Ch 1, 1sc into ea st across, 1 sc into the top of the turning ch, turn.

Row 3: Ch 3, 1 dc into the 2nd st, 1 dc into ea st acorss, turn. Repeat rows 2 and 3 until pocket lining measures 4" ending with row 1. Fasten off.

LEFT FRONT

Using size F needle, work ribbing same as for back to 8¾ (9¾, 10¼, 10¾)". Using size H needle, work 35 (41, 41, 44) dc along long edge of ribbing. Work in pattern until front measures 6½" ending with a wrong side row. Next work 8 (11, 11, 12) sts in est pattern, continuing in est pattern work 17 sts across top of pocket lining, work 10 (13, 13, 15) st in patt. Continue to work in est pattern until front measures 14 (14½, 14½, 15)" ending with a wrong side row.

NECK SHAPING

Work in est patt to the last 2 sts, dc2tog (dec made). Dec 1 st at neck edge every right side row 7 (7, 7, 8) times more, then dec 1 st at neck edge every 2nd right side row 1 (2, 2, 2) times. Work even on 26 (31, 31, 33) sts until front measures 23½ (24½, 25, 26)" with a wrong side row. Fasten off.

RIGHT FRONT

Work the same as right front to 6½". Next row: Work 10 (13, 13, 15) sts, work 17 sts across top of pocket lining, work 8 (11, 11, 12) sts.

Work the same as right front to neck shaping.

NECK SHAPING

Ch2, yo and draw up a loop in the 2nd st, yo, draw thru 2 loops, yo, draw thru 3 loops (dec made), work in est pattern to end of row.

Finish same as right front having neck increases at beg of row.

SLEEVES

Work ribbing same as for back to 7½ (7½, 8, 8)". Using size H needle work 41 (41, 44, 47) dc along long edge of ribbing. Work in pattern and inc 1 st ea end of the row every right side row 14 (16, 16, 17) times, then every 2nd right side row 4 times. Work even on 77 (81, 84, 89) sts until sleeve measures 17½ (18, 18½, 19)" ending with a wrong side row. Fasten off.

FINISHING

Sew pocket lining to inside of fronts. Using size H needle work 1 sc into ea st across the 17 sts of pocket opening, ch 1, work 1 reverse sc into ea st across. Fasten off.

Sew Shoulder Seams: Place a marker 9½ (10, 10½, 11)" below shoulder seam on front and back. Sew sleeve between markers. Sew side and sleeve seams.

Weave in all yarn ends.

FRONT AND NECK BAND

Row 1: With right side facing using size F needle, work 106 (110, 112, 117) sc sts along right front edge, work 1 sc into ea st across back neck, work 106 (110, 112, 117) sc sts along left front edge, turn.

Row 2: Ch1, 1 sc into ea st around, turn.

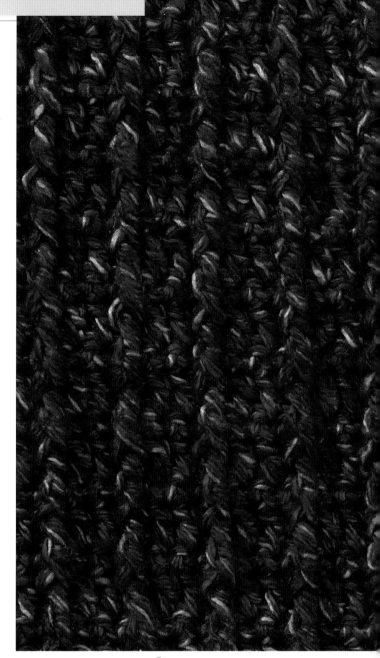

Coats & Clark's Red Heart® Tweed™ yarns come in numerous colors rich in variegated hues such as cranberry, shown above, used in this featured cardigan.

Row 3: Mark 5 buttonholes evenly spaced, the top buttonhole 3 sts below the first neck dec and the bottom buttonhole 3 sts above bottom edge. Ch1 [1 sc into ea st to marker, ch3, skip 3 sc sts] 5 times, 1 sc into ea st to end of row, turn.

Row 4: [1 sc into ea st to the ch3, 1 sc into ea of the 3 ch sts] 5 times, 1 sc into ea st to the end of row, turn.

Row 5: Ch1, 1 sc into each st to end. Finish off.

Chenille Meets Chanel

■ ■ ■

This striped pullover in a 1964 **Workbasket**
issue sports classic Chanel flair. Coats & Clark's similar
version adds a little twist
to the texture with their rich chenille-feel
Baby Teri yarn, soft and subtle in pink and white.

■ **PROJECT**
Powder Puff Sweater, by Coats & Clark

■ **SKILL LEVEL**
Beginner

■ **SIZES**
Small (Medium, Large)
Directions for Small with larger sizes in parentheses.
If there is only one figure, it applies to all sizes.

■ **FINISHED MEASUREMENTS**
To Fit Chest: 32 (36, 40)"
Finished Chest Measurement: 40 (44, 48)"

■ **MATERIALS**
COATS & CLARK Red Heart Baby Teri[®]
3-Ply Light Worsted-Weight Yarn (3 oz. skeins)
CA—7 (8, 8) skeins, White
CB—6 (7, 7) skeins, Pink

■ **NEEDLES**
Size I-9 and K-10.5 SUSAN BATES[®] crochet hooks
OR SIZE TO OBTAIN GAUGE

■ **GAUGE**
22 sts = 9", 25 rows = 12" with larger hook
TAKE TIME TO CHECK GAUGE.

1964 Workbasket

ABBREVIATIONS

beg = begin(ning); **bpdc** = back post double crochet; **ch** = chain; **cont** = continue; **dc** = double crochet; **dec** = decrease; **est** = established; **fpdc** = front post double crochet; **hdc** = half double crochet; **lp** = loop; **pat** = pattern; **rem** = remaining; **rep** = repeat; **sk** = skip; **sp** = space; **st(s)** = stitch(es); **sc** = single crochet; **RS** = right side; **WS** = wrong side; ***** = repeat whatever follows the * as indicated; **yo** = yarn over.

Note: Entire sweater is worked holding 2 strands together. Change colors every 4 rows.

Back & Front Color Sequence: CA & CB, CB & CB, CA & CB, CA & CA.

Sleeve Color Sequence: CA & CA, CA & CB, CB & CB, CA & CB.

DIRECTIONS

BACK

With larger hook using CA & CB ch 50 (56, 60).

Work (sc, dc) in 2nd ch from hook, * sk next ch, (sc, dc) in next ch, rep from * to last 2 ch, sk next ch, sc in last ch; turn—49 (55, 59) st.

Pat Row: Ch 1, * (sc, dc) in sc, sk dc, rep from * to last st, sc in last sc; turn.

Following color sequence rep pat row 22½ (23½, 24½)" from beg.

SHAPE SHOULDERS

Work pat row for 17 (19, 21) st. Fasten off. Skip next 15 (17, 17) st. Attach yarn in next st, ch 1, work pat row across. Fasten off.

FRONT

Work same as back until 6 rows less than back.

FIRST SHOULDER SHAPING

Rep pat row for 21 (23, 25) sts; turn. Cont rep Pat Row, following color sequence until front is same length as back, at the same time, dec 2 st at next edge on next 2 rows. Fasten off.

SECOND SHOULDER SHAPING

Sk next 7 (9, 9) st.

Rep as for First Shoulder.

SLEEVES

Put mark 10 (11, 12)" down from shoulder on front and back. With RS facing, using larger hook, attach CA & CA at mark. Ch 1, work (sc, dc) 24 (27, 29) times evenly spaced between markers, work sc; turn—49 (55, 59) sts.

Following color sequence, work 2 pat rows then 1 dec row 10 (10, 9) times, then work dec row till 27 (29, 29) st rem. Fasten off.

Dec Row: Ch 1, * (sc, dc) in sc, sk dc, rep from * to last 7 st, sc in next sc, yo insert hook in same st as last sc, yo, draw loop through, sk next dc, insert hook in next sc, yo, draw loop through, yo, draw loop through 3 loops on hook, yo, draw through 2 loops on hook, insert hook in last sc used, yo, draw loop through, sk next dc, insert hook in next sc, yo, draw loop through, yo, draw loop through 3 loops on hook, dc in last sc used, sk next dc, sc in last sc; turn—2 st dec.

Sew side and sleeve seams.

SLEEVE & BOTTOM RIBBING

Rnd 1: With RS facing, attach CA & CA at opening, with smaller hook ch 2 (counts as 1 hdc), work an even number of hdc evenly spaced around opening, join in top of beg ch 2.

Rnd 2: Ch 2, * fpdc around post of next st, bpdc around post of next st, rep from * to last st, fpdc around post of last st, join in top of beg ch 2.

Rep Rnd 2 until ribbing is 2". Fasten off.

The powder puff-soft baby Teri yarn, made by Coats & Clark Red Heart, has a unique chenille-like texture and comes in many colors.

NECK RIBBING

With RS facing, attach CA & CA at neck, with smaller hook ch 2 (counts as 1 hdc), work an even number of hdc evenly spaced around neck opening, join in top of beg ch 2. Rep Rnd 2 of sleeve & bottom ribbing for 1½". Fasten off.

Love Triangle

*Fashion has rekindled its love affair with shawls. And why not! They combine Old World romance **and** contemporary casual elegance. This triangle shawl by Lion Brand—reminiscent of one in a 1973* **Workbasket** *issue—is done in glorious lilac Wool Ease. No cold shoulders here!*

■ **PROJECT**
Fringed Triangular Shawl, by Lion Brand

■ **SKILL LEVEL**
Intermediate

■ **SIZES**
One size fits all.

■ **FINISHED MEASUREMENTS**
60" across at widest point

■ **MATERIALS**
LION BRAND Wool-Ease® 4 balls (5 oz/435 yd)
Lilac or color of your choice

■ **NEEDLES**
Size H-8 (5 mm) crochet hook
or size to obtain gauge

■ **GAUGE**
18 sts + 8 rows = 4" in pattern.
TAKE TIME TO CHECK GAUGE.

ABBREVIATIONS

beg = begin(ning); **ch** = chain; **dc** = double crochet; **rep** = repeat(s); **rev** = revers(e)(ing); **st(s)** = stitch(es); **t-ch** = turning chain; **WS** = wrong side.

DIRECTIONS

Row 1: Ch 4, 2 dc in 4th ch from hook—counts as 3 dc.

Row 2: Ch 3 (counts as 1 dc now and each row hereafter), turn. 2 dc in first dc, ch 1, skip 1 dc, 3 dc in 3rd ch of beg-ch of row 1 – 6 dc.

Row 3: Ch 3, turn. 2 dc in first dc, ch 2, dc in ch1-space, ch 2, 3 dc in top of t-ch—7 dc.

Row 4: Ch 3, turn. 2 dc in first dc, ch 1, skip 1 dc, 3 dc in next dc, ch 1, skip (ch 2, dc, ch 2), 3 dc in next dc, ch 1, skip 1 dc, 3 dc in top of t-ch—12 dc.

Row 5: Ch 3, turn. 2 dc in first dc, ch 2, skip 2 dc, 1 dc in ch1-space, ch 2, skip 3 dc, 3 dc in ch1-space, ch 2, skip 3 dc, 1 dc in ch1-space, ch 2, skip 2 dc, 3 dc in top of t-ch—11 dc.

Row 6: Ch 3, turn. 2 dc in first dc, ch 1, skip 1 dc, 3 dc in next dc, * ch1, skip (ch 2, dc, ch 2), 3 dc in next dc, ch 1, skip 1 dc, 3 dc in next dc; rep from *, end last rep 3 dc in top of t-ch.

Row 7: Ch 3, turn. 2 dc in first dc, ch 2, skip 2 dc, * 1 dc in ch1-space, ch 2, skip 3 dc, 3 dc in ch1-space, ch 2, skip 3 dc; rep from *, end last rep dc in ch1-space, ch 2, skip 2 dc, 3 dc in top of t-ch.

Repeat Rows 6 and 7 until shawl measures 60" across, end with Row 6.

Final Row: Ch 3, turn, 1 dc in first dc, ch 1, skip 2 dc, *1 dc in ch1-space, ch 1, skip 3 dc, 3dc in ch1-space, ch 1, skip 3 dc; rep from *, end, 1 dc in ch1-space, ch 1, sk 2 dc, 2 dc in top of t-ch. Work 1 row single crochet evenly across top edge. Fasten off.

FRINGE

Cut strands 16" long. With WS of shawl facing, fold 4 strands in half and draw loops through lowest corner with hook, pull ends through loops and pull knot tight; rep at ends of every other row along short sides of shawl, with last fringe at corner.

Winter Woolies

■ ■ ■

Workbasket's 1970 scarf and fluff-top snowcap are cute, but Berroco's contemporary version in hot Hip Hop yarn sports cache with flair and flashy fringe. And, good news—this set is super easy to make!

■ **PROJECT**
Fringed Scarf, Cap, & Mittens, by Berroco

■ **SKILL LEVEL**
Very Easy

■ **SIZE**
One size fits all

■ **FINISHED MEASUREMENTS**
Finished measurements of scarf: 6" wide (not including fringe) X 64" long.

■ **MATERIALS**
BERROCO HIP HOP (100 g) Zion
Scarf—4 hanks
Hat—2 hanks
Mittens—2 hanks
2 St markers
2 St holders

■ **NEEDLES**
Size 13 straight knitting needles
OR SIZE TO OBTAIN GAUGE
Size 5.5 mm crochet hook
Tapestry needle

■ **GAUGE**
10 sts = 4"; 15 rows = 4" in St st on
size 13 needles
TAKE TIME TO CHECK GAUGE.

1970 Workbasket

beg = begin(ning); **CC** = contrasting color; **ch** = chain; **dc** = double crochet; **dec** = decrease; **inc** = increase; **k** = knit; **lp(s)** = loop(s); **M1**= make one (incr 1); **MC** = main color; **p** = purl; **psso** = pass sl st over k st; **pat(s)** = pattern(s); **rep** = repeat; **RH** = right hand; **RS** = right side; **rnd(s)** = round(s); **sc** = single crochet; **SKP** = sl 1, k 1, psso; **sl** = slip; **st(s)** = stitch(es); **tog** = together; **WS** = wrong side; **yo** = yarn over; **end on WS** = end having just completed a WS row; **end on RS** = end having just completed a RS row.

DIRECTIONS

SCARF

With straight needles, cast on 17 sts.

Row 1 (RS): (K1, p1) twice, k to last 4 sts, end (p1, k1) twice.

Row 2: (P1, k1) twice, p to last 4 sts, end (k1, p1) twice. Rep these 2 rows until piece measures 64" from beg, end on WS. Bind off all sts.

STEAM LIGHTLY: Steam piece lightly by laying piece WS down on a padded surface and move steam iron slowly back and forth 1" above piece. Do not allow iron to touch knitted fabric. Steam will allow knitted fabric to blossom. Selvages and ribbings will lay flat. This method may not allow you to block pieces larger or smaller.

FINISHING: Cut two 12" long strands of yarn. Put strands tog and fold in half. With crochet hook, draw center of strands through end st on first row of scarf, forming a lp. Pull ends of fringe through this lp. In this manner, make fringe in every other row along 1 entire long edge of scarf. Trim fringe to even off if necessary.

Note: For speedier cutting, wrap yarn multiple times around a piece of cardboard that is the desired finished length of the fringe. Cut the lower edge to free wrapped strands.

With RS facing, using crochet hook, work 1 row dc along opposite long edge of scarf from fringe. Ch 2, turn, work 1 dc in each dc across. Fasten off.

HAT

With straight needles, cast on 26 sts.

Row 1 (RS): (K1, p1) twice, k to last 4 sts, (p1, k1) twice.

Row 2: (p1, k1) twice, p to last 4 sts, (k1, p1) twice. Rep these 2 rows until piece measures 19" from beg, end on WS. Bind off all sts.

FINISHING: Steam piece lightly. Fringe one long edge same as for scarf. Sew cast-on edge to bound-off edge. With tapestry needle, weave yarn through fringed edge of hat 1" in from edge. Draw up tightly to gather, then fasten off.

MITTENS

With straight needles, cast on 22 sts.

Row 1 (RS): K2, * p2, k2, rep from * across.

Row 2: P2, * k2, p2, rep from * across. Rep these 2 rows for 4", end on WS. Work even in St st until piece measures 6" from beg, end on WS.

SHAPE THUMB GUSSET: Next Row (RS): K10, place marker, M1k, k2, M1k, place marker, k to end. Continue to inc 1 st after first marker and before second in this manner every RS row twice more, end on WS—28 sts.

THUMB: Next Row (RS): K to first marker and sl these sts onto first holder, drop marker, k8, drop marker, sl remaining 10 sts onto second holder. Work even in St st on 8 sts until thumb measures 2¼", end on WS.

Dec Row (RS): (K2tog) 4 times—4 sts. Break off yarn, leaving an end for sewing. Draw end through 4 sts on needle and pull up tightly. Fasten off. Sew thumb seam.

HAND: Next Row (RS): Sl 10 sts from first holder onto straight needle, join yarn and pick up and k1 st at base of thumb, k10 sts from second holder—21 sts. Work even in St st until hand measures 5" above thumb, end on WS.

SHAPE TOP: Row 1 (RS): *K2tog, rep from * to last st, k1—11 sts. Purl 1 row.

Row 3: * K2tog, rep from * to last st, k1—6 sts. Purl 1 row. Break off yarn, leaving an end for sewing. Draw end through 6 sts on needle and pull up tightly. Fasten off. Sew mitten seam.

Vintage design.

Sassy Satchel

What could be more dramatic than red, except simple black and white in a most striking pattern! Cascade's contemporary fleur-de-lis purse embellished with a Grecian-style geometric border and tassel packs plenty of pizzazz !

■ **PROJECT**
Black & White Fleur-de-lis Purse

■ **SKILL LEVEL**
Intermediate/Advanced

■ **SIZE**
Finished size is 8" across and 5" deep

■ **MATERIALS**
Cascade's Hayfield Yarns (50 g balls)
One ball each White (A) and Black (B)
Next Additions DK Ribbon or any of the Hayfield
DK-weight luxury yarns
One ring marker
One electric hand-mixer (for twisting cord)
One tasseled button
One large snap
Two large paper clips

■ **NEEDLES**
Size 3 (3.25 mm) 16" circular knitting needle

■ **GAUGE**
30 sts = 4"
TAKE TIME TO CHECK GAUGE.

1993 **Workbasket**

ABBREVIATIONS

beg = begin(ning); **bet** = between; **BO** = bind off; **CC** = contrasting color; **ch** = chain; **CO** = cast on; **dc** = double crochet; **dec** = decreas(e)(s)(ing); **eor** = every other row; **hdc** = half double crochet; **inc** = increase(e)(s)(ing); **k** = knit; **lp** = loop; **p** = purl; **pat (s)** = pattern(s) ; **pm** = place marker; **rnd (s)** = round (s); **rem** = remaining; **RS** = right side; **sc** = single crochet; **seq** = sequence; **sk** = skip; **sl st** = slip stitch; **sp** = space; **SSK =** Sl 2 sts knitwise, insert point of LH needle through FRONTS of these 2 sts and k 2 tog; **st(s)** = stitch(es); **St st** = Stockinette stitch; **wyif** = with yarn in front; **wyib** = with yarn in back; **WS** = wrong side; **yo** = yarn over; **end on WS** = end having just completed a WS row; **end on RS** = end having just completed a RS row.

PATTERN STITCHES

PATTERN 1: In-the-round knitting

Rnd 1: With B, knit.

Rnd 2: With B, purl.

Rnd 3: With A; * sl 1, k5, rep from * around.

Rnd 4 and All Subsequent Even Rows: Purl all the same sts worked on previous rnd with the same color; sl all the same sl sts with yarn in *back*.

Rnd 5: With B, k1, sl 1; * k3, sl 1, k1, sl 1; rep from * around end sl 1.

Rnd 7: With A, sl 1; * k3, sl 1, k1, sl 1; rep from * around, end sl 1, k1.

Rnd 9: With B, * k3, sl 1, k1, sl 1; rep from * around.

Rnd 11: With A, k4; * sl 1, k5; rep from * around, end k1.

Rnd 12: Rep rnd 4.

PATTERN I: Row knitting

Rows 1 and All Odd-Numbered Rows (RS): Work as for pat 1 in-the-round version.

Rows 2 and All Even-Numbered Rows (WS): Knit all the same sts worked on previous row with the same color; sl all the same sl sts with yarn in *front*.

Vintage design.

PATTERN II: In-the-round knitting for main section

SSk: Insert right-hand needle in front of first st on left-hand needle, and in back of next st, k these 2 sts tog.

Note: *Rnds 1, 4, 5, and 8 are in B background and Rows 2, 3, 6, and 7 are the A motif.*

Rnd 1: With B, k2; * (k1, yo, k1) in next st making 3 lps in same st, k3; rep from * around, end last rep k1.

Rnd 2: With A, k2; * sl 3 wyib, k3; rep from * around, end last rep k1.

Rnd 3: With A, k1; * k2 tog, sl 1 wyib, ssk, k1; rep from * around, end last rep ssk.

Rnd 4: With B, * sl 1 wyib, k3; rep from * around.

Rnd 5: With B, * (k1, yo, k1) in next st, k3; rep from * around.

Rnd 6: With A, *sl 3 wyib, k3; rep from * around.

Rnd 7: With A, sl 2 wyib; * ssk, k1, k2 tog, sl 1 wyib; rep from * around. ***Note:*** *2nd st of last k2 tog will be the first sl st.*

Rnd 8: With B, k2; * sl 1 wyib, k3; rep from * around, end last rep with k1.

Rep Rnds 1–8 for Pattern II.

DIRECTIONS

PURSE

With B, CO 120 sts; join, being careful not to twist sts. Place marker at beg of rnd and work Pat I Rnds 1–12, then Rnds 1 and 2 once more.

Next work Pat II until 5" from beg, ending after rnd 8.

Next row, BO first 60 sts, then working back and forth in rows, work in pat I for row knitting for 24 rows for front flap. BO all sts.

TWISTED CORDING FOR STRAP

Cut six 90" lengths of yarn to make one corded strap. Hold tog for each drawstring and knot each end. Fasten a large paperclip through one knot and then into the end of the beater of electric hand mixer. Fasten or have someone hold the other end. Run beater until strand is twisted tightly, gradually moving mixer closer to the other end as tension increases. With tension slightly relaxed (when cord begins to twist on itself), fold in half and allow to wind on itself. Finally, knot each of the double ends.

FINISHING

Sew bottom opening shut. Attach each end of the Twisted Cord strap to each side of bag. Sew tasseled button to center flap. Sew large snap inside flap.

Homespun in Heather

■ ■ ■

As crisp and cozy as an autumn day, this smart heather-soft pullover and tunic ensemble was knit in Lion Brand's Homespun yarn. You won't believe how comfy this casual combo is to wear!

■ **PROJECT**
Heather Pullover & Tunic, by Lion Brand

■ **SKILL LEVEL**
Intermediate

■ **SIZES**
Small (Medium, Large, X-Large, XX-Large)
Directions for Small with larger sizes in parentheses.
If there is only one figure, it applies to all sizes.

■ **FINISHED MEASUREMENT**
Finished chest measurements: 36 (40, 44, 48, 52)"

■ **MATERIALS**
MC—LION BRAND Homespun Sierra (6 oz. skeins)
CC—LION BRAND Homespun Williamsburg Blue
PULLOVER: Homespun 5 (5, 6, 6, 7) skeins
TUNIC: Homespun: 4 (4, 4, 5, 5) skeins;
CC—Homespun 1 (1, 1, 1, 1) skein
3 Large stitch holders
Stitch marker

■ **NEEDLES**
Size 10½ circular needle, 24"
Yarn needle

■ **GAUGE**
3 sts and 4 rows = 1" in St st on 10½ needles
TAKE TIME TO CHECK GAUGE.

1981 Workbasket

beg = begin(ning); **CC** = contrasting color; **CO** = cast on; **dec** = decrease; **k** = knit; **M1** = make one (incr 1); **MC** = main color; **p** = purl; **pat** = pattern; **RS** = right side; **ssk** = slip, slip, knit; **sssk** = slip, slip, slip, knit (slip the first, second, and/or third stitch knitwise one at a time, then insert the tip of the left-hand needle into the back of these 2 or 3 sts and knit them together); **st(s)** = stitch(es); **St st** = Stockinette stitch; **tog** = together; **WS** = wrong side.

DIRECTIONS

PULLOVER

Back: ** CO 54 (60, 66, 72, 78) sts. Work 9 rows in k2, p2 rib. Starting with a knit row, work in St st (knit 1 row, purl 1 row) until piece measures 16" from beg or desired length to underarm ending with a purl row.

Armhole Shaping (All Sizes): BO 3 sts at beg of next 2 rows. *For sizes 44, 48, and 52 ONLY:* **Row 1:** ssk, k to last 2 sts, k2tog. **Row 2:** Purl. Repeat Rows 1 and 2 twice more. **

All Sizes: Work even until armhole measures 7 (7½, 8, 8½, 9)".

Neck Shaping: Row 1: k 13 (14, 14, 16, 17), then k 22 (26, 26, 28, 32) and place on large stitch holder, k 13 (14, 14, 16, 17).

Left Shoulder: Row 2: Purl. **Row 3:** ssk, k to end. **Row 4:** Purl. Bind off.

Right Shoulder: With wrong side facing, join yarn at neck edge. **Row 2:** Purl. **Row 3:** k to last 2 sts, k2tog. **Row 4:** Purl. Bind off.

FRONT

Work same as back from ** to **. Then continue working even until armhole measures 6 (6½, 7, 7½, 8)".

Neck Shaping: Row 1: k 15 (16, 16, 18, 19), then k 18 (22, 22, 24, 28) and place on large stitch holder, k 15 (16, 16, 18, 19).

Right shoulder: Row 2: Purl. **Rows 3 and 5:** ssk, k to end. **Rows 4 and 6:** Purl. Bind off.

Left shoulder: Row 2(WS): Join yarn at neck edge, purl across. **Rows 3 and 5:** k to last 2 sts, k2tog. **Rows 4 and 6:** Purl. Bind off.

COLLAR

Sew both shoulder seams. Starting at left shoulder seam, pick up 6 sts along left front neck, k 18 (22, 22, 24, 28) from front stitch holder, pick up 6 sts along right front neck, pick up 4 sts along right back, k 22 (26, 26, 28, 32) from back stitch holder, pick up 4 sts along left back neck: 60 (68, 68, 72, 80) sts. Place marker. Working in rounds, k2, p2 around until collar measures 10". Bind off loosely in rib. Weave in ends.

SLEEVES

CO 28 (28, 28, 32, 32). Work 9 rows in k2, p2 rib.

Row 1 (inc row): K1, M1, k to last st, M1, k1. **Row 2:** Purl. **Row 3:** Knit. **Row 4:** Purl. Rep rows 1–4 3 (4, 5, 6, 6) times more. Then, **Row 1:** K1, M1, k to last st, M1, k1. **Rows 2, 4, and 6:** Purl. **Rows 3 and 5:** Knit. Rep rows 1-6 until you have 48 (52, 54, 58, 60) sts. Work even until sleeve measures 18 (18, 18½, 19, 19)" from beginning. Bind off.

FINISHING

Sew sleeves to armholes between BO sts. *Do not sew upper part of sleeve to the 3 BO sts.* Next, weave or sew BO sts to sides of sleeve. Then, sew side seams and sleeve seams. Weave in ends.

tunic front chart for blue design

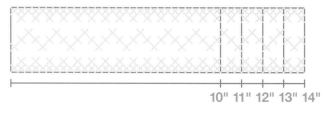

10" 11" 12" 13" 14"

Homespun yarn sample colors

TUNIC

BACK

CO 60 (66, 72, 78, 84) sts. Work 9 rows in k2, p2 rib. Starting with knit row, work in St st until piece measures 22" from beg, ending with a purl row.

Armhole Shaping (all sizes): BO 3 sts at beg of next 2 rows.

Next, for sizes 48, 52, and 56 ONLY:
Row 1: Ssk, k to last 2 sts, k2tog. **Row 2:** Purl. Rep rows 1 and 2 twice more.

All Sizes: Work even in St st until armhole measures 8 (8½, 8½, 9, 9)".

Neck Shaping: Row 1: K 13 (15, 15, 16, 19), then k 28 (30, 30, 34, 34) and place on large stitch holder, k 13 (15, 15, 16, 19).

Left shoulder: **Row 2:** Purl. **Row 3:** SSK, k to end. **Row 4:** Purl. Bind off.

Right shoulder: Row 2(WS): Join yarn at neck edge, purl across. **Row 3:** K to last 2 sts, k2tog. **Row 4:** Purl. Bind off.

LEFT FRONT

** CO 30 (32, 36, 38, 42) sts. Work 9 rows in K2, P2 rib. **Row 1:** Inc 1 sts 0 (1, 0, 1, 0) times, k to end: 30 (33, 36, 39, 42) sts. **Row 2:** Purl. Continue in St st until piece measures 6½" from beg ending with a purl row. Join CC and work Chart A over next 9 rows. Then, continue in St st with MC until piece measures 20½" from beg. ** Work Chart A again and AT THE SAME TIME, when 22" from beg and ending with a *purl* row, start Armhole Shaping as follows:

Row 1: BO 3 sts, work across as established. **Row 2:** Purl across as established.

For sizes 48, 52, and 56 ONLY:

Row 3: ssk, knit across as established. **Row 4:** Purl across as established.

Rep rows 3 and 4 twice more. (Remember to keep in pat until you have finished Chart, then continue in MC.)

All Sizes: Work even until armhole measures 7 (7½, 7½, 8, 8)".

Neck Shaping: Row 1: K 13 (15, 15, 16, 19), k2tog, slip remaining 12 (13, 16, 18, 18) sts onto stitch holder. **Rows 2, 4, and 6:** Purl. **Row 3:** K 12 (14, 14, 15, 18), k2tog. **Row 5:** K 11 (13, 13, 14, 17), k2tog. **Row 7:** Knit. **Row 8:** Purl. Bind off.

RIGHT FRONT

Work same as Left Front from ** to **. Then work Chart and AT THE SAME TIME, when 22" from beg and ending with a knit row, work as follows:

Armhole Shaping: Row 1: BO 3 sts, purl across as established.

Sizes 40 and 44 ONLY:
Row 2: K across as established.

Sizes 48, 52, and 56 ONLY:
Row 2: Work across as established to last 2 sts, k2tog.

Row 3: Purl across as established.

Rep rows 2 and 3 twice more. (Remember to keep in pat until you have finished Chart, then continue in MC.)

All Sizes: Work even until armhole measures 7 (7½, 7½, 8, 8)".

Neck Shaping: Row 1: k 12 (13, 16, 18, 18) sts and place on stitch holder, ssk, k to end: 14 (16, 16, 17, 20) sts on needle. **Rows 2, 4, and 6:** Purl. **Rows 3 and 5:** Ssk, k to end. **Row 7:** Knit. **Row 8:** Purl. Bind off.

NECKBAND

Sew shoulder seams. With right sides facing and beg at right front, k 12 (13, 16, 18, 18) sts from right front stitch holder, pick up 8 sts along right neck to shoulder, pick up 4 sts along right back, k 28 (30, 30, 34, 34) sts from back stitch holder, pick 4 sts along left back to shoulder, pick up 8 sts along left front, k 12 (13, 16, 18, 18) sts from left front stitch holder: 76 (80, 86, 94, 94) sts. Work 3 rows in k2, p2 rib. Bind off loosely in rib.

FRONT BANDS

From right side of work, pick up 92 sts evenly spaced along left front and then right front. Work 3 rows in k2, p2 rib. Bind off in rib.

ARMBANDS

Working between the 3 BO sts, pick up 68 (68, 68, 72, 72) sts. Work 3 rows in k2, p2 rib. Bind off in rib. Sew sides of band to the Bind off sts.

FINISHING

Sew side seams up to armbands. Weave in ends.

Poignant Picots

■ ■ ■

Wedding garters have a long tradition and so does tatting. Try this quick-and-easy but elegant tatted wedding garter with a delicate picot pattern. Designed by Handy Hands based on a Workbasket 1978 design.

■ PROJECT
Tatted Bridal Garter, by Handy Hands

■ SKILL LEVEL
Beginner

■ SIZE
Tat length to fit

■ MATERIALS
Flora size 10 thread, color of your choice
Needle Ribbon, at least a yard (enough to thread through tatted length and tie in graceful bow)
Tatting shuttle or needle

ABBREVIATIONS

R = Ring(s); **Rw** = Row; **Ch** = Chain(s); **Cl** = Close ring.

DIRECTIONS:

Note: *See How-To-Tat Basics beginning on page 120 for more information and diagrams.*

R 8-8 Cl. Rw.

Ch 5-1-1-1-1-1-5 Rw.

R 4-4+ (to center picot of prev. R) 4-4 Cl. Rw.

*Ch 4-1-1-4 Cl.

R 4+ (to last picot of prev. R) 4-4-4 Cl. Rw.*

Repeat for * to * for desired length.

1978 Workbasket

Ch 5-1-1-1-1-1-5 Rw.

R 8+ (to center picot of prev. R) 8 Cl. Rw.

Ch 5-1-1-1-1-1-5 Rw.

R 4-4+ (to center joining picot of prev. R) 4-4 Cl. Rw.

**Ch 4-1-1-4 Cl.

R 4+ (to last picot of prev. R) 4+ (to center picot of corresponding R) 4-4 Cl. Rw. **

Repeat for ** to ** to end.

Ch 5-1-1-1-1-1-5 Rw.

Join to the beginning. Tie/Hide/Cut

Thread ribbon (type and color of your choice) through middle of tatted length. Tie both ends in graceful bow. If desired, can also embellish with tiny silk roses (as shown).

Linear á la Mode

■ ■ ■

Believe it or not, a beginner can make this gorgeous sweater! Echoing a sweater in a 1977 **Workbasket** *issue, the new Tahki Stacy Charles version is in cashmere-soft Micio in seven glorious colors. Earn* **these** *stripes the easy way!*

■ PROJECT
Striped Fuzzy Sweater, by Tahki Stacy Charles

■ SKILL LEVEL
Beginner

■ SIZES
Small (Medium, Large)
Directions for Small with larger sizes in parentheses.
If there is only one figure, it applies to all sizes.

■ FINISHED MEASUREMENTS
Finished Chest: 33 (35, 37)"
Length: 20 (20½, 21)"
Upper Arm: 13 (13, 13½)"

■ MATERIALS
TAHKI STACY CHARLES Collezione Micio yarn (each ball 50 g; approx. 110 yds)
A—3 balls black for all sizes
B—1 ball red for all sizes
C—1 ball rust for all sizes
D—1 ball brown for all sizes
E—1 ball purple for all sizes
F—1 ball olive for all sizes
G—1 ball sage green for all sizes
Stitch holders

■ NEEDLES
Size 8 knitting needles
OR SIZE TO OBTAIN GAUGE
Size 6 needles for neck finishing

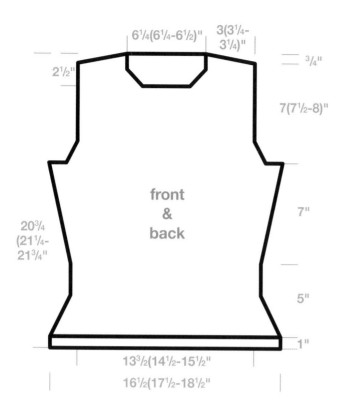

Measurements for front & back:
6¼(6¼-6½)"
3(3¼-3¼)"
2½"
¾"
7(7½-8)"
7"
5"
1"
20¾(21¼-21¾)"
13¾(14½-15½)"
16½(17½-18½)"

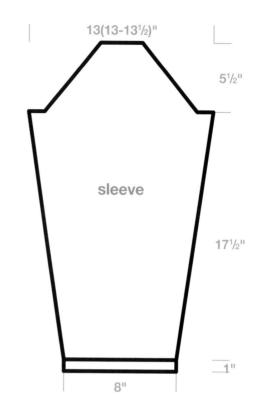

Measurements for sleeve:
13(13-13½)"
5½"
17½"
1"
8"

■ GAUGE

16 sts and 24 rows = 4" in St st using size 8 needles
TAKE TIME TO CHECK GAUGE.

ABBREVIATIONS

beg = begin(ning); **bet** = between; **BO** = bind off; **CC** = contrasting color; **ch** = chain; **CO** = Cast on; **cont** = continue; **dc** = double crochet; **dec** = decreas(e)(s)(ing); **eor** = every other row; **inc** = increase(e)(s)(ing); **k** = knit; **lp** = loop; **MC** = main color; **p** = purl; **pat** = pattern; **pm** = place marker; **rem** = remaining; **RS** = right side; **sc** = single crochet; **seq** = sequence; **sk** = skip; **ssk** = slip, slip, knit; **sssk** = slip, slip, slip, knit (slip the first, second, and/or third stitch knitwise one at the time, then insert the tip of the left-hand needle into the back of these 2 or 3 sts and knit them together); **st(s)** = stitch(es); **St st** = Stockinette stitch; **tog** = together; **wyif** = with yarn in front; **wyib** = with yarn in back; **WS** = wrong side; **yo** = yarn over.

DIRECTIONS

STRIPE SEQUENCE

Working in St st (k 1 row, p 1 row), work *2 rows A, 4 rows B, 2 rows A, 4 rows C, 2 rows A, 4 rows D, 2 rows A, 4 rows E, 2 rows A, 4 rows F, 2 rows A, 4 rows G; rep from * for length.

BACK

Using larger needles and A, cast on 74 (78, 82) sts; work 1" in k2, p2 rib, end WS row. Cont with A, beg Stripe pat, work 2 rows even.

Shape Body: Dec 1 st each side every 4 rows 6 times—62 (66, 70) sts. Work even until piece measures 6" from beg, then inc 1 st each side every 4 rows 6 times—74 (78, 82) sts. Work even in Stripe pat until piece measures 13" from beg, end with 4th row of G.

Shape armhole: Cont in Stripe pat, at each side, bind off 4 sts once, 3 sts once, then 1 st each side every other row 3 (3, 4) times—54 (58, 60) sts. Work even in Stripe pat until armhole measures 7 (7½, 8)", end WS row.

Shape Shoulder: At each shoulder, bind off 6 (7, 7) sts once, 7 (8, 8) sts once; place rem sts on holder for black neck.

FRONT

Work as for back until armhole measures $4\frac{1}{2}$ (5, $5\frac{1}{2}$)", end WS row.

Shape Neck: (RS) Cont in Stripe pat, k18 (20, 20) sts, place next 18 (18, 20) sts on a holder, join a second ball of yarn and work to end. Working each side separately, bind off at each neck edge 3 sts once, then 1 st at each neck edge every other row twice—13 (15, 15) sts each shoulder; when piece measures same as back to shoulder shaping, Shape shoulders as for Back.

SLEEVES

Using larger needles and A, cast on 36 sts; work 4 rows in k2, p2 rib. Beg Stripe pat with 4 rows B.

Shape Sleeve: Cont in Stripe pat, inc 1 st each side every 6 rows 4 (4, 5) times, every 8 rows 7 times— 58 (58, 60) sts. Work even until piece measures approx $18\frac{1}{2}$" from beg, end with 4th row of G.

Shape Cap: At each side, bind off 4 sts once; then 1 st each side every other row until cap measures 5" from beg of shaping; at each side, bind off 2 sts twice; bind off rem sts.

FINISHING

Block pieces very lightly to finished measurements. Sew right shoulder seam.

Mock Turtleneck: RS facing, using smaller needles and A, beg at left front neck edge, pick up and knit approx 68 (68, 72) sts evenly around neck, including sts on holders; work in k2, p2 rib for 3"; bind off in pat.

Sew left shoulder and mock turtleneck. Set in sleeves; sew side and sleeve seams.

Vintage design.

Ripple Effect

Ripples were the rage in '70s fashions and they're back in waves! This dramatic redeux by Lion Brand sports a mesmerizing ripple stitch in rich Wool Ease colors. Sure to make a splash in any circle!

■ **PROJECT**
Ripple Pullover, by Lion Brand

■ **SKILL LEVEL**
Intermediate

■ **SIZES**
Small (Medium, Large, X-Large, XX-Large)
Directions for Small with larger sizes in parentheses.
If there is only one figure, it applies to all sizes.

■ **FINISHED MEASUREMENTS**
Finished chest: 39 (42, 45, 48, 51)"
Length: 24 (24, 25, 25, 26)"

■ **MATERIALS**
Lion Brand Wool-Ease (3 oz. balls, approx. 197 yd)
A/MC—Cranberry 4 (4, 5, 5, 5) balls
B—Butterscotch 2 (2, 3, 3, 3) balls
C—Black 2 (2, 3, 3, 3) balls
D—Seaspray 2 (2, 3, 3, 3) balls
E—Fisherman 2 (2, 3, 3, 3) balls
F—Loden 2 (2, 3, 3, 3) balls

■ **NEEDLES**
Size I-9 (5.5 mm) crochet hook or
SIZE TO OBTAIN GAUGE
Size G-6 (4 mm) crochet hook for joining seams
Large-eyed, blunt needle

■ **GAUGE**
8 "V" sts + 10 rows = 4".
For gauge swatch Ch 34, work "V" st pattern.
TAKE TIME TO CHECK GAUGE.

1975 Workbasket

ABBREVIATIONS

beg = begin(ning); **ch** = chain; **dc** = double crochet; **dec** = decreas(e)(s)(ing); **hdc** = half double crochet; **inc** = increase(e)(s)(ing); **rnd(s)** = round(s); **sc** = single crochet; **st(s)** = stitch(es); **t-ch** = turning chain; **WS** = wrong side; **yo** = yarn over.

DIRECTIONS

"V" STITCH PATTERN (Multiple of 3 +1, plus 3 ch to turn)

Row 1: 2 dc in 5th ch from hook—"V" st made. (Skip 2 ch, 2 dc in next ch) across to last 2 ch. Skip 1 ch, dc in last ch, ch 3, turn.

Row 2: (Skip 2 sts, 2 dc in middle of "V" st below) across, ending with 1 dc in t-ch space. Ch 3, turn.

Repeat Row 2 for pattern.

NOTES

1. 2 dc worked in one space counts as one "V" st.

2. Last dc at end of each row and t-ch at beg of row count as edge sts.

3. When changing colors at end of row, work last dc until 2 loops remain on hook. Tie new color around old color and slide knot close to hook. Draw new color through 2 loops on hook to complete st. Leave 6" yarn ends at edges to be worked with when finishing sweater.

4. To inc 1 "V" st work 2 dc in space formed by edge st.

5. When working sc along row ends, a pattern of (2 sc in space, 1 sc in next space) may be needed to ease in fullness.

6. To dec 1 sc draw up loop in each of next 2 sc, yo, draw through 3 loops on hook.

COLOR SEQUENCE

3 rows	A Cranberry
1 row	B Butterscotch
1 row	C Black
2 rows	D Seaspray
1 row	A Cranberry
1 row	E Fisherman
1 row	F Loden
1 row	A Cranberry
2 rows	B Butterscotch
1 row	D Seaspray
1 row	C Black
1 row	E Fisherman
1 row	F Loden

LION BRAND'S Wool-Ease yarn comes in a vast variety of colors and weights. Shown is just a smattering of Wool-Ease colors and weights.

BACK

With A and larger hook, ch 118 (127, 136, 145, 154). Work in pattern, forming 38 (41, 44, 47, 50) "V" sts across, plus an edge st at each end, changing colors in sequence as indicated, until piece measures 14" (or desired length) to underarm. At end of last row, ch 1, turn.

Shape Armhole: Slip st across first 9 dc, ch 3, continue in "V" st pattern across 30 (33, 36, 39, 42) "V" sts, skip 1 dc, dc in next dc for edge st, ch 3, turn (leaving last 3 full "V" sts unworked). Continue in pattern until piece measures 9 (9½, 10, 10½, 11)" from beg of armhole. Fasten off.

FRONT

Work same as for Back and armhole shaping. Continue in pattern until piece measures 6 (6½, 7, 7½, 8)" from beg of armhole.

Shape Neck: (Note: When changing colors for the following rows, leave long enough yarn ends at neck edge to weave in across entire row toward armhole edge.)

Next Row: Work in pattern across 9 (9, 10, 11, 12) "V" sts, skip 1 dc, dc in next dc for edge st, ch 3, turn. Continue in pattern until piece measures 9 (9½, 10, 10½, 11)" from beg of armhole. Change to A, ch 1, turn, sc in each dc across and in t-ch—20 (20, 22, 24, 26) sc. Fasten off, leaving long yarn end for sewing shoulder seam. Attach yarn to last row worked before neck shaping (WS facing) with slip st in the 42nd (48th, 52nd, 56th, 60th) dc from beg of row, counting t-ch at beg as 1 dc. Ch 3, continue in pattern as for other side, leaving center 10 (13, 14, 15, 16) "V" sts unworked. Fasten off, leaving long yarn end for sewing shoulder seam.

SLEEVES

With A and larger hook, ch 55 (55, 61, 61, 61). Work even in pattern, forming 17 (17, 19, 19, 19) "V" sts across plus an edge st at each end, changing colors in sequence as indicated, for 4 (4, 4, 3, 3)

Vintage design.

rows. Inc 1 "V" st at each end of next row and every 5th (5th, 5th, 4th, 4th) row thereafter until there are 35 (37, 39, 41, 43) "V" sts across. Work even for 5 (0, 0, 6, 2) more rows for a total of 50 rows from beg (approximately 20"). Change to color A yarn, ch 1, turn, sc in each dc across and in t-ch—72 (76, 80, 84, 88) sc. Fasten off, leaving long yarn end for sewing sleeve to body.

FINISHING

Sew shoulder seams.

Neckband: Rnd 1: Join A with slip st at center back neck, ch 1, work sc evenly around neck edge. Join rnd with slip st in first sc, ch 1, turn. **Rnd 2:** Sc in each sc around, decreasing 1 sc at inner curves. Join rnd, ch 1, turn. **Rnd 3:** Hdc in each sc around, join rnd, fasten off.

Armhole and Sleeve Seams: With A, work 1 row sc evenly along armhole edge of body of sweater to correspond with the number of sts along last sleeve row. Set in sleeve and sew to armhole edge.

Sleeve and Seams: With A and smaller hook, and right sides together, attach yarn at cuff edge with slip st through both layers. Working tightly, (ch 3, slip st in next space through both layers) along sleeve seam to underarm and down side seam to lower edge. Hold yarn ends toward back, being careful not to catch them in slip sts.

Lower Edge and Cuff Borders: Join A with slip st at seam, ch 1, work (1 hdc in center of "V" st, 1 hdc in next space) around edge, join rnd with slip st, fasten off.

Yarn Ends: On inside of sweater, tie pairs of corresponding color yarn ends (one each from front and back) together with overhand knots. Yarn ends within 3" to 4" of lower edge and cuffs may be sewn into seams, all others may be trimmed to about 3".

Checkmate!

Workbasket's *1967 checked sweater is fun, but Coats & Clark's contemporary tweed pattern, rendered in Red Heart yarn, has stunning checkerboard charm. Definitely a smart move in the game of style!*

■ **PROJECT**
Checkerboard Sweater, by Coats & Clark

■ **SKILL LEVEL**
Intermediate

■ **SIZE**
Small (Medium, Large)
Directions for Small with larger sizes in parentheses.
If there is only one figure, it applies to all sizes.

■ **FINISHED MEASUREMENTS**
To Fit Chest: 32 (36, 40)"
Finished Chest Measurement: 36 (40, 44)"

■ **MATERIALS**
COATS & CLARK Red Heart Yarn
A—5 (5, 6) skeins, Red Heart Tweed Worsted-Weight
Yarn (4 oz. skeins) Lavender
B—2 (2, 3) skeins, Red Heart Super-Saver Worsted-
Weight (8 oz. skeins) Soft White

■ **NEEDLES**
Susan Bates crochet hooks
Size G-6 (4 mm)
Size H-8 (5 mm)
OR SIZE TO OBTAIN GAUGE.

■ **GAUGE**
13 sts = 4", 33 rows = 7" with larger hook.
TAKE TIME TO CHECK GAUGE.

1967 Workbasket

ABBREVIATIONS

beg = begin(ning); **cont** = continue; **est** = established; **pat** = pattern; **rem** = remaining; **rep** = repeat; **st(s)** = stitch(es); **ch** = chain; **sc** = single crochet; **hdc** = half double crochet; **dc** = double crochet; **fpdc** = front post double crochet; **bpdc** = back post double crochet; **lp** = loop; **sk** = skip; **sp** = space; **dec** = decrease; **RS** = right side; **WS** = wrong side; ***** = repeat whatever follows the * as indicated; **[ ]** = work directions given in brackets the number of times specified.

DIRECTIONS

CHART INSTRUCTIONS

RS rows are worked from right to left. WS rows are worked from left to right. * Work 1 row using A drop loop from hook. Go back to beginning of last row and work 1 row using B working in the same direction. Drop loop from hook. Pick up dropped loop of A. Repeat from * throughout. Begin each row with ch 2 (does not count as a st) and sc in first st even if chart does not have a sc indicated for the first st. End each row with a sc in the last st even if chart does not have a sc indicated for the last st. When working long single crochet = ls, work ls in sc or ls st in row or rows below working over ch st. Never work ls in ch st except in beginning foundation ch.

BACK

With larger hook using A ch 60 (66, 72). Begin by working first sc in second ch from hook.

Follow chart for Back until piece is 22½ (23½, 24½)" ending with a WS A row.

Shape Shoulders: Work next pat row for 20 (22, 24) st. Fasten off. Skip next 19 (21, 23) st. Attach yarn in next st, ch 1, continue across row in est pat. Fasten off. Using A, sc in each st across both shoulders. Fasten off.

FRONT

Work same as Back until 14 rows less than back ending on a WS A row.

First Shoulder Shaping: Work next pat row for 24 (26, 28) st; turn.

Cont working in est pat until 1 row less than Back, at the same time, dec 2 st at next edge on next B row then 1 st at neck edge on next 2 B rows.

Using A, sc in each st across shoulder. Fasten off.

Second Shoulder Shaping: Sk next 11 (13, 15) st. Rep as for First Shoulder.

stitch chart schematic for lavender checkerboard sweater

[Stitch chart grid schematic with repeated S, ls, W, L symbols, marked with "repeat 4 times" at right side in multiple places; bottom markers labeled L, M, S ... S, M, L]

S	SINGLE CROCHET	L SINGLE CROCHET
ls	LONG SINGLE CROCHET	W LONG SINGLE CROCHET
	CHAIN STITCH	

SLEEVES

Put mark 9 (10, 11)" down from shoulder on front and back. With RS facing, using larger hook, attach A at mark. Ch 1, work first row of chart evenly spaced between markers. Cont working chart till 4 (3, 2)" from beg.

Cont working chart, at the same time dec 1 st on end of every B row till 15 (15½, 16)" from beg ending with a B row.

Using A, sc in each st across. Fasten off.

Sew side and sleeve seams.

SLEEVE and BOTTOM RIBBING

Rnd 1: With RS facing, attach A at opening, with smaller hook ch 2 (counts as 1 hdc), work an even number of hdc evenly spaced around opening, join in top of beg ch 2. **Rnd 2:** Ch 2, * fpdc around post of next st, bpdc around post of next st, rep from * to last st, fpdc around post of last st, join in top of beg ch 2.

Rep Rnd 2 till ribbing is 2". Fasten off.

NECK RIBBING

With RS facing, attach A at neck, with smaller hook ch 2 (counts as 1 hdc), work an even number of hdc evenly spaced around neck opening, join in top of beg ch 2. Rep Rnd 2 of Sleeve and Bottom Ribbing for 1". Fasten off.

Sweater-Coat Swank

■ ■ ■

This gorgeously textured sweater with cozy cowl neck by Cascade is done in Magnum wool yarn. Quite similar in design to a **Workbasket** *December 1970 popcorn coat, the svelte sweater-coat look was classic then and still is!*

■ **PROJECT**
Sweater Coat, by Cascade

■ **SKILL LEVEL**
Intermediate

■ **SIZE**
Small (Medium, Large)
Directions for Small with larger sizes in parentheses.
If there is only one figure, it applies to all sizes.

■ **FINISHED MEASUREMENTS**
Finished Chest: 48 (54, 60)"
Length hanging: 48" (Coat can stretch, so plan ahead regarding length.)

■ **MATERIALS**
CASCADE's Magnum yarn 10 (11, 12) skeins
CASCADE 220 yarn 8 (9, 10) skeins
5 large buttons and 3 medium matching buttons

■ **NEEDLES**
Sizes 8, 9, 10, 10½ & 15 (The size 9 must be a long circular needle.)

■ **GAUGE**
In pattern stitch, 7 sts = 13½"
TAKE TIME TO CHECK GAUGE.

1970 Workbasket

ABBREVIATIONS

beg = begin(ning); **bet** = between; **BO** = bind off; **CC** = contrasting color; **ch** = chain; **CO** = Cast on; **dc** = double crochet; **dec** = decreas(e)(s)(ing); **eor** = every other row; **inc** = increase (s)(ing); **k** = knit; **lp** = loop; **MC** = main color; **p** = purl; **pat** = pattern; **pm** = place marker; **rem** = remaining; **RS** = right side; **sc** = single crochet; **seq** = sequence; **sk** = skip; **ssk** = slip, slip, knit; **sssk** = slip, slip, slip, knit (slip the first, second, and/or third stitch knitwise, one at the time, then insert the tip of left-hand needle into the back of these 2 or 3 sts and knit them together); **st(s)** = stitch (es); **St st** = Stockinette stitch; **wyif** = with yarn in front; **wyib** = with yarn in back; **WS** = wrong side; **yo** = yarn over.

DIRECTIONS

PATTERN STITCH

When working with Magnum and 220, always use one strand of each for pattern stitch. The 220 is always used two strands for trim ribbing. For a softer lighter coat, use Magnum alone for pattern stitch, and you will use three skeins less of Cascade 220.

Pattern Stitch for Magnum and 220:
Row 1: (k2, p2) rep. to end
Row 2: Purl
Row 3: (p2, k2) rep. to end
Row 4: Purl

Trim Ribbing:
Row 1: (k2, p2) rep. to end
Row 2: Knit the knits & Purl the purls

Note: Always keep in the Magnum pattern stitch, a selvedge stitch of one knit at the beginning and end of right side rows. Make all increases and decreases inside that edge stitch.

BACK

Cast on very loosely 56 (60, 68) sts and with size 15 needles work pattern stitch. Work pattern decreasing 1 st each end every 6", 4 times 48 (52, 60) sts. When total from beginning is 38", or desired length, shape armholes.

Bind off 3 sts at the beginning of the next 2 rows. Then bind off 1 (2, 3) sts beginning next 2 rows 40 (42, 48) sts. Then decrease 1 st each end every other row 1 (1, 3) times. Work even on 38 (40, 42) sts until armhole measures 9" from the first bind off.

Shape Shoulder: Bind off 4 sts at the beginning of the next 6 rows, then bind off remaining 14 (16, 18) sts.

Vintage design.

LEFT FRONT

Cast on very loosely 26 (28, 32) sts, and work pattern stitch on size 15 needles. Dec 1 st at the armhole edge every 8" 3 times. When the front is the same as the back to the armhole (count your rows, it's easy in this pattern), bind off 1 (2, 3) sts at armhole edge, then decrease 1 (2, 3) sts at armhole edge every other row. When armhole measures 5½", shape neck. Bind off 4 (5, 6) sts, then decrease 1 st on next row. Skip 1 row, decrease 1 st at neck edge. When front measures the same as back, shape shoulders. Bind off 4 sts on armhole edge only 6 times, then bind off remaining sts.

Photo: Courtesy of Cascade Yarns.

POCKETS

Cast on very loosely 10 (12, 12) sts with size 15 needles and work pattern st. At 5 (5½, 5½)" on wrong side row, change to 220 and size 9 needle. Increase 1 st in every stitch. 20 (24, 24) sts. Work in 2/2 rib for 4 rows, bind off loosely. For 2nd pocket, begin pattern st in reverse for 1st size only, and reverse rib pattern for 2nd and 3rd sizes.

FINISHING

Lightly steam all pieces. **Left front border:** with 220 and size 9 needles and right side facing, pick up 128 sts just inside the selvedge edge. For different lengths, pick up 1 st in every row hole, making sure you have an even number. Work 2/2 rib pattern for 9 rows and bind off in pattern loosely. **Right front border:** After placing buttons on left front, work right border same as for left placing buttonholes where needed. (A yarn over buttonhole works well.) Join the front and back shoulder seams.

COLLAR

Note: *Do not pick up sts in the top edges of front borders. A perpendicular border will be put on the collar, which will be joined later.*

With size 8 needles and 220, beginning at Magnum pattern neck edge, with right side facing, pick up 74 (74, 78) sts as follows: 26 (26, 27) along front neck edge, 22 (22, 24) across back of neck, and 26 (26, 27) along front neck edge.

Work in 2/2 rib pattern for 3". Change to size 9 needles and work for another 3". Change to size 10 needles and work for 3" more. Change to size 10½ needles and at 10 (11, 11)" bind off very loosely in rib pattern.

Collar Borders: Left: At front edge of collar with size 9 needles and 220, pick up 38 (42, 42) sts.

(***Note:*** *It may be smoother to pick up in every row and reduce evenly on the first rib row.*) Work 9 rows in 2/2 rib pattern. Bind off loosely in rib pat. Repeat for right edge, placing buttonholes where needed.

Place medium button ½" from outside edge and 2 more 2½" apart.

Sew collar borders to respective front borders. Weave side and sleeve seams. Sew sleeves into armholes.

RIGHT FRONT

Work as for left front, remembering to reverse all shaping.

SLEEVES

Cast on very loosely 22 (24, 26) sts and work pattern st on size 15 needles. Increase 1 st each edge every 2" 6 times. 34 (36, 38) sts. When sleeve measures 16" or desired length to underarm shape, cap as follows:

Bind off 2 (3, 3) sts at beginning of the next 2 rows. Then decrease 1 st each end every other row 6 (6, 7) times (14 sts). Work even for 6 rows. Bind off 2 sts at the beginning of the next 4 rows, then bind off remaining sts.

Retro's the Rage!

*Retro is **de riguer** in fashion today and classic crochet '60s vests are back in spades! Lion Brand's flashy and fashionable jiffy vest, done in luscious lime Microspun, is short on time and effort to make,*

but long on style!

■ **PROJECT:**
60s Jiffy Crochet Vest, by Lion Brand

■ **SKILL LEVEL**
Beginner

■ **SIZE**
One size fits most.
Finished chest: 48"
Tied length: 27"

■ **MATERIALS**
LION BRAND Microspun (2½ oz 168 yd balls)
5 balls Lime or color of your choice

■ **NEEDLES**
Size J-10 (6 mm) crochet hook
OR SIZE TO OBTAIN GAUGE

■ **GAUGE**
17 sts + 8 rows = 4"
TAKE TIME TO CHECK GAUGE.

1967 Workbasket

ABBREVIATIONS

beg = begin(ning); **ch** = chain; **cont** = continu(e)(ing); **dc** = double crochet; **dec** = decreas(e)(s)(ing); **foll** = follow(s)(ing); **rnd(s)** = round(s); **RS** = right side; **sc** = single crochet; **st(s)** = stitch(es); **t-ch** = turning chain; **WS** = wrong side.

DIRECTIONS

NOTE: *Body is worked in one piece.*

PATTERN STITCH

Row 1: 1 dc in 6th ch from hook (counts as 2 sts), *ch 1, skip 1 ch, 1 dc in next ch; rep from * across.

Row 2: Ch 3, turn. *1 dc in ch-1 space, ch 1, skip 1 dc; rep from * across, end 1 dc in ch-1 space, ch 1, 1 dc in 2nd ch of beg ch of previous row.

Row 3: Ch 3, turn. *1 dc in ch-1 space, ch 1, skip 1 dc; rep from * across, end 1 dc in top of t-ch.

Row 4: Ch 3, turn. *1 dc in ch-1 space, ch 1, skip 1 dc; rep from * across, end 1 dc in last ch-space, ch 1, 1 dc in 3rd ch of t-ch.

Rep Rows 3 and 4 for pattern.

BODY

Ch 208. Beg with pattern Row 1 (204) sts, work even until piece measures 15" from beg.

Next Row: Place markers 51 sts from each side for side seams. Cont until piece measures 16" from beg.

Shape V-Neck: Keeping to pattern, dec 1 st at beg and end of each row (center front) 17 times. AT SAME TIME, when piece measures 17" from beg, beg shaping armhole.

Right Front (RS): Work to within 13 sts of right side-seam marker (armhole edge), turn. Dec 1 st at armhole edge every other row 4 times and cont neck decs. Work until armhole measures 10" from beg. Fasten off.

BACK

With RS facing, join yarn 13 sts in from right side-seam marker, ch 3, then keeping to pattern work across to within 13 sts of left side-seam marker, turn. Dec 1 st at beg and end of every other row 4 times for armholes. Work even until armholes measure 10" from beg. Fasten off.

LEFT FRONT

With RS facing, join yarn 13 sts in from left side-seam marker (armhole edge), ch 3 and cont in pat-

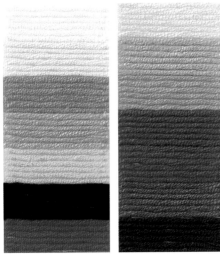

Lion Brand's vest is crocheted in MicroSpun yarn available in a wide range of brilliant colors.

Vintage design: Long Crochet vests were the rage in the '60s and '70s. Shown are just a few of the many Workbasket vest featured.

tern, dec 1 st at armhole edge every other row 4 times and cont neck decs. Work until armhole measures 10" from beg. Fasten off.

FINISHING

Sew fronts to back at shoulders over 17 sts. Work 1 row sc around entire outer edge of Vest, working 3 sc in front corners.

ARMHOLE EDGING

Join yarn at underarm marker and work 1 rnd sc around armhole. Fasten off.

TIES

Make two. Ch 57. **Row 1:** Sc in 2nd ch from hook and in each ch across (56 sc). Fasten off, leaving a long strand to join to Vest at V-neck shaping.

The 'Scoop' on Style

■ ■ ■

*Scoopnecks are sensuous and breezy in **any** color, but Tahki Stacy Charles' dramatic pullover in its variegated Austermann Domani yarn is a veritable whirlwind of splashy tropical hues!*

■ **PROJECT**
Scoopneck Sweater, by Tahki Stacy Charles

■ **SKILL LEVEL**
Intermediate

■ **SIZE:**
Small (Medium)
Directions for Small with Medium size in parentheses.
If there is only one figure, it applies to both sizes.

■ **MATERIALS**
TAHKI STACY CHARLES Austermann Domani Kolibri
5 (6) balls (each ball 50 g)
Stitch holders

■ **NEEDLES**
Size 7 (4.5mm) knitting needles
Size 6 (4 mm) crochet hook

■ **GAUGE**
14 sts and 23 rows = 4" over St st.
TAKE TIME TO CHECK GAUGE.

1985 Workbasket

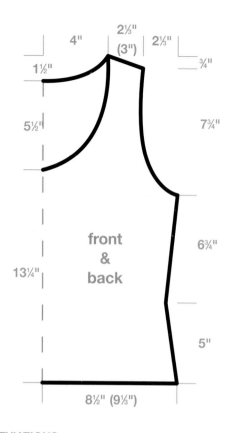

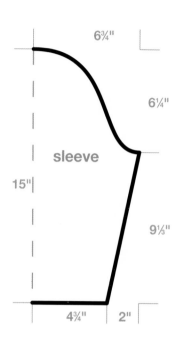

ABBREVIATIONS

beg = begin(ning); **bet** = between; **BO** = bind off; **CC** = contrasting color; **ch** = chain; **CO** = Cast on; **dc** = double crochet; **dec** = decreas(e)(s)(ing); **eor** = every other row; **inc** = increase(e)(s)(ing); **k** = knit; **lp** = loop; **MC** = main color; **p** = purl; **pat** = pattern; **pm** = place marker; **rem** = remaining; **RS** = right side; **sc** = single crochet; **seq** = sequence; **sk** = skip; **ssk** = slip, slip, knit; **sssk** = slip, slip, slip, knit (slip the first, second, and/or third stitch knitwise one at the time, then insert the tip of left-hand needle into the back of these 2 or 3 sts and knit them together); **st(s)** = stitch(es); **St st** = Stockinette stitch; **tog** = together; **wyif** = with yarn in front; **wyib** = with yarn in back; **WS** = wrong side; **yo** = yarn over.

DIRECTIONS

BACK

Cast on 64 (70) sts and work in garter st for 4 rows.

Row 5: 1 selvage st, *K2tog, yo, rep from *, end with 1 selvage st.

Row 6: Purl. Cont in St st, dec 1 st each side every 8th row 3 times = 58 (64) sts. Inc 1 st each side every 13th row 3 times = 64 (70) sts. Work even until piece measures 12" from beg.

Shape Armholes: Bind off 3 sts at beg of next 2 rows, 2 sts at beg of next 2 rows, dec 1 st each side every 2nd row 3 times = 48 (54) sts. Work even until piece measures 19" from beg.

Shape Neck and Shoulder: Bind off center 10 sts and working both sides at once, bind off from each neck edge 4 sts once, 2 sts once and 1 st once. AT THE SAME TIME, when piece measures 19½" from beg, bind off from each shoulder edge 4 (5) sts 3 times.

FRONT

Work same as back until piece measures 13¼" from beg.

Shape Neck: Bind off center 8 sts and, working both sides at once, bind off from each neck edge 3 sts once, 2 sts once and 1 st 3 times. When same length as back to shoulder, shape shoulder same as back.

SLEEVES

Cast on 36 sts and work first 6 rows same as back. Work in St st, inc 1 st each side every 7th row 7 times = 50 sts. Work even until piece measures 9½" from beg.

Shape Cap: Bind off 3 sts at beg of next 4 rows, 1 st at beg of next 2 rows, dec 1 st each side every 4th row 4 times, every 2nd row 4 times and bind off 2 sts at beg of next 4 rows. Bind off rem sts.

Vintage design.

FINISHING

Block pieces to finished measurements. Sew shoulder seams. Set in sleeves. Sew side and sleeve seams. With RS facing and crochet hook, work 1 rnd sc evenly around neck edge.

Cabled Cache

∎ ∎ ∎

This alluring cabled shell with sweeping yoke by Cascade Yarns echoes **Workbasket**'s *1968 design. But the contemporary version is brilliantly updated in bold chartreuse Indulgency yarn. A cable classic in any decade!*

■ **PROJECT**
Cabled Shell with Yoke, by Cascade

■ **SKILL LEVEL**
Advanced

■ **SIZE**
Medium (Large)
Directions for Medium with Large size in parentheses.
If there is only one figure, it applies to both sizes.

■ **FINISHED MEASUREMENTS**
Medium to fit 32" to 36" bust
Large to fit 38" to 42" bust

■ **MATERIALS**
Cascade Indulgency Yarn 3 (4) skeins
Color of your choice

■ **NEEDLES**
Size 7 circular needles, 16" and 24"
Size 4 circular needs, 16" and 24"

■ **GAUGE**
7 sts = #1" over cable pattern on size 7 needles.
TAKE TIME TO CHECK GAUGE.

ABBREVIATIONS

beg = begin(ning); **dec** = decrease; **k** = knit; **p** = purl; **RS** = right side; **st(s)** = stitch(es); **ssk** = slip, slip, knit; **sssk** = slip, slip, slip, knit (slip the first, second, and/or third stitch knitwise one at the time, then insert the tip of left-hand needle into the back of these 2 or 3 sts and knit them together); **WS** = wrong side.

DIRECTIONS

NOTES

Do not stretch to measure your test swatch.

The body is worked in the round up to the armholes.

Ribbings (armbands, bottom) are worked in garter st in the round.

Collar is also garter st in the round.

BODY

With 24" size 4 needles, cast on 205 (240) sts. Work in the round as follows: (knit 1 round, purl 1 round) repeat 2 more times. On the last round, knit and increase to 240 (280) sts evenly spaced. Change to 24" size 7 needles and start working in pattern as follows:

CABLE PATTERN

c8b = slip next 4 sts on cable needle and hold in the back of your work. K 4 sts, then k the 4 sts on the cable needle.

Row 1: p1, (k8, p2) rep around ending with p1.

Row 2: p1, (c8b, p2, k8, p2) rep. around ending with p1.

Row 3: as row 1.

Row 4: as row 1.

Row 5: as row 1.

Row 6: as row 2.

Row 7: as row 1

Row 8: as row 1.

Row 9: as row 1.

Row 10: as row 2.

Row 11: as row 1.

Row 12: as row 1.

Row 13: as row 1.

Row 14: p1 (k8, p2, c8b, p2) rep. around ending with p1.

Row 15: as row 1.

Row 16: as row 1.

Row 17: as row 1.

Row 18: as row 14.

Row 19: as row 1.

Row 20: as row 1.

Row 21: as row 1.

Row 22: as row 14.

Row 23: as row 1.

Row 24: as row 1.

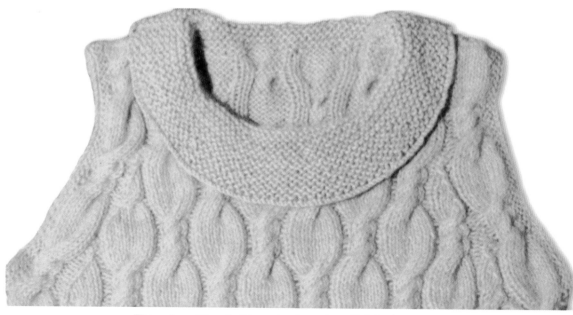

The collar of the shell is a simple garter stitch in the round.

Repeat these 24 rows until sweater measures 15"
long. Break for armholes. Work in pattern on 120
(140) sts only leaving remaining sts on a spare needle or holder to be worked later.

Keeping pattern correct and working back and
forth, decrease 1 st on each side on every other row
after the first and before the last cable as follows:

P1, k8, p1, slip, slip and knit these 2 sts together.
Work to the last 12 sts and knit 2 together then p1,
k8, p1.

Continue to decrease in this manner until there are
100 (120) sts remaining. When armhole measures 8",
put the center 30 sts on a holder. At the neck edge
only, dec 1 st every row 4 times. Bind off remaining
20 (30) sts. Repeat for the other shoulder.

Rejoin yarn to the 120 (140) sts and work the front
as for back until armholes measure 6". Place center
18 sts on a holder. At neck edge only, bind off 2 sts
2 times, then 1 st every other row 6 times. When
front shoulder measures the same as the back, bind
off. Repeat for the other shoulder. Sew shoulder
seams together.

ARM BANDS

With 16" size 4 needles, pick up 80 sts around armholes (p 1 round, k 1 round). Repeat 2 times more.
Bind off loosely.

COLLAR

With 16" size 7 needles, pick up 80 sts around
neck. (p 1 round, k 1 round) repeat 4 more times.
Increase 10 sts evenly spaced on the next round.
Work another 10 rows in garter pattern. Collar
should be approx. 3½" wide. BIND OFF VERY
LOOSELY. For a loose collar, bind off on the collar,
knit 1 st and *pull a loop through this st. Then knit
next st and pass the loop over*. Repeat between *
and *. This extra loop will give the needed ease for
the collar to lay down.

This beauti-
ful cable stitch
boasts graceful
scallops with
intertwining links
that make this
shell a unique
showpiece!

Chevron Chic

■ ■ ■

*Chevrons have long offered a sporty slant on fashion,
as Coats & Clark's contemporary variegated vest attests.
Smartly accented with lots of visual interest,
the dramatic chevron is complemented
with cabling, ribbing, and rich colors.
The "V" stands for "very chic!"*

■ **PROJECT**
Chevron Cabled Vest, by Coats & Clark

■ **SKILL LEVEL**
Intermediate

■ **SIZE**
Small (Medium, Large, X-Large, XX-Large)
Directions for Small with larger sizes in parentheses.
If there is only one figure, it applies to all sizes.

■ **FINISHED MEASUREMENTS**
Finished measurements: 36 (39, 42, 45, 49)"

■ **MATERIALS**
COATS & CLARK Red Heart TLC Essentials
MC—2 skeins Oasis
A—1 skein Country Blue
B—1 skein Aran
2 stitch holders

■ **NEEDLES**
Sizes 5 and 8 knitting needles
OR SIZE TO OBTAIN GAUGE

■ **GAUGE**
16 sts and 23 rows = 4"
TAKE TIME TO CHECK GAUGE.

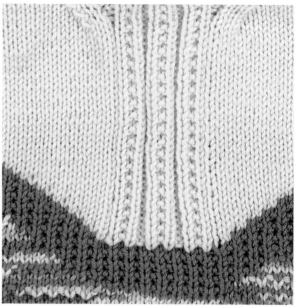

These front details show the striking interplay of the chevron with the vertical cabling banded neck and the rich variegated field of color below.

beg = begin(ning); **bo** = bind off; **bpdc** = back post double crochet; **ch** = chain; **co** = cast on; **cont** = continue; **dc** = double crochet; **dec** = decrease; **eor** = every other row; **est** = established; **fpdc** = front post double crochet; **hdc** = half double crochet; **k** = knit; **lp** = loop; **psso** = pass sl st over k st; **p** = purl; **Pat** = pattern; **rem** = remaining; **rep** = repeat; **RS** = right side; **sc** = single crochet; **sk** = skip; **sl** = slip; **sst(s)** = stitch(es); **St st** = Stockinette stitch; **WS** = wrong side; ***** = repeat whatever follows the * as indicated; **[ ]** = work directions given in brackets the number of times specified.

DIRECTIONS

STITCHES / MOTIFS

BEADED RIBBING:

Row 1: (RS) [p1, k1, p1, k1, p1] across.

Row 2: (WS) [k1, p3, k1] across.

CHEVRON PATTERN:

Row 1: (RS) K across.

Row 2: (WS) [P1, k1] to last st, p 1 st.

BODY PATTERN:

Row 1: (RS) K.

Row 2 and All WS Rows: Purl across.

Row 3: (RS) [K1, p1] across.

Row 4: (WS) Rep Row 2.

NOTE

Patterns are worked with separate balls. Be certain to wrap new color around previous color to prevent holes.

BACK

With smaller needles and MC, co 71, (77, 83, 89, 95) sts.

Row 1: P1, work Row 1 of Beaded Ribbing across, p1.

Row 2: K1, work Row 2 of Beaded Ribbing across, k1.

Repeat Rows 1 and 2 for 2¾", ending with a WS Row, increasing 2 sts evenly spaced on last row—73 (79, 85, 91, 97) sts. Work in Body Pattern until piece measures 10½ (10½, 11, 11, 11½)", begin Underarm: bo 3 (3, 3, 4, 4) sts at beg of next 2 rows, then dec 1 st each side every other row 3 (3, 4, 4, 5) times— 61 (67, 71, 75, 79) sts. Work even.

When piece measures 13 (13, 13¼, 13¾, 13¾)", ending with WS row, fasten off MC, attach A. Work in Chevron Pattern for 9 rows, ending with RS row. Fasten off A, attach B; P across 23, (26, 28, 30, 32) sts, rep [between [ ] = s of WS row of Beaded Ribbing] 3 times; P across rem sts. Keeping center 15 sts in Beaded Ribbing, work even in St st until armhole measures 8¼ (8¼, 8½, 8¾, 9)". Bo 8 sts at beg of next 2 rows; bo 12 sts at beg of next 2 rows. Next Row: bo 3, (6, 8, 10, 12) sts; work in Beaded Ribbing across 15 sts; place on holder, bo rem sts.

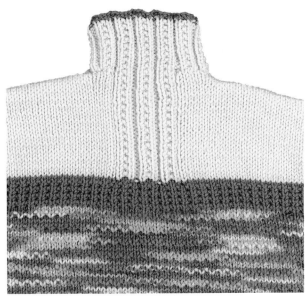

Back of shell showing cabling and color band, which runs straight across the back.

FRONT:

With smaller needles and MC, co 71 (77, 83, 89, 95) sts. Repeat as for back until piece measures 9", ending with a WS row.

Begin Chevron: Work in est pattern across 29 (32, 35, 38, 41) sts, attach A, work Row 1 of Chevron Pattern; with another ball of MC, work across rem sts.

Next Row: With MC, P across 28 (31, 34, 37, 40) sts. With A, work Row 2 of Chevron Pattern across 17 sts. With MC, p across rem sts. Continue inc 1 st in A, (dec 1 st in MC) ea side of Chevron ea row until there are 9 rows completed, ending with RS row.

Next Row: (RS) With MC, work in est pattern to Chevron, work in A across 9 sts. Attach B, Soft White, k1, place marker, rep [between [ ]=s of WS Row of Beaded Ribbing] 3 times. Place marker, k1; with another ball of A, work in Chevron pattern across 9 sts. With MC, work in pattern across rem sts. Following chart, work until all sts are in B, keeping center 15 sts in Beaded Ribbing pattern.

At the same time, when piece measures 10½ (10½, 11, 11, 11½)", begin underarm: bo 3, (3, 3, 4, 4) sts at beg of next 2 rows, then dec 1 st ea side every other row 3 (3, 4, 4, 5) times—61 (67, 71, 75, 79) sts. Work even as established.

When armhole measures 6½ (6½, 6½, 7, 7)", ending with RS row, begin neck shaping: P across 23 (26, 28, 30, 32) sts. Work Row 2 of Beaded Ribbing across center 15 sts, then place on holder; p across rem sts.

Next Row: K across to 3 sts before neck; k2 tog; k 2 (neck dec made). Continue dec at neck edge eor; at the same time, when armhole measures same as back to shoulder at armhole edge, bo 8 sts 1 time; 12 sts 1 time, then any rem sts.

Leaving center sts on holder, attach yarn to right neck; k2; [sl1, k1, psso], k to end. Work as for Left neck, reversing all shaping.

FINISHING

Neck: Sew right shoulder seam. With smaller needles and B, pick up 11, (11, 11, 14, 14) sts along left neck edge, work in RS pattern across 15 sts from front neck holder, 12 (12, 12, 15, 15) sts along right neck edge, 10 (10, 10, 12, 12) sts across bo sts of back to holder, work in RS pattern across 15 sts from back neck holder; pick up 9 (9, 9, 11, 11) across rem bo sts—72 (72, 72, 82, 82) sts.

Next Row: (WS) P3, then Row 2 of Beaded Ribbing around, ending K2. Work in Beaded Ribbing for 2¼", ending with RS row. Fasten off B. With A, working Row 2 of Beaded Ribbing, bo loosely with A in pattern.

Sew neck ribbing seam and left shoulder. With smaller needles and B, pick up 72 (72, 72, 77, 77) sts around armhole. Work [(WS) k1, Row 2 across, k1.

Next Row: (RS) p1, Row 1 across, p1] twice of Beaded Ribbing; fasten off B. With A, work k1, Row 2 across, k1; bo loosely in pattern.

Sew underarm seams. Weave in all loose ends; block lightly.

Pocket Panache

Lion Brand's chill-chasers in downy-soft Homespun yarn aren't just any run-of-the-mill winter wraps. The scarf has built-in hand-warmers that are both fashionable and practical.

Quick, easy, and stylish!

■ **PROJECT**
Tam & Scarf with Pockets, by Lion Brand

■ **SKILL LEVEL**
Beginner

■ **SIZE**
Tam—One size fits most (10" diameter / 32" circumference)
Scarf—Measures 8" x 76", unfinished

■ **MATERIALS**
LION BRAND Homespun (each skein 6 oz)
Barrington or color of your choice
1 skein for the tam
2 skeins for the scarf

■ **NEEDLES**
16" size 8 circular needle
16" size 10 circular needle
Size 10 double-pointed needle
OR SIZE TO OBTAIN GAUGE

■ **GAUGE**
14 St sts = 4" on size 10 needle
TAKE TIME TO CHECK GAUGE.

beg = begin(ning); **dec** = decreas(e)(s)(ing); **DPNs** = double-pointed needles; **k** = knit; **p** = purl; **psso**= pass sl st over k st; **rem** = remain(s)(ing); **rep** = repeat; **rnd(s)** = round(s); **st(s)** = stitch(es); **St st** = Stockinette stitch; **tog** = together.

DIRECTIONS

STITCH EXPLANATIONS

M1 = make 1. An increase worked by lifting the horizontal thread lying between the needles and placing it onto the left needle. Work this new stitch through the back loop.

Sl 2 kwise-k1-p2sso = slip 2 stitches together knit-wise (as though to knit), knit 1, pass 2 slipped stitches over the knit stitch = centered double decrease.

TAM

Using smaller needles, loosely cast on 70 sts. Place marker to indicate beg of rnd.

Rnds 1-7: K1, p1 rib.

Rnd 8: * K2, M1, rep from * across the rnd (105 sts).

Homespun Yarn Samples

Rich in texture and blended hues, LION BRAND's Homespun yarn comes in a glorious range of colors.

Rnd 9: Change to larger needles and work in St st for 3½".

Crown: Decrease as follows (change to DPNs when necessary):

Dec Rnd 1: K 6, * sl 2 kwise-k1-p2sso, k 12, rep from * 6 more times; k6. K 1 rnd.

Dec Rnd 2: K 5, * sl 2 kwise-k1-p2sso, k 10, rep from * 6 more times; k5. K 1 rnd.

Continue decreasing in this manner every other round until 7 sts rem.

Next Rnd: K2tog around until 2 rem. Work 2 rnds on 2 sts. Break yarn and pull through remaining sts. Hide ends. Wet block tam on large dinner plate.

SCARF

With larger needles, cast on 29 sts.

Row 1: Working back and forth, k1, *p1, k1; rep from *.

Repeat Row 1 for 76". Bind off.

Finishing: Laying scarf flat, fold up 8" on each side to form pockets. Sew sides in place invisibly.

Vintage design.

Homespun Yarn Samples

Striped Sensation

■ ■ ■

Turtlenecks are toasty, but Tahki Stacy Charles'
sensational striped turtle in their Fargo yarn
veritably sizzles in red-hot reds and fiery
speckles of orange and cobalt!

■ **PROJECT**
Striped Turtleneck Sweater, by Tahki Stacy Charles

■ **SKILL LEVEL**
Advanced

■ **SIZE**
Small (Medium, Large)
Directions for Small with larger sizes in parentheses.
If there is only one figure, it applies to all sizes.

■ **MATERIALS**
TAHKI STACY CHARLES Fargo (each ball 1¾ oz. 60 yds.)
A—2 balls Multi Pink
B—1 ball Blue
C—2 balls Multi Blue
D—1 ball Orange
E—2 balls Multi Orange
F—3 (3, 4) balls Raspberry
Stitch holders

■ **NEEDLES**
Size 10½ knittng needles
Size 10 circular needle 16"
OR SIZE TO OBTAIN GAUGE

■ **GAUGE**
10 sts and 16 rows = 4" in St st with larger
needles
TAKE TIME TO CHECK GAUGE.

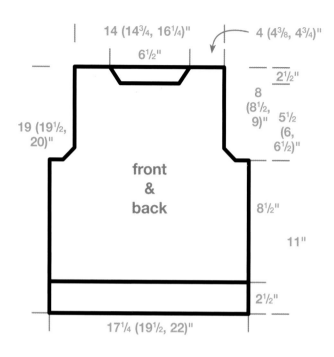

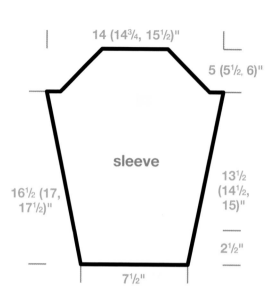

ABBREVIATIONS

beg = begin(ning); **dec** = decreas(e)(s)(ing); **DPNs** = Double-pointed needles; **k** = knit; **p** = purl; **psso** = pass sl st over k st; **rem** = remain(s)(ing); **rep** = repeat; **rnd(s)** = round(s); **RS** = right side; **st(s)** = stitch(es); **St st** = stockinette stitch; **tog** = together; **WSRC** = wrong side row completed; ***** = repeat whatever follows the * as indicated.

DIRECTIONS

PATTERN STITCH

Borders: Rib:

Row 1: (RS) K2, *P3, K3 *, end P3, K2.

Row 2: (WS) P2, *K3, P3 *, end K3, P2.

Body Stripes: (St st) 4 rows A, 2 rows B, 4 rows C, 2 rows D, 4 rows E, 2 rows F.

BACK

With size 10½ needle and F, cast on 43 (49, 55) sts and work even in k3, p3 rib pattern for 2½". End with wrong side row completed (End WSRC). Change to St st and work stripe sequence until piece measures 11". (End WSRC).

Shape Armhole: Maintain color sequence; bind off 2 (3, 4) sts at the beginning of the next 2 rows (always decrease as follows: at the beginning of the row, k2 tog; work to the last 4 sts, slip one as if to knit, knit 1, psso, k2.) Decrease 1 st each end every other row 2 (3, 3) times: 35 (37, 41) sts. Work even until armhole measures 8 (8½, 9)". Bind off 9 (10, 12) sts at the beginning of the next 2 rows. Place center 17 sts on holder.

FRONT

Work exactly as back until armhole measures 6 (6½, 7)". (End WSRC).

Shape Front Neck: Work 12 (13, 15) sts. Place center 11 sts on holder. Join a second ball of yarn and work remaining 12 (13, 15) sts. Decrease 1 st each neck edge every other row 3 times. Work even on each side until armhole measures 8 (8½, 9)". Bind off remaining sts.

Vintage to Vogue: Toasty turtlenecks shown, then and now—*Workbasket's* 1975 version and today's turtle in Tahki Stacy Charles' bold stripes, bold colors, and bold texture.

SLEEVES

With size 10½ needle and F, cast on 19 sts and work even in k3, p3 rib pattern for 2½".

Maintain color sequence as for back and increase 1 st each end on the 7th row and every 6th row 7 (8, 5) times, every 4th row 0 (0, 5) times; 35 (37, 39) sts. Shape cap when piece measures approximately 16 (17, 17½)", ending with same stripe as on back to armhole (end WSRC).

Shape Cap: Bind off 3 sts at the beginning of the next 2 rows. Decrease 1 st each end every other row 8 (9, 10) times, every row 2 times. Bind off all sts.

FINISHING

Block pieces to measurements. Sew shoulder seams. Sew side and sleeve seams; set in sleeves.

Neckband: With size 10 circular needle and F and with right side facing, pick up 42 (42, 48) sts evenly around neck and work in k3, p3 rib pattern for 6"; bind off loosely in pattern.

Learn How—It's Easy!

See why so many are rediscovering the ancient crafts of knitting, crocheting, and tatting. They're easy to learn and provide endless hours of quiet enjoyment and creativity!

Knitting, crochet, and tatting, like their other needlecraft cousins, are ancient crafts, and you're about to learn the basic stitches like so many women and men, girls and boys for thousands of years have done.

This section was designed for beginners and contains step-by-step diagrams with easy-to-understand instructions. Review this section for the meaning of specific terms and diagrams on specific stitches you may find in projects included in this book.

Like most crafts and hobbies, there is a simple language of terms unique to needlework. So let's start there. Following are some simple universal abbreviations used in knitting, crochet, and tatting notation. **Don't be intimidated by the list! You'll only need to learn several abbreviations to do most of the projects in this book.** But some projects will include special stitches, so those notations are also included here.

Special thanks to Coats & Clark for providing these How-To Basics.

ABBREVIATIONS

approx = approximately
beg = begin(ning)
bl = block
CC = contrasting color
ch = chain
cl r = close ring
cn = cable needle
cont = continu(e)(ing)
dc = double crochet
dec = decrease(ing)
ds = double stitch
Dtr = double treble
foll = follow(s)(ing)
incr = increase(ing)
k = knit
LH = left hand
lp = loop

MC = main color
M1 = make 1 (incr 1)
meas = measures
p = purl
P = picot
Pc st = popcorn stitch
pat(s) = pattern(s)
pm = place marker
psso = passs slip st over
rem = remain(ing)
rep = repeat
R = ring
RH = right hand
RS = right side
rw = row
sc = single crochet
sk = skip

sl = slip
sp = space
ssk = slip, slip, knit
st(s) = stitch(es)
St st = Stockinette stitch
tog = together
t-ch = turning chain
tr = treble
Tr tr = triple trebler
WS = wrong side
wyib = with yarn in back
wyif = with yarn in front
yd(s) = yard(s)
yo = yarn over
* = repeat as indicated
[ ] = repeat as indicated

How-To-Knit Basics

Knitting is enjoying an incredible resurgence today and many are discovering the enjoyment creativity and the calming effect of this needlecraft. One of the beauties of knitting is that you need only minimal equipment and you can knit almost anywhere.

EQUIPMENT

Knitting needles are used in pairs to produce a flat knitted fabric. The needles may be made of plastic, wood, steel, or alloy and range in size from 0 (2mm) to 15 (10mm) in diameter. Needles are also made in different lengths. Each project in this book will recommend the types of needles you will need.

Circular and double-pointed needles are used to produce a tubular fabric or flat rounds (such as circular shawls). Circular needles consist of two needles joined by a flexible length of plastic. Double-pointed needles are sold in sets of four or five.

Cable needles are short and double pointed, and they are used to hold the stitches temporarily when knitting cables.

Stitch holders resemble large safety pins and are used to hold stitches while they are not being worked. For example, they are often used to hold a neckline so it doesn't unravel while the front and back pieces are being joined.

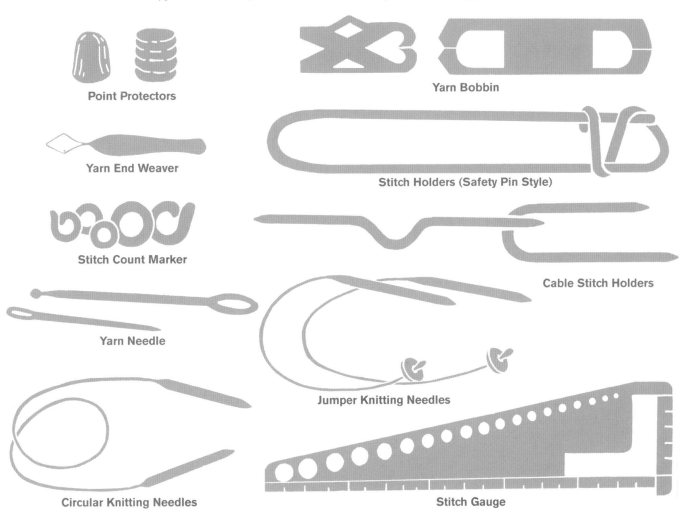

Point Protectors

Yarn Bobbin

Yarn End Weaver

Stitch Holders (Safety Pin Style)

Stitch Count Marker

Cable Stitch Holders

Yarn Needle

Jumper Knitting Needles

Circular Knitting Needles

Stitch Gauge

KNITTING YARNS

The wide array of yarns available today is nothing less than spectacular! The selection in colors, textures, twists, weights, composition, and embellishments is endless. *Vintage to Vogue's* then-and-now fashion examples underscore how exciting contemporary yarns can dramatically alter the way a basic design looks.

We recommend that you use the yarn stated in each project. It is important that you buy all the yarn needed for a project at the same time, as different dye lots can vary subtly in shading, which may show on the finished piece. Most of these yarns should be available at your local yarn shop. However, you can also order yarns featured in these projects through the manufacturer by phone or the Internet. Refer to the "Resources" section beginning on page 123 for details.

Always keep the ball band as a reference. The best way is to pin it to the gauge swatch and keep them together with any left over yarn. That way you can always check the washing instructions and have materials for repairs.

First Steps

MAKING A SLIP KNOT

A slip knot is the starting point for almost everything you do in knitting and is the basis for all casting on techniques. "Casting on" is the simple process of starting a stitch with your needles and yarn.

1. Wind the yarn around two fingers and over the

 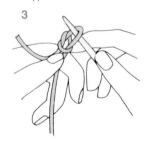

two fingers again to the back of the first thread.

2. Using a knitting needle, pull the back thread through the front one to form a loop.

3. Pull end to tighten the loop.

HOLDING THE NEEDLES

The right needle is held as if holding a pencil. For casting on and working the first few rows, the knitted piece passes over the hand, between the thumb and the index finger.

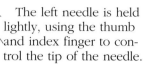

As work progresses, let the thumb slide under the knitted piece, grasping the needle from below.

The left needle is held lightly, using the thumb and index finger to control the tip of the needle.

HOLDING THE YARN

There are various methods of winding the yarn around the fingers to control the tension on the yarn and produce even stitches. In time, you may find your own favorite way, but first try the method shown here.

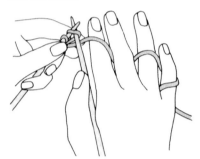

Holding the yarn in your right hand, pass under the little finger, then around the same finger, over the next finger, under the center finger, and over the index finger.

Now use the index finger to pass the yarn around the needle tip.

The yarn circled around the little finger creates the necessary tension for knitting evenly.

CASTING ON

There are two common methods of casting on: (1) Cable or *between* stitches method gives a firm neat finish and is best used before ribbing. (2) The thumb method is best for an elastic edge or when followed by rows in Garter stitch or Stockinettte stitch.

Cable Method

1. Make a slip knot about four inches from the end of the yarn.

2. Insert the right-hand needle through the slip knot and pass the yarn over the right needle.

3. Pull a loop through.

4. Place this loop on the left-hand needle.

5. Insert the right-hand needle between the two stitches on the left-hand needle. Wind yarn around the point of the right-hand needle.

6. Draw a loop through, place this loop on the left-hand needle.

Repeat steps 5 and 6 until the required number of stitches has been cast on.

Thumb Method

1. Make a slip knot about 1 yard (depending on the number of stitches required) from the end of the yarn. Hold the needle in the right hand with the ball end of the yarn over your first finger. *Wind the loose end of the yarn around the left thumb from front to back.

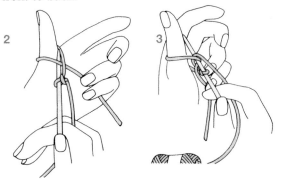

2. Insert the needle through the yarn on the thumb.

3. Take the ball end of yarn with your right forefinger over the point of the needle.

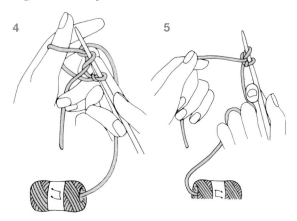

4. Pull a loop through to form the first stitch.

5. Remove your left thumb from the yarn and pull the loose end to secure the stitch.

Repeat from * until the required number of stitches has been cast on.

The Basic Stitches

KNIT STITCHES

1. Hold the needle with the cast on stitches in the left hand. With the yarn at the back of the work, insert the right-hand needle from left to right through the front of the first stitch on the left-hand needle.

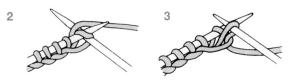

2. Wind the yarn from left to right over the point of the right-hand needle.

3. Draw the yarn back through the stitch, thus forming a loop on the right-hand needle.

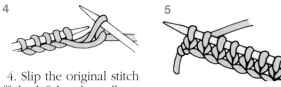

4. Slip the original stitch off the left-hand needle.

To knit a row, repeat steps 1 to 4 until all the stitches have been transferred onto the right needle.

5. Turn the work and transfer the needle with the stitches onto the left hand to work the next row.

When every row is knitted (known as Garter stitch or plain knitting), both sides of the fabric have raised horizontal ridges.

PURL STITCHES

1. With the yarn at the front of the work, insert the right-hand needle from right to left through the front of the first stitch on the left-hand needle.

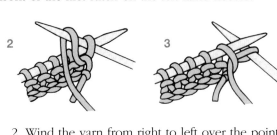

2. Wind the yarn from right to left over the point of the right-hand needle.

3. Draw a loop through onto the right-hand needle.

4. Slip the stitch off the left-hand needle.

To purl a row, repeat steps 1 to 4 until all the stitches are transferred to the right-hand needle,

then turn the work and transfer the needles to work the next row.

Purling every row creates a Garter stitch but can be slower to work than knitting every row.

STOCKINETTE STITCH

The Stockinette stitch is the most widely knitted fabric, comprised of alternate knit and purl horizontal rows. Follow the preceding instructions for Knit Stitches and Purl Stitches with each alternating row.

SINGLE RIB (k1, p1)

This technique is formed by alternately knitting a stitch then purling a stitch to create unbroken vertical lines on each side of the work. It makes a very elastic fabric that is mainly used for borders such as welts, neckbands, and cuffs. When used as an edging, rib is generally worked on a smaller size needle than the main body of the garment to keep it firm and elastic.

1. Knit the first stitch.

2. Bring the yarn forward to the front of the work between the needles and purl the next stitch.

3. Take the yarn to the back of the work between the needles and knit the next stitch.

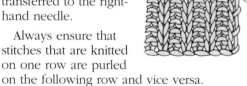

Repeat steps 2 and 3 until all stitches are transferred to the right-hand needle.

Always ensure that stitches that are knitted on one row are purled on the following row and vice versa.

How-To-Crochet Basics

Crocheting is one of the oldest needlework arts. Its name is derived from the French word "croche," meaning a hook. Even a beginner can master intricate laces and designs. Only two items are required for crocheting—a hook and thread or yarn. All crochet designs are only variations of a few basic crochet stitches.

EQUIPMENT

Crochet hooks are usually made from steel, aluminum, or plastic in a range of sizes according to their diameter. As each crochet stitch is worked separately until only one loop remains on the hook, space is not needed to hold stitches, and the hooks are made to a standard convenient length.

Crochet Hook

CROCHET YARNS & THREADS

As with knitting yarns, today's crochet threads and yarns are available in a vast array of thicknesses, twists, and finishes. It's recommended that you use the yarn stated in each project, and it's important that you buy all the yarn needed for a project at the same time, as different dye lots can vary subtly in shading, which may show on the finished piece. Most of these yarns should be available at your local yarn shop. However, you can also order yarns featured in these projects through the manufacturer, by phone or the Internet. Refer to the "Resources" section beginning on page 392 near the back of this book for details.

Always keep the ball band as a reference. Pin it to the gauge swatch and keep them together with any leftover yarn. That way you can always check the washing instructions and have materials for repairs.

HOLDING THE HOOK AND YARN

There are no hard and fast rules as to the best way to hold the hook and yarn. The diagrams below show just one method, but choose whatever way you find most comfortable. The following directions are for right-handers. Left-handers should simply reverse the process, reading left for right and right for left where applicable.

1. The hook is held in the right hand as if holding a pencil.

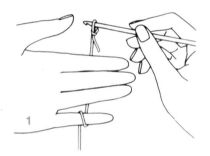

2. To maintain the slight tension in the yarn necessary for easy even working, it's helpful to arrange the yarn around the fingers of the left hand in the way shown below.

3. The left hand holds the work and at the same time controls the yarn supply. The left-hand middle finger is used to manipulate the yarn, while the index finger and thumb hold onto the work.

First Steps

Almost all crochet begins with a base of starting chain, which is a series of chain stitches, beginning with a slip knot.

MAKING A SLIP KNOT

1. Make a loop then hook another loop through it.

2. Tighten gently and slide the knot up to the hook

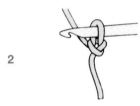

YARN OVER (yo)

Wrap the yarn from back to front over the hook to hold the yarn still and maneuver the hook. This movement of the yarn over the hook is used over and over again in crochet and is usually called "yarn over," abbreviated as "yo."

CHAIN STITCH (ch)

1. Yarn over and draw the yarn through to form a new loop without tightening up the previous one.

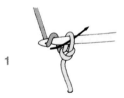

2. Repeat to form as many chains as required. Do not count the slip knot as a stitch.

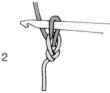

Unless otherwise stated, when working into the starting chain always work under two strands of chain loops as shown in the diagrams.

The Basic Stitches

The following basic stitches are shown worked into a starting chain but the method is the same whatever part of the work the stitch is worked into.

SLIP STITCHES (sl st)

This is the shortest of crochet stitches and, unlike other stitches, it is not used on its own to produce a fabric. It is used for joining, shaping, and, where necessary, carrying the yarn to another part of the fabric for the next stage.

1. Insert the hook into the work (second chain from hook in diagram), yarn over and draw the yarn through both the work and loop on the hook in one movement.

2. To join a chain ring with a slip stitch, insert the hook into the first chain, yarn over, and draw through the work and the loop on the hook.

SINGLE CROCHET (sc)

1. Insert the hook into the work (second chain from hook on starting chain), * yarn over, and draw the yarn through the work only.

2. Yarn over again and draw the yarn through both loops on the hook.

3. 1 sc made. Insert hook into next stitch; repeat from * in step 1.

HALF DOUBLE CROCHET (hdc)

1. Yarn over and insert the hook into the front of the work (third chain from hook on starting chain).

2. * Yarn over again and draw through the work only.

3. Yarn over again and draw through all three loops on the hook.

4. 1 hdc made. Yarn over, insert hook into next stitch; repeat from * in step 2.

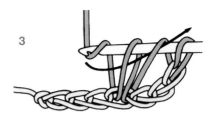

4. Yarn over and draw through the last two loops in the hook.

5. 1 dc made. Yarn over, insert hook into next stitch; repeat from * in step 2.

DOUBLE CROCHET (dc)

1. Yarn over and insert the hook into the work

(fourth chain from hook on starting chain).

2. * Yarn over again and draw through the work only.

3. Yarn over and draw through all two loops only.

How-To-Tat Basics

Tatting is an ancient needlecraft that was practiced in Europe and the Far East for thousands of years. In the 1700s, European nobility took up tatting as a genteel artform. Decorative tatted laces and edgings were thus customarily used to decorate gowns as a fashion statement. The Pilgrims brought the needlecraft to the Colonies, and it remained popular in the United States until World War I. Today, tatting is being rediscovered, especially for teen chokers, anklets, and belts.

EQUIPMENT

A simple tool called a shuttle is used in tatting. Shuttles can be made of various materials such plastic or steel, with or without a hook at the end. The hook is especially helpful when joining rings or picots of thread, which are the basis of tatting. Tatting can also be done with a needle, but a shuttle makes it much easier.

Very simply, tatting is done by winding loops or knots of thread around a length of thread with the shuttle. Do not wind the thread beyond the edge of the shuttle. When making different motifs or patterns, count the number of turns of thread around the shuttle so you can assess the amount of thread you need for each motif. This way you won't have to do unnecessary joining of thread ends in the middle of a motif.

THREADS

Fine threads are usually used for tatting. Clark's Big Ball sizes 20, 30, and 40 are ideally suited for this work. South Maid and J. & P. Coats 'Knit-Cro-Sheen' size 10 are available in a range of lovely colors and are suitable for heavier work.

BEFORE YOU BEGIN

Tatting is composed of just a few basic techniques, such as the double stitch, rings, picots, and chains. Practice these simple techniques first to become proficient, and your work will go much faster when you begin an actual project.

ABBREVIATIONS

Tatting uses tatting and also crochet terminology. Following is a brief list of abbreviations used specifically in tatting directions.

ch = chain	**cl** = close
dc = double crochet	**ds** = double stitch
dtr = double treble	**j** = join
lp = long picot	**lr** = long ring
p(s) = picot(s)	**R** = ring
rw = reverse work	**sc** = separated
sep = separated	**smp** = small picot
sp = space	**sr** = small ring
ss = slip stitch	**tog** = together
tr = treble	***** = repeat as indicated
( ) = repeat as indicated	

The Basic Stitches

THE DOUBLE STITCH (ds)

1. Let approximately 15 inches of the shuttle thread hang loose from the back of the shuttle. Hold the shuttle in the right hand and the free end of the shuttle thread between the thumb and forefinger of the left hand.

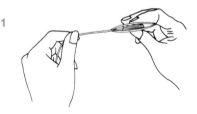

2. Bring the thread around the fingers of the left hand to form a circle. Bend the ring and little finger of the left hand to catch the thread against the palm.

3. Pass the shuttle thread around the back of the little finger of the right hand.

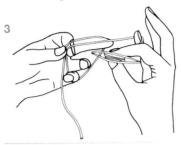

4. Move the shuttle forward, passing it under the shuttle thread and through the circle of thread.

5. Bring the shuttle back over the circle of thread and under the shuttle thread.

6. Drop the thread from the little finger of the right hand and draw the shuttle thread taut with a sharp jerk. As you pull with the right hand, relax the index and ring fingers of the left hand to ensure that the knot forms on the shuttle thread. Slide the loop into position between thumb and forefinger. This completes the first half of the double stitch.

7. Pass the shuttle over the circle of thread and under the shuttle thread.

8. Draw your shuttle thread taut with a sharp jerk. As you pull with the right hand, relax the index and ring fingers of the left hand to ensure that the knot forms on the shuttle thread. Slide the loop into position next to the first half of the stitch. This completes the second half of the double stitch. Hold the double stitch between thumb and forefinger until the next stitch is made.

Note: *The shuttle thread must pull both ways through the double stitch. When the ring around the left hand becomes too small, pull through more of the shuttle thread. When the ring is completed, close it by pulling the shuttle thread tight.*

RINGS and PICOTS

1. To make a sample ring, make four double stitches. Then make the first half of a double stitch, leaving a gap of about ¼ inch from the previous stitch. Then complete the stitch.

2. Push the whole stitch next to the previous stitch, creating an open loop that extends above the row of stitches. This open loop is called a picot.

3. Make three more double stitches (one double stitch has already been completed at the base of the picot, making four double stitches between each picot). Continue this process, making four double stitches between each picot, until you have created three picots.

4. To create a ring, connect the two shuttled ends by holding the work firmly in the left hand and drawing the shuttle thread until the first and last stitches meet, forming a ring.

Note: *The abbreviated instructions for this basic ring with three picots are: R of 4 ds, 3 ps sep by 4ds, 4ds cl. The translation: Ring of 4 double stitches, 3 picots separated by 4 double stitches, 4 double stitches closed.*

TATTING A CONNECTING CHAIN

1. A chain connects two rings and is made the same way as a ring with three picots, but the two ends are not connected to form a ring. Instead, the loose end of the chain is connected to another ring, as shown below.

2. Working with two threads allows a wider range of patterns. You can join a second thread by using a knot to fasten in a new thread at the base of a ring. Then work the double stitches and picots over the shuttle thread in the same way your first ring was created.

TATTING A SECOND RING

1. Tat four double stitches next to the finished chain. Now instead of making a picot, join the thread to the last picot in the previous ring to connect the first and second ring. To join the picot, hold the first ring in the left hand. With the right hand, insert the shuttle end into the last picot of the first ring and pull the circle of thread through. Pull the loop large enough to insert the shuttle. Draw the shuttle through the loop and pull the shuttle thread tight. This joins the rings and takes the place of the first picot on the second ring.

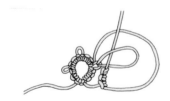

2. Continue completing the second ring and join the end at the base to close the second ring.

3. Continue the above process, tatting connecting chains between rings connected by shared picots.

REVERSING WORK

Turn work so that the base of the ring or chain just completed faces downwards. The next ring or chain is then worked in the usual way, with the rounded edge facing upwards.

FINISHING ENDS

Make a knot to close the base of the last ring or chain. Do not cut off ends. With a single strand of thread, over sew the ends on the wrong side of the work.

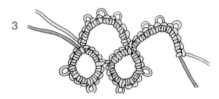

Resources

The contemporary fashions in this book were designed by some of the world's top designers and yarn manufacturers, featuring some of their premiere yarns. Refer to this section for information about the companies, products, and other patterns you can purchase from these fine manufacturers, as well as other helpful information sources.

Coats & Clark

8 Shelter Drive
Greer, SC 29650
Phone: 864.848.5610
Fax: 864.848.5609
Web site: www.coatsandclark.com

COATS & CLARK PROJECTS FEATURED IN THIS BOOK:

- Divine Duster, page 288
- Button-Front Tweed Cardigan, page 318
- Powder Puff Sweater, page 322
- Checkerboard Sweater, page 350
- Chevron Cabled Vest, page 370

Special thanks to Coats & Clark for the use of their directions and illustrations on how to knit, crochet, and tat, on pages 382 to 392. These instructions and many additional stitches may be found in Coats and Clark's *Learn How Book*, published by Lyric Books Limited, 1993.

ABOUT THE COMPANY:

Coats & Clark has long been a household name among needlecrafters. Today Coats & Clark is the largest textile/thread manufacturing company in the world, with products sold in over 150 countries.

The company was established more than 180 years ago in Paisley, Scotland, where its weavers first reproduced the rare Kashmir shawls of India. The Clark family built a thriving loom equipment business and began selling silk threads, as well.

The "Clark" part of the partnership had its start in 1806, when Napoleon blockaded Great Britain and silk was no longer available. Patrick Clark created a method of twisting cotton yarns together to produce a thread that was so strong and smooth it could be substituted for the silk. The Clarks opened the first factory for making cotton sewing thread in 1812.

In 1896, the Coats' and the Clarks' interests were consolidated, however they retained separate identities. In 1952 J. & P. Coats and the Clark Thread Co. merged to become Coats & Clark Inc.

Today the company sells a wide line of products from Red Heart® and other yarns, to crochet threads, embroidery floss, threads, zippers, trims, and other products.

PRODUCT INFORMATION:

Over the years, the product range has expanded to additionally include specialty Threads, Zippers, Tapes and Trims, Needlework Accessories, specialty Hand Knitting and Craft Yarns, Crochet Threads, and Embroidery Floss. Today major brands include Dual Duty Plus®, Red Heart®, Anchor®, J. & P. Coats, South Maid®, Susan Bates®, and Aunt Lydia®.

WEB SITE:

Coats & Clark's Web site at www.coatsandclark.com is an extensive site full of consumer and product information, in addition to an extensive offering of patterns and books, many of which are free!

MORE PATTERNS & PATTERN BOOKS:

Coats & Clark offers a wide range of CD-ROMs on Crochet, Knitting, Embroidery, and Crafts. Millions of consumers have used their "Learn How" books to teach themselves enjoyable new skills. Pattern books cover everything from afghans to apparel for the entire family, at all skill levels.

In addition, the Coats & Clark Web site offers a long list of FREE leaflets of knitting and crochet projects, including vests, afghans, women's, men's and children's pullovers, crochet purses, home decorating, and much more!

Lion Brand Yarn Company

34 West 15th Street
New York, NY 10011
Phone: 800.258.YARN (9276)
Fax: 212.627.8154
Web site: www.LionBrandYarn.com

LION BRAND PROJECTS FEATURED IN THIS BOOK:

- Mondrian Cardigan, page 292
- Granny Squares Cardigan & Shell, page 302
- Triangle Shawl, page 326
- Heather Pullover & Tunic, page 336
- Ripple Pullover, page 346
- 60s Jiffy Crochet Vest, page 358
- Tam & Scarf with Pockets, page 374

ABOUT THE COMPANY:

At 123 years and counting, Lion Brand Yarn Company is the oldest American yarn brand. From the beginning in 1878, the Lion Brand philosophy was to provide a quality product at an affordable price. This tradition is still carried on by the fourth generation Blumenthal family members, producing yarns and patterns for today's lifestyles.

Lion Brand has long been a trendsetter in the industry. Lion Brand was the first to receive the Woolmark for hand-knitting yarns, the first to offer free patterns on the back of labels and the first to offer blended-fiber and novelty yarns at popular prices.

Each Lion Brand yarn has its own personality and is designed in a palette of colors that is appropriate to its texture and use. Lion Brand's mission is to excite and motivate needlecrafters to create handmade heirlooms that will be treasured for generations.

PRODUCT INFORMATION:

Lion Brand Yarn Company offers an expansive selection of yarns, knitting and crochet tools, patterns, books, and tools. Included is a wonderful FREE catalog that can be ordered online or over the phone.

WEB SITE:

Lion Brand's Web site www.LionBrandYarn.com offers a vast array of products, patterns, information, helpful tips, and even a gallery of customer projects. Lion Brand's site is very user-friendly and offers a long list of free downloadable patterns.

MORE PATTERNS & PATTERN BOOKS:

Lion Brand offers a wide range of books on crochet, knitting, crafts, tools, yarns, needles, and patterns.

FREE STUFF!

In addition, the Lion Brand's Web site offers numerous FREE patterns, which are downloadable.

BERROCO

Berroco, Inc.

14 Elmdale Road
P.O. Box 367
Uxbridge, MA 01569-0367
Phone: 800.343.4948
Fax: 508.278.2461
Web site: www.berroco.com

BERROCO PROJECTS FEATURED IN THIS BOOK:

- Timeless Tee, page 284
- Button Cardigan with Fluff Collar & Cuffs, 312
- Fringed Scarf, Cap, & Mittens, page 328

ABOUT THE COMPANY:

Berroco's story begins in the year 1810 when the great-great-great-grandfather of Warren Wheelock, Berroco's president today, opened the first of the Wheelock mills in rural Massachusetts, one of the first in the fledgling United States to produce woolen cloth. He began an enterprise that would grow and change and endure through six generations. Over the years, the Stanley Woolen Company mills sold to such manufacturers as Evan Picone, Perry Ellis, Brooks Brothers, and Hager.

In 1968, the Wheelock family formed a new handknitting subsidiary called Stanley Berroco, a name forged from the names of three business associates. This new firm grew to become one of the largest importers and wholesalers of handknitting yarns, patterns, and supplies in the United States. Importing yarns from the United Kingdom, Switzerland, Germany, France, Italy, New Zealand, Japan, Brazil, and Uruguay, Berroco also produces a full range of handknitting books and patterns.

Berroco patterns and yarns have been featured in such magazines as *Woman's Day, Family Circle, Redbook, Vogue Knitting, Knitters, Knitting Digest,* and *McCall's.* In 1995, Berroco became a US distributor of top-quality Inox and Clover knitting needles rounding out their offering to the handknitter.

The year 1992 brought further change to the company. Warren Wheelock, president of Berroco since 1987, created the Handeze Glove Division, becoming the master distributor of the Handeze glove in the craft industry.

Operating on the site of one of the Wheelock family's original woolen mills, Berroco, Inc., continues the family tradition of changing with the needs of the times to provide top-quality products.

PRODUCT INFORMATION:

Berroco offers a wide range of products from their mainstay in yarns, including a lovely array of specialty and exotic yarns, books, tools, knitting needle, patterns, and the Handeze glove, manufactured by the Handeze Glove Division.

WEB SITE:

Berroco's Web site, www.berroco.com, provides a wide range of information, books, products, and patterns, including numerous FREE patterns.

MORE PATTERNS & PATTERN BOOKS:

Berroco's offers a very extensive online pattern library of both FREE and retail patterns and pattern books. Furthermore, patterns are divided by skill levels, yarn types, or fashion categories, such as women's, men's, children, home decorating, etc.

FREE STUFF!

Berroco features one of the most extensive lines of FREE patterns. In addition, it also offers a FREE online newsletter that contains product, how-to and pattern information for consumers.

Tahki Stacy Charles, Inc.

8000 Cooper Ave. Building 1
Glendale, NY 11385
Phone: 800.338.YARN (9276)
Fax: 718.326.5017
Web site: www.tahkistacycharles.com

TSC PROJECTS FEATURED IN THIS BOOK:

- Casca Sage Shag Pullover, page 280
- Scarlet Shag Shell, page 296
- Loose-knit Red Pullover, page 308
- Striped Fuzzy Sweater, page 342
- Scoopneck Sweater, page 362
- Striped Turtleneck Sweater, page 378

ABOUT THE COMPANY:

Stacy Charles Inc. and Tahki Imports LTD. merged on January 10, 2000. The new company became known as Tahki Stacy Charles, Inc. Stacy Charles, Inc. was originally launched in 1984 as a high-end luxury and novelty yarn supplier and formed a longstanding relationship with the world-renowned Filatura Di Crosa Mill. To this day, the brand names of Filatura Di Crosa and S. Charles Collezione are synonymous with superior quality and fashion.

Tahki Imports LTD. was established in 1968 and became known for its classic and quality yarns imported from Ireland, England, Greece, France, and Italy. Classic yarns like Donegal Tweed, Cotton Classic, and New Tweed continue to be mainstays for the company.

Today, TSC offers classic yarns at value prices, as well as luxurious and fashion-forward novelty yarns and fashions.

PRODUCT INFORMATION:

Tahki Stacy Charles distributes an extensive line of yarns from all over the world, including Tahki Yarns, Austermann, Filatura di Crosa, and S. Charles Collezione. TSC also offers a wonderful line of patterns and pattern books that feature international and classic European and American styles.

WEB SITE:

TSC's Web site, www.tahkistacycharles.com, provides in-depth information about their extensive product line, numerous pattern books, and a directory of shops in each state that sells TSC yarns. In addition, needlecrafters can sign up to receive a FREE pattern.

MORE PATTERNS & PATTERN BOOKS:

Tahki Stacy Charles sells numerous pattern books, featuring styles from around the work, especially Europe and the United States. Individual projects featured in each book can be viewed on the Web site.

FREE STUFF!

Visitors to TSC's Web site can sign up for a FREE pattern.

Cascade Yarns

1224 Andover Park East
Tukwila, WA 98188
Phone: 800.548.1048
Fax: 888.855.9276
Web site: www.cascadeyarns.com

CASCADE PROJECTS FEATURED IN THIS BOOK:

- Multicolor Bulky Cardigan, page 298
- Ivory Turtleneck, page 306
- Fleur-de-Lis Purse, page 332
- Sweater Coat, page 354
- Cabled Shell with Yoke, page 366

ABOUT THE COMPANY:

Cascade Yarns offers a very wide selection of yarns from all over the world, including:

- Alpaca/wool and alpaca/cotton blends from the Andes Mountains of Peru.
- Kid mohair/silk blends from the spinners of Italy.
- Fabulous baby yarns from the gifted spinners of England.
- Many brands of yarns with exotic names, such as Indulgence, Lana D'Oro, Cherub, Pastaza, Sierra, King Cole, Magnum, Confetti, Merino, and Madil.

Cascade yarns also features other needlecraft product lines, such as Jean Greenhouse's many whimsical knitting project including "Little Dumpling Dolls," clowns, toys, hedgehogs, and other animals.

PRODUCT INFORMATION:

Cascade Yarn's Web site, www.cascadeyarn.com, features numerous types of yarns from all over the world and includes close-up photographs of the colors, textures, and weights of the yarns. In addition, Cascade offers an online service in which consumers can find the nearest store that sells each brand. Cascade's site also includes an extensive offering of patterns.

MORE PATTERNS & PATTERN BOOKS:

Find a wide array of pattern offerings featuring many different types of yarns and styles from around the world.

Handy Hands

Handy Hands, Inc.

577 N 1800
Paxton, IL 60957
Phone: 217.379.3802
Fax: 800.617.8626
Web site: www.hhtatting.com

HANDY HANDS PROJECTS FEATURED IN THIS BOOK:

- Tatted Choker & Earrings, page 316
- Tatted Bridal Garter, page 340

ABOUT THE COMPANY:

Handy Hands specializes specifically in tatting and offers a wonderful online and printed catalog, featuring all things tatting, including hundreds of books and a wide array of tools and supplies. The catalog also contains books, tools, and supplies for lace crochet, lace knitting, and bobbin lace.

The back section of the catalog has a special treat: A wide selection of shuttles, both decorative and functional, in all types of imaginative shapes, colors, and materials. Included are exotic shuttles made of everything from water buffalo horn to bone, embossed sterling silver to bronze, abalone to Mother of Pearl, and many types of colorful stones and colorfully dyed woods. You'll want to start tatting just so you can buy a beautiful shuttle!

PRODUCT INFORMATION:

Handy Hands provides nearly everything needed for tatting: shuttles, needles, tools, yarns, books, and other information, as well as tools and materials for other needlecrafts, such as bobbin lace-making and crocheting.

MORE PATTERNS:

Handy Hands online catalog features hundreds of how-to books from beginner to advanced tatting projects and patterns.

FREE STUFF!

Go to Handy Hands, Web site, www.hhtatting.com, for FREE tatting projects, wonderful how-to basics, complete with photographs, and even a question-and-answer service. You can also subscribe to an inexpensive newsletter service.

Helpful Web Sites

Visit these Web sites for more helpful information:

- Craft Yarn Council of America
  www.craftyarncouncil.com

- Crochet Guild of America
  www.crochet.com

- The Knitters Guild of America
  www.tkga.com

- The National Needlework Association
  www.tnna.org

- American Quilter's Society
  www.aqsquilt.com

- American Sewing Guild
  www.asg.org

- Hobby Industry Association
  www.i-craft.com

- Home Sewing Association
  www.sewing.org

- Sew Young/Sew Fun
  www.sewyoungsewfun.com

- The Knitting Needle
  www.knittingneedle.com

- Tatting and Design
  www.tatting.co.uk

Helpful Magazines

- *Cast On Magazine*
  www.wellroundedknitter.com

- *Knitters Magazine*
  www.knittinguniverse.com

- *Interweave Knits Magazine*
  www.interweave.com

- *Knitting Digest*
  www.knittingdigest.com

- *Knit 'N Style*
  www.knitnstyle.com

- *Vogue Knitting*
  www.vogueknitting.com

- *Family Circle Easy Knitting*
  www.fceasyknitting.com

gallery

The material in this compilation appeared in the
following previously published Krause Publications,
and appears here by permission of the authors.

(The initial page numbers given refer to pages in
the original work; page numbers in parentheses
refer to pages in this book.)

Colucci, Mary & Holmes, Christina
Knitting in the Fast Lane c. 2001
1, 3–126 (275–399)

Krause Publications
Vintage to Vogue c. 2003
1, 3–142 (133–274)

Michler, J. Marsha
Design & Knit the Sweater of Your Dreams
c. 2002
1, 3–128 (5–132)

COVER DESIGNER:
Marissa Bowers

PRODUCTION EDITOR:
Jennifer Ziegler

PRODUCTION COORDINATOR:
Kristen Heller

fw
F+W PUBLICATIONS, INC.

Other fine KP books are available from your local
bookstore, craft store or direct from the publisher.

09 08 07 06 05 5 4 3 2 1

Easy Knitting
0-89689-279-4

All works of art reproduced in this book have been
previously copyrighted by the individual artists.